SIR LAWRENCE ALMA-TADEMA 1836–1912

SIR LAWRENCE ALMA-TADEMA 1836–1912

Van Gogh Museum, Amsterdam
Walker Art Gallery, Liverpool

SIR LAWRENCE
ALMA-TADEMA

Editors

Edwin Becker

Edward Morris
Elizabeth Prettejohn
Julian Treuherz

Authors

Elizabeth Prettejohn

Rosemary Barrow
Edwin Becker
Dianne Sachko Macleod
Teio Meedendorp
Edward Morris
Luuk Pijl
Ulrich Pohlmann
Julian Treuherz
Jon Whiteley

RIZZOLI
NEW YORK

Lenders

Belgium
Koninklijk Museum voor Schone Kunsten, Antwerpen

France
Musée d'Orsay, Paris

Germany
Hamburger Kunsthalle, Hamburg

Great Britain
The Trustees of the Cecil Higgins Art Gallery, Bedford

Birmingham Museum & Art Gallery

University of Birmingham

Bristol City Museum & Art Gallery

Towneley Hall Art Gallery & Museums, Burnley Borough Council

The Syndics of the Fitzwilliam Museum, Cambridge

National Museum of Wales, Cardiff

Dick Institute, Kilmarnock, Scotland

The British Museum, London

Guildhall Art Gallery, Corporation of London

Royal Academy of Arts, London

Royal Watercolour Society, London

Tate Gallery, London

Board of Trustees of the Victoria & Albert Museum, London

Manchester City Art Gallery

Board of Trustees of the National Museums & Galleries on
Merseyside (Walker Art Gallery, Liverpool; Sudley House,
Liverpool; Lady Lever Art Gallery, Port Sunlight)

Ashmolean Museum, Oxford

William Morris Gallery, London Borough of Waltham Forest

Stanley J. Allen

John Constable, Esq.

Italy
Galleria degli Uffizi, Collezione degli Autoritratti, Florence

The Netherlands
Van Gogh Museum, Amsterdam

Rijksmuseum, Amsterdam

Rijksprentenkabinet, Amsterdam

Stedelijk Museum, Amsterdam

Dordrechts Museum, Dordrecht

Groninger Museum, Groningen

Fries Museum, Leeuwarden

Museum Mesdag, The Hague

Royal Collections, The Hague (by gracious permission
   of H.R.H. Princess Juliana of the Netherlands)

Poland
Muzeum Narodowe w Warszawie, Warsaw

United States
Walters Art Gallery, Baltimore

Hood Museum of Art, Dartmouth College, Hanover, New Hampshire

Frances Lehman Loeb Art Center, Vassar College,
   Poughkeepsie, New York

Philadelphia Museum of Art

Museum of Art, Brigham Young University, Provo, Utah

Sterling and Francine Clark Art Institute, Williamstown

Zanesville Art Center, Zanesville, Ohio

An anonymous lady, Texas

Haussner Family Limited Partnership

J. Nicholson, Beverly Hills, California

and the many private owners who wish to remain anonymous

Contents

Foreword and acknowledgements

The exhibition of Lawrence Alma-Tadema's work enables us to re-assess a painter whose reputation has with the passage of time suffered alarmingly extreme vicissitudes. Though his work was at first not uniformly well received by contemporaries, he became one of the most highly-praised, successful and wealthy of all Victorian painters, celebrated for serious archaeological and architectural learning as well as for supreme technical brillance. Yet immediately after his death, his reputation sank and it was only in the 1960s that it began to rise again. Now images of his classical subjects have wide popular currency and the originals are keenly sought after by collectors, but he is still not taken seriously either by much of the art historical community or the gallery-going public.

Though there have been a number of small exhibitions of his work in the 1970s and a medium-sized show in the USA in 1991, this is the first really large and representative selection of his work to be shown since the Memorial Exhibition held at the Royal Academy in 1913, the year after his death. Our exhibition is also the first to portray Alma-Tadema as a European figure. For Alma-Tadema was more than a pillar of the British Royal Academy. He was born in Friesland in the Northern Netherlands; he studied in Antwerp, lived for a time in Brussels and exhibited in Amsterdam, Brussels, Paris, Berlin and Munich. Though he moved to London in 1870 and became a naturalized British citizen in 1873, he might just as easily have settled in any other European capital. He continued to exhibit throughout the continent, and was showered with honours and medals by many countries and academies.

The idea for the exhibition was originally proposed by two Dutch art historians, Teio Meedendorp and Luuk Pijl, to Rik Vos of the Fries Museum in Leeuwarden. First contacts with the National Museums & Galleries on Merseyside (NMGM) were laid to establish a future cooperation. Sadly, the Fries Museum was unable to proceed but the Van Gogh Museum stepped in and has collaborated on the show with the Walker Art Gallery, Liverpool, part of the NMGM, which has an important collection of Victorian art, including some masterworks by Alma-Tadema in the Lady Lever Art Gallery and Sudley House in addition to the Walker Art Gallery itself. The staff of the Van Gogh Museum enthusiastically took up the project, intrigued by the possibility of devoting a retrospective to Holland's most successful painter of the 19th century in the museum dedicated to an artist who could only have dreamed of a comparable life-time appreciation. Within its exhibition programme Alma-Tadema is third in a series of quite individual interpretations of the classical heritage. After the Frenchman Pierre Puvis de Chavannes and his arcadian visions, and the Bavarian Franz von Stuck with his rather Dionysiac approach, Alma-Tadema perhaps represents the archaeological will to truth, filtered, of course, by Victorian taste.

Julian Treuherz and Edward Morris of the Walker Art Gallery, and Andreas Blühm and Edwin Becker of the Van Gogh Museum formed a team to plan the exhibition. The latter acted as the project's coordinator, ably supported by Aly Noordermeer and Sandra Sihan in Amsterdam as well as David McNeff in Liverpool. Together we are proud to have assembled a team of Dutch, British, German and American scholars who have contributed to the catalogue, with Elizabeth Prettejohn undertaking a large share of the work. Their contributions enable us to take a fresh and penetrating look at a major Victorian painter whose vision has moulded our perception of the classical age. Everyone involved with this project would like to pay tribute to the pioneering scholarship of Professor Vern Swanson, whose biography and catalogue of the artist's work has been of fundamental importance to the exhibition.

The exhibition itself would not have been possible without the generosity of institutional and private lenders from Europe, North and Central America. All recipients of our requests were unanimously in favour of our project and helped to bring together the finest collection of works by Alma-Tadema ever.

We would also like to thank Caroline Arscott, Robyn Asleson, Joanna Barnes, Frédéric Bastet, Steven Bayley, Martin Beisly (Christie's, London), Piotr Bienkowski, Jo-Anne Birnie-Danzker, Susan Bourne, Caroline Breunesse, Judith Bronkhurst, Lucilla Burn, Tim Butchard (The British Council, Amsterdam), Richard D. Cacchione, Jeanette Canavan, Melva Croal, Sara Dodgson, John Edmondson, Catharine Edwards, Thomas Elsaesser, Gert Elzinga, Joan Esch, Charlotte Gere, Francis Greenacre, Barbara Guggenheim, Veronique Gunner, Penelope Gurland, Julian Hartnoll,

Freek Heijbroek, Sorrel Hershberg, Colin Jackson, Heleen de Jong, Daniëlle Kisluk-Grosheide, Vivien Knight, Tim Knox, Philip Alan LaDouceur, Helmut Leppien, Michael Liversidge, Henri Loyrette, Sandra Martin, Charles Martindale, David Mason, Freda Matassa, Leela Meinertas, Sir David Miers (British Embassy, The Netherlands), John Millard, Dominic Montserrat, James Mundy, Jenny Newall, Rianne Norbart, Barry Norman, Léonee Ormond, Christine Penney and the staff of the Heslop Room (Main Library, University of Birmingham), Richard Rand, Yvette S. Robbins, James Robson, Christopher Rose-Innes, Katie Sambrook, George T.M. Shackelford, Jeanne Sheehy, Michael Silk, Sotheby's Inc. New York, Claire H. Stewart, Roxana Velásquez, Geoffrey Waywell, Lilian Widdershoven, Christopher Wood, Lucy Wood. Thanks are also due to Air UK, The British Council and to Christie's, London, for sponsorship.

It remains to wish the visitors to the exhibition, as well as the readers of the catalogue, both the enlightening experience and the pleasure the organizers had while studying the art of Sir Lawrence Alma-Tadema.

Ronald de Leeuw
Director Van Gogh Museum

Richard Foster
Director National Museums & Galleries on Merseyside

Introduction to Alma-Tadema

Julian Treuherz

Sir Lawrence Alma-Tadema's sunny visions of Roman luxury offered the Victorians a beguiling fantasy, an escape from darkest London, from fogs and social problems, from constricting dress and rigid social codes. Looking at these paintings, the Victorians were transported into a seemingly realistic world of filmy draperies and clear blue skies, where toga-clad senators debated the merits of a vase or bronze statuette, where girls bathed beneath lofty architectural vaults or idled on white marble benches overlooking the sea.

So popular was his work during his lifetime, so compelling was this vision of the past, that according to the *Dictionary of National Biography* 'no public gallery of any importance in Europe, America or Australia is without at least one example of his handiwork, nor can any private collection of modern art be deemed representative, which has nothing of his to show'.[1] He exhibited regularly in London at the Royal Academy and at exhibitions in other European capitals. He was industrious and prolific: from 1872 he numbered his pictures, signing each one with an 'opus number' to prevent forgeries, also retrospectively giving numbers to his earlier works. In all he produced more than 400 pictures, a large number especially considering their high finish, delicate touch and painstaking detail.

Today Alma-Tadema's work is known from a relatively few images of the kind described above, often reproduced on greetings cards and calendars, but his range is wider than these might suggest. His output includes many portraits, and a few startlingly vivid landscapes besides his characteristic scenes of Greek and Roman antiquity. But his earliest historical subjects depict the Merovingians, the dynasty which dominated northern Europe in the dark ages after the fall of the Roman Empire, and he also painted ancient Egypt as well as 15th-, 16th- and 17th-century Flemish scenes. Some of his works show known historical personages, often decadent characters such as the emperor Caligula [23], or the perverted Heliogabalus killing his courtiers by suffocating them with rose petals [69]. A number of his subjects are tragic, such as *An Egyptian widow in the time of Diocletian* or *The death of the first-born* [27 28]; but by far the majority are happy, inconsequential everyday incidents in the lives of anonymous though well-to-do inhabitants of Rome or Pompeii. The paintings lack drama or strong feeling: figures are in repose or gentle movement, faces are impassive and not distorted by strong emotion; Alma-Tadema's people lead contented, calm and prosperous lives.

Alma-Tadema felt that art was closely bound up with daily life: 'All great art must in some form or other bear relation to life – be in accord with the things we daily see and feel'.[2] Hence his use of everyday events as his principal subject matter, though set in ancient times, for he believed that 'there is not such a great difference between the ancients and the moderns as we are apt to suppose ... the old Romans were human flesh and blood like ourselves, moved by much the same passions and emotions'.[3] In choosing for the most part to depict ordinary events such as mothers and children, flirting couples or women admiring flowers, he was placing the emphasis on the differences between ancient and modern civilization, as he saw it: not differences of outlook or philosophy but material differences: the architecture, the costumes, the objects, the local customs, the details. And it was the thorough understanding of the details of architecture and accessories, rather than anything deeper, that enabled him to create a convincing illusion of the tangibility of the ancient world. The way Alma-Tadema painted the sheen of marble, the glint of light on precious metals or the minute appearance of flowers seduces the eye. His technique owes a great deal to his Dutch artistic forbears and has led to comparisons with the *fijnschilders* (fine painters), the school of 17th-century painters such as Dou and Metsu, famous for their minute touch. Alma-Tadema's highly sophisticated compositions, which draw the spectator into the picture also show awareness of 17th-century Dutch interior paintings:[4] his pictures demonstrate a facility for space-construction and perspective, creating intriguing views through one space into another, with further space beyond indicated by a brightly lit view through a door or window. Alma-Tadema's most original compositional devices develop this feeling for space beyond its Dutch origins into the vertiginous architectural perpectives of his later works, with steep views up or down from one level to another, and abrupt contrasts between foreground and distance. He was also adept at using the up-to-date tricks of realist painters, such as the snapshot-like close-up, using the edge of the picture to cut off part of a figure or a detail. It may have been such modern features which made his work appeal to Degas, who in a letter written to the London dealer Charles Deschamps, mentioned Alma-Tadema as one of a number of British painters with whom he wished to exhibit in London.[5]

Alma-Tadema was a perfectionist. He ruthlessly destroyed the result of days of work if he found it unsatisfactory, scraping off and repainting detail tirelessly until he was happy with it. 'Nothing can be done well without taking trouble' he said. 'No half measures ... no hesitation or uncertainty ... it must, it shall be right and exact; if you are sure of the facts, why hesitate to state them definitely?'[6] In a lecture on art training he stressed the importance of knowing one's subject thoroughly, even those parts of it not seen in the painting. 'A gardener in midwinter will tell you which is an apple tree and which is a pear tree. How many landscape painters are there who would be able to do the same?'[7] It was said of the architecture in Alma-Tadema's pictures, and even in his stage designs, a field where trickery and illusion were paramount, that they showed a thorough knowledge of building construction and the properties of the various materials used.[8]

His care for even the smallest details is seen in his dealings with the engravers who made reproductive etchings of his work. Leopold Lowenstam's daughter complained about the unreasonable demands Alma-Tadema made on her father,[9] and this is borne out by the instructions written by Alma-Tadema to the etcher Paul Adolphe Rajon on his proof after the watercolour *Strigils and sponges* [1] [52]. The painter asks for minute amendments to the tiniest of details: 'too much light in the jet of water ... the strigil in the shade darker ... a bit more drawing in the hair on the bronze ... the sponge should have more variously shaped and deeper holes'.[10]

This perfectionism seems to have been acquired early in his career. Biographical details of his youth are largely anecdotal, for the artist was a great raconteur, but they reveal a struggle against his family's wishes.[11] The Tademas were Mennonites (strict Protestants) from Friesland, the northernmost province of Holland. Lawrence was born in the small village of Dronrijp, where his father was the village notary. The family moved to the larger town of Leeuwarden in 1837 but three years later Alma-Tadema's father died, leaving his mother to bring him up with her sister and three half brothers. Though poor, she was supported in her efforts to educate her family by her brothers-in-law, Lourens and Adrianus Alma, Amsterdam apothecaries who were godfathers to young Alma-Tadema. It was after the former that he was christened Lourens Alma, his first name later anglicized to Lawrence; the surname is the Dutch equivalent of Adamson, and it and the middle name were often hyphenated as 'Alma-Tadema' allegedly so that it would be listed at the beginning of exhibition catalogues rather than at the end.

Alma-Tadema showed precocious talent for art but was directed by his father's will towards a career as a lawyer. The strain of trying to practise art in his spare time whilst keeping up his academic studies led to a serious breakdown. He was diagnosed as consumptive, and because he was not given long to live, the doctors recommended that he should be able to do what he wanted. The experience of painting and drawing unencumbered by other pressures led to the complete restoration of his health, and he was then allowed to pursue a career in art, justifying his early determination to become a painter.

Alma-Tadema's training in Antwerp (see pp. 21-27) brought him into contact with two influential artists from whom he learned the virtue of thoroughness. Louis de Taeye (1822-1890), a minor painter, in whose house Alma-Tadema lodged from 1856 to 1858, was Professor of Archaeology at the Antwerp Academy where he taught history and historical costume. From him, Alma-Tadema learned a rigorous approach to attaining archaeological accuracy, and was able to explore authentic source material in De Taeye's extensive archaeological library.

Alma-Tadema's second mentor was Baron Henri Leys (1815-1869), a well-known painter of 16th-century Flemish historical subjects, in a deliberately archaizing style, flat, stiff and decorative, yet full of convincing detail. With Leys, Alma-Tadema gained solid experience of studio practice, assisting him with his murals at Antwerp Town Hall. Two anecdotes later told by Alma-Tadema illustrate what he gained from Leys. At his master's request, the young artist painted a table in one of Leys's paintings. 'That is not my idea of a table', said Leys, 'it ought to be so constructed that everyone knocks his knees to pieces on it'. And on seeing Alma-Tadema working on his own *The education of the children of Clovis* [3] Leys remarked 'That marble is cheese'.[12] The implication is that Alma-Tadema learned from Leys the need for absolute accuracy, the need to understand a thing thoroughly to be able to paint it, and the willingness to reject unsatisfactory work. All these lessons Alma-Tadema emphasized in his later writings and interviews. Such perfectionism was foreign to most English painters, whose artistic education lacked the rigours of continental academic technique or the discipline of apprenticeship.

In the mid 1860s two significant events occurred which were to shape his career. In 1863 he visited Florence, Rome, Naples and Pompeii whilst on his honeymoon following his marriage to the Frenchwoman Marie Pauline Gressin Dumoulin de Boisgirard. 'My first visit to Italy was a revelation to me. It extended my archaeological learning to such a degree that my brain soon became hungry for it'.[13] At this time he had been painting historical subjects from the various epochs introduced to him by De Taeye and Leys, but the discovery especially of Pompeii stimulated his imagination, and ultimately led him to concentrate exclusively

1   *Strigils and sponges*, 1879, etching by Paul Rajon after the watercolour by Alma-Tadema, The British Museum, London

on scenes of classical life. On this and subsequent visits he made measured drawings of the ruins [2], examined excavated artefacts in the Naples Museum, and collected photographs and information about classical antiquities and architecture in general. The following year, 1864, he met the art dealer Ernest Gambart (see pp. 26-27).[14] Gambart and his successors Pilgeram and Lefèvre were to be crucial in marketing Alma-Tadema's work to an increasing number of wealthy patrons (see pp. 91-98).

Between 1865 and 1870 he lived in Brussels, exhibiting in London, Brussels, Paris and Amsterdam, but in 1870 he finally decided to come to London, partly for medical reasons, partly for personal reasons, but mainly because London was the most promising market for his pictures (see pp. 28-30). In 1870, his work was not particularly well-known in Britain, even though he had exhibited in London at the Academy in 1869 and from 1865 at Gambart's French Gallery. The type of painting with which he made his name in Britain was a foreign import, quite unlike anything by native British painters: historical genre painting had been popular in Britain for decades, but genre painting set in classical or Pompeian times was not well known in Britain. It was of French origin, exemplified by the work of Gérôme and the 'néo-Grec' school, which had been shown in Paris from the late 1840s (see pp. 69-76). Alma-Tadema's thorough and archaeological approach to the recreation of a historical period was quite different from that of the English painters of historical genre, such as William Powell Frith and Edward Matthew Ward whose 17th- and 18th-century scenes were stagey and unconvincing; or the Pre-Raphaelites, whose medieval subjects were less literal and more inventive than Alma-Tadema's in their use of historical detail, and were based on poetry and imagination rather than everyday life. Alma-Tadema's methods came from his Belgian training: he was a European artist and exemplified the increasing internationalism of the art world in the last quarter of the 19th century.

Alma-Tadema soon established himself on the British art scene and in the London society. He married Laura Epps, daughter of a London doctor, in 1871 (his first wife had died in 1869). Laura, who had been his pupil, also practised as an artist and exhibited at the Academy and elsewhere, painting mainly domestic subjects, often in 16th- or 17th-century period costume [5], employing a similarly detailed syle to that of her husband. Alma-Tadema was naturalized in 1873. He exhibited regularly at the Royal Academy, becoming an Associate Member in 1876 and a full Royal Academician in 1879. His lavish Tuesday evening musical parties, first at Townshend House, near Regent's Park and later at his St. John's Wood studio house were legendary, as were the houses themselves (see pp. 45-56) and his pictures sold well. By the 1890s he was wealthy, famous and part of the British establishment: knighted in 1899, awarded the Order of Merit in 1905 and the Royal Institute of British Architects Gold Medal in 1906, and buried at St. Paul's Cathedral in 1912.

2　*Alma-Tadema measuring the House of Sallust*, Pompeii, c. 1862-63, University of Birmingham (CXXIII, 11161)

Alma-Tadema accumulated an immense fund of knowledge of classical archaeology and architecture, which became a key ingredient in his paintings. He was regarded by contemporaries as an authority: the architect Sir Matthew Digby Wyatt said of him 'That painter knows more of Roman architecture than any Roman architect of any period'.[15] Alma-Tadema collected a library of books and photographs which forms a uniquely surviving example of the archive of a 19th-century painter (it was given by his daughters to the Victoria & Albert Museum in 1915, but transferred to the University of Birmingham in 1947). The library includes the works of classical authors, transactions of Archaeological Academies and Societies in France, Germany and Britain, museum catalogues of antiquities, and books of engravings, measured drawings and accounts of antiquities from the late 18th century onwards. The photographs are sorted into portfolios classified by subject, such as altars, bulls, cats, dogs, triumphal arches, cinerary urns, costume, flowers, sculptures of various gods and heroes, glass, mosaics and so on, also including a smaller amount of Egyptian, Japanese, Asian and Medieval material (see pp. 111-124). The portfolios were kept in his studio so that they could be readily referred to when a particular detail was required. 'Photography is a great boon undoubtedly to the artist of today who has any concern for accuracy in details'.[16] The other British classical painters occasionally incorporated a vase or architectural motif into their pictures but their principal aim was High Art not authenticity (see pp. 59-66); and Alma-Tadema's followers, such as John William Godward and John Reinhard Weguelin, did not share his passion for archaeology. Alma-Tadema filled his pictures with detail culled from his photographic collection, especially during the period immediately after his first visit to Pompeii when his pictures typically show dark, Pompeian-red interiors filled with vases, statues and other objects jostling for attention, as if to show off the artists' knowledge. The later works, often set out-of-doors in bright sunlight, with pale, iridescent colour schemes and more daring use of space and scale, refer to classical sources in a more sophisticated and allusive way (see pp. 33-42).

Because of Alma-Tadema's reputation as an authority on classical antiquity, he was asked to design a number of stage productions by managers such as Sir Henry Irving, who spearheaded a new movement in the late Victorian theatre which rejected the hazy approximation of historical period for elaborately realistic and authentic-looking stage pictures. Alma-Tadema's finest achievement in this field was Irving's production of Shakespeare's *Coriolanus* starring Ellen Terry at the Lyceum Theatre, 1901 [81].[17] What impressed audiences, critics, actors, producers and scene-painters alike was the artist's learning. An associate of Irving recalled him using his knowledge of statuary to transform the theatrical toga. 'And the result? Not a flimsy covering which would have become draggle-tailed in a day or an hour of strenuous work, but a huge garment of heavy cloth which would allow infinite varieties of wearing ... he knew how a velarium should be made, and of what, and how adorned; how it should be put up and secured. He was learned of boats and chariots; of carts and carriages, and of the trappings of horses. Implements of agriculture and trade and manufacture and for domestic use were familiar to him'.[18] Alma-Tadema also designed two productions for Sir Herbert Beerbohm Tree. For Tree's *Hypatia* at the Haymarket Theatre in 1893 the actress Julia Neilsen noted Alma-Tadema's care for detail in designing for her a Greek coiffure and in coming round in the interval to correct the drapery of her costume.[19] Similar thoroughness is evident in Alma-

3   Giovanni Battista Amendola, *Laura Alma-Tadema in her rocking chair*, 1879, coll. Richard Cacchione, New York

Tadema's sets for Tree's *Julius Caesar* at Her Majesty's Theatre (1898) which were highly praised for their striking architectural designs [7].[20]

The way Alma-Tadema used his sources was not however literal or authentic, it was creative. He combined objects from different periods and from different parts of the classical world; he loved to play with scale, enlarging or reducing motifs, transforming part of a sarcophagus into an architectural frieze or a statuette into a life-sized figure; he used marble busts or painted portraits as sources for facial types, but equally gave some of his ancient Romans the features of his friends and family, deliberately manipulating his material for aesthetic or symbolic reasons. This constant playing with sources which alluded not just to the past, but to the survival and interpretation of knowledge of the past, was not lost on his more knowledgable contemporaries. The art critic Cosmo Monkhouse commented on the paradoxical modernity of his work. 'Nor could this unique artist's strange imagination have done its special work in any other of former generations. His art is essentially the product of its time. His ground was prepared for him by hundreds of patient archaeologists and scholars, and his work, deal as it does with "ages ago" is as modern as an Edison lamp'.[21] It is the same attitude, not slavishly historicist but using the past for a contemporary purpose, which led the archi-

4   *Ask me no more*, 1906, private collection

5   Laura Alma-Tadema, *Sweet industry*, 1904, Manchester
     City Art Gallery

tect Alfred Waterhouse to write of his Gothic revival masterpiece Manchester Town Hall as 'essentially nineteenth century'.[22]

A closer analogy lies in the work of Georg Ebers (1837-1898), a German Egyptologist, Professor of Egyptology at Jena and then at Leipzig, and a friend of Alma-Tadema's.[23] Ebers wrote many serious books and articles about ancient Egypt but was perhaps best known as a popularizer, through illustrated books such as *Aegypten in Bild und Wort* (1880) and Baedeker's *Egypt* (1877). Ebers also wrote historical novels: his *Eine ägyptische Königstochter* (1864) translated into English as *An Egyptian princess* (known to Alma-Tadema, see p. 26) had by 1928 sold 400,000 copies in sixteen languages. It is very similar to Alma-Tadema's paintings in that it is a work of fiction set in ancient times, based on surviving evidence of customs and artefacts. It places fictional characters in everyday situations, against a background of known buildings, places and historical personages. Both writer and painter parade the archaeological basis of their work, Ebers explicitly through detailed scholarly footnotes and Alma-Tadema through the accumulation of visual quotations.

The extent to which Alma-Tadema's public understood his sources in detail is not easy to gauge. Specialists undoubtedly recognized his references, but though his businessmen collectors and the gallery-going public were impressed by his learning, it does not seem

likely that they appreciated every nuance. Nevertheless a general acquaintance with the classics was part of the culture of the educated classes in 19th-century Britain: Greek and Latin were taught at public schools, and literary journals such as the *Athenaeum* published weekly accounts of the proceedings of archaeological societies and descriptions of the latest discoveries.

There is a strong sexual element in some of Alma-Tadema's paintings, which has led to modern critics describing him as a painter of soft pornography.[24] This eroticism is at its most explicit in *Tepidarium* [58], a reclining nude female caressing a phallically-shaped strigil, an implement commonly used by the ancients for scraping oil from the body; the sexual suggestiveness of the figure is barely legitimized by the classical context, which could for the Victorians confer respectability on scenes sometimes regarded as 'unwholesome'. Alma-Tadema could however be more subtle; most people seeing his bacchantes, bathers or flower girls would miss the connotations of sexual abandon or prostitution, familiar to the classical scholar. The painting *Spring* [6] includes references to satyrs and maenads, personifications of sexual energy, represented in relief sculpture, and he even incorporates a Latin inscription dedicated to Priapus, but the casual viewer sees only a procession of virginal young girls bearing flowers.[25] There is some evidence too of a kind of deliberate disingenuousness by contemporaries as for instance when Ellen Gosse described the sadistic act of cruelty shown in *The roses of Heliogabalus* [69] as 'a practical joke on a large scale'.[26]

Ellen Gosse, the artist's sister-in-law, was in fact a most perceptive writer on Alma-Tadema as well as a friend, familiar with his practice and personality.[27] She described his astonishing technical facility, working directly onto the canvas or panel without the preparatory drawings used by most academically trained painters to work out figure compositions or try out poses and details. She stated that he painted his figures direct from the live model; he also worked out his architectural backgrounds straight onto the canvas or panel, having unsuccessfully tried using an architectural assistant to draw out the perspective actual size on paper beforehand. Drawings by Alma-Tadema are rare, and tend not to be preparatory works, but records of a head or pose done for pleasure in fine pencil, after perfecting them on the canvas or panel [4].[28] However, a small number of rough studies for figures and compositions survives [8], suggesting that his methods were more conventional than Gosse implies.[29] Alma-Tadema was equally skilled at watercolour, and was elected an Associate of the Royal Society of Painters in Water-Colours in 1873; he used watercolour in very much the same highly finished way as oil, but preferred oil as it was more profitable.[30]

His perfectionism was indeed obsessive: Gosse observed a side of the artist hidden from the guests at his famous parties when he played the genial host, showing visitors round the studio, delighting in his collection of mechanical toys and laughing at his own jokes, told in a thick Dutch accent.[31] She saw how every drapery, brush and pen-knife in the studio was arranged with extreme neatness so that if a visitor disturbed the slightest thing it caused agony to his highly strung nerves. She saw the tension of the perfectionist at work: 'When an important picture approaches completion, the whole household is aware of the painter's excitement ... Professional models are insufficient to supply the demand, and a friend is called upon at night or some member of the family in the very early morning ... During these critical times Mr. Alma-Tadema's intensity is something formidable'.[32]

Alma-Tadema himself felt the pressures of success. 'Bah! My friends, the public, won't let me progress', he told C.L. Hind. 'I paint a bit of marble, and they always want marble; a blue sky, and they

6   *Spring*, 1894, The J. Paul Getty Museum, Malibu

7   *The Forum*, from *Julius Caesar*, Her Majesty's Theatre, 1898, photograph, Theatre Museum, London

17

8   Sketch for *The vintage festival*, 1870, private collection

always want blue skies; Agrippa, and they always want Agrippas; an Oleander, and they want nothing but Oleanders. Bah! A man isn't a machine!'.[33] There are signs that he felt trapped by the need to maintain an extravagant style of life and to keep up his social standing with patrons, both necessary to sell his work.

Perhaps Alma-Tadema sometimes shared Gosse's wish to escape: 'a little longing comes over us for a little repose from all this crowded perfection of detail; a wish creeps into the mind for a little dimness and a slight mist over it all', she wrote.[34] Alma-Tadema was lucky to be painting at a time when a ready market existed for pictures full of detail, but it was also a time when a fundamental change was occurring in the development of art. Though a supporter might write of the Memorial Exhibition held after his death that 'there is more real sunlight and *joie de vivre* in a single square inch of [his] painting ... than in the entire output of the Impressionist School'[35], Alma-Tadema's reputation plummeted rapidly. Yet his vision of antiquity would not die; even before the revival of our own day, it was taken up by Hollywood producers such as Cecil B. DeMille[36], whose epic films, such as *Cleopatra* (1934), recreate in moving images the spectacular processions and crowd scenes of Alma-Tadema's paintings [9].

9   Publicity still of *Caesar's triumphal entry into Rome* from *Cleopatra* (1934) by Cecil B. DeMille, Universal Pictures, A Division of Universal City Studio's, Inc.

Alma-Tadema's artistic training

Critics on the continent 1852–1870

Teio Meedendorp & Luuk Pijl

The edition of the weekly *De Amsterdammer* published on 10 February 1895 contained a striking cartoon entitled *The English bait* [10].[1] The Dutch maiden watches with mixed feelings as a typical Englishman – tweed suit, sideburns, gaiters and top hat – fishes in her pool. A fish labelled W. Kes is about to bite. Closer inspection of the bait leaves no room for doubt: three worms have interlaced to form the abbreviations for English currency of the time: pounds (£), shillings (s), and pence (d). Three fish have already been landed. The fattest of the three bears the name Alma-Tadema, who had moved to London in 1870. The other two are the graphic artist Petrus J. Arendzen, who had crossed the Channel in the 1880s, and the sculptor Joseph H. Teixeira de Mattos, who followed in his footsteps a decade later. The conductor Willem Kes also fell for the bait; he became leader of the Scottish Orchestra in 1895 as the successor to George Henschel, a good friend of Alma-Tadema [55].[2]

Artists who are unable to resist the temptation of big money are often viewed disparagingly. Art is supposed to arise from an indescribable inner source with a passion which blinds the artist to such incidental matters as material prosperity. The romantic view that an artist must suffer in order to produce his best work is certainly not applicable to Alma-Tadema. In 1895 he was home and dry, and although he had been through more difficult periods at first, he managed to keep luck on his side. The fact that his fortune was not to be sought in his own country is due to the low level of Dutch interest in historical painting in general, and in classicizing representations in particular, including Alma-Tadema's genre-like approach.

The cartoon in *De Amsterdammer* is typical of the troubled relation which Alma-Tadema had with the Netherlands throughout his life. In 1852, at the age of sixteen, he moved to Belgium to study at the Royal Academy of Fine Arts in Antwerp, after being rejected in Amsterdam and The Hague.[3] He developed his style and conception of painting in Antwerp and later in Brussels, where he moved in 1865. Although he regularly submitted work for exhibitions in the Netherlands during this period and later, he rarely sold anything there. 'Holland only has three of my paintings', he complained in 1885, 'and only one of them is genuinely important'.[4] He is referring to his *Queen Fredegonda at the death-bed of Bishop Praetextatus* of 1864 [12], now in the Fries Museum in Leeuwarden and unfortunately not able to be exhibited because of the extensive bitumen craquelure. His work is still barely represented in Dutch collections today, although the two Alma-Tademas from the Rijksmuseum [27 28] now are on permanent display in the new wing and the Van Gogh Museum recently acquired three of his paintings [31 34 55].

10   Johan Braakensiek, *The English bait*, published in
De Amsterdammer, 10 February 1895

The Belgian artistic climate

Alma-Tadema arrived in Antwerp in the summer of 1852, just in time to enrol for the winter course in the academy. At this time the director was still the historical painter Gustaaf Wappers (1803-1874), who left for Paris in 1853 after thirteen years at the head of the academy. Wappers was a key figure in what is known as Flemish Romanticism: he freed the Antwerp school of painting from Dutch influence and Neo-Classicism.[5]

Belgium had been an independent kingdom since 1831. The academy was organized during Dutch rule (1815-31), with an emphasis on Dutch art from the 16th and 17th centuries. Before then French Classicism had been the dominant tendency both in the Antwerp academy and in its traditional counterpart, the Royal Academy of Fine Arts in Brussels. The Brussels academy was not marked by any Dutch interference and adhered to the French line under the direction of François-Joseph Navez, a pupil of Jacques-Louis David. In Antwerp the focus shifted from Dutch to Flemish themes, reinforcing the predilection for a cultural identity of its own and a national historical awareness. Wappers, his successor Nicaise de Keyser, and Joseph Laurent Dyckmans were the most important exponents of this tendency. The opposition between the two schools is symptomatic of the division between Flanders and the French-speaking Belgian South.[6]

Many young Dutch artists felt attracted to study art in the liberal Belgian climate, not least because education there was free of charge.[7] Alma-Tadema spent four years at the academy before joining the studio of Louis de Taeye. De Taeye also offered him board in his house and introduced him to Henri Leys, whose studio he entered as an assistant in 1859. Both painters exerted a strong influence on the painter's development in their own ways. De Taeye, a painter as well as a lecturer in history and archaeology at the academy, had a reputation for his phenomenal knowledge of antiquity. He was an important authority who could be consulted on the accuracy of the historical details which Alma-Tadema included in his paintings. De Taeye had little influence as a painter and was much less well-known than Leys.

'On finishing my term as a student, I was lucky enough to come under the influence of Leys, the famous historical painter of Belgium', Alma-Tadema recalls in his memoirs.[8] Leys was an extremely critical tutor and placed great emphasis on the rendering of material. As a result of the importance that Leys attributed to the accurate historical detail and his precise method of working, from the 1840s he found himself somewhat of an outsider to the academic tradition in

11   Henri Leys, *Announcement of the Edict of Charles V*, c. 1861, Walters Art Gallery, Baltimore

Antwerp. His treatment of paint differs from that of Wappers or De Keyser, who followed their great model Rubens in using the brush in a more flamboyant, lyrical manner. Leys, on the other hand, increasingly shunned heroic rhetoric in his themes and concentrated on simpler, serene compositions with a subdued range of tints but displaying a great sensitivity to local colour. He shifted attention to the detail, drawing his inspiration above all from the 17th-century Dutch genre painters. His style underwent a further change after a journey through Germany in the early 1850s, when he was profoundly impressed by old German masters like Cranach, Holbein and Dürer, as well as by the Nazarenes. It prompted him to study the Flemish Primitives closer to home in more detail, and from now on his work was characterized by an even harder, linear realism, clear-cut contours, sharp individual expression in the rendering of features which gave them an increased psychological depth, and skilfully arranged group compositions in an architectural setting. His choice of themes was totally given over to 16th-century Flemish history, particularly scenes from the history of Antwerp [11]. It led one critic to remark: 'Leys is basically just a Renaissance realist'.[9]

This typical style, also known as 'Leys style', gives his paintings a distinctive appearance with their reference to the 'primitive' drapery folds, static poses and facial expressions full of character, but it often also led to a degree of stiffness. The figures are frozen in their action as if in a *tableau vivant*. Nevertheless, the change in his style brought him great success and enhanced his reputation at home and abroad. He influenced not only Alma-Tadema but also painters like Matthijs Maris and James Tissot.[10] The city of Antwerp honoured him with a gold laurel wreath when he won a *médaille d'honneur* at the Exposition Universelle in Paris in 1855.[11] This must have given him a measure of satisfaction, as two years earlier he had been passed over as a successor to Wappers at the academy in favour of Nicaise de Keyser. Antwerp honoured Leys again by commissioning him to decorate the reception room of the Town Hall with historical scenes in 1859. Leys worked on this project from 1863 until his death in 1869, assisted by Alma-Tadema, even after the latter had moved to Brussels in 1865.[12]

12   *Queen Fredegonda at the death-bed of Bishop Praetextatus*, 1864, Fries Museum, Leeuwarden

History brought closer

The cooperation with Leys and the influence of De Taeye formed the basis of Alma-Tadema's first major success. This was at the exhibition which accompanied a large international arts conference held in Antwerp in 1861. Alma-Tadema's contribution to the exhibition was his *The education of the children of Clovis* [3], a subject from 6th-century French history under the Merovingian dynasty. Few artists had drawn on the Merovingians as a source before, and this enabled him to set out in a direction of his own.[13] Before 1861 his choice of themes was determined by late medieval and Renaissance national history, apart from a few subjects from the more remote past, including the classical period, such as *Marius on the ruins of Carthage* (1858), *The death of Hippolytus* (1860), *The death of Attila* (1859) and *The sad father: the unfavourable oracle* (1859, s 40).[14] The theme of the last painting, a biblical subject set in Egypt, depicting the pharaoh mourning the loss of his eldest son, was taken up again at a later date [28]. He had also executed a painting of a Merovingian subject in 1858, *Clotilde at the tomb of her grandchildren* (s 35). It could be claimed that the themes from antiquity, Egypt and the Merovingian period – which were eventually to make him so popular – were already latent.

Under the influence of Leys, Alma-Tadema gradually freed himself from the traditional academic conventions in the choice and treatment of his themes. He

13 *Pastimes in ancient Egypt 3000 years ago*, 1863,
Harris Museum & Art Gallery, Preston

shifted the focus of attention from the centre of the stage to the wings of world history and was not interested in glorious heroes or famous battles. He was much more interested in giving an impression of the surroundings in which people used to live in the past by painting them in an extremely precise way. He was not out to idealise history, but to make it something that could be imagined and emotionally experienced. The Merovingian paintings were the first step in this direction.

Besides the paintings mentioned above, Alma-Tadema painted four other works on Merovingian themes between 1862 and 1865 [5]. For the history of the illustrious people he drew on the erudition of De Taeye, who familiarized him with Gregory of Tours's *History of the Franks* and with the writings of the French historian Augustin Thierry (1795-1856). The work of Gregory, bishop of Tours from 573 to 594, is a stirring contemporary account of the intrigues and bloody struggle for power in the land of the Franks. It was the main source for Thierry's *Récits des temps mérovingiens* (1840). Alma-Tadema had both a recent French translation of Gregory's original Latin text and a copy of the *Récits*.[15]

What appealed to him in this still rather murky period of medieval history? He stated to his friend Carel Vosmaer that, though the Franks were a curious people, they were picturesque and interesting.[16] He probably felt strongly attracted by the historiographical style of the writings in question. The *History of the Franks* is full of juicy anecdotes, and the fact that Gregory allows the main characters to have their say in direct speech adds to the liveliness of the account. Thierry does the same in his *Récits*. In the preface he emphasizes his 'picturesque' conception of the writing of history, which he shared with a number of other historians from the early 19th century, including Chateaubriand. The latter admired Thierry for his '... depiction of the way of life of certain characters from an old world which ends in a world which is beginning'.[17] Thierry himself regarded his *Récits* as a 'work of art' rather than as a 'work of historical science'.[18] Both historians practised a montage-like way of writing history, putting together a lively story from a smattering of sources. To quote Chateaubriand again: 'What is good and honest about descriptive history is that it gives the periods their own words'.[19] If we replace 'history' by 'painting' and 'words' by 'pictures', we come pretty close to what Alma-Tadema must have had in mind. Thierry painted with the pen, Alma-Tadema wrote with the brush. His painstaking depiction of architecture, clothing, jewellery, furniture and other accessories was supposed to evoke a realistic picture of the period. His paintings often contain parts which could function as independent still lifes. It is only natural for the eye to linger over skilfully painted pottery executed in a way which recalls the *fijnschilderkunst* (fine painting) of the 17th century. This attention to detail was often at the expense of the figures in his paintings, which particularly in the early work display the same stiffness as those of Henri Leys.

The critics and the appeal to the imagination

Not many people, however, outside a circle of historians were familiar with the world of Clovis, Clotilde and the many who succeeded them. The critics were not slow to point this out, which was probably one of the reasons why Alma-Tadema rarely touched the theme again after 1865. His *Queen Fredegonda at the death-bed of Bishop Praetextatus* [12] was on display at the Paris Salon of that year. 'Queen Fredegonda, weighed down by all the evil that had been done under the rule of her husband', in Thierry's words, had given her followers instructions to kill Praetextatus, Bishop of Rouen, after she had had a heated argument with him.[20] In the year 585 he was stabbed with a dagger during matins in church and was carried to his room by a few of the faithful. Fredegonda immediately appeared on the scene with two dukes (the figures on the left of the painting) and offered the dying bishop the medical assistance of her highly skilled court physicians. She hypocritically added that she hoped the perpetrator would not escape his just deserts. Alma-Tadema has chosen the moment when the dying Praetextatus points an accusing finger at the queen. According to Gregory, his last words were: 'Who has done this? ... No one but he who has killed our kings, who far too often has shed innocent blood, and has been responsible for many crimes in this kingdom.'[21] Thierry adds a detail to Gregory's account: that Praetextatus rose up in bed when he spoke these words. This can clearly be seen in the painting, which follows the written sources very closely on the whole – an unusual practice for Alma-Tadema. It is also unusual for him to give pride of place to the dramatic climax of the meeting, the exchange of words shortly before Praetextatus expires. This also struck Paul Mantz, a critic of the *Gazette des Beaux-Arts*. 'There is thus a drama in Mr Alma-Tadema's painting, but a drama that is stifled and lost in skilfully combined details of Merovingian bric-à-brac. We are absolutely not competent enough to assess the accuracy of the items of furniture, clothing, jewels and weapons, and we can only regret the fact that Augustin Thierry is no longer with us to appreciate the verisimilitude of a work that would certainly have aroused his interest'.[22] Mantz warned Alma-Tadema to beware of relying too much on his erudition: 'He looks for his themes in remote history, and to understand them properly one would really have to be a member of the Academy of inscriptions'.[23] A similar warning was issued when the painting was exhibited in Antwerp in the previous year. The rich details could lead to the work's being appreciated for its 'archaeological correctness' rather than for its 'praiseworthy execution'.[24] Alma-Tadema often met with remarks in this vein during his life. The appeal to a comprehensive factual knowledge of the past did not immediately put the average viewer at ease, but the overwhelming attention to detail often compelled admiration for the masterly execution.

14   *Leaving church in the fifteenth century*, 1864, private collection

Alma-Tadema later expressed his views on art in an interview with the art critic Helen Zimmern. Art, he claimed, must primarily stimulate the imagination: art lovers were such because their imagination was stirred. Still, one had to possess some knowledge in order to be able to look properly.[25] However, the imagination can be stirred in different ways. Here lies an important distinction between the work of Alma-Tadema and the characteristics of the modern artistic currents which were emerging in the second half of the 19th century, such as Impressionism. One could say that, in the case of Impressionism, the viewer is proffered a picture which is not yet finished, and which can be supplemented in accordance with the viewer's own temperament. The same can be said of naturalistic landscape painting, which above all creates a mood – the fashionable term of the time – that the viewer can test against his own world of experience. Truth to nature is no longer situated at the level of a tangible reality, but a felt one. Alma-Tadema appeals to a very different imagination: that of an archaeologist who pokes around in the ground to reconstruct the past. The artefacts that he finds are 'real'; it is their combination which is a reconstruction. Everything hinges on making the past tangible. In the work of Alma-Tadema, what is at stake is a 'genuine-ness' which by means of a correct, detailed depiction of historical artefacts was meant to convince and arouse the viewer's imagination so that the viewer felt a natural urge to walk around in that world. By further concentrating on everyday life in antiquity instead of the well-known major events, and by taking the archaeological artefacts out of the museum showcases so that they could once again fulfil their utilitarian function on the canvas, he reduced the distance between people and their past. It is a picture of history in which not people but their surroundings have changed.

We find the same approach in the group of paintings on themes from ancient Egypt. In contrast to the Merovingian subjects, Alma-Tadema returned to these on a number of occasions during his life [91] [27 28]. He visited London for the first time in 1862, where his teacher Leys caused a stir at the International Exhibition. He took advantage of the opportunity to visit the British Museum as well, and admired both the Elgin marbles from the Parthenon and the Egyptian art treasures. Under their inspiration, he completed the painting *Pastimes in ancient Egypt 3000 years ago* in 1863, which originally bore the more prosaic title *How people amused themselves 3000 years ago* [13]. The subject demonstrates his interest in the customs and rituals of contemporary life in the land of the pharaohs. The Orient had already attracted the attention of a number of European artists, such as Eugène Delacroix and Jean-Léon Gérôme in France, Frederick Goodall in England, and Jean-François Portaels in Belgium, but Alma-Tadema, unlike these artists, had never visited the East. He was not so interested in the Bedouin, camels and harem women (Arabia of the thousand-and-one-nights) as in the archaeological background. For this he was dependent on academic textbooks and objects from museums, which he copied and of which he collected photographs. The Egyptologist and historical novelist Georg Ebers, who established a friendship with Alma-Tadema after coming into contact with his work at exhibitions in Germany in the late 1860s or 1870s, was struck by the scientific quality of the subjects, which kindled his imagination. He included five works by Alma-Tadema in his de luxe publication *Aegypten in Bild und Wort* (1880).[26]

Turbulent developments: overture to success

Early in 1863 Alma-Tadema's mother died. She and his sister Artje had come to live with him four years earlier. He married the aristocratic Frenchwoman Marie Pauline Gressin Dumoulin de Boisgirard in the same year. Until then he had probably been financially dependent on his family to a large extent.[27] He was not yet in a position to live from his painting alone, but this situation changed in the following year.

The year 1864 was a very important one for Alma-Tadema in more ways than one. During the winter of 1863-64, on his first trip to Italy, he discovered the treasures of the ancient Roman empire, and a visit to the excavations at Pompeii, which made great progress precisely in the 1860s, left an indelible impression.[28] From 1865 on, classical Roman themes and scenes from everyday life in a Pompeian setting formed the larger part of his oeuvre. The year 1864 also marked his debut at the Paris Salon, where he was awarded the gold medal for the painting *Pastimes in ancient Egypt 3000 years ago*. But probably the most important event took place in the summer, when the famous art dealer of Belgian origin, Ernest Gambart, honoured him with a visit. 'Gambart, the picture-dealer whose smile or frown meant so much to the young painters of the time', in the words of Alma-Tadema's biographer, Percy Cross Standing, was based in London, where he had been presenting not only English but also French, Belgian, Dutch and German artists in his French Gallery in Pall Mall since the 1850s.[29] It was he who was responsible for introducing Leys in England. He had branches in the main European art centres and as an assiduous visitor of studios he maintained contacts with many painters. His astute and no-nonsense manner made him a charismatic figure and an influential dealer, whose many nicknames ranged from 'prince of picture-dealers' to 'Vampire Gambart'.[30] Jeremy Maas, who published a biography of his 19th-century colleague, claims that he made the reputations of two artists: Rosa Bonheur and Alma-Tadema.

The story has it that Gambart ended up in Alma-Tadema's studio by mistake.[31] His carriage was deliberately sent to Alma-Tadema's address by friends of the painter, instead of to that of the genre painter Joseph

15 *Proclaiming Claudius Emperor*, 1867,
   whereabouts unknown

Dyckmans, one of Alma-Tadema's former teachers at the academy. Gambart treated the deception in a sporting fashion, examined the work, and was so impressed by the painting that stood on the easel that he bought it on the spot even though it was intended for a different dealer. Without a doubt it is an attractive story, but Gambart must have heard of the artist earlier. After all, he had known Leys for some time and must have discussed his talented pupil with him. Nor is he likely to have missed the gold medal at the Paris Salon, some two months before the meeting. It appears that Rosa Bonheur drew his attention to Alma-Tadema at the time.[32]

The meeting had serious repercussions, which go some way to confirming that Gambart could make reputations. He offered the thirty-year old artist a contract for twenty-four paintings. He increased the price for each painting, resulting in an average price for the whole commission of £ 80 per painting. Although this was not an exceptionally high sum, it was certainly a lucrative basis on which to set up as an independent painter. This was especially so because Alma-Tadema completed the commission in a little more than three years, which meant a regular gross income of around £ 270 a year (slightly more than 3000 guilders in Dutch currency.)[33] By comparison with the earnings of Dutch artists at the time, he belonged to the upper middle class, on a par with the famous painter of church interiors Johannes Bosboom, who earned between 1800 and 4500 guilders a year.[34] Alma-Tadema could certainly use the money. A son, Eugène, was born in the summer, though he died in

October, and some financial elbow-room was very welcome at that time. He had only managed to sell a few works before his meeting with Gambart. The largest amount that he received was £ 64 (about 800 guilders) in 1861 for *The education of the children of Clovis* [3], but works which had already won a medal, *Venantius Fortunatus reading his poems to Radegonda VI* [5] and *Pastimes in ancient Egypt 3000 years ago* [13], had still not found buyers.

However, Gambart stipulated one condition that turned out badly for the artist. The painting on the easel which had so appealed to him was *Leaving church in the fifteenth century* [14] [7]. Gambart must have thought that he was engaging a second Leys and proposed to Alma-Tadema that he produce paintings on a similar theme. Alma-Tadema, however, had discovered the Egyptians the previous year and was about to embark on Pompeian subjects. In the end he managed to convince Gambart of the new direction he had taken and the commission was eventually to include only three subjects from Flemish history. The fact that Gambart conceded was connected with the interest which had arisen at precisely that time in England for the work of Frederic Leighton and other Neo-Classical painters.[35] The genre-like approach of Alma-Tadema's paintings and their explicit knowledge of factual details set them apart from the more idealized works of someone like Leighton, conferring on them a special place within classicizing circles.

Partly at the instigation of Gambart, the artist moved to the more fashionable city of Brussels in the spring of 1865. Another contributory factor to the move was that it brought the couple closer to the family of Marie Pauline, who regularly suffered from poor health. She gave birth to two daughters, Laurense (1865) and Anna (1867), and died of smallpox in May 1869. In the 1860s Brussels had expanded to become a welcome alternative to Paris for those who wanted to set up as artists. A direct rail link with the French capital had brought it closer too. Many important art dealers had a branch there, and the Brussels Salon was on a much larger scale than its Antwerp counterpart, as can be seen from the considerable attention that it paid to French art, for example.[36]

Alma-Tadema's five years in Brussels were marked by an unprecedented productivity. Three-quarters of the almost eighty paintings that he produced in Belgium and later provided with an opus number were created in Brussels. The (Antwerp) period of apprenticeship was over, and he now concentrated on establishing his reputation, making welcome use of the contacts that he maintained with different artists to this end. For instance, another painter from Friesland, Christoffel Bisschop, helped to secure his participation in the Exposition Universelle in Paris in 1867.[37] Bisschop was a member of the Pulchri Studio association of artists in The Hague and of the commission responsible for the Dutch contribution to the exposition. His correspondence with Alma-Tadema reveals that the latter had many friends among Dutch artists. They visited one another and kept one another informed of what was going on in Belgium and the Netherlands. Around 1867 Alma-Tadema began to organize soirées at home. Among the guests were artists like Félicien Rops and the successful salon painter Jan Verhas (see p. 46) [27]. These soirées must also have been attended by his cousin, Hendrik Willem Mesdag, who was later to become a famous maritime painter. Mesdag had come to Brussels in 1866 to learn the art of painting under the guidance of Alma-Tadema and the landscape painter Willem Roelofs.[38] Alma-Tadema's contacts with other artists were not confined to figures who all shared the same conception of art. This can be seen, for example, from his support for the progressive Brussels association of artists Société Libre des Beaux-Arts.[39] It was not in his nature to make critical statements about artists who worked in a different style. On the contrary, he was often appreciated by his fellow artists for his craftsmanship and for his technical mastery rather than for his subject matter.

On the basis of various pieces of evidence it may be concluded that Alma-Tadema had secured a permanent place in the art world by about 1868. At first his work was slow in finding buyers. This can be seen from his amazement during an evening party at Gambart's in London in May 1866 when he noticed that most of the paintings which he had been commissioned to produce were hanging on the wall.[40] This situation soon changed. The sales figures on each painting which Swanson compiled in his catalogue raisonné indicate that from the second half of 1866 most of the paintings found a buyer within a couple of months (and in one case after only one week). This must have considerably increased the

men's confidence in one another and prompted Gambart to commission another fifty-two works from the artist in 1868, once again with an increase in price.[41] In the same year Alma-Tadema began making two versions of a few paintings. Another piece of evidence for the reputation that he was beginning to build up can be found in a letter to Mesdag dated 8 June 1868, in which he writes: '... if an art-lover has asked about my painting, believe me, it is more to own a work by me than because he likes it'.[42] The same letter contains more information which is worth quoting: 'One thing is certain: my reputation in Paris is greater than in Holland and Belgium. Everyone knows me there. I have even met a gentleman who has offered to build me a house on his land to suit my wishes and needs and drawings ... I did not immediately take him up on it, as it is not yet entirely suitable for me. We have been to see a few houses which were very charming and suitable, all for a rent of around 5, 6 or 7 thousand francs, near the Rue de Boulogne, Rue de Bruxelles, Rue Laval, etc., in the heart of Paris. So I have discovered that it is quite possible to live in an entire house with a garden in Paris. However, we have postponed the matter for a while, as there is no hurry and we have the time'. The amount of money that he was able to pay for renting a house is substantial. Apparently success made him set his sights on Paris, where he had already won three medals.[43] What was the situation like in the Netherlands?

The situation in the Netherlands and the choice of England

Appreciation of Alma-Tadema in his own country oscillated between two extremes in the 1860s: in 1862 he was awarded a gold medal at the exhibition of Living Masters in Amsterdam for his painting *Venantius Fortunatus reading his poems to Radegonda VI* [5], one of the few paintings to be sold in the Netherlands, albeit five years later. He was also offered membership of the Dutch Royal Academy on this occasion. King Willem III knighted him in 1868 for his general contribution to Dutch art, two years after Leopold II of Belgium had made him a Knight of the Order of Leopold.

On the other hand, the criticism in the main Dutch art journals of the day was by no means lavish. Positive aspects of his work were pointed out, such as the

16   *Portrait of Carel Vosmaer*, 1871, Rijksprentenkabinet, Amsterdam

technical execution and the display of erudition, but a universal complaint was the low level of conviction of the whole and the fact that he used his talents to depict scenes set in a classical past. The glory of the 17th-century Dutch masters determined the direction of painting in the Netherlands to a large extent, and new developments in landscape painting found their way from Barbizon to the North.[44] In the exhibitions of Living Masters in the Netherlands, in which Alma-Tadema regularly participated, historical paintings accounted for a mere two per cent of the total number of paintings on sale in the period between 1858 and 1896. Genre paintings, figure compositions and landscapes together accounted for more than sixty per cent.[45] In 1866 a critic in *Kunstkronijk* noted: 'Less attuned to the national movement in art, and not at all recalling Dutch everyday life in subject matter, is Alma Tadema, the artist from Friesland ... who has chosen his theme from Greek or Roman antiquity', adding the complaint that the painter was too much concerned with details and accessories.[46] Alma-Tadema must have been astonished when even Rembrandt passed judgement on his work. The latter's statue had come to life to inspect the exhibition of Living Masters in Amsterdam in 1867. As he stood before the painting *Proclaiming Claudius Emperor* [15], the master uttered the words: 'It must have been commissioned for the library of some archaeologist or other ... because that is not the vocation of art: it has no soul, even though all the ancient bric-à-brac is displayed with an undeniable professionalism'.[47]

Particularly after 1870 Alma-Tadema found an enthusiastic defender of his art in the Netherlands in the figure of the writer and classicist mentioned earlier, Carel Vosmaer (1826-1888) [16]. Alma-Tadema got to know Vosmaer around 1869. The two men began a lively correspondence, and in the mid-1870s Vosmaer began the compilation of an oeuvre catalogue.[48] He was also the author of the first Dutch-language biography of the painter of any length in 1885. Both men approached history in the same way, and Vosmaer never tired of the many details in the paintings, on which he remarked: 'We must read them from beginning to end like a page'.[49] Time and again he put pen to paper to defend the painter, who became naturalized as a British citizen in 1873. The greatest honour that Vosmaer paid to Alma-Tadema was to use him as a model for one of the protagonists in his popular novel *The amazon* (1880), the painter Siwart Aisma.[50]

Given the nature of his work, classicizing genre painting, in the Netherlands Alma-Tadema would have had to rely in the first instance on public commissions. However, the Dutch government, particularly the Prime Minister J.P. Thorbecke, had stated in no uncertain terms that art was not a concern for the government. The backing of well-disposed individuals or associations would have to suffice to support budding artistic talent. In his view, material assistance did not promote genius, and nothing was more fatal to an artist's independence than intervention by a government or monarch.[51] Vosmaer too noted in 1867, with regret, that 'in accordance with government policy' public buildings were not decorated with historical paintings.[52] An extremely virulent rejection of this branch of painting was published in *De Nederlandsche Spectator* in 1869: 'Historical art is nonsense', according to a certain J. Maalman: when it came down to it, the Dutch were a natural and simple people, and art should be the same.[53]

In the light of his contacts with various Dutch artists, Alma-Tadema must have been aware of the hostile artistic climate, if he had not already drawn the same conclusion from the low sales of his paintings in his native country. He was therefore probably surprised when he was invited in 1870 to become the director and first professor of the newly established Rijksacademie in Amsterdam, the successor to the Royal Academy after the closure of the latter. The draft plan contained a profile of a young, talented artist who already enjoyed the necessary prestige.[54] Alma-Tadema matched the description, although his reputation had mainly been established abroad. He was flattered, but discreetly indicated that he was not interested in the position. 'After much deliberation, I must confess that it would be rash for a young man like myself, who is engaged in making a name for himself and thus has little experience, as well as only limited resources at his disposal, to take up a position as head of the art academy that must officially be recognized as the leading one in our country', was his reply to the minister responsible.[55]

He deliberately opted for an independent career abroad, no doubt based on the success of his sales in England. His director's salary would have been 3000 guilders a year, the equivalent of two paintings for Gambart, and he was not yet even halfway through the second commission. What is more, his annual income at the time was two or three times as much, which put the temptation of a civil servant's pension in a different light. He could also have chosen France, but the death of his French wife and the outbreak of the Franco-Prussian war in July 1870 probably deterred him. Although he was very well known in France, interest in collecting his work was as low there as in the Netherlands.

There was another factor involved as well. On the advice of Gambart, he had consulted the London physician Sir Henry Thompson [85] for problems with his bladder. He visited Thompson in the winter of 1869-70, and Gambart took advantage of the opportunity to introduce him to a few painters, including John Everett Millais, Dante Gabriel Rossetti and George Frederic Watts. In a letter to his friend, the Belgian livestock and maritime painter Alfred Verwee, he wrote: 'They are a rough crowd. I already know the whole Pre-Raphaelite clique'.[56] A dinner was organized in his honour and he was surprised to see how much prestige Gambart enjoyed among the assembled guests. This must have reinforced his confidence in his art dealer even more. Finally, an event took place during a dancing party at Ford Madox Brown's which made up his mind to leave for England: he fell in love at first sight with the seventeen-year old Laura Theresa Epps and married her eighteen months later.[57]

England became Alma-Tadema's second fatherland. The continent had given him a measure of recognition, but it had not provided a retail market. The cartoon from *De Amsterdammer* thus contains a core of truth. During the last quarter of the 19th century, the style of painting which attracted the most attention in the Netherlands was mainly that of the genre and landscape painters of the Hague School. A younger generation of artists and writers associated with the revolutionary monthly *De Nieuwe Gids* elevated 'mood' and 'atmosphere' to the status of the most important properties of authentic art. Its major critic, the artist Jan Veth, wrote Alma-Tadema's work off as soulless labour.[58] The archaeologist got in the way of the artist. Veth compared *Hadrian in England: visiting a Romano-British pottery* [63-65] with a 'careless' watercolour by Jozef Israëls, the most important Dutch painter of the lives of farmers and fishermen at the time. According to Veth, Israëls's suggestive impressionistic touch contained far more spirituality and material for reflection: 'Let someone engage you for a long time in the most cultured style in the world, with skilful transitions, with taste, with a perfect grasp of his subject, on interesting events from the life of antiquity, until a suspicion begins to dawn on you that he is not direct in his intentions, and that he is actually using his exceptional knowledge and his polished and smooth delivery to conceal the poverty of his soul, – you will finally turn away from him and find more pleasure in another who, though his language may be deficient at times, blurts out a great human perception with deep feeling and childlike respect'.[59]

What people admired in Alma-Tadema's work was his archaeological knowledge, his technical expertise, and also the fact that by now he had made a name for himself abroad. His fellow countrymen liked to be received by him in the luxurious mansions that he had built in London. But few of them were excited by the themes of his paintings, with the exception of people like Vosmaer, and the exaggerated display of craftsmanship emphatically blocked authentic empathy, genuine involvement in the representation. Many preferred the small-scale sentiment of the Dutch interior or the atmospheric landscapes of the Hague School to the richly decorated life of an ancient past.

Antiquity fragmented and reconstructed

Alma-Tadema's compositions

Elizabeth Prettejohn

Alma-Tadema's first English critics found the accumulation of archaeological detail in his pictures compellingly 'realistic'. As Tom Taylor, art critic for *The Times*, observed in 1870, the artist appeared to be 'reviving the inner life of the later Romans, and does it certainly in a very wonderful way, and with extraordinary minuteness and range of antiquarian knowledge'. At the same time, Taylor was struck by the unfamiliarity of the ancient world as reconstructed in Alma-Tadema's paintings: 'after all', he concluded, 'their strangeness and remoteness is calculated to make such pictures more curious than pleasing'.[1] The artefacts seemed vividly present and immediate, yet their assemblage produced a world that was felt to be oddly distant.

One reason for this apparent paradox was that, however authentic were his classical artefacts, Alma-Tadema organized them into compositions that were flagrantly unclassical, by the standards of academic art theory. The pictures were crowded with minutely detailed artefacts in a fashion foreign both to the simplicity of classical painting in the traditional grand manner, such as the paintings of Jacques-Louis David and his school, and to the precepts of academic art theories, most familiar in England through Sir Joshua Reynolds's *Discourses* to the students of the Royal Academy (1769-90). Alma-Tadema's compositions came closer to the characteristics associated, in theory, with the painting of everyday life, or 'genre'. This might have been interpreted as appropriate to the artist's Dutch origins, or indeed to the small scale of many of the pictures, but critics found it strange in the context of classical subject-painting, invariably associated with the grand manner in academic art theory.

Instead of establishing a clear hierarchy among figure groups, as demanded in theories such as Reynolds's, Alma-Tadema's compositions often divide the attention among two or more groups. In *A Roman emperor, A.D. 41* [23], the action is dispersed to the extreme left, where an unruly mob of looting soldiers and inquisitive women surge into the room, and the right, where the Praetorian guard bows in mock reverence before Claudius, ignobly hiding behind the curtain. In the central position traditionally reserved for the 'hero' of a history painting, there is nothing but a heap of corpses, abruptly foreshortened and surmounted by a terminal portrait of Augustus, whose sculptured features are the only ones to display the dignity appropriate to a Roman hero. The disruption of the compositional order expected of a Roman history painting makes it patent that this is a scene of historical disorder.

The precepts of academic art theory required a composition organized to offer the spectator an ideal view, as if from the centre of the stalls in a theatre. Alma-Tadema's compositions, by contrast, often oblige the spectator to view the depicted scene from one side or from an angle, as in *Phidias showing the frieze of the Parthenon to his friends* [13] or *The picture gallery* [36]. The decentred point of view disturbed the critic Sidney Colvin, who in 1877 complained about Alma-Tadema's 'trick of eccentric composition, and of looking at nature, for the purposes of his picture, as it were through some queer slit or out of some queer corner'.[2] This characterizes the spectator's view as that of an illicit voyeur, not a privileged audience.

Traditional compositional techniques oriented the scene to appear an integral whole, rationally bounded by the four sides of the frame. In Alma-Tadema's work, though, the boundaries often appear arbitrary, with figures and objects cut off without warning at the edges.

17 *The flower market*, 1868, Manchester City Art Gallery

The critics of the Royal Academy exhibition of 1873 were startled by the disembodied heads and hands of two figures, cut off by the lower right corner of *The death of the first-born* [28]. In *A reading from Homer* of 1885 [67], the figure farthest to the left is severed almost in half, making his relation to the depicted event enigmatic. In other cases, figures are partially obscured. The arm of the female vase painter in *Pottery painting* [25] bisects the head of her male colleague, and only the disconnected arm of an attendant is visible behind the huge central artefact in *The sculpture gallery* [35]. In *Thermae Antoninianae* of 1899 [26], a gigantic column is cut off abruptly at the top, and obstructs more than one-third of the view of the swimming bath, perplexing at least one critic: 'further work is not likely to modify the intrusion of the monster column – or prove to those who do not look at the base that it is a column and not a slab'.[3]

These devices deprive the spectator of intellectual mastery over the depicted scene; spectators can never be sure whether they are witnessing the entire scene, or only a fragment of it. At the same time, they are 'realist' devices; the cut-offs imply that there is a larger 'real' scene, extending beyond the borders of the picture, and happened upon by chance. As one contemporary critic put it, the compositions appeared to represent 'bits out of a real world of which [Alma-Tadema] had been an

eye-witness'.[4] Displaced from the centre of the stalls, the spectator is denied comprehensive knowledge of the scene; on the other hand, the glimpse appears not to have been stage-managed or edited. This helps to account for the simultaneous sense of presence and distance that critics experienced.

Art historians have frequently noted analogous compositional techniques in 19th-century paintings of contemporary life, particularly the modern-life pictures of the French Impressionists; the 'realist' effects and the decentring of the spectator's viewpoint have been associated with the representation of 'modernity'.[5] It is possible that Alma-Tadema was drawing on this set of associations, to present antiquity with the vividness of 'modernity'. However, the compositional techniques have special resonances in the context of classical antiquity. At one level, they characterize the 'decadent' world of Imperial Rome as one that is dislocated, disordered, and unfathomable, in abrupt opposition to traditional notions of the classical past as a realm of stability, order, and comprehensibility. In this respect Alma-Tadema's work can be related to that of certain contemporary painters in France who were experimenting with non-traditional approaches to ancient subject-matter, particularly Jean-Léon Gérôme, as well as anti-classical approaches to medieval subject-

18 *Reconstruction of a Pompeian shop*, from: François
Mazois, *Les ruines de Pompéi*, Paris 1824-38, vol. 2

matter, such as that of Paul Delaroche earlier in the
century (see pp. 69-76).

Alma-Tadema's passionate interest in the debates
of contemporary archaeology suggests further levels of
interpretation. In some cases, a cut-off alludes to a specific lacuna in the archaeological evidence. For example, the famous Pompeian mosaic, the *Battle of Issus*, is
drastically curtailed at the left edge of *The picture
gallery*, so that only a few inches of its right side are
visible. Moreover, Alma-Tadema shows not a mosaic,
but a painting; the implication is that the picture gallery is displaying the lost original painting, of which the
Pompeian mosaic was understood to be a copy. By rendering the painting a fragment, Alma-Tadema reminds
the spectator that modern knowledge of the original
painting is partial, deducible only from the incomplete
evidence provided by the mosaic copy. In *The picture
gallery*, the theme of non-survival is also hinted by the
presentation of the picture on the easel with its back
turned: although this painting is the principal object of
attention for the figures in the picture, it is lost to the
view of the modern spectator [36]. The absences and
omissions, suggested by compositional means, serve as
reminders of the lost data, unrecovered or unrecoverable by archaeology [59 78].

Alma-Tadema's subtlest references to gaps in the
archaeological record would have been comprehensible
only to spectators with a special interest in classical
archaeology. However, his practices of presenting the
scene from a 'queer' angle and cropping it unexpectedly
serve as more general reminders that even 'scientific'
archaeology provides only partial information about the
ancient past, however vivid and 'life-like' that information may be. Alma-Tadema incorporated abundant
archaeological 'truths' even in his smallest pictures, but
his compositions prevent the spectator from concluding
that they are witnessing the 'whole truth': the spectator
can only guess what may lie beyond the picture's borders,
or what another viewpoint might reveal. The comments
of contemporary critics attest to the startling impact of
these effects, on 19th-century observers more accustomed
to paintings that presented the classical world as one of
wholeness and complete comprehensibility.

Alma-Tadema used unconventional viewpoints,
non-hierarchical groupings, and unexpected cut-offs
throughout his career. However, his approaches to composition changed appreciably over the course of his
career. In early pictures such as *The flower market* of
1868 [17] [14], the emphasis is on the accumulation of
diverse artefacts, in a Pompeian environment characterized by abundance of detail; in later pictures such as
Unconscious rivals of 1893 [23] [78], Alma-Tadema
focusses attention on fewer artefacts, grander in scale, in
a more magnificent Roman environment. A comparison
of these two examples may elucidate the shifts in the
artist's approach, as both his own interests and the
debates of classical archaeology changed between the
1860s and the 1890s.

The flower market uses a basic compositional formula that Alma-Tadema favoured throughout his career,
with a shallow foreground on the right and a sharp perspective recession on the extreme left [61 79]. It measures approximately 42 by 58 centimetres, the standard
dimensions for Alma-Tadema's early pictures, executed
on commission for the dealer Ernest Gambart. Within
this small format, though, the artist combines data from
the widest variety of sources. Virtually everything in the
picture, including the figural characterisations, can be
verified by reference to a specific source; the picture
might be described as a collection of what Stephen Bann
has called 'invisible footnotes', vouching for the authenticity of every detail.[6]

The Pompeian setting gives the impression that it is directly observed from life, but it is pieced together from diverse fragments of data. The stepping-stones crossing the narrow street are a conspicuous feature of the Pompeian topography, immediately recognizable to anyone who has visited the site. The wine-shop on the right is also based on the remains at Pompeii, but its depiction depends on an intermediary source, a reconstruction by the French draughtsman François Mazois first published in his book, *Les ruines de Pompéi* (1824-38), of which Alma-Tadema owned a copy. Mazois's shop-front is reproduced meticulously, including the garlands of foliage invented by the draughtsman [18]. However, the inscription in red lettering on the corner post is Alma-Tadema's interpolation, derived from an inscription on a different building in Pompeii, of which he had made a delicate pencil drawing (CLX, E.2846).[7]

On the right of the wine-shop's counter is a portable stove, instantly recognizable to contemporary critics as a famous Pompeian artefact in the Naples Museum; Alma-Tadema's collection includes several photographs of the stove [19]. Other objects are either based on particular artefacts, or made to resemble common types of artefact, such as the drinking bowls, the amphorae that the workmen are lifting at the left, and the rustic well, made minuscule by the perspective recession at the very end of the narrow side-street. Alma-Tadema owned a number of photographs of simple, workaday wells similar to this one (Portfolio XI); his concern for authenticity extended even to such thoroughly mundane artefacts. On the left wall, seen in receding perspective, is a reconstruction of an ancient notice-board; the division by pilasters into pedimented sections and the red lettering in elongated capitals are typical of notice-boards found at Pompeii.[8]

The critic Arthur Clutton Brock, reviewing Alma-Tadema's memorial exhibition in 1913, took issue with the artist's procedure of filling his pictures with 'documentary evidence', objecting that 'there is one kind of document that necessarily fails him. In Rome there are many kinds of Roman handiwork to be seen, but the Romans themselves have long been dust'.[9] The figures in *The flower market* are therefore inventions of the artist's; but Clutton Brock was wrong to suggest that they do not refer to 'documentary evidence'. The style of hair and beard of the older man at extreme left, as well as his

straight nose and the general cast of his features, recall Greek portrait sculptures, perhaps suggesting that the man is one of the many Greeks who inhabited Pompeii. The hairstyle of his female companion, with its roll of curls at the front, is borrowed from the fashions of the Flavian and later periods, often attacked as frivolous by the Roman satirists; the hairstyle probably represents the latest fashion, since such styles were still new at the time of the eruption of Vesuvius in A.D. 79. Among Alma-Tadema's drawings are several that catalogue female coiffures from Imperial portrait busts [19]. However, the physiognomy and facial hair of the young man, standing to left of centre, do not resemble portrait sculptures; at first glance they appear closer to the young male types seen in the 'Fayum portraits' unearthed in Egypt.[10] Although the Fayum portraits did not come to light until the late 1880s, a double portrait including a similar male type had been excavated in Pompeii shortly before Alma-Tadema painted *The flower market*. The large, dark eyes, heavy eyebrows, cropped hair, moustache and wispy beard resemble the male figure in this double portrait, of which Alma-Tadema eventually owned a photograph [20]; the artist seems to have visited Pompeii in the first half of 1868, and may have been there when the artefact was unearthed.[11] Although other sources are certainly possible, it is intriguing to speculate that Alma-Tadema was drawing on the very latest archaeological find. In many cases he incorporated artefacts that had been recently unearthed [35 40 68]. The inclusion of the latest archaeological discoveries enhanced the sense of immediacy, for spectators who could recognize the artefacts.

19 *Table and brazier*, 1st century A.D. (Museo Archeologico Nazionale, Naples), photograph by Robert Rive (attributed) from Alma-Tadema's collection, University of Birmingham (CXIX, 11089)

However, there is also a different kind of 'source' for the figures' characterizations – 19th-century historical novels about Rome. Many such novels include scenes set in wine-shops, presented as places for class mixing, gambling, and brawling, as well as intoxication; the disreputable shop of Burbo in the founding novel of the genre, Edward Bulwer-Lytton's *The last days of Pompeii* of 1834, was the prototype for many similar scenes in later novels. Marketplace scenes were also frequent. In particular, there is a scene set in an ancient flower market in the novel by Georg Ebers, *An Egyptian princess*, first published four years before *The flower market* was painted. Although Ebers's scene is set in a Greek colony in Egypt several centuries before the notional date of Alma-Tadema's Pompeian scene, the juxtaposition of a female flower seller with a male purchaser of higher social class closely parallels the scene in the novel. More broadly, the picture's inclusion of figures from all social classes of ancient life, from workmen to patricians, is analogous to the casts of characters in historical novels. Historical fiction drew extensively on the researches of social historians, as well as culling data about ancient life from the traditional classical texts. Although Alma-Tadema's library contained few contemporary works on Roman social history, and only a fairly standard range of classical texts, he had access to research of this kind through his friendships with classical scholars, including Ebers himself.[12]

Indeed, the picture amounts to a Victorian text on Roman social history, displaying abundant data about ancient commerce and labour; in addition to the shop and the marketplace, it includes the masculine manual labour of transporting amphorae and the feminine manual labour of drawing water from a well. The inscriptions on the walls allude to the ancient equivalent of advertising, expanding on the general theme of bustling commercial activity. Although the lettering on the left wall is not legible, it refers to the well-known Roman practice of inscribing notices ranging from official announcements to advertisements for theatrical entertainments and gladiatorial games. The inscription on the corner of the wine-shop is only partially legible, but names can be deciphered, indicating that it is an election poster of a kind common at Pompeii: Suedius Clemens is recommending Marcus Epidius Sabinus for office. Both men are historical, known from inscriptions and other evidence.[13]

20 *Double portrait of a man and wife*, mural painting from Pompeii, photograph by Robert Rive from Alma-Tadema's collection, University of Birmingham (CXXXII, 11451)

This introduces an intriguing contrast between documented – but unseen – historical figures and the 'fictional' figures, representatives of the multitude of Romans who 'have long been dust'. Paradoxically, it is the latter who come to life in the picture; although lost to the written historical record, they are 'resuscitated' as examples of characteristic types from ancient Roman social life. There are indications of social status in the contrast between the togas of the patrician figures, all standing, and the simpler costumes of the working figures, seated or bending to their labours. Moreover, there is a significant exchange of glances between the patrician young man and the plebeian flower girl. Vern Swanson cites the artist's own explanation, in a letter to a patron, that the man is buying flowers for his beloved, presumably a respectable woman of his own social class. However, Swanson also notes a comment by Alma-Tadema's friend, Carel Vosmaer, linking the episode with an epigram by Dionysius, implying that the flower girl is selling her sexual favours as well as the flowers;[14] this obscure Hellenistic epigram is included in the Greek Anthology. In his later study of the artist, Georg Ebers noted the same epigram as a source for both *The flower market* and the analogous scene in his own novel, *An Egyptian princess*: 'What dost thou sell? The flowers? Thyself? Or both, my pretty maiden?'[15] Indeed, the scene in *An Egyptian princess* suggests that the discrepancy between Alma-Tadema's statement and the classical epigram is only apparent. The flower girls in the novel approach the young noblemen by asking them to buy flowers for their sweethearts, but this turns out to be a ploy: the flower girls are prostitutes in search of clients.

Nonetheless, Alma-Tadema may have been deliberately offering a 'respectable' reading for the picture, for the benefit of the patron, a Mr. Markham, who owned *The flower market* at the beginning of the 20th century. This did not, of course, deter initiated observers such as Vosmaer and Ebers from proposing a more salacious reading for the picture; indeed, it is probable that the artist would have sanctioned the salacious alternative reading as well as the one he offered to Markham. Many of his pictures are amenable to this kind of double reading: a 'respectable' reading for the general public, as well as a more risqué or subversive meaning for initiates [29 41 50]. In the case of *The flower market*, the recorded comments of Alma-Tadema, Vosmaer, and Ebers provide particularly strong evidence for the existence of alternative readings for the same scene.

If the classical epigram can be considered one of the 'sources' for the picture, it is the most traditional of the sources Alma-Tadema draws upon, despite its salacious suggestion; the subjects of traditional classical paintings were ordinarily drawn from the ancient literary texts that formed the basis of the gentleman's classical education. However, *The flower market* combines this reference to a classical text with the widest variety of other kinds of 'source'; the ones named above may be only a fraction of those on which the artist drew. Even this list, though, is remarkably diverse, including literary texts ancient and modern, ancient artefacts and modern reconstructions, with tenuous dividing-lines between 'fact' and 'fiction'; Alma-Tadema juxtaposes and recombines fragments of data with considerable freedom.

In some cases this requires considerable alteration to the 'sources'. For example, Mazois's reconstructed shop had sold food, not wine. The wall painting of Ceres on the corner post, faithfully reproduced from Mazois, made rather more sense in the context of a food shop, since Ceres is the goddess of corn. However, Alma-Tadema's addition of the stove, used for heating wine, helps to effect the transposition. Although Alma-Tadema was always noted for the 'accuracy' of his arte-

21 *Sphinx decoration*, probably from a piece of Roman furniture, photograph from Alma-Tadema's collection, University of Birmingham (CXIX, 11082)

facts, he routinely recast them in ways that suited the contexts of his pictures. He might, for instance, borrow the sphinx, commonly found as a decorative motif on ancient tables or chairs [21], increasing its scale and changing its function to become the fountain in *A bath* of 1876 [43]; or he might transform a Pompeian table into a lectern for the Greek poetess *Sappho* [22 98]. One reason for these transpositions was expediency: in the absence of an appropriate surviving artefact, the artist simply adapted another artefact to suit the requirements of his picture. However, the game-playing with 'sources' must also have been intended to delight and tease the erudite spectator; to recognize the sphinx motif from a piece of furniture, blown up to huge scale and spouting water, produces a pleasurable surprise.

In a broader sense, Alma-Tadema's compositional procedures systematically transformed the functions and contexts of the individual artefacts, by providing them with new roles in the assemblages invented by the artist. The 'authentic' artefacts were thus recombined into a whole scene that was pure fiction. Nonetheless, contemporary critics saw this as a laudable effort to make sense of the archaeological data, vividly illustrating the roles that individual artefacts might have served in ancient everyday life. In a sense, *The flower market* reenacts the

22　Table with pedestal figure of winged Victory, from
　　Pompeii, photograph from Alma-Tadema's collection,
　　University of Birmingham (CXIX, 11066)

archaeologist's procedure of piecing together a coherent
conception of the ancient material world from fragmentary and disconnected data. Indeed, the multiplication of
artefacts within the picture creates a kind of catalogue or
inventory of the various kinds of data about the ancient
world that were available to the modern scholar.

In early pictures such as *The flower market*, the
emphasis is on the accumulation of data to produce the
illusion of a coherent environment. Nonetheless, the composition employs the artist's characteristic devices for
suggesting that the scene is only a fragment after all. The
lines of the paving stones in the foreground show that the
scene is seen from a slight angle. The notice-board, the
botanically specific flowers and plants,[16] and the buildings are all cut off at the edges, reminding the spectator
that this is only one tiny corner of a thriving ancient
town; indeed, it is an insignificant corner, with just a
glimpse of grander buildings, rising in sunlight in the distance beyond the end of the side street. The principal
incident, the transaction between the young man and the
flower girl, occurs off-centre and on a diagonal; other figures, including the patrician pair, are pushed to the
extreme left. Moreover, the foreground male figure and
the canopy to the left of the wine-shop obstruct the view
down the side street; the potentially disreputable

actions of the carousing figures, in the wine shop and
just outside it to the left, remain enigmatic, since nearly all are partially concealed by some intervening figure
or object.

The flower market is characteristic of Alma-
Tadema's early works in the abundance and diversity of
its artefacts, and the multiple plays on their 'authenticity'. *The sculpture gallery* and *The picture gallery* [35 36],
Alma-Tadema's twin magna opera of the mid-1870s,
mark the culmination of this approach, presenting elaborate collections of artefacts at grand scale. However, the
artefacts are more homogeneous than before; the individual paintings and sculptures are variations on one overall theme. Later pictures such as *Unconscious rivals* of
1893 [23] continued the tendency to concentration, often
presenting only a few significant artefacts, increasingly
large in scale, and deployed in more magnificent settings.

Although *Unconscious rivals* is somewhat larger
than *The flower market*, it includes far fewer artefacts,
and these are organized into a simplified juxtaposition
between the vast curve of the vault and the rectilinear
space of the foreground. The Roman environment is
more overtly beautiful than before; the red colour harmonies of the majestic barrel vault, with its gradually
diminishing illumination, make a ravishing contrast
with the bravura display of shades of white in the foreground marbles. Despite the 'aestheticizing' of the setting, the references to the archaeological fragment are
much bolder: the architectural elements imply a vast
space, but the vault is curtailed just to the left of its
apex, and there is no clue to the length of its potential
extension into the spectator's space.

In contrast to the socially specific commercial
environment of *The flower market*, the setting of
Unconscious rivals is enigmatic; the architecture may
suggest either a public building of unspecified function
or a particularly lavish private villa. In either case, the
environment is much grander than that of provincial
Pompeii, hinting at the opulence associated with the
highest ranking Romans; most of the artefacts derive
from examples in Rome itself, which helps to explain
their large scale in comparison with the humbler artefacts of the Pompeian excavations, seen in earlier pictures. The barrel vault, inexplicably deprived of its end
wall, leads at an angle to a view of a sunlit landscape
which is largely hidden by the foreground azalea tree and

sculpture, but the deep blue-green water and the fragments of villa architecture suggest the Bay of Naples, where the wealthiest urban Romans had their country houses [79]. At the corner where the barrel vault meets the foreground parapet, Alma-Tadema introduces a minuscule detail, a tiny fragment of a sloping, red-tiled roof. There is no obvious formal or narrative reason for this detail; instead it enhances the illusion that the scene has been painted from direct observation, faithfully reproducing a detail that becomes virtually illegible from the particular perspective chosen for the painting.

This is only one of a number of perspectives or views suggested in the picture, without quite being gratified. The standing woman gazes over the parapet, but the spectator cannot be certain what she sees; the seated woman looks toward the spectator but does not reveal her thoughts; the sculptured amorino raises a theatrical mask from his face, but his huge marble eyes are blank. Most dramatic of all is the implied, but unseen, gaze of the sculpture to the right, one of the most audacious examples of Alma-Tadema's practice of edge-cropping. The statue is cut off so that only disconnected limbs are visible, but when the spectator's imagination supplies the remainder of the figure, the colossal male figure appears to be keeping watch over the scene.

Although it is easy enough to propose a straightforward narrative reading, in which the two women are 'unconscious rivals' for the attentions of the same man, this remains a hint, in contrast to the legible interactions among the figures in *The flower market*; there are no subsidiary figures and incidents analogous to those in *The flower market*, with its variations on the theme of ancient commerce. Nor can the sculptures be dismissed as mere accessories to an anecdote. The two large statues are based on identifiable artefacts represented in Alma-Tadema's photograph collection, as is the sculptured parapet, adapted from an ancient bas-relief [24]. However, they are not comparable to the useful objects, such as the stove or the notice-board, which help to illustrate ancient customs in *The flower market*; they transcend accessory status to vie with the human figures for the spectator's attention. Indeed, the gigantesque babyhood of the amorino and the heroic virility of the fragmentary limbs on the right preside over the scene by virtue of their huge scale, elevated positions, and their masculinity.

Comparison with Alma-Tadema's photograph of the 'real' artefact on which the right-hand statue was based shows how carefully the artist has erased the traces of age, supplying a missing hand, and repairing the worn places on thumb and heel [25]. Alma-Tadema

23 *Unconscious rivals*, 1893, Bristol City Museum & Art Gallery

24 *Marble relief with Bacchanalian decorative motifs* (Museo Archeologico Nazionale, Naples), photograph by Robert Rive (attributed) from Alma-Tadema's collection, University of Birmingham (CXLII, 11835)

25 *Statue of a seated gladiator*, photograph by James Robertson (attributed) from Alma-Tadema's collection, University of Birmingham (LXX, 9618)

makes the statue perfect. introducing exquisite details such as the yellow highlights on the restored toes; however, he simultaneously renders it a fragment by cutting it off abruptly just above the knee. This parallels the way in which the statue's gaze is notionally authoritative, yet literally absent from view. The combination of the theme of the curtailed gaze with the references to fragmentation keeps the spectator aware that this view into the past is only a partial one.

There is perhaps an even subtler play on the tension between survival and ephemerality. As contemporary accounts of excavations stressed, the ancient statues as they were unearthed retained traces of the painted colouring that originally adorned most classical sculpture, according to the latest theories of 19th-century archaeologists.[17] Alma-Tadema was fully aware of contemporary debates on the issue, having introduced a vividly-coloured 'reconstruction' of a section of the Parthenon frieze in *Phidias showing the frieze of the Parthenon to his friends* of 1868 [13 16 59]. In *Unconscious rivals* and other late works, though, he chose repeatedly to represent pure white sculptures; although they are restored to pristine perfection of form, they are deprived of their original colouring. This removes the statues to a timeless realm, where they appear neither in their original state nor in time-worn condition, but in an idealized combination of formal perfection and the purity of whiteness.

A purely visual explanation can be advanced for the juxtaposition of the white marble sculptures with the reds of the barrel vault. However, the picture's colour scheme might also be read as a meditation on transience. The warm colouring of the barrel vault recalls the painted decorations of the vaults of Nero's Golden House (*Domus Aurea*), famous from ancient descriptions and excavated from the 16th century onwards. However, the colouring of Nero's vaults was ephemeral; many of the paintings that had impressed the artists of the Renaissance had vanished by Alma-Tadema's time [78]. In a more general sense, the delicacy of the painted decorations, fading in the brighter distance, suggests the 19th-century preoccupation with the non-survival of much ancient painting, an issue emphasized in Victorian texts on ancient art [36].[18]

Equally colourful, and equally ephemeral, are the living things in the picture, the flowering tree and the two women, the precise details of whose intrigue seem to have been lost forever. The light catches the standing woman's red hair, skilfully relieving it against the red barrel vault; the flesh-tint of her foreshortened arm makes an intriguing rhyme with the cold marble arm of the statue to the right. The contrast between the warm colour of living or ephemeral things and the cool whiteness of eternal marble suggests a reflection on the theme of survival: it is the sculptures, not the living things, that will endure as testimony to the lost 'reality' of the ancient past.

The sculptures are also larger than life, as measured by the scale of the human figures. In many of Alma-Tadema's late pictures, the pure white sculptures are gigantic in scale. No longer simply one element in a catalogue of artefacts, they become monuments to the tan-

26 *Thermae Antoninianae (baths of Caracalla)*, 1899, private collection

gibility and durability of the physical remains of the past, counterpointed against the frivolity and ephemerality of the human figures. Even the 'monster column' in *Thermae Antoninianae* [26] becomes an emblem of survival, towering over the lighthearted antics of the bathing figures. Alma-Tadema's critics frequently objected to the prominence given to material objects in his pictures, but material objects are all that archaeology can recover of past 'reality'.

The monumentality of the artefacts in Alma-Tadema's late pictures reflects contemporary developments in classical archaeology, as interest shifted from the Pompeian excavations, centred on the humble paraphernalia of everyday life, to those of Rome itself, unearthing the grander remains of the Imperial capital, in the last quarter of the 19th century. More broadly, Alma-Tadema's later pictures gave vivid visible form to the late Victorian fascination with the opulence and decadence of the wealthiest classes of Imperial society [26] [69]. These pictures also presented the world of the Roman Empire as one of compelling beauty. Accordingly, they have often been treated as Imperialist fantasies, presenting the late Victorian citizens of the British Empire with a glamorous mirror of their own wealth and luxury.

However, this is to ignore the increasing boldness of Alma-Tadema's techniques of edge-cropping, vertiginous perspective, and bizarre contrasts of scale [43 63-65 72 79]. Such techniques enhanced the immediacy of the glimpse of Imperial life, so that contemporary observers could still greet the pictures as compellingly 'realistic'. Nonetheless, the same techniques present the Roman Empire as a world of unexpected disjunctures and curtailments. Although the Roman environment of *Unconscious rivals* appears more beautiful than that of *The flower market*, the later picture presents a vision of classical antiquity that is less fathomable than the socially specific representation of ancient customs in the earlier picture. In this sense, Alma-Tadema's late work moved even farther from traditional notions of the classical past as a realm of comprehensibility and stability. *The flower market* can be read as a comprehensive exploration of the available evidence about ancient commercial life. However, the fragmentation of the seated statue, in *Unconscious rivals*, is not only inadmissible according to the precepts of academic art theory, but frustrates any attempt to read the picture's Roman environment as a self-contained world wholly available to the gaze of the modern spectator.

Alma-Tadema's fascination with the material remains of the ancient world never diminished, over the course of a career spanning half a century. The artefacts in *Unconscious rivals*, although fewer in number than those of *The flower market*, are still conscientiously imitated from surviving examples, establishing contact with the 'real' ancient world at the level of immediate sensory experience. However, the artefacts that had served as accessories for human use, in Alma-Tadema's early pictures, dwarf the human figures in later pictures. The satirical edge of pictures such as *The flower market*, with its references to the more disreputable customs of ancient social life, may seem absent from the beautiful Imperial settings of the later pictures. However, it is not necessary to understand Alma-Tadema's more sophisticated plays on the archaeological evidence to sense the ambiguity of his vision of Imperial Rome. The colossal fragments of sculpture and architecture present the Roman Empire as a world where material splendour, beautiful as it is, threatens to overwhelm the merely human concerns of the figures.

Alma-Tadema, aesthete, architect and interior designer

Julian Treuherz

Alma-Tadema was an aesthete. A shrewd businessman, keenly aware of the saleability of a sensational historical subject, a sentimental anecdote or even a suggestive nude, he can hardly be said to have purified his art of extraneous, non-artistic values. Nevertheless, paintings such as *A favourite poet* [71] or *In my studio* [77] are not so very different from the 'subjectless' pictures of Albert Joseph Moore and James McNeill Whistler: they place decoratively posed females in self-consciously beautiful surroundings, amongst rich fabrics, precious objects, statuary and flowers, all painted with a fastidious touch in carefully chosen colours. In these paintings anecdote and human relationships may be suggested, but the eye of the spectator is struck first and foremost by the sense of beauty and the artistic effect of form, design and colour.

Like many of his contemporaries, Alma-Tadema sought to exercise his aesthetic sense not only in two dimensions but in three, in the creation of settings for his daily life and work. 'I have always found that the light and colour in a studio had great influence upon me in my work', he wrote in 1899. 'I first painted in a studio with panels of black decoration. Then in my studio in Brussels I was surrounded by bright red and in London – at Townshend House, Regent's Park – I worked under the influence of a light green tint. During the winter I spent in Rome in 1875-6 – when I was obliged to leave my London house by the destructive effect of the Regent's Canal explosion – I tried the effect of a white studio. Now, as you see, the prevailing hue is silvery white, and that, I think, best agrees with my present temperament, artistically speaking'.[1]

His biographer and friend Georg Ebers noted that he had been interested in designing beautiful surroundings from an early age. 'From boyhood he has known how to fit up his work-room in a way that satisfied his sense of beauty. Even in Brussels his studio, 51 Rue du Palais, obtained a certain degree of celebrity on account of its thoroughly artistic and extremely peculiar style of decoration'.[2] A glimpse of the interior of his Brussels studio with its deep red walls can be seen in *My studio* [10]. His interest in decorating his studio may have been stimulated by his teacher, Baron Henri Leys, whose own studio house in Antwerp contained a celebrated dining room with murals depicting guests arriving and partaking of a feast.[3]

Alma-Tadema was in Brussels from 1865 to 1870, just at the time when in Britain pioneering studio houses were being built for a few artists, including Val Prinsep and George Price Boyce, whose residences were designed by the architect Philip Webb in 1864-65 and 1868-69; and Frederic Leighton, for whom George Aitchison designed an 'artistic home' in 1864-66.[4] It was not until the mid 70s that the fashion began to be more widespread with the development of the Melbury Road estate by Norman Shaw and others.[5] By this time Alma-Tadema had moved to London and was well advanced with the creation of his first London home, Townshend House, near Regent's Park.

The artists' houses that grew up in late 19th-century London were an integral part of the economics of the late Victorian art world. They were built for entertaining and impressing patrons as much as for painting or living in. They acted as a discreet shop window for an artist's work; but the role of the studio was more subtle than simply as a place to sell pictures, a function which could also be undertaken at an art dealer's gallery or a public exhibition. The studios were lavishly contrived to

27 Jan Verhas, *Interior of Townshend House*, 1870,
private collection

show off the artists' taste in decoration and *objets d'art*
as well as to display their own paintings. The effect was
to enhance the status of the painters as cultural and
social arbiters, and thus to increase the desirability of
owning an example of their work.

Alma-Tadema's two London studio houses (he
lived at Townshend House from 1870 until 1886, when he
moved to 17 Grove End Road, which he occupied
until his death in 1912) functioned in this way, but
otherwise they were exceptional. Firstly, unlike most
other painters, Alma-Tadema did not turn to a professional architect, several of whom specialized in artists'
houses: Alma-Tadema acted as his own designer, using
draughtsmen, tradesmen or technicians to assist him in
realizing his ideas.[6] Secondly, his houses were not new-
built. This in itself was not unique, for Dante Gabriel
Rossetti, Edward Burne-Jones, Walter Crane and other
artists lived in old houses, which they redecorated in
their own fashion, but Alma-Tadema took existing houses and completely transformed them, spatially as well as
decoratively, removing doors, knocking down walls,
changing the alignment of rooms and introducing old
panelling and other features from elsewhere. Thirdly, his
houses were eclectic in a highly original way, not only
combining objects and styles of different periods, but
using exotic materials such as brass, aluminium and
onyx to create unusual effects. The results were quite
different from the standard look of the Victorian artists'
studio with its Queen Anne or Old English interiors furnished with a tasteful mixture of Persian rugs, Japanese
fans and blue and white pots.

Alma-Tadema's houses had more in common with
the studio houses built by non-British artists of the 1880s
and 1890s, such as the neo-Renaissance house built in
Munich by Franz von Lenbach, the austere but eclectic
Villa Khnopff in Brussels built by Fernand Khnopff, and
the Villa Stuck, Munich home of Franz von Stuck, neo-
antique but in a *fin-de-siècle* manner quite different in
effect from the classicism of Alma-Tadema's houses.
Each is very different in style, but in conception they are
alike: because in addition to being practical places in
which to live and work, they also reflect the imaginative
inner world of their creators.

Townshend House

When Alma-Tadema settled in London in September
1870 he stayed in Camden Square in the house and studio of the artist Frederick Goodall, who was then travelling in Egypt. Alma-Tadema soon moved to Townshend
House, an 'ordinary, somewhat commonplace London
residence'[7] opposite the North Gate of Regent's Park, in
St. John's Wood, not far from the home of Gambart, and
in an area popular with artists. The earliest interior
view of Townshend House, by the Belgian painter Jan
Verhas, a fellow student of Alma-Tadema's at Antwerp,
is dated 1870 [27]. It shows a modish interior and a
modishly dressed visitor, probably the future Mrs.
Alma-Tadema.[8] The walls are hung frame to frame
with photographic prints of Alma-Tadema's paintings
and the room includes several Oriental *objets d'art*,
part of what was to become a large collection: Alma-
Tadema was described in 1871 by William Michael
Rossetti as 'a devoted admirer of Japanese art – going,
I think, as far as anyone I know'.[9]

Though carpet and furniture were conventional,
the matting dado and draped doorway were then at the
height of fashion. Moncure Daniel Conway, an American
writer resident in London, described a number of leading artistic houses in his book *Travels in South
Kensington*. He noted the use of a matting dado at the
Ionides' house in Holland Park, as well as at Alma-
Tadema's, and illustrated a sketch of a draped doorway
at Townshend House similar to that in the painting,
recommending artistic home-owners 'to tear away doors
that divide a drawing-room and substitute a draping, or
else frame it round with looped and corded drapery,

which, having in itself an artistic effect, shall change the barrier into beauty'.[10]

Later descriptions of Townshend House remark on this lack of doors, a precursor of the flowing, inter-connected spaces of the Arts and Crafts movement, and a more distant ancestor of the 20th-century open-plan. 'I will only mention specially its numerous divisions, and absence, or concealment of doors, so that as in his pictures there are vistas everywhere, and from each room you can see another, if not more. This is not only characteristic of his own art, but of that of his nation', wrote Cosmo Monkhouse.[11] The same spatial effect is seen in Verhas's painting, which looks through an intermediate dark room into a brightly lit conservatory.

The evidence provided by Conway and Verhas is of particular importance as all other views and descriptions of Townshend House date from its reconstruction after 2 October 1874, when it was partially destroyed by the explosion of a barge carrying over four tons of explosives along the Regent's Canal nearby.[12] The artist and his wife were travelling home from Scotland at the time and so were unharmed, but their two young daughters narrowly escaped injury, waking to find a sash window lying on the bed and the house littered with hundreds of hazelnuts, part of the barge's cargo. Doors, windows and roofs were blown off but luckily none of Alma-Tadema's paintings was damaged (in 1866 his *Pastimes in ancient Egypt 3000 years ago* [13] had been ruined by another explosion, in this case caused by a gas leak in Gambart's house in Avenue Road, but Alma-Tadema, who was staying there, miraculously survived).

After the disaster of 1874 Alma-Tadema consulted at least one professional architect, George E. Street, who dismissed the house as a 'made up trumpery'.[13] The artist and his family had to move out while the house was reconstructed but they returned the following year and set about recreating the interiors, using where possible materials salvaged from the ruins. The refurbished house was extensively described and illustrated.[14] Most of these accounts remark on the small size of Townshend House as compared to the large premises of other artists, on its bright interior colours contrasted with the dull tertiary colours then currently in vogue, its collections of antiques, still unusual at this date, and above all on its originality. In this latter respect it was only rivalled amongst the London studio houses by Leighton House, with its Arab Hall, added by Aitchison 1877-79.

Most original of all was Alma-Tadema's studio on the first floor [28]. It was smaller than those of other painters and its square shape contrasted with the inde-terminate, doorless spaces elsewhere in the house. The decorations of the studio, painted by the artist himself [38], were in the Pompeian style, with a dark red ceiling and red and yellow wall panels, ornamented with arabesques, garlands and medallions. At one end were shelves and pigeon-holes for draperies, properties and for the artists portfolios of photographs (see pp. 111-124): these shelves were decorated by Alma-Tadema with fantastic birds and figures. The tints on walls and ceilings, 'somewhat expressionless' according to the *Magazine of Art* were, as Ebers explained, deliberately subdued to match ancient mosaics, whose colours, he wrote, do not fade.[15]

Tadema's copying of Pompeian wall paintings was of course appropriate to his art and central to his interests. Nevertheless it was unusual at this date to use the style for interior decoration, and almost unique in Britain. Alma-Tadema may have been encouraged to adopt the style by the example of the Maison Pompéienne, Paris (1856-60), built by Prince Napoleon, who sold it in 1866, after which it became a museum.[16] Alma-Tadema may also have known of it through

28   Joe Parkin Mayall, *Alma-Tadema in his studio at Townshend House*, 1884, photo-engraving, National Portrait Gallery, London

29 Gustave Boulanger, *The rehearsal of 'The Flute Player'
in the atrium of the house of H.I.H. the Prince Napoleon*,
1861, Musée national du Château de Versailles

Gustave Boulanger's painting of *The rehearsal of 'The
Flute Player' in the atrium of the house of H.I.H. the
Prince Napoleon* [29] (Salon 1861); which shows the atrium of the Maison Pompéienne lined with wall paintings
in the Pompeian manner, with the Prince and his literary and theatrical friends acting in a play based on a
painting in the House of the Tragic Poet in Pompeii. The
resemblance between the Boulanger and some of Alma-
Tadema's own paintings. for example cat. 20 and S 120,
suggest he must have seen it.

Even more idiosyncratic than the use of the
Pompeian style for his studio was the eclectic sequence
of little drawing rooms leading from it. First was the
Column Drawing-Room. furnished with chairs and
couches heaped up with cushions of Oriental stuffs,
recreating a room with Persian divans and rugs
described by Conway in the house prior to the explosion.[17] It is here that the architecture of the original
house was at its clearest: the room contained a standard
pair of what must have been scagliola columns of the
kind common in English houses of the early 19th century. Perhaps because they jarred with the exotica
of Alma-Tadema's furnishings. artists recording the
room usually managed to find viewpoints that concealed them.[18]

A section of this room was hung with a piece of
Persian appliqué work on crimson velvet, seen in
the alcove at the back of fig. 30 (a painting by Alma-
Tadema's daughter Anna, exhibited at the Royal
Academy in 1885). Another antique textile, a curtain of
embroidered Chinese silk, is shown in the painting.
dividing this room from the next. Also visible is the

30 Anna Alma-Tadema, *The drawing room at Townshend
House*, 1885, Royal Academy of Arts, London

Alhambra style ceiling. and the ornamental birdcage.
which reappears in views of the artist's next house [46].[19]
The room from which this view is taken was known as
the Gold Room after the unvarnished gold leaf on walls
and ceiling. Other features of this room included a
Byzantine-style dado supporting ornaments and a miniature copy of the Parthenon frieze in ivory. mounted in
ebony. Through all these spaces ran a stylish floor inlaid
with parquetry of ebony and maple.

Off the Gold Room was a kind of alcove [31.
another of Anna's paintings] also divided from it by an
antique textile curtain. seen in the background of the
portrait of Alice Lewis [66]. The alcove, lit by a window
formed from small geometrical-shaped panes of translucent Mexican onyx. housed Alma-Tadema's grand piano
with its matching throne, jammed right up against the
fireplace. another relic of the pre-Alma-Tadema interior.
The piano was made for him in 1878 by Broadwood and
it is noteworthy that when the *Athenaeum* named Alma-
Tadema as the designer. he took the trouble to ensure a
correction was published, stating the design was by
George Fox, 'who has been engaged on works at
Warwick Castle'.[20] The piano was a massive instrument
in the Byzantine style. made of oak inlaid with rosewood. mahogany, ebony, ivory, tortoiseshell and mother

31   Anna Alma-Tadema, *The grand piano in the Gold Room*, *Townshend House*, c. 1885, The Nelson-Atkins Museum of Art, Kansas City

32   Anna Alma-Tadema, *The library, Townshend House*, 1884, private collection

of pearl, and decorated with *opus Alexandrinum* patterns, monograms of the artist's initials, acanthus leaves, birds and lines of music. Beneath the lid were large panels of ivory which received the autographs of many famous musicians whom the artist persuaded to perform at his famous Tuesday evening receptions, including Clara Schumann, Joseph Joachim, Anton Rubinstein, Camille Saint-Saëns and Pablo de Sarasate. (Ignacy Jan Paderewski [75] signed the piano but refused to play it and when he was the star of the Tuesday recitals, a van from Erard's would call to deliver an upright.[21]) Sadly Alma-Tadema's grand piano was destroyed in an air raid during the Second World War, whilst it was in a London warehouse.[22]

The last room in the sequence at Townshend House was the Dutch Room, lined with wooden panelling, allegedly reusing the remains of a collection of old Dutch cabinets salvaged from the ruins after the explosion. Lit from lattice windows with wooden shutters, the room had a groin-vaulted plaster ceiling. Self-contained and surprisingly different in character from the rest of the house, it echoed the Dutch-style interior paintings of Laura Alma-Tadema, the artist's wife. Her studio was on the ground floor, reached via the staircase, hung with William Morris's Pomegranate paper and photographs of

her husband's paintings.[23] Laura Alma-Tadema's studio was furnished with Japanese fans and a cottage piano with painted decoration.[24] Also on the ground floor was the dining room, with a matting dado, and the library [32] with simple furniture and a chandelier to Alma-Tadema's own design. The decoration included a dado of batik fabric,[25] Japanese matting on the floor, Japanese fans and, on the ceiling of the section to the left (probably an extension to the original house), a Chinese lantern; there were also Chinese lanterns in the Conservatory. The library doors, on the left of fig. 32, were picked out in colours, and similar work can be seen on the painted doors in the background to the portrait of the artist's daughter [60]. The medallion portraits represent Alma-Tadema and his wife, and were amongst the items salvaged from the explosion. Alma-Tadema loved to personalize his house: the monogram LAT, his wife's initials as well as his own, was incorporated into the decoration in several rooms and over the drawing room door was an inscription recording the chief events in their lives.

The Marquand music room

Alma-Tadema was also associated with another spectacular piano. In 1884 he was commissioned to provide a suite of furniture for the music room [33] of Henry Marquand, a New York financier and art collector who was a trustee and then President of the Metropolitan Museum.[26] Marquand's New York mansion was designed by the architect William Morris Hunt. It had rooms in various styles, a Japanese room, a Moorish smoking room, an English Renaissance dining room and a classical music room. These expensive and somewhat charmless interiors make an instructive contrast with those of Townshend house; the Marquand rooms were much more orderly and 'correct' in style than the 'artistic' clutter of Alma-Tadema's rooms, where styles and epochs are mixed in a way which contradicts the popular view of his house as a miniature Pompeian palace. The contrast shows the difference between the eye of the professional decorator and that of the artist.

The suite of furniture Alma-Tadema designed for Marquand and made by the London firm of Johnstone, Norman and Company consists of 18 pieces including settees, chairs [34], stools, tripod tables, cabinets including one for music, and a grand piano.[27] The furniture was made of exotic woods, ivory, mother of pearl and brass with inlaid and low-relief decoration in stylish Grecian patterns. The piano was particularly spectacular, with Marquand monograms and Greek mottoes on the lid, and front legs in the form of winged beasts. The seat furniture had embroidered upholstery echoing the inlaid patterns, and there were curtains and portières to match. The furniture was exhibited in London

before being shipped to New York; most of the pieces were shown in 1885 except the grand piano which was not ready until 1887.

The inside of the keyboard cover of the piano was painted by Edward John Poynter with *The wandering minstrels*, a composition he later developed into an exhibited painting *Horae serenae* (1894, Bristol City Museum & Art Gallery). Alma-Tadema brought in Poynter and other artist friends to collaborate on the Marquand commission. The sculptor Edward Onslow Ford executed in bronze Alma-Tadema's design for a fender and a pair of andirons, the latter based on a favourite antique motif of Alma-Tadema's, a 1st-century marble term of a flute-player in the British Museum. Frederic Leighton provided a painting of the muses Melpomene, Mnemosyne and Thalia for the ceiling.[28] Two of Alma-Tadema's own paintings, *A reading from Homer* [67] and *Amo te ama me* (S 273) also hung in the room.

The form of the armchair may perhaps have been loosely based on an antique porphyry bathing chair from the Vatican Museum, a photograph of which exists in Alma-Tadema's reference collection [35]. This would

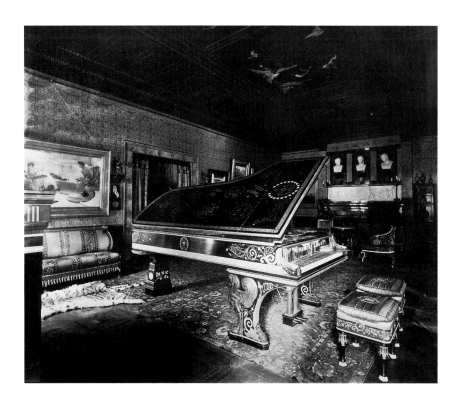

33   *Music room in the Henry Marquand residence,*
photograph, The Metropolitan Museum of Art, New York

34 *Armchair* designed by Alma-Tadema for Henry Marquand, 1884, Victoria & Albert Museum, London

35 *Porphyry bathing chair* in the Vatican Museum, photograph from Alma-Tadema's collection, University of Birmingham (XI, 7975)

suggest that in this case Alma-Tadema took the lead in the design process. The furniture was described as having been designed under the artist's supervision by W.C. Codman. who is known to have made detail drawings for the carving. inlay and embroidery:[29] Alma-Tadema probably explained what he wanted by means of sketches. getting Codman to provide finished drawings from which the craftsmen could work.

Grove End Road

A similar process was described by an interviewer with reference to the furnishing for Alma-Tadema's new house at Grove End Road: 'When his present home was under construction. he was continually drawing designs in delicate outline for such details as the turning of an ivory handle or the decoration of some inlaid panel: or again. plans were made for couches with strange and elaborate legs, or for other articles of furniture, which his workmen would carry out from his designs'.[30] The description of the couches suggests the writer had in mind the pair of studio seats (c. 1890). of which one is now in the Victoria & Albert Museum. each Pompeian on one side and Egyptian on the other [87].[31] The Pompeian side was inspired by an antique bronze bed

discovered at Pompeii in 1868: a photograph of the bed. in the Naples museum. is in the artist's reference collection [148].

Alma-Tadema moved to his second London studio-house at 17 Grove End Road in 1886.[32] For this house. the names of those who helped to realize the artist's ideas are known from the signatures on the set of 30 architectural drawings which survives [36 37 38]. These drawings were agreed on 12 August 1885 by Alma-Tadema and his contractor William C. Downs. Alma-Tadema's signature was witnessed by Alfred Calderon. the son of the painter Philip H. Calderon. who lived next door at 16 Grove End Road: Calderon's role is clarified by the *Art Journal*. which described the house as 'entirely designed by Alma-Tadema himself. with the technical assistance of Mr. Alfred Calderon'.[33] The witness for Downs's signature was J.J. Gaul. who may well have been the draughtsman for the architectural drawings. Gaul was in Pompeii with Alma-Tadema in May 1883. for Gaul's signature also appears on several measured drawings of details drawn at Pompeii. now in the Alma-Tadema archive.[34] Another draughtsman may have been the architect J. Elmsly Inglis whose outline sketches of 17 Grove End Road appeared in the *Art Journal* in 1886.[35]

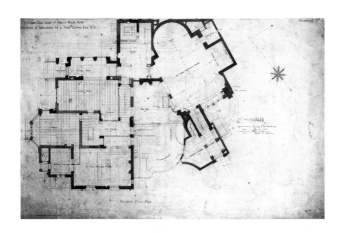

36 *Plan of the ground floor of Alma-Tadema's House in St. John's Wood, 17 Grove End Road, 1884, Royal Institute of British Architects Drawings Collection, London*

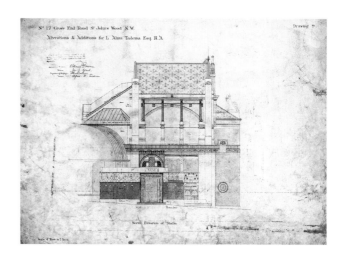

38 *Drawing of the north elevation of the studio of Alma-Tadema's House in St. John's Wood, 17 Grove End Road, 1884, Royal Institute of British Architects Drawings Collection, London*

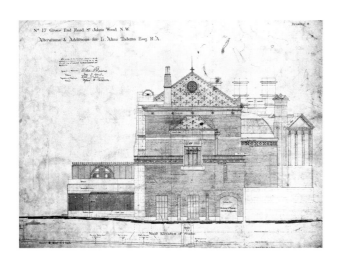

37 *Drawing of the west elevation of the studio of Alma-Tadema's House in St. John's Wood, 17 Grove End Road, 1884, Royal Institute of British Architects Drawings Collection, London*

Alma-Tadema decided to move to Grove End Road partly because of the small size of Townshend House;[36] the new house was much bigger and contained greatly enlarged studios for himself and his wife, and also a studio for his daughter Anna. His involvement in the Marquand commission may also have been a factor, making him hanker after grander surroundings. Like his previous home, 17 Grove End Road was a conversion, but a much more ambitious one, and much less dependent on the pre-existing plan. The house was formerly owned by the painter James Tissot, but Tissot's house, designed by the architect J.J. Stevenson, was completely encased, and almost doubled in area, forming a completely new layout. Of Tissot's interiors hardly anything was retained: a panelled room with a bay window based on the Trafalgar Tavern at Greenwich, was moved to an upper room, and Alma-Tadema also preserved Tissot's garden colonnade, loosely inspired by that at Malmaison;[37] some of Tissot's outbuildings were converted into a garden studio where woodwork, monogrammed LAT and dated 1885, still survives. From Townshend House, Alma-Tadema brought his growing collections of classical, oriental and Dutch antiques, and installed them with the same eclecticism and idiosyncratic use of materials, but the clutter was thinned out: the new house was more ordered, with a carefully planned sequence of spaces leading up to the spectacular studio.[38]

Today the house, long divided into flats, is in a sorry state, but its remarkable exterior still gives a good idea of its original aspect. It has a slightly diminutive appearance, lacking the breadth and scale to match its ambitious form. The studio, double height and raised up one storey above street level, was set at an angle to the rest of the house to obtain a north light [39]. The main studio window, exceptionally tall, was divided by fluted

39   North side of 17 Grove End Road, showing studio
     window, from *The Architect*, 31 May 1889

40   Entrance loggia of 17 Grove End Road, from
     The Architect, 31 May 1889

columns on high bases, and below it, the entrance passage was faced in marble panels with a curious frieze of
irregular chequerboard tiling. High above was a weather vane by A. Newman & Co. in the form of a palette and
mahlstick.[39]

The house was entered from the road through a
doorway set into the garden wall. A loggia [40] with a
glazed roof and tesselated pavement led to the entrance,
with its carved surround, antique mask doorknocker
and welcoming inscription 'Salve' on the lintel. From
here, a steep staircase lined in burnished brass led
straight up to the studio; or visitors could turn left
(see plan [36]), pass through the conservatory (a relic of
Tissot's house) into the hall and the domestic side of the
house. Behind the hall was an atrium with a gallery
around the top. The studio could be entered from both
levels of the atrium and from the hall as well as from the
front entrance: these openings afforded dramatic vistas
from the generally lower spaces of the house through
into the lofty studio.

An unusual feature of the hall was the fireplace
alcove, painted ivory white [41]. Its walls were inset
with tall narrow paintings given by artist friends, some
of them already installed in Townshend House.[40]
Eventually totalling 45 paintings, they were described as
an autograph album or a collection of artistic calling
cards, and most of the subjects were characteristic vig-

41   Entrance hall, fireplace, of 17 Grove End Road, from
     The Architect, 31 May 1889

42   Seven panels by various artists, formerly in the entrance hall of 17 Grove End Road, now private collection; from left to right: Edward John Poynter, *Grecian moonlight*, 1903; Marcus Stone, *In the garden*, c. 1901-02; Emily Williams, *The drawing room, Townshend House*, 1885; John Collier, *The temple at Philae*; Alfred Parsons, *Wild roses*; Charles Green, *A bit of old Hampstead*; John MacWhirter, *Silver birches*.

nettes of each artist's style; for example there were a Grecian view by Poynter, an Egyptian scene by Alma-Tadema's pupil John Collier, *A bit of old Hampstead* by the illustrator Charles Green, flowers by Alfred Parsons, silver birches by John MacWhirter and a garden scene by Marcus Stone. There was also a memento of Townshend House painted by Emily Williams [42]. Leighton presented his friend with the first version of his celebrated *Bath of Psyche* [52] and the musician George Henschel [55] designed the floor tiles. The chimneypiece was lettered 'I count myself in nothing else so happy. As in a soul remembering my good friends', one of many inscriptions throughout the house: 'Good morrow' inside a bedroom, 'God keep you' outside it, and in the studio 'Ars Longa, Vita Brevis' and the artist's favourite motto 'As the sun colours flowers so art colours life'.

The studio itself was the climax of the house. It was a large, lofty room with a curved groin vault and a semi-domed apse at the south end [43]. The general effect recalled the Early Christian basilicas which the artist had admired as a young man in Rome [6]. The lower part of the apse was lined with a long semicircular upholstered bench, identical in design to the Marquand furniture. Over it hung the Persian appliqué embroidery from the drawing room at Townshend House. On the right hand wall was an alcove lit by an enlarged version of the onyx window from Townshend House [44]. Below it stood the grand piano, behind which was a Chinese screen which appears in the background to many portraits [75 80]. To the left of the apse was a raised gallery [45]. Views from this overlooking the studio may have assisted the artist in devising the unusual viewpoint of *Unconscious rivals* [78]. The frieze along the gallery front was a relief by the sculptor Sir William Reynolds-Stephens based on Alma-Tadema's painting *The women of Amphissa* [68]. The most striking feature of the studio was the silvery light reflected from the inner surface of the apse, which was covered in aluminium paint[41] (the lower walls were faced in marble and the rest of the vault was painted white). Many artists complained about the poor light in London, especially in the winter, and built conservatory-like 'winter studios' to try and counteract this, but only Alma-Tadema sought to maximize the light by using a reflective surface. The influence of the silvery white hue thus produced is evident in the iridescent colours and brilliantly high key of paintings such as *Silver favourites* [83].

The studio gallery gave on to a balcony in the upper part of the atrium, at the back of the house, its glazed roof hidden by a muslin velarium over the marble basin of the impluvium below. In the atrium were bookcases of exotic woods, maple, pear, holly, rosewood and walnut. The atrium linked the studio to the smoking room, with cedar skirtings, marble facings and couches. With the dining room, the Pompeian style came to an end; it was lined with wooden panelling from the Dutch room at Townshend House and lit by a stained glass window of *Peonies in bloom in the wind* by the American John La Farge, a differently coloured version of that made for Marquand for his summer residence Lindon Gate at Newport, Rhode Island.[42] The Dutch theme continued into Laura Alma-Tadema's studio [46], fitted with oak panelling, stained glass in hinged casements, and a beamed ceiling re-using antique carvings and corbels. Adjoining this was the 'antique bedroom', with four poster bed and leather wall-panels. Furnished with oak coffers and presses, a virginals,[43] pewter and brass dishes and Delft tiles, these two rooms looked like period rooms in a museum rather than rooms for daily use.

44 *Studio alcove of 17 Grove End Road,* from *The Architect,* 31 May 1889

43 *Studio apse of 17 Grove End Road,* from *The Architect,* 31 May 1889

45 *Studio, showing gallery, of 17 Grove End Road,* from *The Architect,* 31 May 1889

Something of the bohemian charm of Townshend House had been lost.

17 Grove End Road became famous through its publication in art and architectural magazines. Perhaps because of this, Alma-Tadema was asked to advise on re-decorating the Athenaeum Club, London, of which he was a member. In 1890 a Decoration Sub-Committee was formed consisting of himself, and his fellow artists Edward John Poynter and Arthur Lucas. By 1893 their schemes were completed.[44] Alma-Tadema was responsible for the hall and staircase, the drawing room and the smoking room lobby. The coloured marble facings on the dado of the entrance hall and staircase survive, but the rest has disappeared, including the Pompeian motifs in the coffered ceilings of the entrance hall, the green and white smoking room lobby, and the sumptuous drawing room, with green brocade walls, gilded capitals, painted friezes of Pompeian garlands and leaves, and much use of aluminium on ceiling mouldings and beams. Some documents and drawings connected with the scheme are preserved in the Athenaeum Club archives. The drawings are in a number of hands but there are several for Pompeian style ornaments which appear to be by Alma-Tadema himself.[45] Two letters written by the architect J. Elmsly Inglis mention measured drawings and scale plans supplied to Alma-Tadema to 'enable him to scheme the decorations' for the drawing room.[46]

In 1906 Alma-Tadema was awarded the annual Gold Medal of the Royal Institute of British Architects, for services to architecture. He was only the second painter to receive the honour (it had been given to Lord Leighton in 1894). Alma-Tadema's achievement in designing his own house was specifically cited by John Belcher, President of the RIBA, when making the presentation, as well as the authoritative reconstructions of ancient architecture in his paintings.[47] It was a signal honour for one who was not a trained architect.

46   *Laura Alma-Tadema's studio of 17 Grove End Road*, from
      The Architect, 31 May 1889

Alma-Tadema and the English Classical Revival

Edward Morris

Most contemporary critics linked Alma-Tadema closely with the English Classical Revival of 1860-90 simply by virtue of his principal subject matter during his years in London – the history and everyday life of ancient Rome. The relationship was indeed highly significant for both parties but the tensions between them were more important than their stylistic or personal similarities. Establishing, however, the precise nature and membership of the Classical Revival is difficult because its origins did not depend on a group of close knit artists similar to those which formed the Pre-Raphaelite Brotherhood twenty years earlier or the contemporary St. John's Wood Clique. Frederic Leighton and Edward John Poynter had, however, met in Rome as early as 1853; Poynter and Thomas Armstrong had studied together in Paris between 1856 and 1858; Albert Joseph Moore, Henry Holiday, Simeon Solomon and William Blake Richmond knew each other as students at the Royal Academy Schools around 1857-58; Leighton and George Frederic Watts were close friends by 1855; Walter Crane was participating in the busy social and professional life mutually enjoyed by most of these artists, except Moore, in London in the 1860s and 1870s. Certain common principles can therefore be established. Above all compositions and individual figures had to be beautiful – or decorative to use the contemporary term – in their own right. Narrative content, expressive force, technical virtuosity, colour, light and shade and even truth to nature, were sacrificed to the higher demands of an abstract harmony or rhythm of arrangement of colours and shapes. Edward Armitage, a representative of the old academic school, but superficially influenced by the new ideas, made the same sharp distinction between 'decorative or semi-decorative work where

grandeur and harmony of line is the great desideratum, the graphic rendering of the subject being of minor importance', and 'all easel paintings which aspire to represent some historical event or to illustrate some anecdote – in these pictures the graphic rendering of the subject is the first desideratum and the pleasant harmony of line only the second'.[1] Artists found they could achieve this new freedom to compose decoratively most easily within subjects from classical history or mythology and they believed that this freedom to cultivate beauty primarily for its own sake had been first and most decisively asserted in ancient Greece. They did not for the most part exploit classical subjects for the moral or political messages within them in the manner of the late 18th-century Neo-Classical movement. 'It is not Greeks or Romans we wish specially to paint', wrote Poynter, 'it is humanity in the form which gives us the best opportunity of displaying its beauty ... it is not that the treatment of a modern subject is incapable of beauty or interest; what we have to consider is that subjects called classical are capable of a much higher beauty'.[2]

Classical reference, in a broader sense, was, however, essential to their art because it provided a vocabulary, a language well understood by their public who could thereby understand and appreciate the meaning and emotion implicit in their paintings. At a superficial level classicism permitted, even encouraged, the use of the nude and of beautiful and expressive drapery, revealing the underlying form, and yet also with an emotional force of its own in its smooth, rippling or agitated folds. At a deeper level classical mythology embraced a wider range of human experience and emotion than modern, medieval or even Biblical imagery could offer. This was the higher beauty to which Poynter was refer-

47   Frederic Lord Leighton, *Daphnephoria*, 1874-76, Board
      of Trustees of the National Museums & Galleries on
      Merseyside, Lady Lever Art Gallery, Port Sunlight

ring. In no sense were the classicists pursuing an exclusively 'aesthetic' or 'abstract' art and the extent to which they were even aware of theories encouraging art for art's sake remains uncertain. In a much quoted letter, Leighton wrote: 'My growing love for Form ... led me ... to a class of subjects or more accurately to a set of conditions in which supreme scope is left to pure artistic qualities ... These conditions classic subjects afford and, as vehicles therefore of abstract form which is a thing not of one time but of all time, these subjects can never be obsolete'.[3] But here Leighton was simply explaining his repudiation of medieval subjects in his early maturity. When he analyzed in depth the relationship between art and morality, between art and life, he concluded that 'so closely overlaid is the simple aesthetic sensation with elements of ethic or intellectual emotion by these constant and manifold accretions of associated ideas that it is difficult to conceive of it independently of this precious overgrowth'.[4] The career of Albert Moore, apparently the most 'subjectless' artist of the group and possibly through Whistler the most open to advanced aesthetic theories, can be divided up into 'abstract' periods and into 'emotional' periods, but even his most abstract figures were seen, probably rightly, as exquisite modern variants in paint of the Greek sculpture he admired so intensely and thus carried with them all the connotations of the ease, delicacy, grace and freedom of ancient civilization. Similarly, Leighton certainly criticized Watts's intensely moral allegories but

his concern was that Watts was trying to proclaim truths unsuited for pictorial representation, not that art could never convey ideas. Indeed the artists of the Classical Revival believed that their decorative and harmonious arrangements of rather blank, expressionless figures could, by virtue of their mood, their composition, their classical references, their poses and draperies reveal deeper truths and more profound emotions than were contained in the simplistic dramas and anecdotes of earlier genre and history painters.

Their decorative impulse sprang not from any contempt for subject matter but from a desire to paint murals on a grand scale in which, inevitably, meaning would be carried rather by composition, mood and pose than by narrative, facial expression, colour, light and shade. In practice they had few such opportunities although some of their grander easel paintings were clearly intended for the ample walls of museums or of their patrons' great houses – and some of their smaller paintings had not a few of the meretricious charms they so much despised. They came from cultured middle class homes and benefited from the intensive classical – and specifically Greek – erudition of the best English public and grammar schools. With the notable exceptions of Solomon and Moore they moved gracefully through the drawing rooms of cultured London upper class society and through the committee rooms of the academic and official art establishment: Poynter, Leighton, Crane, Richmond and Armstrong all held important official posts as teachers or administrators. Classicism suited the academic world and was the natural language of instruction – although the Royal Academy itself was initially hostile to the new move-

48 William Blake Richmond, *Venus and Anchises*, 1889-90,
    Board of Trustees of the National Museums & Galleries
    on Merseyside, Walker Art Gallery, Liverpool

ment and its adherents took generally longer to achieve academic honours than the very much less gifted artists of the St. John's Wood Clique. Like Pre-Raphaelitism the English Classical Revival had its prophet – Sidney Colvin, who indeed believed as an undergraduate that he was to become 'something like a Ruskin and a Matthew Arnold rolled into one'.[5] Colvin saw Pre-Raphaelitism as providing British art with intellect and Classicism as giving it style - 'those ulterior acquisitions, to some extent voluntary and communicable, which give to the formal embodiments of art, elevation, modulation, dignity with nature and grace with science and which are summed up in the word Style'.[6]

It was style in this sense of the word that Alma-Tadema most conspicuously lacked. His technical gifts were immense – in his ability to render surfaces and textures, in his command of oblique and vertiginous perspectives, in his control of tone and of light and shade and in his grasp of narrative and drama – but these were all qualities despised by the artists of the Classical Revival. The issue went deeper than style and technique. The classicists, like many of the Pre-Raphaelites, hated their own late 19th-century environment which they saw as dominated by industry, machinery, commerce and as profoundly hostile to serious art – hence their love of Italy where, at least until its modernization after 1870, beauty still lingered.[7] Their own real artistic world was outside and aloof from everyday reality – even if this sense of personal detachment and disdain was expressed

in very different ways by Leighton, Poynter, Watts, Moore and Richmond – and did not prevent active careers and social life. By contrast those who knew Alma-Tadema always emphasized his uninhibited immersion in and demonstrative enjoyment of everyday life. 'The sickliness of humanism has never clouded the healthy sunshine of this gay and wholesome spirit for so much as a moment', observed E.W. Gosse,[8] while W.B. Scott noted that Alma-Tadema was 'troubled by no metaphysic believing in no intellect or more soul than can look out of the actor's eye'.[9] Alma-Tadema's loud and exuberant behaviour on social occasions was notorious and it is not entirely fanciful to see this *joie de vivre* reflected in his brilliant and vivacious compositions and textures.

The same lack of propriety, of moral inhibition, is visible in Alma-Tadema's choice of subject matter. The artists of the Classical Revival preferred Greek history and mythology to Roman; they liked unusual subjects

49 George Frederic Watts, *Orpheus and Eurydice*, c. 1869,
    Forbes Magazine Collection, New York

50　Edward John Poynter, *A corner of the villa*, 1889, whereabouts unknown

from obscure sources rather than the hackneyed gods and goddesses of Ovid: their aim was a new and fresh poetic and emotional impact whether derived from the subjectless figures of Moore, the complex allegories of Watts, the historical reconstructions of Poynter or the classical subjects of Leighton and Richmond. Above all, they disliked Imperial Roman art and culture for, as Leighton put it, 'that craving for display and luxury which pervaded Roman society already in the last century of the Republic and merging in the general appetite for unbridled self indulgence helped to bring about under the Empire that moral turpitude and putrescence on which the wrath of Juvenal and shameless Martial's jibes have thrown so fierce a light'.[10] Yet it was figures, generally disreputable, from just this period – Caracalla, Caligula, Catiline, Cleopatra, Heliogabalus – that most attracted Alma-Tadema [23 69], while 'display and luxury' were the very essence of his art. In the same way he demonstrated his contempt for those icons of the Classical Revival, ancient sculpture and the Elgin marbles in particular, by reducing them in his various versions of *The sculpture gallery* [35] and in his *Phidias showing the frieze of the Parthenon to his friends* [13] to the status of elegant *objets d'art* in a dealer's shop. As for ancient religion which inspired some of the grandest and most passionate paintings of the Classical Revival – Leighton's *Daphnephoria* [47], Richmond's *Venus and Anchises* [48], Watts's *Orpheus and Eurydice* [49] – for Alma-Tadema only the female adherents of Bacchus in a state of wild intoxication or subsequent vulnerable stupor [34 68] had any real meaning for him. 'And it is the last corruption of this Roman state, and its Bacchanalian

frenzy, which M. Alma-Tadema seems to hold it his heavenly mission to pourtray', wrote Ruskin who praised Leighton as a Goth and condemned Alma-Tadema as not classical enough.[11]

The gulf, however, between the Classical Revival and Alma-Tadema was never in practice as deep as it should have been in theory. He himself observed that the symbolic grandeur of Greek art may have been superior to the colour, realism, individuality and picturesque qualities of Roman art, but that 19th-century British patrons preferred the latter.[12] Leighton had wealthy parents, Poynter could live off his official salaries, Watts could live off his friends, Richmond could paint commissioned portraits, Holiday could design stained glass, Crane could do decorative work and Moore could simply lead a retired and frugal life. But there remained the dilemma posed by Haydon's suicide – highlighted by Tom Taylor's dramatic and detailed account of it published in 1853 – that High Art did not pay in England, but that Alma-Tadema's art most emphatically did. Poynter's lectures were of course

51　Frederic Lord Leighton, *Old Damascus: Jews' quarter* or *Gathering citrons*, 1873-74, coll. Michael F. Price

aimed primarily at his own art students and were completed before he was forty, but his repeated attacks on realism and demand for 'the high beauties that lie beneath the surface of nature' – although partly just a defence of Michelangelo and a condemnation of Ruskin – still scarcely correspond with the imitations of Alma-Tadema's work which he was producing for much of his later career.[13] For Poynter it was clearly a sensitive issue. He wrote to his most notable patron, Lord Wharncliffe, in 1885, that he could not paint Cleopatra as Alma-Tadema had just done one.[14] When Cosmo Monkhouse wrote his official account of Poynter's career in 1897 to celebrate Poynter's election as President of the Royal Academy, he tried to demonstrate that Poynter's *A corner of the villa* [50] and similar paintings, were quite different from the work of Alma-Tadema, arguing that Poynter had a 'purer style' while Alma-Tadema had a 'livelier humanity'.[15] None of his readers can have been deceived. Similarly even Leighton had to paint the 'fatal inevitable pot-boilers' – as in 1873 he described to his father some of his small Arab genre paintings [51].[16] Leighton was, however, careful, unlike Poynter, to avoid settings for these scenes similar to those employed by Alma-Tadema, while his blander, more generalized handling was far removed from Alma-Tadema's sparkling brushwork emphasizing the surface and texture of individual objects. He gave the first version of his *Bath of Psyche* [52] to Alma-Tadema for the decoration of Alma-Tadema's house in Grove End Road and this painting certainly has a superficial resemblance to Alma-Tadema's work, but the obvious reference to classical sculpture in Psyche's pose and the conspicuous attention paid by Leighton to pattern and composition in the positioning of the figure, the architecture and the drapery, clearly demonstrate the gulf between his art and that of Alma-Tadema.

Albert Moore's *The musicians* of 1867 [54] has both the small format and some of the anecdotal and archaeological emphasis of Alma-Tadema, but thereafter he gradually reduced both incident and identifiable settings from his art. His friend and pupil, Alfred Lys Baldry, commented that he deliberately avoided 'the fatal mistake of attempting by the use of archaeological knowledge necessarily imperfect to reconstruct ancient performances' – undoubtedly a direct reference to and criticism of Alma-Tadema.[17] Like Leighton and Moore,

52 Frederic Lord Leighton, *Bath of Psyche*, c. 1886, whereabouts unknown

53 *A sculptor's model (Venus Esquilina)*, 1877, private collection

Richmond was also experimenting with classical genre just at the moment when Alma-Tadema was beginning to become well known in Britain. His *The bowlers* of 1870-71 [57] was less conversational and more carefully grouped and arranged than similar work by Alma-Tadema and it owes a more obvious debt to Moore. Thereafter, however, Richmond started imitating the more elevated art of Leighton and (briefly) of George Mason, eliminating the slightest reference to Alma-Tadema. Simeon Solomon's *The toilette of a Roman lady* of 1869 [56] was condemned at the Royal Academy of that year for imitating the decadent period of the later

Roman Empire – a criticism frequently levelled at Alma-Tadema – and he too did not return again to classical genre painting.[18] Crane was specializing in solemn processional scenes by the 1870s and Watts too seems never to have been tempted by Alma-Tadema's success. Both men became more interested in Symbolism and Watts was even more emphatic than Leighton or Poynter in denouncing dexterity, brilliant effects and naturalism as destructive of poetry in art; for him decadence in Greek art began when Praxiteles became more concerned with surface than with form, trying 'to suggest texture and sheen of the particular fabric'.[19]

Alma-Tadema became the principal representative in England of the continental 'néo-Grec' style – although in fact he was by no means faithful to all its principles – and the artists of the British Classical Revival with the notable exception of Poynter, well aware that they could not match his technical virtuosity

56   Simeon Solomon, *The toilette of a Roman lady*, 1869, whereabouts unknown

54   Albert Joseph Moore, *The musicians*, c. 1866-67, Yale Center for British Art, New Haven

55   *A favourite poet*, 1888, Board of Trustees of the National Museums & Galleries on Merseyside, Lady Lever Art Gallery, Port Sunlight

in daring perspectives, in the physical rendering of surfaces and textures and in the control of tone and of light and shade, largely abandoned the promising field of classical genre to him. The consequences for grand classical history painting in Britain were considerable. It has recently been argued that the cause of history painting in France was fatally undermined by the triumph of historical genre particularly at the 1867 Exposition Universelle in Paris.[20] More recent research indicates that this theory may be a considerable over-simplification and that the Third Republic after 1871 continued to encourage monumental history painting of certain types.[21] Nonetheless it is remarkable that Leighton, Richmond, Watts, Moore, Crane and even occasionally Poynter – not to mention lesser artists such as Armitage, Holiday, Long and others – continued to produce large exalted classical paintings at least until the 1890s. Official patronage from galleries and other British and colonial public bodies was on a modest scale compared with French state and church commissions, and practical support from 'Hellenism' in literature and philosophy has never been easy to demonstrate. Watts, Richmond and Crane seem to have sold few of their more elevated works; even Leighton had to struggle to dispose of his great *Captive Andromache* (Manchester City Art Gallery); Moore produced little and had a

57   William Blake Richmond, *The bowlers*, 1870,
private collection

58   William Blake Richmond, *The procession of Bacchus at the
time of the vintage*, 1866-69, private collection

devoted patron in William Connal; Poynter and Armstrong largely abandoned painting in the 1880s and the £ 3,000 that Poynter received from Sydney for his *Queen of Sheba's visit to King Solomon* (Art Gallery of New South Wales, Sydney), completed in 1890, cannot have repaid his work on it – any more than did the £ 4,000 obtained by Leighton for his *Captive Andromache* from Manchester a year earlier, bearing in mind that as early as the 1870s he could earn over £ 500 for a small single figure genre painting.[22] Competition with Alma-Tadema in classical and historical genre – even for an artist with the technical gifts and solid academic training of Poynter – was too hazardous and all that was left for the English Classical Revival was the rarefied air of High Art.

If the nature of the impact of Alma-Tadema on the English Classical Revival must remain largely conjectural more certainty attaches to the influence of that movement on him. He emerged in the 1860s as a student and imitator of Henri Leys whose style was well known in England through the success of his own paintings at the International Exhibitions of 1855 and 1862 and at Gambart's London exhibitions and through the paintings exhibited in London by two of his other students, James Tissot and Charles Hemy. Leys's style with its stiff archaic poses and draperies, its distorted perspective, its

unrelated and disjoined figures and its 'primitive', awkward compositions had certain similarities in feeling – but not in subject matter or technique – with early Pre-Raphaelitism but nothing in common with English classicism. Alma-Tadema always remained more independent of Leys than Tissot or Hemy and would have no doubt repudiated his master as rapidly as they did – but probably in the direction of Courbet's realism which in different forms largely replaced the style of Leys in Belgium. But Alma-Tadema was looking at England. He was in London in 1862 and following his contract with Gambart of 1864, began to exhibit there in 1865. His Egyptian paintings of the 1860s [13 126] paralleled the exactly contemporary Egyptian subjects of Poynter and they may indeed have had a common source in Charles Gleyre's studio. It is unclear whether it was Gambart or Alma-Tadema who decided that most of Gambart's huge commission should consist of classical subjects rather than Egyptian or Merovingian history, but it is clear that both men appreciated that if these pictures were to sell in London, their subjects should be classical. Alma-Tadema's exact motives for settling in London in 1870 are no clearer but it cannot have been a coincidence that his paintings at the 1869 Royal Academy exhibition [16] were well received and that that exhibition, hung by Leighton and Watts who were given a very free hand by the Academy Council, witnessed the triumph of the Classical Revival in England. The Royal Academy's exhibitions moved in 1869 from cramped accommodation in the National Gallery to their new and much larger purpose built galleries at Burlington House, but Leighton and Watts took advantage of the extra walls not to hang more pictures but to space out to greater effect their own classical masterpieces and those of their friends. Indeed J.B. Atkinson began his detailed account of the paintings in the exhibition with the comment: 'We proceed to notice the decisive classic revival which has set in under Mr Watts, Mr Leighton, Mr Albert Moore, Mr Simeon Solomon and others'.[23]

By 1869 Alma-Tadema was known in England as one of a group of French and Belgian genre and landscape artists popularized not by the Royal Academy exhibitions which were biased against foreign artists, but by a number of annual exhibitions in London sponsored by dealers, most notably Ernest Gambart but also including Thomas McLean, Arthur Tooth and Everard of Brussels. At these exhibitions Alma-Tadema's paintings were particularly admired for their narrative skill – rather than for the residual influence of Leys which they demonstrated. Thus the *Athenaeum* critic[24] was able to exactly assess the moral and social stature of the two women in the *Entrance to a Roman theatre* [9], when he reviewed it at Gambart's French Gallery in 1866 and, on a slightly higher level, William Bell Scott could weave into a description of *The education of the children of Clovis* [3], the entire story behind the picture noting, for example, that the debased Corinthian capitals must have been rescued by the Franks from earlier Roman buildings.[25] Narrative and anecdote were as alien to the Classical Revival as Alma-Tadema's vivacity and spontaneity of facial expression – so different from the blank, far-off, detached gaze favoured by Leighton, Watts, Richmond, Moore and even Solomon and derived by them from Greek sculpture. Like Ernest Meissonier in France, Alma-Tadema looks back to the 18th-century French tradition of the informal 'speaking' portrait with all its naturalism and immediacy. Alma-Tadema seems to have considered moving to London in 1869 when his first wife died and he was recommended to an English surgeon for a major operation; he must therefore have been alarmed to see at the 1869 Royal Academy exhibition the triumph of the English Classical Revival –

a movement so alien to many of his own principles. Among the most striking of the classical paintings at this exhibition was *The procession of Bacchus at the time of the vintage* [58] by Richmond. William Blake Richmond was already well known as a portrait painter but this was his first great academic subject painting and, with its slow and measured processional rhythm, its religious solemnity and ideal beauty of pose and composition, it was – for all its immaturity of technique – one of the most typical and important masterpieces of the Classical Revival in England. Alma-Tadema's *The vintage festival* of 1871 [21] must surely have been a direct response to it. Here is the young Netherlandish artist trying to come to terms with the English Classical Revival. The subject is similar and in both paintings the procession moves directly across the painting without any of Alma-Tadema's usual oblique views and perspectives. But Alma-Tadema was not fundamentally sympathetic to the steady and deliberate introspective grace and gravity of Richmond's painting. The result is theatre, not religion; the emphasis is on technical skill not on ideal beauty. The symbolism is richer and more exalted in Alma-Tadema's much later processional *Spring* of 1894 [6] but the profusion and crowding of incident, figures and architecture and the claustrophobic, massed advance of the figures apparently about to engulf the spectator are far removed from the organized and spacious grace of Leighton's processional masterpieces [47]. On the one hand there is the physical immediacy of a rich and sensational display; on the other hand there is the intellectual detachment of a calm and organized philosophy. Victorian art critics – and in this respect modernist theorists merely followed their lead – always favoured mind over matter, theory over practice. It is, however, possible to keep an open mind.

Alma-Tadema and the néo-Grecs

Jon Whiteley

Although Alma-Tadema occupies a secure place in the succession of illustrious artists from continental Europe who have been adopted by the British, he was the least British. Among the painters of the Classical Revival round Leighton, he stands apart as a realist who never lost touch with his early training in the traditional skills of Dutch and Belgian art. Although he spent most of his life in England and became a naturalized citizen, his art was formed outside his country of adoption, mostly in Antwerp, where Baron Henri Leys taught him the art of composing pictures with simple, static elements and Louis de Taeye introduced him to Gregory of Tours's *Historia Francorum* and Augustin Thierry's *Récits des temps mérovingiens*. He also read Sir J. Gardner Wilkinson's *Manners and customs of the ancient Egyptians* which provided him with some local colour for his first surviving Egyptian composition, *The death of the first-born* of 1859 (cf. the later version [28]). His earliest work was mostly based on texts, particularly his Merovingian subjects, but as his interests turned from history towards material culture, his art became less directly dependent on written sources.

From textbooks to artefacts was a short step, facilitated by the great museum collections which had reached Europe in the 19th century. The Egyptian collection in the British Museum, visited by Alma-Tadema in 1862, provided him with the details for his *Pastimes in ancient Egypt 3000 years ago* [13], exhibited at Brussels in 1863 and in Paris in 1864. He did not have an opportunity to visit the Louvre until 1864, on return to Antwerp via Paris from his honeymoon in Italy, and by this date, his interest in Egypt had given way to the inspiration of Pompeii and the antiquities in the Museo Nazionale in Naples which turned his attention defini-

tively in the direction of the ancient Romans. Later in life, he would remark that he began to paint Egyptian subjects as a prelude to painting later history. As a literal statement, this is an unlikely explanation for his early interest in the world of the pharaohs, although true in his fascination with the artefacts of ancient Egypt and the use he made of them in his first Egyptian pictures prepared him for the revelation of Pompeii.

The influence of Naples appeared almost instantly in Alma-Tadema's art, following his return from Italy, in *Catullus at Lesbia's* [59], completed in Brussels with a richly coloured Pompeian interior. The bucket on Lesbia's table is based on one in the Museo Nazionale, the first of a great range of Roman artefacts and works of art which Alma-Tadema introduced into his paintings from 1865 onwards. The Museo Nazionale was his favourite source. The statue of the infant Hercules in *The sculpture gallery* [35], the bronze sphinx in *A bath* [43] and most of the works of *The picture gallery* [36] were based on objects in the Naples museum. The sculp-

59   *Catullus at Lesbia's*, 1865, private collection

ture in the Vatican gave him a source for the statue of Augustus in *An audience at Agrippa's* [40] and the bust of Pericles in *The sculpture gallery*; the Uffizi provided him with the models for the group of wrestlers in *Prose* [53], San Giovanni Laterano in Rome with the original of the gladiator in *Unconscious rivals* [78] and the Capitoline Museum was the likely source of the bronze statue, the Younger Furietti Centaur, in *A dedication to Bacchus* [72]. From the British Museum, he took the frieze from the Temple of Apollo at Bassae in the same picture and the Parthenon frieze for his painting of *Phidias showing the frieze of the Parthenon to his friends* [13]. Like other 19th-century artists, Alma-Tadema had a collection of his own which he used as a source of props, including a replica of the silver crater from the Hildesheim hoard which appears in *A dedication to Bacchus*, *A favourite custom* [84] and in other compositions.

Alma-Tadema's use of detail was supported by a growing literature on the archaeology of the ancient world in scholarly and popular books and articles. From the 1820s, a wealth of information was published which gradually transformed the idea of the Roman world available to artists and provided them with an alternative to the literary texts which had previously been their main source of inspiration. Alma-Tadema used Rodolfo Lanciani's *The ruins and excavations of ancient Rome*, in reconstructing the Baths of Caracalla [26]; *Phidias showing the frieze of the Parthenon to his*

friends indicates his knowledge of the recent proofs of colour in antique statuary; the paintings in *The picture gallery*, show that he was aware of the argument that these compositions in fresco and mosaic were derived from a number of lost masterpieces by Greek painters. How much further his scholarship went or how much he cared is difficult to assess. He did not, as a rule, introduce polychromy into pictures which featured antique statues, preferring the whiteness of marble to the evidence of the archaeologists. His attitude, as he told a visitor to his studio in the 1880s was 'that archaeology must be absolutely correct in so far as it forms part of the picture and that if it be not expressive or necessary, it need not be insisted upon'.[1] His archive of photographs, now in the Heslop Room in the University of Birmingham, provided him with his chief documentary source of information about buildings, works of art and artefacts although, as Louise Lippincott points out, the collection is strictly sorted according to classes of subject matter and not by date and place as an archaeologist might have organized it. 'This method of organization, which clearly grew out of the painter's artistic process, enabled him to locate appropriate motifs as needed. Since few of the photographs are individually identified, however, it also made egregious anachronisms possible, such as combining objects made hundreds of years – and miles – apart or using them in contexts unimagined in ancient Rome'.[2] The typological division of the collection, with little reference to the historical

60   Paul Delaroche, *Assassination of the Duc de Guise*, 1835,
Musée Condé, Chantilly

61   Jean-Auguste-Dominique Ingres, *Antiochus and
      Stratonice*, 1840, Musée Condé, Chantilly

context of the objects, also indicates that historical accuracy was not a matter of over-riding concern for the painter by comparison with the artistic effect which they imparted to his compositions.

While Alma-Tadema's interest in antique themes can be linked to developments in archaeology, the artistic framework within which he developed his new range of subjects came chiefly from France where artists had evolved a similar range of subjects based upon the discoveries at Pompeii and Herculaneum and painted with a naturalism which excluded the idealism, heroism and theatricality of neoclassical history painting. Paul Delaroche (1797-1856) was the main influence upon this tendency, although he almost never, himself, painted subjects taken from antique sources and was rightly seen by his comtemporaries as one of the chief influences in undermining the fashion for antique themes in the early 1830s when his cabinet-sized pictures of French and English historical themes were widely reproduced and imitated. A visitor to the Salon in the early 30s in Paris might well have assumed that the antique art and literature which had been the main source of inspiration

in French studios for three centuries had been irrevocably expelled in favour of the works of Scott, Byron, Goethe and the historical chronicles of modern Europe. Yet Delaroche, like many of his fellow artists, was a passionate Hellenist. Critics, too, who were mostly classicists by education, did not repudiate Homer and Virgil but turned against their imitators and illustrators, those who in the critical parlance of the period, were dismissed as the 'classiques'. Théophile Gautier, whose Pompeian novels found an echo in the work of Delaroche's pupils, detested David and his closest followers not because they painted antique subjects but because, in his eyes, they had reduced the world of ancient Greece and Rome to absurdity and ridicule.[3]

Although Delaroche did not himself paint Greek and Roman subjects, he provided a framework for others who did. Ingres who had, for a time, exploited themes from French and Italian history and admired the art of Delaroche, was the first artist to adapt Delaroche's historicism in illustrating an antique theme. Painted as a pendant to Paul Delaroche's *Assassination of the Duc de Guise* [60], between 1834 and 1840, Ingres's *Antiochus and Stratonice* [61],[4] set in an interior decorated with wall paintings from Herculaneum, became the great model for other artists,

62 Hippolyte Flandrin, *Theseus recognized by his father*, 1832, Ecole nationale supérieure des Beaux-Arts, Paris

64 Jean-Auguste-Dominique Ingres, Study for *Tu Marcellus eris*, 1830, Fogg Art Museum, Cambridge, Massachusetts

63 Charles-François Jalabert, *Virgil, Horace and Varius at the house of Maecenas*, 1844-46, Musée des Beaux-Arts, Nîmes

particularly in the studio of Delaroche where the lessons of Ingres's mock Pompeian interior were more easily absorbed than elsewhere.

Despite the success of *Antiochus and Stratonice*, it had few immediate imitators. The catastrophe which had overwhelmed the Davidians in the late 1820s and early 30s left artists and dealers wary of antique sub-jects and, despite the presence of a few substantial works by artists like Delacroix who had never lost their taste for high-minded dramatic subjects of ancient history, the recovery was not really evident in the annual state exhibitions until the late 1840s. In the interim, the annu-al Rome Prize, awarded by an academic jury on the basis of a set subject, maintained a sub-current of inter-est in the antique themes which were often, although not invariably, set for the competition. The painting with which Ingres's pupil, Hippolyte Flandrin, won the com-petition in 1832 [62], includes a scholarly array of pate-rae, oinoichoi and kantharoi and a Pompeian chair with turned, spindly legs, anticipating the furnishings of Alma-Tadema's pictures by three decades.[5] The novelty of Flandrin's picture which marked the break with the art of his Davidian predecessors, was acknowledged at the time, but there was nothing similar in French art until *Antiochus and Stratonice* appeared in Paris in 1840.

Most of the subjects set for the Rome Prize in the 1830s were taken from the Bible. The choice, probably dictated by the increasing importance of Church art in the lives of academically trained artists, increased the sense that antique subjects were out of favour. In the 1840s, when antique subjects were again set for the prize with regularity, the pupils of Delaroche were becoming an important force in the competition. Taking part was

65 Jean-Léon Gérôme, *Cock-fight*, 1846, Musée d'Orsay, Paris

often as significant as winning in turning the attention of students towards the study of ancient Greece and Rome. Charles-François Jalabert's *Virgil, Horace and Varius at the house of Maecenas* [63], which forms an bridge between Ingres's *Tu Marcellus eris* [64] and Alma-Tadema's *Catullus at Lesbia's*, was painted by him in Rome where he went at his own expense after three unsuccessful attempts at the prize.[6] Jean-Léon Gérôme's *Cock-fight* [65] began life as a figure study, painted in the run-up to the Rome competition, to which Gérôme added a second figure, a couple of fighting cocks, a luminous landscape, based, it is said, upon the Bay of Naples, and a few antique accessories.[7] The painting is essentially an academic study, posed in imitation of Chaudet's marble *Eros* in the Louvre, but the rest of the picture, painted with an unexpected freshness and realism, ensured its success with the critics and the public. The response encouraged Gérôme to abandon the Rome Prize and exploit pastoral and mythological themes set in antiquity. He was joined by several fellow students from Delaroche's studio who, throughout the 1850s, produced a series of pictures illustrating historical events or episodes from daily life among the ancients, taking Ingres's compositions as a common point of departure and furnishing their compositions with accessories based on their studies in and around Naples.

66 Théodore Chassériau, *The tepidarium*, 1853, Musée du Louvre, Paris

Not all the 'néo-Grecs', as the writer Claude Vignon named them in 1852,[8] were convinced archaeologists and those who were, notably Gérôme and Gustave Boulanger, were not exclusively painters of ancient themes. The art of Jean-Louis Hamon, who evolved his vaporous style and anacreontic range of subjects while working for the Sèvres porcelain factory, forms a distinct branch of the Pompeian revival, more decorative than scholarly. At the same time, several pictures of the Second Empire – of which Théodore Chassériau's *Tepidarium* [66] in the Louvre is the most

67   Jean-Léon Gérôme, *King Candaules: Queen Rodolphe observed by Gyges*, 1859, Museo de Arte de Ponce, Puerto Rico

68   Gustave Boulanger, *The rehearsal in the House of the Tragic Poet*, 1855, The Hermitage Museum, St. Petersburg

famous – were painted by artists who were not members of the 'néo-Grec' community, but by artists touched by the general enthusiasm which the 'néo-Grecs' had provoked. Nor were all paintings which were inspired by the antique in the Second Empire, connected with the 'néo-Grecs'. Other movements in the French art world seemed to converge on a popular rediscovery of antique themes and forms, supported particularly by the decorative commissions of Haussmann's Paris and by the breadth of the movement which found expression in the novels and poems of Théophile Gautier, the plays of Emile Augier and the music of Hector Berlioz.

There is, among the paintings of the 'néo-Grecs', a sense of composition which suggests a revival of interest in the pictures of the First Empire but this is no more than a consequence of the influence of Ingres whose paintings often echo the types of composition in fashion in his youth. The composition of *Antiochus and Stratonice*, with its long parentage in French art became the model for Gérôme's *King Candaules* of 1859 [67][9] and for Gustave Boulanger's *The rehearsal in the House of the Tragic Poet* of 1855 [68] which developed into his famous *The rehearsal of 'The Flute Player'* of 1861 [29]. These artists did not admire Ingres's art because of its links with Neo-Classicism, which they disliked, but because it gave them a model for treating antique themes in the manner of Delaroche. Gérôme's *Dead Caesar* of 1859, commissioned by the editor, Adolphe Goupil, for sale in reproduction as pendant to a photograph of the *Assassination of the Duc de Guise*, acknowledges his debt to Delaroche not just in the composition but in the polished realism of the detail, giving the kind of direct access to the subject which both artists admired in photography.[10]

When Alma-Tadema arrived in Paris on return from Italy in 1864, the interest in the 'néo-Grecs' had begun to subside and although the artists who had formed the core of the movement in their studios at the Rue Notre-Dame de Champs continued to paint occasional antique compositions, the group had broken up and the interests of the members diversified. But, following his recent visit to Naples, Alma-Tadema must have found Gérôme's formula difficult to resist. Alfred Stevens, the Belgian genre painter, introduced the two artists.[11] They seem to have discussed technique but direct links between the art of Gérôme and Alma-Tadema are hard to find, partly because Alma-Tadema placed a high value on originality but also because antique themes formed a small percentage of Gérôme's work, even in the 1850s. There is a likely connection between Alma-Tadema's *A Roman emperor A.D. 41* [23] and Gérôme's *The death of Caesar* [69],[12] but the figure of Claudius behind the curtain suggests, also, a debt to the figure of Henri III in Delaroche's *Assassination of the Duc de Guise*. Later in life, Alma-Tadema paid tribute to Gérôme by including a cast of his statuette of the *Hoop-dancer*, along with his crater from Hildesheim, in the *Golden hours* (s 419), a painting of a favourite model, posed with two of his studio

artefacts.[13] But he was too independent an artist to borrow more explicitly from Gérôme.

If Gérôme did not leave much trace on the art of Alma-Tadema, there are a few hints similarly vague, which seem to confirm his links with the painters in Gérôme's circle. His first 'néo-Grec' picture, *Catullus at Lesbia's*, the first of a series of pictures of antique poets, appears to derive from Jalabert's *Virgil, Horace and Varius at the house of Maecenas*, connecting Alma-Tadema's picture, indirectly, to the tradition of Ingres's work which is, otherwise, not very visible in his art. Gustave Boulanger's *The rehearsal of 'The Flute Player'*, featuring a group of writers and actors rehearsing a play by Augier in the atrium of the Prince Napoleon's Pompeian house in Paris, anticipates several of Alma-Tadema's series of pictures of art lovers where there is a similar ambiguity between portraits of contemporaries and the antique roles which they are playing. Alphonse Isambert's *Greek vases* may have suggested the theme of Alma-Tadema's *Pottery painting* [25] and Jean-Louis Hamon's *Idyll: my sister is not there* [139] must have suggested Alma-Tadema's very different picture on the same theme [56].[14]

Like the 'néo-Grecs', Alma-Tadema painted a Suetonian view of Roman history, illustrating the cor-

69   Jean-Léon Gérôme, *The death of Caesar*, 1867, Walters Art Gallery, Baltimore

ruption of Imperial power, but these incursions into history are not frequent among his English pictures, probably because he had lost his taste for subjects based on textual sources and built his pictures increasingly round the accessories. The theme of the art collector, common in his early work, allowed him extensive scope to indulge his taste for pictures furnished from his photographs of ancient works of art [70] [36]. The theme of the potter [25 63-65] permitted him to paint humbler artefacts. Flowers dictated many compositions, from the charming *The flower market* of 1868 [14] to the astonishing *The Roses of Heliogabalus* of 1888 [69]. Even in the last decades when he became more interested in the theme of the human figure and eliminated much of his detail, his talent for painting translucent marble in the Mediterranean sunlight continued to play a major role in dictating his choice of subject-matter. In this sense, his art was rooted in an anti-classical, Franco-Dutch tradition, originating with the so-called Troubadours in the studio of David in the early 19th-century[15] and continued by Delaroche and his pupils, in which the inspiration of the artefacts and of historical actuality was of more importance to the artist in originating compositions than the textual themes.

70   *The picture gallery*, 1874, Towneley Hall Art Gallery & Museums, Burnley Borough Council

The soul of things

Alma-Tadema and Symbolism

Edwin Becker

'Everything has its suggestive purpose. There is no point which our eye fixes at once as the central, most important, and the meaning of the whole may often be hidden in some accessory that the ordinary observer is apt to overlook' writes Helen Zimmern in 1902 in her short biography of Alma-Tadema.[1] With these words she highlights an aspect that lies at the foundation of Symbolism, especially Symbolism with a literary orientation. At the same time, she provides a rejoinder to the many critics who regarded Alma-Tadema's work as empty and devoid of content, 'an extreme of mental and imaginative laziness'.[2] Although his characters should perhaps be seen rather as types without psychological profundity ('the general lack of attraction of his figures is due to their complete denial of spirituality'[3]), his themes are anything but lacking in content and are often less superficial than they may appear at first sight. Besides, Alma-Tadema's own view of the matter was: 'Art is imagination and an art lover is so because the viewing of a painting stirs the viewer's imagination and sets him thinking; this is how art heightens the mind'.[4]

The present essay investigates the link between Alma-Tadema's work and Symbolism by concentrating on two Symbolist protagonists: Gustav Klimt and Fernand Khnopff. These two *fin-de-siècle* artists, fascinated by archaeology and ancient works of art, not only incorporated classical objects and themes in their work, as Alma-Tadema did too, but they also integrated his unconventional compositional devices. This involves both a brief outline of Alma-Tadema's influence and an explanation of the hidden symbolism of some of his paintings. These allegorical and symbolic references were further developed by Klimt and Khnopff and received an extra dimension through their highly personal interpretation. Alma-Tadema may be said to have provided the framework on which they embroidered and with which they could give shape to their idiosyncratic ideas.

Life as a theatre

From 1886 to 1888 Gustav Klimt, his brother Ernst and the painter Franz von Matsch worked on the ceiling paintings for the staircase of the Burgtheater in Vienna. The theme was the history of the theatre from antiquity to the 'modernity' era. Klimt was responsible for the following pictures: *In front of the Theatre of Taormina in Sicily*, *The altar of Dionysus*, *The Thespis chariot*, and *The Globe Theatre in London during a performance of William Shakespeare's 'Romeo and Juliet'*.[5] While Klimt's earlier works from the period 1878-85 still evidence a baroque historicism in the style of Hans Makart, stylistic and compositional characteristics can be seen in the Burgtheater which are clearly derived from Alma-Tadema. It was precisely for those scenes bearing on the origin of classical theatre that Klimt had recourse to the famous Victorian painter who was unparalleled in his ability to conjure up such an (apparently) historically faithful picture of antiquity. Alma-Tadema had become a household name within a short time and had secured a prominent position alongside the painters of the English Classical Revival. Not only had his paintings been exhibited successfully in various cities (including London, Paris, Berlin, Munich), but they were also extremely popular through frequent engravings.

In particular, Klimt's *In front of the Theatre of Taormina in Sicily* [71] is unmistakeably influenced by Alma-Tadema in terms of both theme and composition.

71   Gustav Klimt, *In front of the Theatre of Taormina in Sicily*, 1886-88, Burgtheater, Vienna

The right-hand side of the painting is taken up by a very realistic depiction of a marble portico with colossal columns and statues of Victory. In the foreground we see two men of different ages reclining on a triclinium as they watch a slender, attractive young woman dancing. The left-hand side offers a panorama of the bay of Sicily, in contrast to the closed, cool and linear style of the marble. The same opposition between an artificial world (the constructed architecture) and a natural one is often present in Alma-Tadema's work: a view of the deep blue waters from the stairway of a Roman villa (*A kiss* [76]), or a vista of the clear sky through an atrium (*The vintage festival* [21]). Even the way in which the silhouette of the olive tree is set off against the light-blue sky recalls Alma-Tadema (*Sappho* [98]). Moreover, the illusionism of the space is kept under control by a taut composition in Klimt's painting too.

This low degree of recession in the perspective can be seen even more clearly in Klimt's *Altar of Dionysus* [72], where the emphasis is on line and field, two elements which will be of decisive importance for Klimt's further development.[6] To the left a devotee of Dionysus is lying with a tambourine in his hand. His pose recalls that of the spellbound boy in Alma-

Tadema's *A reading from Homer* [73][67]. In the centre of the composition a maenad is offering a sculpture of Athene at the altar, dedicated to Dionysus, while another lies exhausted on the stairs in a state of ecstatic euphoria. Their porcelain-like quality recalls that of Alma-Tadema's figures, and the positioning of the sharply delineated figures against the marble background is identical.

Like Alma-Tadema, Klimt is here playing with fiction and reality. We are presented with a stage production which casts us in the role of spectator. While Alma-Tadema's obsessive realism confers on the scene from antiquity a high level of authenticity, he represents his classical figures without profound human emotions. Likewise, Klimt's human figures in the Burgtheater paintings look like statues which have come to life, or like people who have been turned to stone.[7] This contrast is all the greater in that he often sets 'real' people beside or in front of the décor of 'dead' sculpture. As Helen Zimmern correctly points out with regard to Alma-Tadema, it was often '... as though he had painted accessories with even more care than he bestowed upon his men and women ...'[8] The emphasis is mainly on the beauty of the inanimate objects rather than on that of the living characters.

Such inaccessible, almost petrified figures are also the main actors in the dreamed reality of the Belgian Symbolist Fernand Khnopff. This 'over-refined aesthete, who only experiences life through the medium of ancient art', arranges the expressionless female figures in his *Memories* [74] like waxworks.[9] The same mask-like facial expression and artificial pose recurs in the portrait of Khnopff's unapproachable, introverted sister Marguerite (1887, Fondation Roi Baudouin, Brussels), or in his lithograph *Through the ages* in *The Studio* (1894) on the theme of the confusing similarity and amorous relationship between a marble bust and a young woman.[10] It led the Viennese critic Ludwig Hevesi to remark: 'He turns statues into people and people into statues'.[11]

The confusion between fiction and reality is a typical phenomenon of the fin-de-siècle and plays an important part in Vienna in particular. Writers like Hugo von Hofmannsthal warned of the danger of this escape from reality in works such as his novella *Der Tod des Tizian* (The death of Titian, 1892), and the *Idylle*

72 Gustav Klimt, *The altar of Dionysus*, 1886-1888,
Burgtheater, Vienna

'73 *A reading from Homer* (detail), 1885, Philadelphia
Museum of Art

nach einem antiken Vasenbild (Idyll on an ancient vase painting, 1893), a rejoinder to Keats's *Ode on a Grecian Urn*: an attempt to escape from the fossilized beauty and to awaken the life of the instincts. In *Der Tod des Tizian*, for instance, Tizianello complains: 'I have simply lost the ability to feel', to which Antonello adds: 'Arouse us, turn us into a Bacchanal!'.[12] Humanity, imprisoned in aestheticism, unable to bear reality and therefore seeking an escape in art, had to be liberated.[13]

The philosopher Nietzsche also rejected this morality of escapism and stressed the need to enjoy life as it is. The symbol of this unfettered lust for life is the figure of Dionysus, the spirit of tragedy, instinct, libido, in opposition to arid and controlled reason. This train of thought, which was developed in Nietzsche's *Die Geburt der Tragödie aus dem Geiste der Musik* (The birth of tragedy from the spirit of music, 1872), influenced Klimt's painting of *The altar of Dionysus* and his colleague Franz von Matsch's rendering of *The altar of Apollo*.[14] According to Nietzsche, drama arose in ancient Greece from two mutually opposing aesthetic impulses: the Apollonian, characterized by order and self-control, and the Dionysiac, characterized by wild, unbridled ecstasy.

The numerous devotees of the cult of Dionysus, known under a variety of names (bacchantes, thyades,

maenads) display this lawless, unrestrained side of human life in Alma-Tadema's works as well (*Une fête intime*, s 135, *Exhausted maenides after the dance* [34], *A bacchante* [39], *Autumn* [46], *The women of Amphissa* [68]). But while Klimt slowly but surely manages to escape from the stifling beauty of the purely aesthetic to represent the inner psyche, Alma-Tadema and Khnopff continue to cultivate an idealized beauty. Alma-Tadema's Dionysiac themes are still imprisoned within the Victorian corset, and only subtle references and hidden symbolism can reveal the erotic (and other) implications to insiders.

Klimt returns to the opposition of life versus art, reality versus appearance, vitality versus inanimate matter, in a drawing for *Ver Sacrum, Alte und Neue Kunst* (Ancient and modern art) [75]. The opposition here is between a petrified past, symbolized by the male stele, and a dynamic future, personified by the mischievously laughing woman who rests her head against a marble column. The Latin inscription reinforces the contrast between the two, between ancient and modern art, by

74 Fernand Khnopff, *Memories*, 1889, Musées royaux des
Beaux-Arts de Belgique, Brussels

75 Gustav Klimt, *Duo quum faciunt idem. non est idem*,
published in *Ver Sacrum* 1 (1898), no. 1

76 *A well-protected slumber* (*Silence!*), 1879, whereabouts
unknown

stating that when two people do the same thing. it does
not mean the same thing.[15] Not only are the various elements of the drawing. such as the grave-marker and the
marble plaquette with the inscription. derived from
works by Alma-Tadema. but so is the composition and
the arrangement of the picture plane. A small panel [76]
that Alma-Tadema painted in 1879 entitled 'Silence!'
was illustrated in the *Art Journal*. exhibited in Munich in
1883. and circulated as an engraving. Like the Klimt
sketch. it too has a male bust on the left on a rectangu-
lar column. a homage to the ancestors. and the visual
field is dominated by an open. empty space in the middle. surrounded by various classical attributes grouped
as marginal decoration.

The combination of a herm (for that is what this
bust and column are based on) with the theme of 'silence' is hardly surprising. The word 'herm'. originally
applied to a boundary-marker. comes from Hermes. the
messenger of the gods. In the occult tradition. which was
especially popular at the end of the 19th century. this
god was associated with silence and inspiration which
enable people to attain a different. more spiritual
world.[16] What is going on behind the curtains of Alma-
Tadema's painting is thus probably not so banal or
naughty as one might expect. and its significance is closer to Symbolist works like the *Silences* of Odilon Redon
(1911. Museum of Modern Art. New York). Lucien Lévy-
Dhurmer (1895. private collection). or Khnopff (1890.
Musées royaux des Beaux-Arts de Belgique. Brussels).
where the protagonists use a similar gesture as a sum-
mons to (inner) quiet and retrospection.

For Gustav Klimt it was not so much the icono-
graphical motif as the striking central area. so conspicuously present in Alma-Tadema's painting. which was of
key importance. This compositional element is even
more emphatically present than in the *Ver Sacrum* drawing in Klimt's poster design for the First Secession
Exhibition in Vienna in 1898 [77]. The upper area of the
poster contains the combat between Theseus and the
Minotaur. symbol for resistance to the status quo. On the
right is the silhouette of Pallas Athene. patron goddess of
the arts. who confers her approval on the emergence of
the new art. The physical combat between Theseus and
the Minotaur is set in the background. as if on a stage.
and the depiction of Athene in profile. like a figure in the
wings. emphasizes the theatrical character of the scene.

77   Gustav Klimt, *Poster for the 1st exhibition of the Vienna
Secession*, 1898, private collection

78   Gustav Klimt, *Allegory of sculpture*, 1896, Historisches
Museum der Stadt Wien, Vienna

Many of Alma-Tadema's works display a similar-
ly theatrical approach. In works like *The vintage festival*
[21] or *On the road to the temple of Ceres: a spring
festival* (s 254), the procession of dancing figures seems
to be proceeding over a stage or cat-walk, with the surrounding events in the background like a drop-curtain.
Klimt takes up this idea by projecting the symbolic allusions to a frieze in the background, as in Alma-Tadema's
A favourite poet [71], where the relief medallions clarify
the interpretation of the work (see p. 239). The overall
composition of Klimt's poster is centred on the open
frame, which is not only the largest of the visual elements, but, like the drawing *Alte und Neue Kunst*, is
enclosed by the masculine (the warrior Theseus) and the
feminine (Pallas Athene). What Theseus is fighting for
with the support of Athene – artistic innovation – is thus
symbolized, as it were, by the blank area, waiting to be
filled in by the artist's innovative ideas. It is here literally claimed by the artist through the inclusion of his signature. The same applies to Klimt's drawing for
Allegories, new series, where the woman, this time portrayed as Eve, is set as a living sculpture against the
background of 'dead' statues [78]. Koloman Moser, who
also supplied drawings for this collective work with a

new allegorical interpretation, was surprised by Klimt's
Sculpture: '... complete emptiness ... something entirely
new ... pure Klimt style'.[17]

Michael Pabst contrasts this vacuum with the
exaggerated penchant for sumptuous decoration of
Makart-style Historicism, which not only served to satisfy bourgeois vanity, but was also intended to fill an
inner emptiness.[18] The pristine vacuum has a different
symbolic value from the vast expanses of marble in
Alma-Tadema's paintings like *Expectations* (s 304), *A
kiss* [76], *Under the roof of blue Ionian weather* (s 400),
or *Silver favourites* [83], but it is not less important or
dominant within the total composition. It is noteworthy
that both in *Sculpture* and in the drawing for *Ver
Sacrum* and the Secession poster, the empty area contains a frame and functions as a kind of stone wall.
While the cold marble of Alma-Tadema underlines the
psychological emptiness of his characters, Klimt often
uses it as a symbol of the spiritual. Without decoration,
uncluttered by an extensive range of accessories, Klimt
displays a virginal, blank interior. The mask has been
removed: theatre yields to the true psyche, the naked
truth (*nuda veritas*).[19]

79   *The last roses*, 1872, private collection

Spring blossom and the flowers of evil

'Flowers had impressed his imagination and gained precedence over the human beings with whom they were associated', according to Helen Zimmern.[20] In all kinds of variations, from oleander blossom to rose petals, from lilies to anemones, from sunflowers to azaleas, flowers populate Alma-Tadema's paintings. They often serve not just as a colourful enlivening of the scene, or as a purely compositional element, but to emphasize the transience of life in general, and of love in particular. These symbolic interpretations are not surprising: it was particularly in the second half of the 19th century that people fell 'under the spell of the flower and a specific floral language developed relatively quickly in which it was even claimed that the flower reveals the structure of the human spirit'.[21]

Georg Ebers refers to the symbolic meaning of the flower a number of times in his essay on Alma-Tadema. The flower-girl in Alma-Tadema's painting *The flower market* [14], for example, reminds him of an epigram of Dionysius.[22] Four years earlier, Carel Vosmaer had already referred to this poem: 'The *flower market* in Pompeii skilfully reconstructed a street and a shop in that city, with one of those charming flower-girls of whom the poet Dionysius said: Tell, red-cheeked

maid, what have you for sale in your basket. Roses or yourself? Perhaps both together?'[23] Although Swanson denies that Alma-Tadema deliberately had this interpretation in mind, other works show that Alma-Tadema certainly does allude to sexual matters (see pp. 37-38).[24] In *A silent greeting* [73], a Roman in armour takes his leave of a sleeping young woman and lays a bunch of flowers in her lap just before leaving. The roses, which will soon wilt, emphasize the transience of his visit and his action. The needle and thread which the young woman has clasped between her fingers and the ball of yarn at her feet indicate that this affair could put her in a difficult situation.[25]

Ebers also paraphrases Alma-Tadema's *The last roses* [79] [32] in terms of transience: '"Like this floral garland", a poet from the Anthology sings to his Rhodoklea, "you blossom and wither too". The Greek woman who lays late autumn roses as a pious offering on the marble altar in "The last roses" will also lose her bloom'.[26] The poppies, which were so popular among the Symbolists because of their connotations of death and decay, emphasize the vanitas idea and contrast menacingly with the white marble. The woman, sunk in thought in front of the altar tomb, staring at the last rose petals, here personifies melancholy, the mood associated with autumn.

The idea of the offering in relation to blossoming and decay is also used by Klimt and Khnopff. Fernand Khnopff's *The offering* [80], with its exceptionally elongated format and large, empty marble surfaces recalling the horizontal compositions of works like *A reading from Homer* [67], exudes a cool and mysterious atmosphere. Hevesi effectively puts this 'deathly' mood into words and describes its unworldly character: 'A long woman's arm which lays a flower in front of a marble bust. The arm is attached to a shoulder, and above this is a head with red-gold hair, a modern-English-ancient face with the proud expression of a soul who has settled accounts with everyday life and whose symbol has become an artificial (!) flower, which she offers to a marble (!) human bust'.[27] Hevesi inserts the two exclamation marks to emphasize the key terms: marble and artificial. While Alma-Tadema used flowers that were still 'real', even though wilted, as a symbol of transience, it has become an artificial flower with Khnopff to avoid any connection at all with worldliness.

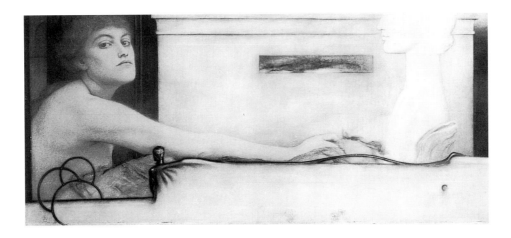

80   Fernand Khnopff, *The offering*, 1891, The Museum of
Modern Art, New York

A watercolour by Klimt entitled *In the morning* [81], dating from 1892, shows a young woman standing beside a Roman table, gazing dreamily at a bunch of roses in a bronze vase. Janus-headed vases like these, with a satyr on one side and a maenad on the other, were often found in Etruscan tombs. Here they underline the dualism of the scene: eros versus thanatos. The young woman, who is on the threshold of womanhood, reflects on the previous night of love: a happy smile plays around her lips. Everything seems to suggest fertility and renewal, but at the same time she is well aware of the brevity of this happiness. As if we could read her thoughts, we see an ancient frieze in the background with horses and warriors, symbols of virility. A similar group of riders provided the background to Alma-Tadema's watercolour version of *The last roses* [32]. But in contrast to the emphasis on the transitory nature of love and the melancholy autumnal mood of Alma-Tadema, Klimt chooses the flourishing happiness of youth as his main motif. This idea of spring was the basis of the avant-garde Viennese Secession movement, and was chosen as the title of their own publication *Ver Sacrum* (Holy spring) to symbolize the budding of modern art.

It is not that Alma-Tadema was impervious to the sensation of spring: in *The Pomona festival* (S 245) a ring of exuberant dancers circle an apple tree in full blossom. But here too it is not pure spring joy, for in the background an older man (a self-portrait of Alma-Tadema) seems to be viewing the scene sceptically. He is aware of the transience and brevity not only of the flowering of nature, but also of the happiness of human life. The painting *Spring* [82] is based on the same idea. The

female protagonist in this work, which has unfortunately been lost, gazes pensively at an anemone which she has just plucked. She is still in the full bloom of her life, on the border between youth and adulthood, but she is already aware that the fragile happiness of youth will not last for ever.

A similar melancholy mood, this time even more sombre, is evoked in Alma-Tadema's *Autumn* [37]. This exceptionally elongated watercolour tackles a theme which was very popular among Romantic and Symbolist artists: the life-cycle, the different stages of human life. To the left, a young man seated on the exedra looks dreamily in front of him, while his companion is lost in thought because of the uncertain future awaiting him as an adolescent. On the extreme right a middle-aged courting couple faces life full of confidence. In the middle of the bench is an old man, who resignedly looks us straight in the eye: he stands for the autumn of life. The sad, somewhat oppressive mood, accentuated by the composition and the isolation of the figures, each of whom is lost in his own unreal world, resembles the ethereal, arcadian landscapes of French Symbolists like Puvis de Chavannes or Alphonse Osbert, who also had a preference for the narrow, frieze-like format.

The vanitas idea is subtly present in Alma-Tadema's *Spring* of 1894 [83]. Four lines of verse by Algernon Charles Swinburne, in the spirit of the Aesthetic Movement, are written on the frame: 'In a land of clear colours and stories / In a region of shadowless hours / Where earth has a garment of glories / And a murmur of musical flowers (Dedication to Burne-Jones in 1865)'. Although Alma-Tadema seems to con-

81 Gustav Klimt, *In the morning*, 1892, whereabouts unknown

82 Lawrence Alma-Tadema, *Spring*, 1877, lost

fine himself to the sunny side of the verse, entirely in line with his favourite motto 'As the sun colours flowers so art colours life', there are elements displaying parallels with the lines of verse which refer to the 'artist's melancholy task of describing beautiful things before they are lost to the forces of time'.[28] Alma-Tadema associates the procession of young people who pass dancing and singing through the streets with the theme of the Victorian May processions. 'Innocent' teenage girls were usually banned from these processions, however, because they could easily degenerate into immoral behaviour. Most viewers will have missed these erotically tinged associations: 'There is here no hint of the excessive merriment, drinking, and lascivious games ...' or, as F.G. Stephens noted, it is only present 'for those who care for such things'.[29] But satyrs and maenads crop up, concealed in capitals or on reliefs; associated with the cult of Dionysus, they embody the mood of psychological ecstasy and the sexual dangers which are lurking everywhere.

This unbridled lust for life, proceeding from the unrestrained, almost animal instincts, was the main theme of the Munich 'prince of artists', Franz von Stuck, who created a furore with paintings like *The seesaw* (Museum Villa Stuck, Munich) or *Fighting fauns* (Neue Pinakothek, Munich).[30] Like Alma-Tadema,

Stuck lived in a villa that he had designed himself, complete with many reminiscences of antiquity. It is therefore hardly surprising that Alma-Tadema's extensive library contained one of the first accounts of the Villa Stuck.[31] Each of these two *fin-de-siècle* artists created his own empire of beauty, but they both viewed classical antiquity as the ideal starting-point. The city of Munich, hailed as the modern Athens, with its many Neo-Classical buildings, must have been a real source of inspiration for Alma-Tadema. In addition, the Starnberger See was nearby, and he regularly visited his good friend Georg Ebers who had a villa on the lake [76]. A high spot in the Munich revival of classical antiquity was reached at the arcadian festivities of the Allotria artists' association, at which all those present wore ancient dress. Alma-Tadema must have felt at home in these surroundings, accompanied by the society painters Franz von Lenbach and Franz von Stuck, and the festive processions certainly did not fail to leave their mark on paintings like *Spring*.

In Alma-Tadema's *Spring*, the colourful flowers, branches of blossom and calla lilies (like those carried by the female spectator on the lower left-hand side) are symbols of blossoming love, while the satyrs, carried in the procession as a silver statue along with the child Bacchus, do not only wink mischievously, they even pose a threat to the innocence of the girls. The theme of the satyr in a state of arousal (as a herm with a phallus mounted by a lascivious woman) is also a Leitmotiv in the work of the Belgian artist Félicien Rops, whom Alma-Tadema met in person during his Brussels period.[32] While Rops boldly and explicitly portrays the act of copulation itself, Alma-Tadema's paintings give the appearance of purity and chastity. All the same, we should not be deceived by Alma-Tadema's seemingly refined, aesthetic scenes. The inscription on the standard in the middle of the composition of *Spring* explains the nature of the procession: a veneration of the god Priapus, the ithyphallic god of nature, gardens, and fertility.

The most exuberant display of flowers is in the painting *The roses of Heliogabalus* [84] [69]. The most decadent of all the Roman emperors, who is really still an adolescent and has certainly not reached adult maturity, treats his guests to a waterfall of rose petals. With a bored smirk of satisfaction at his ploy, Heliogabalus watches as the crowd beneath him is bur-

83　*Spring* (detail), 1894, The J. Paul Getty Museum, Malibu

ied under the roses and borne along in this prodigality. It is striking that everyone is involved in this curious spectacle in one form or another except the young woman in the lower right, who stares at us with a fixed gaze. It is as if she, the real source of all evil, has suddenly woken up to this crazy scene and wants to warn us against its decadence. With a pomegranate in her right hand and a serpent armband on her left forearm, she is the likeness of Eve and thus also refers to the Fall. The pomegranate evokes the figure of Persephone (Proserpina), as in the numerous versions painted by Dante Gabriel Rossetti (including one in 1877, private collection). Persephone, daughter of Demeter, ate from the pomegranate and so could no longer return to the earth. Pictured by Rossetti as a seductive woman with a captivating gaze and full red lips, she became a precursor of the Symbolist *femme fatale*. Because she had eaten from the forbidden fruit, humanity was burdened with a winter season, equivalent to the period spent by Persephone in Hades, the underworld.

Pandora, whom Alma-Tadema painted in watercolours in 1881 [57], is another in the series of *femmes fatales* besides Eve and Persephone. As the first mortal woman, she had gifts heaped on her, including a box which was to remain closed. When she removed the lid of the box in her foolish curiosity, the contents flew out: every conceivable kind of evil was cast out into the world. Only hope remained inside, a poor consolation. The sphinx on Alma-Tadema's watercolour further emphasizes the secret that was concealed in the box, as well as connecting the story of Pandora with her own all-consuming desire, which leads man to his ruin.

Upon closer inspection, many of the women in Alma-Tadema's works turn out to correspond to the Symbolist *femme fatale*. Often they are unruly bacchantes whose ecstatic behaviour and hysterical attacks make them dangerous, like *Bacchante* (1907, S 417), where the inscription in the background, 'dulce periculum', makes further explanation redundant. They may be figures like *Fredegonda* (1864 [12] and 1878, S 240), who derive great enjoyment from their crime. Other women are adepts at a vain 'dolce far niente', as a painting from 1882 (S 280) is entitled: but beware, even if they seem to be innocently fishing on the shore, men are their main prey (*Fishing* [33]).

Although the young emperor is responsible for the decadent party in *The roses of Heliogabalus*, the leading character is still the *femme fatale* in the right-hand corner. Because of her attributes (serpent armband, pomegranate, abundance of roses – the flower of love) and her expression and attitude, she dominates not only the composition but also the message of the painting.

The soul of details

In 1915 Fernand Khnopff described an earlier visit to the sumptuous home of Alma-Tadema in London. It was one of several visits, and there must have been a stronger bond between the two painters than mere superficial acquaintance, as was also the case with Burne-Jones and Khnopff.[33] While the narcissistic and decadent dream world of Khnopff seems at first sight to be far removed from the Victorian classical arcadia of Alma-Tadema, there are a number of striking parallels.

Both artists were extremely progressive in the framing of their compositions by overlapping and abrupt breaks at the edge of the picture. This compositional device is often regarded as an unusual feature of both Khnopff and his source of inspiration, Alma-Tadema. Fernand Khnopff had not earned the nickname 'Maître des fronts coupés' (master of the truncated foreheads) for nothing, and Richard Muther had the following to say about Alma-Tadema's unconventional demarcations:

'Instead of emphasizing regularity as the French do, he accentuates the fortuitous [although with deliberate calculation]. Often there is only a single figure, positioned completely out of symmetry, in the large space. Or beneath a head a hand juts straight out into the picture'.[34]

This fragmented character of the work of the two artists is not only influenced by their predilection for the art of the Japanese print, but it is above all a direct consequence of the use of photographs as an aid in the composition of the paintings (see pp. 111-124). Moreover, this through-the-lens perspective encouraged an extremely precise, photographic attention to detail. In the case of Khnopff, who followed Albert Mockel's adage that a symbol must remain hidden and ambiguous, otherwise it would become an allegory,[35] this exact, photographic style of representation seems, at first sight, to be at odds with his themes, which still puzzle many a viewer. Khnopff's attention to detail is considerably due to his admiration for Gothic painting and the refined English style of painting: 'this sustained and moving precision ... To sum up, the field of observation of English art is very wide, for it extends from the delicate study of everyday life, the religious interpretation of nature, the ingenious restitution of antiquity, to the most lyrical and precious Symbolism'.[36] According to Khnopff, the 'foreigner' Alma-Tadema had adapted completely to this English aesthetic without betraying his origins: the subtle light effects and the portrayal of textures, as well as the fondness for detail, reminded him of 17th-century Netherlandish painting.

Khnopff's fascination with details was also connected with his vision of 'the soul of things'. 'In order to symbolize', he said to his friend Du Jardin, 'you must regard a tangible object as something spiritual'.[37] 'I would like everything to have a meaning and a significance'.[38] The physical, material aspect of the object was thus only superficial and subservient to the idea. Alma-Tadema's paintings had such an appeal for Khnopff, because besides the unconventional composition they proceeded from the same almost obsessive attention to detail.

Characteristic of their love for detail is the following anecdote.[39] During one of his visits to Alma-Tadema, Fernand Khnopff saw on the easel an almost exact copy of the mirror from Jan van Eyck's famous *Arnolfini portrait* (1434, National Gallery, London). Alma-Tadema told Khnopff that, despite all the accuracy, Van Eyck had forgotten to paint one detail, and he asked the Belgian painter whether he knew which one it was. Khnopff immediately rushed off to the National Gallery and discovered that Van Eyck had forgotten to represent the reflection of a few oranges (the size of a pinhead!).

We have seen from the examples discussed above that Alma-Tadema's details are more than mere accessories, and that they may contain the symbolic meaning of the whole painting. I have also tried to modify the one-sided view of his work as 'Victorian genre painting with classical themes' by drawing parallels with works by Klimt, Khnopff and others. Alma-Tadema often took his motifs from the same world of ideas as the Symbolists did, and raised them above the level of the purely anecdotal. 'His manipulation of this detail for subtextual purposes has never been properly acknowledged. It goes beyond historical recreation to symbolic creation'.[40]

84   *The roses of Heliogabalus* (detail), 1888, private collection

The new centurions

Alma-Tadema's international patrons

Dianne Sachko Macleod

Sir Lawrence Alma-Tadema's paintings graced the walls of drawing rooms from Moscow to Melbourne. They were purchased by international financiers and members of the rising professional class who, like the prosperous Romans featured in the artist's paintings, wanted to surround themselves with objects of luxury. Men such as Sir Henry Thompson, the Marqués de Santurce, Sir Ernest Cassel, and Sir John Aird were members of an aristocracy of wealth who earned rather than inherited their titles. Ownership of Alma-Tadema's classical subjects afforded them the opportunity to claim a cultural lineage with the ancient world, to convey an impression of classical learning, and to escape from the pressures of the moment into an untroubled bygone world. Late-Victorian and Edwardian magnates, even those as far afield as South Africa and Canada, felt compelled to include a representative work by Alma-Tadema in their private galleries.

Although Alma-Tadema's patrons enjoyed displaying the perquisites of wealth, they were not self-made upstarts, but were helped along by their fathers and grandfathers. The artist's Victorian clients included sherry merchant Frederick Cozens, chemical manufacturer Hilton Philipson, woollen merchant David Price, and inventor of submarine telegraphy Sir John Pender, each of whom could boast of belonging to families who had possessed wealth for at least three generations.[1] While Alma-Tadema's Edwardian collectors were cast from a similar mould, they ventured forth more ambitiously as international capitalists in this age of Empire building. The composite portrait which emerges of Alma-Tadema's patrons reveals a cosmopolitan and sophisticated gathering of wealthy individualists of both sexes.

The majority of Alma-Tadema's collectors, however, resided in Great Britain where they had easy access to his art through the enthusiastic agency of the dealer Ernest Gambart. After meeting the artist in Antwerp in 1864, Gambart immediately commissioned him to paint twenty-four pictures which the dealer successfully offered for sale at his French Gallery in London. Encouraged by this positive response, Alma-Tadema emigrated to England in 1870 after Gambart had greeted him with a commission for an additional fifty-two pictures.[2] While this particular arrangement was beneficial to both artist and dealer, it distanced Alma-Tadema from his patrons. Unlike the devotees of Aesthetic Movement artists, who depended on Edward Burne-Jones and Dante Gabriel Rossetti to interpret their abstruse subjects for them, Alma-Tadema's clients could more easily grasp his meaning on their own, and thus apparently did not consider a personal alliance with the artist a necessary component of ownership.

An exception to this rule was one of Alma-Tadema's first English patrons, Sir Henry Thompson, who became well-acquainted with the artist as his personal doctor. They first met in 1869 when Gambart referred the artist to Thompson for surgery.[3] Over the next nine years, Thompson acquired eight of Alma-Tadema's pictures, either through Gambart or as gifts from the artist. In addition to a portrait of himself [85] and two of his son [42], Thompson owned a broad range of the artist's work spanning his Egyptian, Roman, and nature subjects. The paintings in his collection included *Cleopatra* (S 184), *Tarquinius Superbus* (S 91) and *Haystacks* (S 192). An explanation for Thompson's ecumenical taste rests in the fact that he was an amateur artist himself and had taken lessons from Alma-Tadema.

Presumably he wished to study the professional artist's more skilful touch. Within two years of meeting Alma-Tadema, Thompson's still lifes and travel scenes were accepted for exhibition at the Royal Academy where he continued to display his efforts until 1901. The versatile surgeon also found time to publish his drawings in an illustrated catalogue of his extensive collection of blue and white porcelain in collaboration with James McNeill Whistler.[4] Thompson enjoyed a relationship with artist John Everett Millais as well, whose portrait he sketched in 1879 (National Portrait Gallery, London).[5]

Acquainted with most of the leading artists of his day, Thompson frequently entertained them along with writers, musicians, and politicians, such as the Prince of Wales, Arthur Conan Doyle, and Robert Browning at his celebrated 'Octaves' or dinners for eight persons invited for eight o'clock. As he explained: 'I regarded my guests as the series of eight musical notes, forming the scale of C major, considering myself as the staff which retains them or brings them together'.[6] Sharing Alma-Tadema's propensity for musical designations, Thompson prepared personal menus for his guests which he labelled 'Allegro Vivace' and decorated with musical notes.

The international financiers who owned paintings by Alma-Tadema, on the other hand, were collectors rather than patrons in that they did not forge a personal link with the artist. These men did not expect art to satisfy their affective needs as did patrons of the Aesthetic Movement, but were content with owning well-crafted evocations of the classical world.[7] Alma-Tadema's finely detailed canvases appealed to merchant bankers such as José de Murrieta, Baron Sir John Henry Schröder, and Sir Ernest Cassel who not only recognized a good investment when they saw one, but respected the degree of labor and professionalism evident in the artist's work. According to Edwardian banker H. Osborne O'Hagan, the men in his field were a hard-working lot. He elaborated: 'Success rarely comes to those who take to their offices, their sports, their theatricals, or other amusements. To really succeed, a man must make his work his first love'.[8] Such dedication to labour was mirrored in Alma-Tadema's highly-prized images.

José Murrieta del Campo Mello y Urrutia, the owner of twenty pictures by Alma-Tadema, was born in London in 1833, the son of Cristobel de Murrieta, a City

85   *Sir Henry Thompson, Bart.*, 1878, Fitzwilliam Museum, Cambridge

merchant banker of Spanish descent who had made a fortune through trading and investing in South America before emigrating to London in the early part of the century.[9] José de Murrieta became head of the family bank following his father's death in 1868 and was elevated to the nobility nine years later as the first Marqués de Santurce by King Alfonso XII in gratitude for his assistance in acquiring loans for Spain.[10]

The success of the Murrietas' financial schemes can be measured by the extravagance of their private residences. In 1855 the ground lease of No. 11 Kensington Palace Gardens was granted to José and his brother Mariano who agreed to spend £ 4,000 on a first class structure. They chose the architect Sydney Smirke to design the spacious house which is now the residence of the French Ambassador. Known as 'Millionaires' Row', Kensington Palace Gardens was characterized by the *Metropolitan* in 1890 as the '*facile princeps* in the estimation of our merchant princes, bankers, and other leaders of the world of finance'.[11] Not to be outdone by neighbouring foreign financiers such as Charles F. Huth and Gustav C. Schwabe whose homes featured art collections, the Murrietas hired the artist Alfred Stevens to paint panels illustrating ten heroines from *The Fairie Queene* on the drawing room walls in grisaille on blue and to create a design emblematic of the four seasons on the ceiling of the morning room.[12] The house was made even more lavish in 1873 when José hired the architect Edward Tarver to add a ballroom and art gallery to the south side to display his expanding collection and called in Walter Crane to paint a decorative frieze of animals and birds.[13]

Tarver, who had trained with William Burges, was summoned by the Murrietas again in the 1870s to enlarge a modest eighteenth-century house on the extensive Wadhurst Park estate they had purchased in East Sussex. Reproduced in *Building News* in 1875 [86], Tarver's design reveals a turreted red-brick mansion in the 'Olde English' style popularized by Richard Norman Shaw which cost three times as much to construct as the Murrietas' Kensington Palace Gardens residence.[14] In a first-hand account, Thomas Escott, who enjoyed the Murrietas' hospitality, observes: 'Wadhurst Hall, under the Murietta [sic] dispensation, formed the earliest instance of an English country home whose arrangements were modelled upon those of a fashionable restaurant or a Pall Mall club. To begin with, breakfast was served at any hour liked by the individual guest. As a fact, we most of us had it between eleven and twelve in an apartment which daily, till noon, looked like the coffee-room at a Metropole Hotel. In each was a little table, presently spread, with more than club or hotel speed, with the English breakfast or the French *déjeuner*'.[15] One wonders to what extent this casual atmosphere was intended to entice the Prince of Wales to traverse the seven miles from Tunbridge Wells to Wadhurst Hall. Members of the Marlborough House set, the Murrietas dispensed the kind of sybaritic comfort enjoyed by the future Edward VII. Wadhurst Park offered excellent shooting as well as a thirty-three acre lake, tea house, tennis courts, and an ice rink, while the interior of the house featured lavish furnishings and many of the gems of José de Murrieta's art collection.[16]

Murrieta's taste covered the gamut from early-Victorian watercolours by David Cox, Vicat Cole, and J.M.W. Turner to mid-Victorian figurative subjects by John Phillip, Frederick Goodall, and the Faeds, to 19th-century French landscapes by Barbizon artists Troyon, Daubigny, and Dupré. In this regard he was characteristic of other businessmen in Britain's age of Empire building who, unlike their xenophobic early-Victorian predecessors, did not limit themselves to collecting the works

of the English school of art, but expanded their vision to reflect the internationalism of their financial enterprises. This, in part, explains Murrieta's attraction to the art of Dutch-born Alma-Tadema which represented the largest body of work by a single artist in his collection.

Even though Murrieta purchased all twenty of his Alma-Tademas through Gambart and his successors, the dealers Pilgeram and Lefèvre, he appears to have desired to sustain the illusion that he was part of the creative process.[17] Four of the canvases he owned depict either connoisseurs admiring works of art or artists making them, suggesting that Murrieta perceived himself as instrumental to the production and reception of art. In *Antistius Labeon, A.D. 75* (S 174), a female connoisseur leans forward to inspect a small painted panel, whereas in *A Roman lover of art* (S 102), a male patron expounds on the merits of a gold and lapis lazuli statue of the *Venus of Arles*. Both artist and collector are present in *A Roman art lover* (S 120): a bearded patriarch directs a sculptor to adjust the base of the *Amazon runner* (Vatican Museum), while friends and family look on.[18] An artist again appears in *Pottery painting* [25] where a woman painter concentrates on her design for a red figure vase.

The desire to be perceived as a knowledgeable *mécène* was not unprecedented in the international set. The American transportation magnate William Henry Vanderbilt also owned a series of pictures featuring various stages of the creative process, from artists at work in their studios to patrons admiring the finished product. His canvases included Baron Henri Leys's *Lucas*

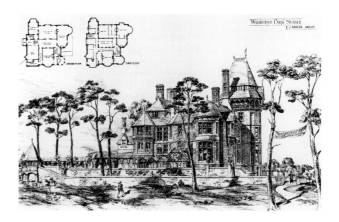

86   Edward J. Tarver, *Wadhurst Hall, Wadhurst Park, Sussex, residence of the Murrieta family*, from *Building News*, 9 April 1875

87   *Private picture gallery, residence of William Henry*
      Vanderbilt, New York, from Magazine of Art *6 (1883)*

88   *Private picture gallery, The Dell, Berkshire, residence of*
      Baron Sir John Henry Schröder, c. 1900, *photograph,*
      Hamburger Kunsthalle, Hamburg

Cranach painting the portrait of Martin Luther, Vincent Palmaroli y Gonzales' *In the studio,* and Ernest Meissonier's *Artist at work,* in addition to two Alma-Tademas depicting connoisseurs, *A picture gallery* (s 157) and *A sculpture gallery* (s 89), reduced versions of cats. 35 and 36.[19] Part of a group of five Alma-Tademas which Vanderbilt purchased between 1877 and 1897, this pair of paintings echoes the subject matter of Murrieta's, even though he, too, was not a direct patron of the artist but relied on the services of an intermediary, the dealer Samuel P. Avery.[20]

Although Vanderbilt and Murrieta lived on different sides of the Atlantic, they shared many similarities. Both were beneficiaries of ambitious fathers who passed on their fortunes to them. Commodore Cornelius Vanderbilt established a railway and shipping empire which produced sufficient surplus capital for his son to spend $ 1,500,000 on the construction of a marble palace on Fifth Avenue in New York and to build a palatial villa in Newport, Rhode Island. Like Murrieta, Vanderbilt had a private picture gallery installed in his home to show off his enormous collection [87]. Its opulence was described with some awe to the English readers of the *Magazine of Art* in 1883: 'The Gallery is divided into two apartments: a principal hall with a smaller showroom *en suite.* The main entrance is a deep alcove, containing a noble mantel and chimney-piece of carved wood. The floor is paved with paly-tinted marbles, and the lofty wainscoting of ebonised Circassian wood har-

monizes well with the rich maroon hangings, which are stamped with gilded designs ... The smaller Gallery includes, half-way up, a second gallery, devoted to water-colour paintings'.[21]

Murrieta and Vanderbilt had more in common than their private picture galleries and their desire to be construed as patrons, despite their reliance on dealers.[22] Their propensity for classical subjects by Alma-Tadema, William-Adolphe Bouguereau, and Jean-Léon Gérôme links them to the new centurions' identification with the ancient world. Scholars of late 19th-century taste have observed, that 'For the educated and literati, no subject or era had more distinction than classicism'.[23] Moreover, as successful international businessmen, Vanderbilt and Murrieta valued evidence of time-consuming labour in the paintings they bought. Alma-Tadema's painstaking technique satisfied this requirement as did Meissonier's meticulously rendered surfaces. Both men owned versions of Ernest Meissonier's *Friedland,* a painting which American novelist Henry James noted 'represents an immense amount of labour, and of acquired science and skill'.[24] They differed, however, in their financial strategies: Vanderbilt substantially increased the fortune he inherited, whereas Murrieta suffered the ignominy of bankruptcy.

Perhaps it was neglect of the gospel of hard work – too much time spent entertaining house guests – that led to Murrieta's financial woes in 1892. Ostensibly a casualty of the Baring banking crises which commenced when Argentina and Uruguay defaulted on loans because of poor harvests and political instability, the Murrietas' fortune quickly crumbled, unlike Schröder's and Cassel's which remained intact. In his study of merchant banking, Stanley Chapman attributes the latters' stability to their industrious management style, noting that 'German clerks worked sixty, seventy and even more hours a week'.[25] Whether Murrieta's more relaxed lifestyle contributed to his downfall, or whether it was simply a matter of unfortunate business decisions, C. de Murrieta & Co was one of only two merchant banks to go under as a result of the crisis, but not before José and Mariano turned it into a limited liability company in 1891 to protect their personal assets.[26] After selling off their vast collections of paintings, *objets d'art*, and furniture, the Murrietas vanished from English society.[27]

Conversely, Baron Sir Henry Schröder's social position was improved as a result of the Baring crisis: he was made a baronet in 1892 in recognition for his efforts on behalf of the German community in England.[28] Having already been conferred the German title of baron, he was henceforth known as Baron Sir John Henry William Schröder. The son of Johann Heinrich Schröder, a Hamburg merchant banker who founded the London branch of the family firm in 1818, the young Schröder was made a full partner in 1849 at the age of twenty four. One of his more successful financial endeavors involved the underwriting of American rail-way construction, an endeavor that was dear to Vanderbilt's heart.

While we do not know if the two financiers ever met on Vanderbilt's frequent visits to Europe, they shared an interest in contemporary continental artists, such as Ary Scheffer, Ernest Meissonier, Henri Leys, and members of the Barbizon school.[29] A receipt that has been preserved among Schröder's private papers discloses that he paid the dealers Pilgeram and Lefèvre just over £3,673 for two paintings in 1875, Louis Gallait's *Vargàs taking the oath* and Leys's *Going to church* (both Hamburger Kunsthalle, Hamburg). Schröder, however, was to pay almost double that amount for a single painting by Alma-Tadema a few years later, *A dedication to Bacchus* [89] [72]. It was one of ten paintings he purchased by the artist over two decades, beginning in the 1870s, and which he displayed in a private picture gallery in his home, The Dell, in Berkshire.[30] In a photograph taken around the year 1900 [88] we recognize *The vintage festival* [21], on the lower row to the right, which had inspired Schröder to commission *A dedication to Bacchus* as its pendant from Gambart in 1889 for £7,000. The high price reflects the time invested by the artist in detailing sixty individual figures in his composition, an effort which a financier like Schröder could appreciate in terms of the time-labour equation. Furthermore Alma-Tadema's reputation had become even more bankable following the retrospective exhibi-

89   *A dedication to Bacchus*, 1889, Hamburger Kunsthalle, Hamburg

90 *The back drawing room, 14 Hyde Park Terrace, London residence of Sir John and Lady Sarah Aird, from Art Journal,* May 1891

tion of his paintings at the Grosvenor Gallery in 1882. Yet one cannot accuse Schröder of wanting to turn a profit on his investment in Alma-Tademas paintings: he bequeathed them, along with the rest of his collection to the Hamburger Kunsthalle.[31]

Nor did merchant banker Ernest Cassel sell his art collection: he willed it to his descendants who today include members of the British royal family.[32] Known as 'Windsor Cassel' because of his close ties to King Edward VII, Cassel expressed his affinity with the classical world by transforming Brook House, his home on Park Lane, into a marble and lapis lazuli-lined palace.[33] There he displayed the two Alma-Tademas he purchased in 1897 and 1901, *Her eyes are with her thoughts, and they are far away* (s 382) and *Under the roof of blue Ionian weather* (s 400), alongside his collections of Old Master paintings, rare books, Renaissance bronzes, Dresden china, Chinese jade, and English silver which he purchased with the advice of dealer Joseph Duveen.[34] Knighted in 1899 for his contribution to the economy, Cassel had ventured forth as a new centurion two years earlier when he agreed to extend the influence of the British Empire in Egypt by providing the financing for the Aswan Dam on the River Nile.[35]

Cassel awarded the lucrative contract for the construction of the Aswan Dam to a fellow Alma-Tadema collector, Sir John Aird. In many ways, Aird was the logical choice for the building of this monument to Britain's technological might. Trained in the firm founded by his father which had erected the Great Exhibition building

and later moved it to Sydenham, Aird went on to construct the Berlin Waterworks and a series of docks including the Royal Albert and those at Avonmouth and Hull.[36] But it was Sir John's work on the Aswan Dam that earned him his baronetcy in 1901. After discovering that he and Alma-Tadema shared an interest in Egyptology, Aird invited the artist to accompany him to the dedication ceremonies of the dam in 1902. Aird clearly enjoyed Alma-Tadema's company and reciprocated by commissioning an Egyptian subject, *The finding of Moses* [91], for the generous sum of £ 5,250 plus expenses, to commemorate their journey together. Although Aird is also credited with commissioning the better known *The roses of Heliogabalus* [69], the fact that this painting was not displayed in any of the public rooms in his house on Hyde Park Terrace, but in the back drawing room, which was his wife Sarah's private sanctum, might suggest her involvement in its selection.[37]

Little has been written about the role of women in art collecting. Relegated to the private domestic sphere, women were expected to be involved in the decoration of their homes. Artistic pursuits were considered a defining feature of femininity and most upper-middle-class women were trained in visual culture from an early age.[38] Yet their names rarely appear in artists' account books or dealers' ledgers. Given the strictures of the laws governing married women's property, any art selections they made were attributed to the men who controlled their assets.[39] But as Leonore Davidoff and Catherine Hall have demonstrated in their study of middle-class women, wives were often complicit in this arrangement in order to benefit the family as a whole by expediting their husband's rise in public prominence.[40] Moreover art collecting was often an interactive pursuit that was pleasurably indulged in by both husband and wife, particularly among couples who enjoyed mutually satisfying relationships, such as Queen Victoria and Prince Albert or several of the patrons of the Pre-Raphaelite artists.[41] As I contend in my book on Victorian art collectors, it was only a small leap for women from their old place in the discourse on domesticity to their new place in the discourse on beauty after the artists and craftsmen associated with the Aesthetic Movement developed designs for tapestries and embroideries for them to embellish the home.[42] In the absence of documents, often it is only by examining the contents of an art collection and its meth-

91   *The finding of Moses*, 1904, private collection

od of display that one can detect the presence of a guiding female hand.

Such is the case with the Aird collection. A sketch of the back drawing room of their home on Hyde Park Terrace which appeared in the *Art Journal* [90] shows Sarah Aird seated at a cloth-covered table with one of her seven daughters at her side, while another is engaged in writing at a table beneath *The roses of Heliogabalus* and a small prepatory study for it [69 70]. Frank Dicksee's *Chivalry* (Forbes Magazine Collection, New York) appears above the mantelpiece, and in between it and the two Alma-Tademas is a group of paintings including Briton Rivière's *Envy, hatred, and malice* (Royal Academy 1881) which represents a young girl holding a puppy surrounded by a pleading posse of collies, spaniels, hounds, and terriers. Sarah Smith Aird's touch is evident in the choice of pictures for this room, the rows of miniatures, and in the placement of the embroidery screen next to the comfortable armchair by the fireplace. Her husband's study, by contrast, contained a masculine assortment of desks and mezzotints that he purchased at Benjamin Disraeli's sale, along with a life-size statue of Rob Roy to designate his Scots ancestry.[43]

The gendering of interior space in the Aird household perplexed the *Art Journal* critic who reviewed their collection in 1891. J.F. Boyes noted the unusually high preponderance of women artists in this collection, who included Clara Montalba, Sophie Anderson, Jessica Hayllar, and Helen Allingham, and puzzled over the

emphasis on the decorative arts in this home, observing that 'Mr. Aird is no collector of curios, though ... "bits" of porcelain, glass, metalwork, lace, embroidery, and so forth, are plentiful throughout the house'.[44] Interpreting the presence of these examples of the 'lesser arts' as an inconsistency in Aird's taste, the critic did not entertain the possibility that Sarah Aird or her daughters may have been responsible for their presence. Women tended to view collecting as an integral aspect of their daily lives and therefore blended together paintings of subjects that pleased them with *objets d'art* and textiles, rather than segregating pictures in a private gallery.

Another instance of shared collecting occurred when Sir Henry Tate commissioned two Alma-Tademas for his second wife Amy Fanny Hislop, who was thirty-one years his junior. Prominently displayed on an easel in their drawing room at Park Hill, Streatham, Alma-Tadema's *A foregone conclusion* [145] was intended as a wedding present from Tate for his new bride. It appropriately depicts a Roman approaching his beloved with an engagement ring in his hand. At Sir Henry Tate's request, Alma-Tadema painted another courtship scene, *A silent greeting* [73], as a companion picture.

Only one Englishwoman is actually recorded as a purchaser of Alma-Tadema and she, significantly, was the wife of an art dealer. Mrs. Charles Wertheimer was married to the brother of Bond Street dealer Asher Wertheimer. Pivoted into the limelight after his home was burgled in 1907, Charles Wertheimer suffered the loss of a Reynolds and a Gainsborough, as well as a valuable collection of snuff boxes.[45] Since he preferred to work out of their palatial home on Park Lane or to consummate deals between hands of whist at his club, it is likely that his wife was acting at his behest when she bid for three Alma-Tademas (e.g., *The dinner* [29]) at the Frederick Turner sale at Christie's in 1878 and sold them once again two years later.[46]

More American women are recorded as clients of Alma-Tadema than any other nationality. One reason is because many American men abdicated from the cultural sphere in favour of their wives in order to distance themselves from the effete connotations conveyed by Anglophiles such as James McNeill Whistler, John Singer Sargent, and Henry James.[47] Another explanation for the higher visibility of American women as art collectors rests in their claim to independence earlier than their European sisters. The three women who are recorded owners of Alma-Tadema's paintings in the United States were among the richest women in the country. Harriet Foote Armour, who commissioned him to paint her portrait, married into a meat packing and banking fortune and was a benefactor of Princeton University.[48] Mary Jane Sexton Morgan inherited a substantial portion of the $ 7,500,000 estate left by her husband Charles. A younger second wife like Amy Tate, Morgan did not begin to collect art until she was widowed in 1878. She purchased Alma-Tadema's *Water pets* (s 186) and *On the road to the temple of Ceres* (s 254) soon afterwards, which she displayed in her New York home in Madison Square alongside French paintings which have been described as 'the finest collection of modern French pictures assembled in New York in the 1880s'.[49] Alma-Tadema's third American woman collector was Lilia Babbitt Hyde who bought *Coign of vantage* [79] through the artist's New York dealer, Knoedler's in 1895.

Lilia Babbitt Hyde's fortune was similar in origin to that of two English collectors of Alma-Tadema: Thomas Barratt and William Lever, 1st Viscount Leverhulme. Her father, Benjamin Talbot Babbitt, invented and manufactured a new formula for soap which he marketed as 'Babbitt's Best Soap'. This brand became a household word and brought Babbitt an immense fortune due to his celebrated advertising skills.[50] Lever, in fact, is said to have imitated American strategies in promoting his own product.[51]

Lever was also influenced by the American practice of endowing private museums. After becoming aware of bequests made by collectors such as William Thompson Walters in Baltimore, who owned seven Alma-Tademas, Lever developed his plans for the Lady Lever Art Gallery in Port Sunlight.[52] A civil engineer by training, Walters discovered that the international trade in liquor was a more profitable field of enterprise. Other American men who were collectors of Alma-Tadema included the department store owner Rodman Wanamaker, the banker Henry Marquand, the transportation czar Charles Yerkes, Judge Samuel Bronson, and Senator George Oliver. As a group they displayed a wider range of professional occupations than his English clients. Alma-Tadema's American collectors, with the exception of Walters, Vanderbilt, and Marquand, made no particular effort to learn more about the individual talent whose subjects blended so well with their classical and academic paintings by other European artists. Often the third or fourth registered owners of the Alma-Tademas that they bid on at auction or bought through dealers, they were geographically and psychologically further removed from the artist.

Despite these differences, Alma-Tadema's meticulously rendered surfaces fared equally as well across the Atlantic for much the same reasons: Americans were in agreement with the English about the equation between value and visible evidence of labour. Even well into this century, when Hollywood producer Allen Funt exhibited his thirty-five Alma-Tademas at the Metropolitan Museum of Art in 1973 prior to selling them, he pithily observed: 'every canvas seems to show an artist trying hard to give his viewer his money's worth. Every inch is crowded with interesting and beautiful detail'.[53] Although the Victorians and Edwardians were silent about their reasons for collecting the art of Alma-Tadema, Funt's explanation cannot be too far off the mark. He strikes at the heart of the work ethic that fuelled the cult of success in both countries, at the same time he acknowledges the aesthetic appeal of the artist's creations. The only element missing is the less expressible psychic release enjoyed by those who allowed themselves to be drawn backward in time by Alma-Tadema's classical fantasies.

Art and 'materialism'

English critical responses to Alma-Tadema 1865–1913

Elizabeth Prettejohn

In 1881, Edmund Gosse described the pitfalls that awaited Alma-Tadema's critics: 'It is very tiresome to praise the painting of a cithera [sic], and then find out that it really was a phorminx, or to be obliged to display a hopeless uncertainty as to the difference between a chlamys and a pallium'.[1] Alma-Tadema's pictures could serve as glorious opportunities for critics to display erudite knowledge of classical archaeology, or they could prove embarrassing to critics unable even to describe their contents without recourse to a dictionary of antiquities; this helps to account for the extremes of adulation and derision that the artist's work inspired, both during his lifetime and after his death. Beyond the mundane problem of distinguishing a cithara from a phorminx, however, was a larger issue: what was the status of an artistic project that brought such distinctions to the fore? Critics rarely questioned Alma-Tadema's sophistication as an archaeologist.[2] At issue, instead, was the cultural value of representing the ancient material environment in archaeologically specific detail. As critical value-systems changed over the half-century of the artist's career, so did responses to his work. However, the problem of locating Alma-Tadema's 'materialistic' project in the realm of 'High' or 'fine' art recurred in diverse ways throughout his career.

The published commentary on Alma-Tadema's work during his lifetime was not only vast, but heterogeneous, since the artist exhibited in all of the important European art centres, as well as his native Holland and his adopted England. This essay will concentrate on the critical response in England, where Alma-Tadema exhibited most consistently and frequently between his first London appearance in 1865 and his memorial exhibition in 1913. However, responses in the many other contemporary forums for the artist's work deserve further study; although beyond the scope of the present essay, such a study would yield fascinating insights not only about Alma-Tadema's own career, but about the complexity of the international art world in the later 19th century.

English critics had some exposure to archaeologically specific paintings of the ancient world before Alma-Tadema's work appeared. At the London International Exhibition of 1862, critics had encountered the works of the French 'néo-Grec' painters (see pp. 69-76), and a few English painters, such as Edward John Poynter, had begun to explore classical archaeology in their works of the 1860s.[3] Nonetheless, Alma-Tadema's paintings seemed novel when they appeared, at first in the exhibitions of continental pictures held by his dealer, Ernest Gambart; the earliest responses stressed the 'originality' of the artist's approach.[4] From 1869, Alma-Tadema's work was shown at the Royal Academy, the exhibition most extensively covered in all sections of the

92   Wal Paget, *Press-day in the Royal Academy*, from *Magazine of Art*, March 1892

101

English periodical press. Critics were now obliged to develop methodologies for evaluating a kind of art that had hitherto been treated as a foreign product.

Royal Academy critics quickly established a distinctive vocabulary for describing Alma-Tadema's paintings, emphasizing words beginning with the prefix 're-': the pictures were described as 'reanimating', 'recovering', or 'restoring' the ancient world. Tom Taylor of *The Times* depended heavily on such words in his notice of *An Egyptian widow in the time of Diocletian* in 1872 [27]: 'This is one of those complete archaeological resuscitations in which the painter delights .... It is wonderful to see the past revived with such perfect realization'.[5] Some critics elaborated the 'resuscitation' vocabulary to describe the depicted scene as if it were literally coming to life before the spectator's eyes. As the *Art-Journal* put it in 1869, 'The picture restores to life what has been dead in antiquarian detail; the old Roman citizen now walks before us, treading on ancient mosaics and surrounded by antique bronzes and classic columns'.[6] The phraseology suggests that the 'life-like' effect of Alma-Tadema's pictures was closely associated with the vivid depiction of the Roman material environment. For W.B. Scott, noticing *The vintage festival* in 1871 [21], it was the sense that 'every single object had been painted from nature, that conveys so decided a feeling of reality and veracity'.[7]

The egalitarian treatment accorded to 'every single object' impressed Scott as compellingly 'life-like'. However, other critics complained that the vivid treatment of inanimate objects threatened to compete with the human figures for the spectator's attention. As the *Illustrated London News* noted in 1871, 'the only too-skilfully-painted accessories have almost the same pictorial value as the figures'.[8] The elevation of accessory objects to equality with human figures violated the prescriptions of 'High Art' theories, such as that of Reynolds's *Discourses*, for the hierarchical subordination of the less to the more important elements of the design.[9] Conservative critics found this particularly worrying in the context of classical subject-painting, traditionally the highest of pictorial categories, and therefore the one in which hierarchical subordination was expected to be most scrupulously maintained.

A Roman emperor, A.D. 41 [93] [23] was the artist's first Academy picture with a subject from Roman history proper. Its exhibition in 1871 elicited this response from the conservative *Art-Journal*: 'In his pictures human figures are apt to be borne down, and all but annihilated, by realism and materialism. Marbles and mosaics, though painted to illusive perfection, can never have the worth and dignity of historic Art. The great painters of this class have always made the palace subordinate to the emperor'.[10] In *A Roman emperor A.D. 41*, the material

93   *A Roman emperor, A.D. 41*, 1871, Walters Art Gallery, Baltimore

94 *The sculpture gallery*, 1874, Hood Museum of Art, Dartmouth College, Hanover, New Hampshire

95 *The picture gallery*, 1874, Towneley Hall Art Gallery & Museums, Burnley Borough Council

splendour of the palace interior is deliberately calculated to upstage the cowardly Emperor Claudius, in order to dramatize a historical event in which greed and brute force triumph over the heroism expected of a Roman political leader. Nonetheless, the *Art-Journal* critic felt bound to apply the standards of 'High Art' theory to a Roman history subject; by those standards, the picture could not qualify as an example of 'historic Art'.

It was not until 1875 that Alma-Tadema's work came under the notice of the most famous of Victorian art critics, but John Ruskin's *Academy Notes* of that year included a forceful denunciation of the artist's disregard for hierarchical subordination. Commenting on *The sculpture gallery* [94] [35], Ruskin wrote: 'The artistic skill has succeeded with all its objects in the degree of their unimportance. The piece of silver plate is painted best; the griffin bas-relief it stands on, second best; the statue of the empress worse than the griffins, and the living personages worse than the statue'. Furthermore, Ruskin made explicit what had been implicit in the *Art-Journal*'s comment – the connection between traditional pictorial hierarchies and traditional structures of political authority. Ruskin associated egalitarianism of pictorial treatment with its political counterpart, to describe Alma-Tadema as a 'modern Republican'.[11] In a lecture delivered at Oxford in 1883, he elaborated: 'M. Alma Tadema does but represent – or rather, has haplessly got

96 *Caricature of The picture gallery: The Apotheosis of E. Gambart, Esquire*, vignette from 'Recollections of the Royal Academy', in *Fun*, 23 May 1874

himself entangled in, – the vast vortex of recent Italian and French revolutionary rage against all that resists, or ever did resist, its licence; in a word, against all priesthood and knighthood'.[12] For Ruskin, overturning pictorial hierarchies was tantamount to advocating the overthrow of traditional political and social hierarchies.

Ruskin's quarrel was not only with Alma-Tadema's neglect of hierarchical subordination. Like some other critics, he objected to the choice of subject-matter from the 'decadent' period of the Roman Empire: 'it is the last corruption of this Roman state, and its Bacchanalian phrenzy, which M. Alma Tadema seems to hold it his heavenly mission to pourtray'.[13] Indeed, the two complaints were related, since Alma-Tadema's characterization of Roman 'decadence' involved presenting the Romans as obsessed with material luxury; the 'materialism' of his stylistic emphasis on Roman artefacts was inseparable from his thematic emphasis on the 'materialism' of Roman social life. Ruskin's comment on *The sculpture gallery*, although intended to be derogatory, captures a crucial implication of the picture's subject: in a Roman Imperial world of extravagant luxury, it is appropriate to lavish attention on a 'piece of silver plate'. Alma-Tadema accordingly places this object in a prominent position near the centre foreground.

The sculpture gallery might be interpreted as a challenge to the critics who had insisted on evaluating the artist's work against the standards of 'High Art' theory. Almost alone among Alma-Tadema's pictures, it approaches the huge dimensions associated with history painting in the grand manner, yet it places a material object in the central position traditionally reserved for the highest-ranking human figure. However, the terms of the critical debate were shifting by 1875, when *The sculpture gallery* appeared at the Royal Academy; descriptions of the picture concentrated less on the prominence of the material objects than on the skill with which they were painted, and many critics dwelt on the technical tour de force of relieving white against white. Alma-Tadema consolidated this success with another spectacular white marble interior the next year, in *An audience at Agrippa's* [97][40], perhaps the most universally admired work of his entire career. From this point, the artist's sheer technical skill became a dominant motif in the criticism of his work.

This was partly in response to developments in the artist's practice, as he moved away from the meticulous craftsmanship of his early 'Pompeian' pictures toward the more bravura style of his later work. However, it also reflects more general trends in English critical writing. As progressive critics increasingly stressed the discernment of technical and visual qualities as a sign of their own professional expertise, they placed higher value on Alma-Tadema's skill as a 'painter *per se*'.[14] Emphasizing the immediate visual qualities of paintings over their anecdotal content or moral implications, they applauded the visual splendour of Alma-Tadema's Roman world without censuring its 'decadence'. Alma-Tadema had formerly been treated as a foreign artist, but he was now discussed alongside English painters associated with aestheticism, such as Frederic Leighton and Albert Moore; in 1879, Wilfrid Meynell linked Alma-Tadema's work with the term 'art for art's sake'.[15] For some critics, the 'Greek' ideal beauty associated with the work of Leighton and Moore remained higher in status than the material luxury of Alma-Tadema's Roman world. Nonetheless, the 'aestheticizing' standards of progressive criticism permitted a positive valuation of Alma-Tadema's 'materialism', on grounds of both technical skill and visual sumptuousness. In 1877, Sidney Colvin noted the 'masterly painting in pavements, mosaics, hangings, draperies, the patina of metals and quality of tissues'.[16]

Despite Ruskin's objections, then, Alma-Tadema's critical reputation reached a peak by the late 1870s; perhaps there is no inconsistency, since Alma-Tadema's champions came from the new generation of critics who were striving to present their evaluations as more progressive than Ruskin's. The artist's high status in 'advanced' art criticism must have been one reason that he was one of the first artists to be honoured with a large retrospective exhibition at the Grosvenor Gallery, the exhibiting institution that had been seen as the stronghold of aestheticism since its first exhibition in 1877.[17] However, the retrospective provided an opportunity for conservative as well as progressive critics to publish more detailed evaluations than ever before. Held in the winter of 1882-83, the exhibition covered Alma-Tadema's entire career, from the self-portrait of 1852 [1] to a work finished and added after the exhibition had already opened (s 283). The Grosvenor showing challenged critics to judge the artist's entire oeuvre, as if he were an old master.

By 1882 it seemed inconceivable to question Alma-Tadema's technical skill. However, negative notices turned this against the artist, to claim that there was some sort of absence, behind the superficially faultless facade of technical brilliance. Some critics concentrated on the figures, finding a failure in psychological or emotional profundity. The *Art-Journal* thought that 'the general lack of attraction in his figures is due to their complete denial of spirituality',[18] while Harry Quilter of the *Spectator* asked: 'Is there a single man or woman that this artist has ever painted, whose face expresses to us anything of the inner character, – on which we care to dwell to find out its meaning?'[19]

A related charge was that Alma-Tadema failed to penetrate beneath the superficial luxury of the Roman world, to fathom the spiritual degeneracy of Imperial society. *The Times* complained that Alma-Tadema neglected to show the enervation and world-weariness that attended the excesses of the Roman 'decadence': 'Nor has he ever looked below the shining surface of wealth and ease and culture upon the dark foundations of society, that hopeless mass of slaves who toiled and hated'.[20] Similarly, the *Art-Journal* objected to the artist's 'resolute suppression of the ghastly truths underlying "the grandeur that was Rome", – of the tyrannies, the hopelessness, the defilement and despair'.[21]

Such views elaborated the old complaint about Alma-Tadema's 'materialism'; now not only the accessories, but also the figural characterizations were attacked as capturing only physical appearances, to the neglect of a spiritual dimension. Quilter summed up this critical attitude, writing that Alma-Tadema 'imagined a body, and forgot the soul; he has given us the face of antique life, but not the heart'.[22] However, critics no longer measured Alma-Tadema's 'materialism' against the standards of 'High Art' theory. Instead, they asked whether it required 'imagination' to record the purely physical appearance of the Roman world and its people. As Quilter put it, 'The power of reproducing, bit by bit, the accessories, down to the minutest detail, of an ancient civilization, is not necessarily an imaginative one'.[23] J.B. Atkinson of *Blackwood's Edinburgh Magazine* described the pictures as 'concretions': 'they are wrought as mosaics out of infinite *tesserae*. Accordingly they come, not as visions of the mind, or as offsprings of the imagination'.[24]

Atkinson's comparison to a mosaic was not inapt as a description of Alma-Tadema's compositional approach (see pp. 33-42), but it was intended to be slighting. Both he and Quilter represented conservative positions in the art world; they refused to consider compositional skill an 'imaginative' quality in the absence of the dramatic and expressive power they valued in contemporary painting. However, progressive critics

97 *An audience at Agrippa's*, 1875, Dick Institute, Kilmarnock, Scotland

were prepared not only to praise the 'aesthetic' appeal of Alma-Tadema's Roman artefacts, but to find 'imagination' in his ability to combine them into effective pictorial compositions. Writing in the *Academy*, a highbrow periodical that consistently supported aestheticism in painting, Cosmo Monkhouse coined the term 'constructive imagination' to describe the way Alma-Tadema 'puts together the broken pieces of an old world [so] that you cannot detect a flaw'. Monkhouse noted the artist's 'fragmentary style of composition', but unlike Atkinson he found this purposeful, creating the impression that the scenes were 'bits out of a real world of which he had been an eye-witness'.[25]

Most of the reviews of 1882-83 were neither as hostile as Quilter's nor as laudatory as Monkhouse's, but the character of the opinions perhaps mattered less than the sheer volume of verbiage published in connection with the Grosvenor exhibition. Although retrospective exhibitions of the works of living artists are now the most familiar of art world events, they were a novelty in the 1880s. The Grosvenor had initiated the practice with an exhibition in the winter of 1881-82 devoted to the work of the respected elder statesman, George Frederic Watts; for Alma-Tadema to receive the same honour the next winter was a mark of exceptional distinction. The extensive press coverage confirmed the artist's celebrity status.

98   *Sappho*, 1881, Walters Art Gallery, Baltimore

99   *Caricature of Sappho, 'Sap-pho-tography', from Punch,*
14 May 1881

Indeed, after the Grosvenor retrospective the habit of praising Alma-Tadema's consummate technique moved from the rarefied realm of 'advanced' art criticism into that of critical cliché. Critics singled out certain technical features, such as the depiction of tessellated floors in receding perspective, and particularly the representation of white marble. Eulogies of Alma-Tadema's marble became so repetitive that critics adopted an elliptical figure of speech: 'Of the extraordinary truthfulness with which the marbles are rendered nothing need be said', observed one critic with reference to *A dedication to Bacchus* [72].[26] Only Ruskin dissented: in his Oxford lecture of 1883, he accused Alma-Tadema of

superficiality even in the representation of the material object for which he was most famous: 'with me, the translucency and glow of marble is the principal character of its substance, while with M. Tadema it is chiefly the superficial lustre and veining which seem to attract him'.[27] This objection failed to stem the tide of the comments on marble, already so ubiquitous that they had become a target for parody. In response to *Sappho* of 1881 [98], *Punch* advised: 'Look closely at the Marble! Marbellous!'[28] More than a decade later, the joke still appealed: in *Punch*'s imaginary account of the conversations of spectators at the New Gallery in 1893, where Alma-Tadema was exhibiting *Unconscious rivals* [78], a woman is made to exclaim: 'Oh! I see it's a Tadema, so of *course* it's marble. He's the great *man* for it, you know!'[29]

By the late 1880s, it was no longer a mark of a critic's progressive credentials to comment on the technical qualities that every popular newspaper was eulogizing. Morever, other changes in the art world contributed to a shift in perceptions of Alma-Tadema's technique; the more progressive younger painters of the 1880s, such as those who showed at the New English Art Club from its first exhibition in 1886, were adopting the sketchier styles associated with the term 'impressionism'. In 1889, the *Magazine of Art* characterized Alma-Tadema's careful craftsmanship as serving 'to resist that threatens to undermine the art-constitution of many of the rising artists of the day'.[30] Alma-Tadema's technique had abruptly shifted in art-political orientation; henceforth it would be championed by conservative critics in specific opposition to 'impressionism'.

After this date, a new divide appeared in the criticism of Alma-Tadema's work. While conservative critics continued to review his paintings in much the same terms as before, progressive critics tended to ignore them altogether. In 1894, *The Times* remarked: '"Advanced" people, however – and there are so many of them nowadays! – are inclined to take [Leighton] and Mr. Poynter, and even Mr. Tadema, very much for granted'.[31] On the rare occasions when 'advanced' critics did offer a comment on Alma-Tadema's work, they tended to be disparaging, and in terms not so different from those that had been applied throughout the artist's career. D.S. MacColl of the *Spectator*, responding to *Unconscious rivals* of 1893 [78], wrote that 'It is to great painting what an elaborate and skilful catalogue of precious objects is to a poet's description'.[32]

After Alma-Tadema's death, the Royal Academy held a large memorial exhibition of his work, opening in January 1913. This was reviewed in virtually all of the periodicals that covered art, but the response showed that the formerly celebrated artist's critical reputation had undergone a decline and fall as precipitous as that of the Roman Empire itself. Although most reviews made at least a condescending reference to Alma-Tadema's skill in the painting of marble and other inanimate objects, few of the critics of 1913 were prepared to consider the representation of the Roman material world a valid aim for fine art. The only unequivocally favourable reviews therefore came from critics with a particular interest in classical archaeology, such as R. Phené Spiers, writing in the *Architectural Review*.[33] However, writers in the specialist art periodicals that were beginning to proliferate in the early 20th century were unwilling to admit an artistic project based on classical archaeology into the realm of 'fine' art. Writing in the prestigious new art periodical, the *Burlington Magazine*, Arthur Clutton Brock refused even to take seriously the pictures' claim to document the material remains of the ancient past: 'The aim of his pictures, I take it, was to give pleasure by the closest possible imitation of a number of things all commonly considered agreeable in themselves; and they are, in fact, collections of such objects, the classical theme being a pretext for collecting them'.[34]

As this passage suggests, the critical objections of 1913, like so many of those that had preceded them, centred on the pictures' 'materialism'; phrases such as 'collections of objects', 'compilations of elaborate properties', or 'atmosphere of inanimate perfection' recurred frequently.[35] The critic for the *Connoisseur*, in fact one of the least derogatory of 1913, did not hesitate to assign Alma-Tadema to 'that class of artists who transmit the material rather than the spiritual vision'.[36] However, once again the 'spiritual' quality, to be opposed to Alma-Tadema's 'materialism', had changed character: the critics of 1913 no longer worried about the absence of psychological penetration in the artist's characterization of the ancient Romans, still less about his glossing over the degeneracy of Roman Imperial society. Instead, they missed signs of self-expression, a quality that would never have occurred to the critics of Alma-Tadema's earlier years. As the critic for the *Connoisseur* put it, 'Advanced modern critics deplore in [Alma-Tadema's work] an absence of personal revelation and vitality, which, in their eyes, reduces it from art to craftsmanship, superlative of its kind, but still only craftsmanship'.[37]

Many critics reversed the opinions of the critics of the 1870s, who had found Alma-Tadema's work distinguished for 'purely aesthetic' qualities; now the pictures were accused of lacking 'design', another new preoccupation of early 20th-century critics. The critic who commented on Alma-Tadema's 'hopeless indifference to the large plastic facts of the scene' was drawing on the latest critical terminology; *The Studio* regretted that the artist's 'miraculous skill was frittered away upon dainty triviality at the expense of the decorative and dramatic intent of his canvas as a whole'.[38] In one sense it is surprising that the critics of 1913 did not respond to Alma-Tadema's compositional ingenuity; this was perhaps partly because they had little sympathy with his plays on the compositional placement of particular Roman artefacts. Moreover, the organizational principles associated with the new catchword, 'design', stressed overall compositional shapes over telling juxtapositions among individual elements. Ironically, this attitude toward composition had more in common with the emphasis on simplicity and grandeur in the old 'High Art' tradition than with Alma-Tadema's 'fragmentary style of composition' (see pp. 33-35).

It was Roger Fry, the critic most closely associated with 'design', who gave a final twist to the 'materialism' theme in his famous article for the *Nation*, asserting that all of Alma-Tadema's figures and objects were 'made of highly-scented soap'. The phrase could scarcely have been chosen more cleverly to ridicule the adulation of previous generations. Fry's article transformed the durability and opulence of Alma-Tadema's marble, which earlier critics had thought would perpetuate his reputation for generations to come, into the evanescence and frivolity of 'scented soap'. Soap was the quintessential commercial product, the one most associated with advertising, and this too is central to Fry's denunciation: 'the case of Sir Lawrence Alma Tadema is only an extreme instance of the commercial materialism of our civilization'. Indeed, Fry's contempt was less for Alma-Tadema's work *per se*, than for its marketability among a class he considered philistine; he reserved his greatest ire for 'the half-educated members of the lower middle-class' who, he claimed, were prepared to accept 'scented soap' in lieu of fine art.[39]

It may be pure coincidence that Alma-Tadema's two most strident opponents were also the two most skilful writers among his critics. None of the many eulogies of the artist's work are as quotable as Roger Fry's comments about 'scented soap' or Ruskin's famous denunciation of *A Pyrrhic dance* [16] as 'a microscopic view of a small detachment of black-beetles, in search of a dead rat'.[40] It is notable, though, that Alma-Tadema's work inspired both critics to write some of their most vivid prose.

Ruskin saw Alma-Tadema as a dangerous radical, Fry saw him as a dangerous reactionary. The shift might be described as the inevitable fate of an artist whose career spanned half a century; as the *Athenaeum* remarked in 1909, 'to become old-fashioned is the ultimate fate of every one, and there is something fine in fighting to the last in a losing cause'.[41] However, it was premature to describe Alma-Tadema's project as a 'losing cause'. Fry in 1913, as well as Ruskin in 1883, associated Alma-Tadema's 'materialism' with contemporary issues they thought urgent. Indeed, both writers linked Alma-Tadema with larger social trends or groups they

100 Felician Freiherr von Myrbach, *An Alma Tadema*, published in *Art Journal*, December 1891

detested, Ruskin with 'the vast vortex of French and Italian revolutionary rage' and Fry with 'the half-educated members of the lower middle-class'. The distinction between a cithara and a phorminx, trivial in itself, had implications that were the reverse of trivial. Critical responses to Alma-Tadema's work offered a series of shifting perspectives on the role of 'High' or 'fine' art in a world of 'commercial materialism'; the debate thus involved cultural issues that critics thought fundamental, in 1913 as in the 1860s.

However, after the flurry of responses to the 1913 memorial exhibition, Alma-Tadema's reputation sank suddenly into oblivion, suggesting that the issues raised by his work no longer seemed relevant in an art world preoccupied by the debates of 'modernism'; the story of his neglect by 20th-century art historians has often been told (see p. 18). Since the 1970s, a significant revival of interest has taken place, resulting in several exhibitions and a substantial catalogue raisonné by Vern G. Swanson.[42] The simultaneous appearance of coffee-table books, with glossy colour reproductions of Alma-Tadema's pictures, suggests that his work retains popular appeal. At the end of the 20th century, then, debate continues about the status of Alma-Tadema's archaeological project: should it be considered 'High Art' or popular entertainment? The present exhibition aims to demonstrate that Alma-Tadema's archaeological sophistication, as well as his popular appeal, continue to deserve the serious attention accorded them by their first critics.

Alma-Tadema and photography

Ulrich Pohlmann

The almost photographic qualities in Sir Lawrence Alma-Tadema's paintings of Greek and Roman antiquity were already being remarked upon by contemporary critics during his lifetime. This impression of photographic realism was substantiated in particular by the artist's detailed reproduction and illusionistic presentation of accessories. The deceptive authenticity with which he was able to reproduce the texture of materials such as marble in his paintings gained Alma-Tadema the reputation of being an all-rounder, while also earning him the criticism that his painting subscribed solely to the visual cult of the beautiful and the superficial reproduction of appearances. Although there are various indicators that Alma-Tadema used photographs as studies for his paintings, the existence of a photographic archive in his estate seems to have gone practically unnoticed or even been ignored in the relevant research on the relationship between painting and photography.[1] Only recently have the origins of Alma-Tadema's photographic archive and the relationship between painting and photography in his work become the object of special scrutiny.[2]

To begin with, the fact that Alma-Tadema had an extensive photographic archive at his disposal is in no way unusual. In England, the homeland of the medium, photography was held in particularly great esteem and had patrons in the highest social circles. Not only the royal family, in the persons of Prince Albert and Queen Victoria, showed considerable interest in the progress of photography both as a science and as an art,[3] but a large number of artists were also very enthusiastic about this 'most remarkable invention of modern times'.[4] What is more, a first impressive presentation of its products had been on show at the Great Exhibition in London in 1851. Among the many and varied functions the medium of photography had was that of providing artists with studies of architecture, landscapes, portraits and clouds:[5] 'With art, doubtless, its future destiny will be closely linked: but so far from becoming a rival, it will prove a most useful auxiliary, and a means by which the artist of merit may rise higher in reputation and eminence. By using photography as a means of replacing the purely mechanical parts of his labour, the work of the artist may be much lightened'.[6] In an age of progress-oriented positivism there was widespread willingness on the part of artists to avail themselves of scientific and mechanical aids such as photography. Their aim in doing so was to achieve a deeper understanding of their subjects. As comprehensive research has in the meantime shown, numerous painters, draughtsmen and sculptors collected photographs, among them the Pre-Raphaelite artists Ford Madox Brown, Dante Gabriel Rossetti, William Holman Hunt and John Everett Millais, all of whom had repeated recourse to them as studies for their paintings.[7] Millais is reputed to have said that 'all artists use photographs now',[8] a statement which as of 1880 is valid not only for English but also for German painting.[9] Alma-Tadema too made no secret of his high regard for photography. In 1893, on the occasion of a survey undertaken by the art periodical *The Studio*, the artist replied quite candidly to the question as to whether he saw in the camera a friend or a foe of art: 'I am convinced that the camera has had a very salutary and useful influence on art. It is of great use to artists'.[10]

Despite this public admission of indebtedness to photography, only in the rarest of cases have complete photographic archives been preserved in artists' estates. For this reason Alma-Tadema's collection is an exception to the rule, both in its extent and in its specific structure.

This becomes even more evident when it is compared with the archives of other artists such as Franz von Lenbach, Fernand Khnopff or Franz von Stuck.[11] Unlike the latter, who staged and recorded scenes for prospective paintings in their studios with the support of professional and amateur photographers or occasionally even took up a camera themselves, Alma-Tadema had recourse exclusively to photographs which were commercially available. It is not possible to endorse the repeated claim that Alma-Tadema was an active photographer himself.[12] With the exception of a none too clearly designated photography handbook in Italian, *Manuale di fotografia*, the artist's library contained no other relevant literature of this kind. Amateur snapshots supposedly taken by Alma-Tadema with the first Kodak camera to come onto the market in 1888 have not been preserved.[13]

The order of things

Due to a lack of sources and the absence of confirmed statements by the artist, the genesis of his photograph collection remains very uncertain. However, as the earliest examples date from around 1850, there can be little doubt that the archive was not assembled at the time the photographs were taken. The collection embraces a total of 5,300 vintage prints from the period between 1851 and 1910. In 1915 the photographs were given to the Victoria & Albert Museum but in 1947 they were transferred to Birmingham University Library, where they are stored today in 167 portfolios in the Heslop Room.[14] Art reproductions and photographs of architecture account for the largest section of the archive. These photographs are mainly of Egyptian, Greek and Roman, Byzantine, Medieval and Renaissance works of art preserved in Italian, English, Egyptian and German museums.[15] While reproductions of paintings are almost totally absent, except for the wall frescoes in Pompeii, the archive has a rich selection of photographs of sculptures. From the technical point of view, most of these photographs are albumen prints commonly used in the 19th century. These were taken from negatives produced in the wet collodion process. Salt paper prints from glass or paper negatives, also common up to 1860, are rare, and there are no Daguerreotypes or costly positive process prints such as carbon prints in the collection of the artist. Alma-Tadema seems to have had no interest in stereoscopes, which were very popular in the 19th century. A broad selection of these – over 100,000 different motifs – was available as early as 1858 from the London Stereoscopic and Photographic Company. The thematic structure and order imposed on this imaginary museum is the work of Alma-Tadema himself, whereas cataloguing of the photograph collection was undertaken three years after the artist's death in 1915 by the Victoria & Albert Museum, London. The portfolios bring together a comprehensive spectrum of themes which ranges from motifs such as Roman aqueducts, triumphal arches, catacombs, prehistoric art, and Egyptian architecture, to studies of flowers, trees and animals. The combination of the respective typologies was dictated by the principle of comparison and swift accessibility. This principle resulted in images from very different stylistic epochs being filed together, irrespective of the date of their origins and their context in the history of art. This principle of decontextualization becomes especially obvious in the case of one particular cardboard sheet (XXXVIII, 8893) which carries not only a photograph of an unidentified Medieval church portal but also three engravings of a portal arch in the church of St. Agostino in Palermo, the inside of the church of St. Sebastian in Magdeburg, and part of a plan of Cologne cathedral. It is characteristic of Alma-Tadema's eclectic filing system that he even split up inherently linked series of photographs by Maxime Du Camp, Francis Bedford, Guglielmo Plüschow or Giorgio Sommer in favour of his own subdivision according to his themes.

Alma-Tadema bought most of these photographs as individual items which he later mounted on sheets of cardboard, the acid content of which is unfortunately responsible for the poor condition of many of the photographs today. Occasionally he also purchased photographs in the widely available *carte de visite* or cabinet card format, mounting them on cardboard at a later stage alongside his own drawings, ground plans, wood engravings etc. Wherever signatures and inscriptions have been preserved it is of course possible to identify clearly the respective authors. However, as Alma-Tadema often made no note on the cardboard sheets, many of the photographers remain anonymous. The artist's main interest was obviously not in the photograph as a work of art but as a highly detailed reproduction of a particular motif which was of documentary value to him.

101 Robert Rive (attributed), *New excavations in Pompeii*, c. 1880, photograph from Alma-Tadema's collection, University of Birmingham (CXXII, 11128)

102 *Lawrence Alma-Tadema (?) drawing in the House of Sallust*, Pompeii, 1862-63, photograph, University of Birmingham (CXXIII, 11162)

103 Giorgio Sommer, *House of Meleager*, Pompeii, c. 1865, photograph from Alma-Tadema's collection, University of Birmingham (CXXII, 11129)

104 Guglielmo Plüschow, *Street in Pompeii*, photograph from Alma-Tadema's collection, University of Birmimgham (CLIX, 12420)

The imaginary museum

It is more than likely that Alma-Tadema's initial preoccupation with photography was inspired by the reproductions which professional photographers made of his paintings. As from 1860 this was general practice among artists, the reproductions being sent to collectors, galleries or museums as illustrative material. We know from various reports that the walls of Townshend House, his first London home, were decorated with reproductions of paintings by Alma-Tadema [27].[16] Another function these photographs of paintings had was to record various stages in the progress of a work of art. So as to be able to study the development of his own works, at the latest from 1866 onwards Alma-Tadema cooperated with the photographer J. Dupont who captured his paintings at different moments in their genesis.[17]

In all probability, Alma-Tadema began his collecting activities in the early 1860s,[18] although according to Richard Tomlinson the greater part of the photographic archive was put together after the artist moved to London in 1871.[19] Alma-Tadema may well have visited the extensive photographic section at the International Exhibition in London in 1862, in which numerous photographic studies of other artists were on display. However, the most decisive event for his archive was certainly his honeymoon trip to Italy in 1863 with his first wife Marie Pauline Gressin Dumoulin de Boisgirard. The newly wedded couple spent two months visiting Florence, Rome, Naples, and in particular Pompeii. While there, Alma-Tadema became completely enthralled by Roman antiquity which he captured in the form of measured drawings and photographs. The extraordinary fascination which the ancient ruins of Pompeii held for him is demonstrated in a number of portrait photographs of the artist. These portraits were possibly commissioned and show him in the middle of the ruins of the House of Sallust thoroughly preoccupied with surveying and sketching the exact proportions of the buildings [2 102].[20]

Alma-Tadema's particular interest in archaeology as a science resulted in him informing himself thoroughly about the latest excavations as well as acquiring photographic documentation of them.[21] As in his paintings, the most prominent motifs in the photographs are ancient Roman architecture, art, and artefacts, with ancient Greek, Egyptian and Medieval art cropping up less frequently. His particular preference was for the excavations at Pompeii and Herculaneum, and he repeatedly visited these sites up until 1900. The ruins of ancient Pompeii had already been captured in calotypes by English photographers such as Calvert Richard Jones and George Wilson Bridges (1846) and James Graham (1858-64).[22] However, commercial photographic records of the city only became available during the intensive excavations undertaken in the early 1860s. Photographs of ancient remains and architecture taken by the photographers Michele Amodio, Giorgio Sommer, Robert Rive, all of whom lived in Naples, and later Alinari, James Anderson and Giacomo Brogi, were on sale locally as individual items or in albums. The tightly-knit distribution network through which original photographs of Pompeii and other ancient Italian cities could be acquired included the book and art dealers Negesborn & Bowinkel and Alberto Detken in Naples, the premises of Joseph Spithöfer, Hermann Loescher, Edmondo Behles and the travel agent Cook in Rome, Celestino Degoix in Genoa, Carlo Ponti and Carlo Naya in Venice, J. Brecker in Florence, and Ludwig Niernberger and Oscar Kramer in Vienna. Alma-Tadema made great use of this commercial availability, as proven by the large number of photographs by Sommer, Amodio and Rive in his archive.

Particularly in vogue were views and art reproductions by the photographer Giorgio Sommer, who was born in Frankfurt am Main. From 1857 onwards Sommer worked as a successful photographer and entrepreneur in Naples, and from 1860 he photographed in close cooperation with Giuseppe Fiorelli, director of excavations at Pompeii. His architectural photographs, be they views and art reproductions of the Stabian Baths, the Temple of Mercury or the House of the Tragic Poet, were renowned for their extraordinary quality [103]. Sommer also took photographs of the artworks and archaeological finds – altars, tripods, frescos, lanterns, vases, mummies etc. – preserved in the Vatican Museums in Rome, as well as in the Museo Nazionale (the National Archeological Museum) in Naples.[23] Alma-Tadema's collection contains a rich selection of these photographs as both small and large format prints. When something was of particular interest to the artist he was not content with just one view of it. Instead he purchased numerous

105 *Theatre at Pompeii*, c. 1880, photograph from Alma-
Tadema's collection, University of Birmingham
(CXLIX, 12070)

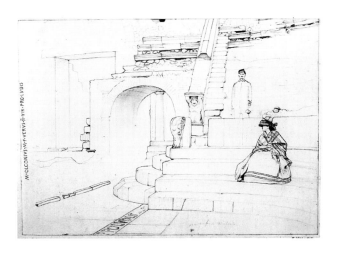

106 *Theatre at Pompeii*, drawing by Alma-Tadema after the
photograph, 1883, University of Birmingham
(CXLIX, E.2823)

107 John Parker (ed.), *Ostia Cornice*, c. 1870, photograph
from Alma-Tadema's collection, University of Birmingham
(XIV, 8089)

108 John Parker (ed.), *Excavations in Rome*, c. 1870, photograph from Alma-Tadema's collection, University of
Birmingham (C, 10486)

versions, as in the case of the bronze figure of the drunken faun discovered in 1880 during excavations in Pompeii and preserved in the Museo Nazionale in Naples. Alma-Tadema also devoted great attention to the architectural details of specific buildings such as the triumphal arches or the amphitheatres in Rome and Pompeii, as demonstrated by the large number of photographs by Sommer, Amodio, Ludovico Tuminello, Michele Mang, James Anderson and Simelli in his archive. In 1883 the artist made an almost identical copy of a photograph of the rows of seating in the Pompeian amphitheatre in an outline drawing [105 106]. His obsessive preoccupation with ornaments and fragments can be seen in the innumerable photographs of the capitals, bases and mouldings of columns which he collected [107].

Between 1865 and 1870, his so-called Pompeian period, Alma-Tadema had repeated recourse to photographs of the ruins of that southern Italian city for the paintings. It is also possible that he used study material in the form of replicas of terracotta, bronze and marble objects from the excavations at Pompeii. A whole range of more than 200 different small statues in the original size had been copied in Sommer's workshop, for example, those of Silenus, Narcissus, Seneca, Plato or the Dancing Faun. Sommer had these on sale, together with his photographs, in his shop on the Piazza Vittorio, in the Museo Nazionale in Naples, and through mail order catalogues and advertisements in illustrated magazines [see repr. p. 109].

Whereas the photographs of Pompeian architecture produced by professional studios were taken mainly to suit the taste and requirement of people on the so-called grand tour, that is to say, of an aristocratic and bourgeois clientele, the scientific utilization of photography in the field of archaeology adhered to quite different criteria. This particular application cultivated a certain preference for the representation of the fragment, designed for the more analytical eye which focused on the architectonic detail. The German Heinrich Schliemann[24] and the Englishman John Henry Parker, who lived in Rome,[25] were among the first archaeologists to recognize the value of the systematic utilization of photography in recording discoveries. Between 1864 and 1877 Parker, who was vice-president of the British and American Archaeological Society of Rome, commissioned Carlo Baldassare Simelli, Giovanni Battista

Colamedici, Filippo Lais, Charles Smeaton, Francesco Sidoli, A. De Bonis, Filippo Spina and other photographers whose reputations have not endured to record the medieval and ancient Roman constructions and artworks which came to light during the excavations on the Palatine Hill in Rome and in Naples and Pompeii. Unlike the tourist views, these photographs served primarily archaeological interests. Parker made copious use of them in his 13-volume work *Archaeology of Rome* and offered them for sale with the aid of various mail order catalogues containing all the 3,391 motifs. Alma-Tadema's library contained a copy of one such catalogue.[26] Numerous photographs from his archive originate from Parker's collection, for example, the photographs of structural details of the wall of the city of Rome, the aqueducts by Simelli or the Ostia Cornice by Colamedici [107].[27] One characteristic feature of this archaeological study of parts of the marble entablature is that it indicates the proportions with the aid of a metric system. However, Parker's photographic documentation not only captured precise moments in the excavation but also contained romantic panoramic views in which the monuments are presented in their natural surroundings.[28]

The approximately 30 photographs by the German photographer Guglielmo Plüschow contained in Alma-Tadema's archive exemplify a completely different method of re-staging scenes of life in ancient times [104 109 112 124].[29] Plüschow was a relative of the cosmopolitan Baron Wilhelm von Gloeden who also lived and worked as a photographer in Taormina. Plüschow had emigrated to Italy around 1880. At first he settled as a photographer in Naples and from there took 'photographs from life' in the Imperial Roman villas of Tivoli, in the ruins of Pompeii, and the Greek temples in Paestum. For his 'living images' taken in the House of Meleager or the House of Marcus Lucretius, he had youthful models dressed in pseudo-ancient robes pose as musicians and 'celebrants', as the original inscription on the cardboard sheets in Alma-Tadema's collection put it. Depictions of this kind were published in the 1890s in English magazines such as *The Studio* and *The Photogram* and were highly praised by archaeologists such as the German Rudolf Hauser as successful attempts to reconstruct ancient life.[30] It is conceivable – among other things given Alma-Tadema's preference for

109 Guglielmo Plüschow, *Nude boy with a lion-legged pedestal*, Naples, c. 1885, photograph from Alma-Tadema's collection, University of Birmingham (CXVIII, 11053)

110 Giacomo Caneva, *Young girl in Roman costume*, c. 1852, photograph from Alma-Tadema's collection, University of Birmingham (LX, 9253)

111 Ernest Benecke, *Christian costumes in Bethlehem. Convent of the Scourging, Jerusalem*, 1852, photograph from Alma-Tadema's collection, University of Birmingham (CII, 10567)

112 Guglielmo Plüschow, *Four boys at a Pompeian altar*, c. 1885, photograph from Alma-Tadema's collection, University of Birmingham (I, 7646)

terraced scenes with marble seats – that Plüschow's photographs functioned as inspiration for the paintings *A reading from Homer* [67] and *Amo te ama me* (s 273).

At the same time there is a conspicuous absence in Alma-Tadema's photographic archive of both figure and nude studies and of genre scenes. The few that exist are oriental costume studies of various traders, musicians or dancing dervishes taken by Antonio Beato, Francis Frith, Naya & Schoefft, or Ch. Lallemand (Galerie Universelle des Peuples). Two studies of a Roman artist's model are the work of Giacomo Caneva and date from around 1850-52 [110]. Caneva belonged to the international circle in Rome which produced some of the first art photographers. He also experimented with the Blanquart-Evrard calotype process.[31] Other costume studies are obviously the work of the photographer Ernest Benecke who undertook a series of *Costumes chrétiennes* in Egypt in 1852 [111]. Today these are among the most sought-after photographs of the Orient, not only because of their beauty but also because of their scarcity. However, Alma-Tadema mainly sketched and painted from living models. Occasionally members of his circle of friends or his family posed for him in Roman robes.[32] Despite being 'studies from nature', these figures have often been criticized as failures, as being stiff and too 'modern' in their whole physiognomy.[33] It was only under the influence of Eadweard Muybridge's famous instantaneous photographs of people in motion, available in a book published in 1901, that Alma-Tadema is said to have paid greater attention to reproducing more spontaneous forms of expression in the human body.[34] The artist had been all in favour of Muybridge holding a lecture on his work in the Royal Academy in 1889, and he is sure to have known the article on instantaneous photography which appeared in 1882 in the *Magazine of Art* and which sang the praises of the advantages of instantaneous photography for painting.[35]

Early publications of photographs of the Near East

The earliest photographs contained in Alma-Tadema's collection were taken in Egypt, Palestine, Syria and the Holy Land. This group also includes several interior views (probably reproductions of daguerreotypes) of the Egyptian Section in the Crystal Palace showing reconstructions of the colossal statue of Ramses II near Abu Simbel and of the Temple of Beni Hasan. However, a place of special prominence in his collection is held by photographs from the archaeological folios by Maxime Du Camp and Auguste Salzmann which were produced at the Imprimerie Photographique of Louis-Désiré Blanquart-Evrard in Lille.[36] The French journalist Maxime Du Camp, a pupil of the photographer Gustave Le Gray, took about 200 calotypes during a trip to the Orient which he undertook between 1849 and 1851 in the company of the novelist Gustave Flaubert. In 1852 he had a selection of 125 motifs published by Gide and Baudry in Paris in an album entitled *Egypte, Nubie, Palestine et Syrie; dessins photographiques recueillis pendant les années 1849, 1850 et 1851*. Du Camp, whose photographic journey followed the route taken by the Champollion expedition in 1829, was mainly concerned with a scientific documentation for archaeological purposes. For this reason his photographs, produced in the wax paper negative process, and noble in their sober composition, appear free of any romanticising tendencies and were greatly praised for their perfection and beauty. Occasionally Du Camp's Corsican servant Sassetti is to be seen on photographs of the hieroglyph walls or buildings, but he is included there less as a picturesque accessory and more to demonstrate size and proportion [123]. 150 to 200 copies of Du Camp's photographs were published, 25 sets of five motifs each. They were advertised by means of brochures and sold for 20 francs per set or five francs per individual motif.

The artist and photographer Auguste Salzmann (1824-1872), who travelled to Egypt, Palestine and Syria in 1854 and recorded Christian, Islamic and Jewish cultural monuments in more than 200 architectural photographs using the calotype process, also pursued obviously scientific ends. In his own words, he wanted to 'do a true service' to archaeology 'by reproducing through photography all the monuments in Jerusalem, in particular those of which the origins are controversial'.[37] A selection of 174 of Salzmann's motifs was published from 1854 onwards in the three-volume work *Jérusalem, époques judaïque, romaine, chrétienne, arabe: explorations photographiques*. Although aimed primarily at experts and scientists, the photographs are of great artistic quality and combine in a unique manner artistic vision and archaeological documentation. This is surely

113 Auguste Salzmann, *Holy Sepulchre, Jerusalem*, c. 1850, photograph from Alma-Tadema's collection, University of Birmingham (XXIV, 8477)

114 Maxime Du Camp, *Golden Gate, Jerusalem*, c. 1852, photograph from Alma-Tadema's collection, University of Birmingham (CI, 10520)

115 Francis Bedford, *Olive trees in the Garden of Gethsemane near Jerusalem*, 1862, photograph from Alma-Tadema's collection, University of Birmingham (LXIV, 9352)

116 James Robertson and Felice Beato, *Jews at the Wailing Wall*, Jerusalem, c. 1857, photograph from Alma-Tadema's collection, University of Birmingham (CI, 10518)

one reason for Alma-Tadema's special liking for these particular photographs. He purchased several individual items from a smaller edition of 40 of the most beautiful and interesting motifs which appeared in 1856 [113].[38] These could be obtained through the Parisian publishers Gide and J. Baudry in sets of four photographs at a price of 12 francs, or as individual motifs at four francs each.[39]

Blanquart-Evrard too was highly active in promoting distribution of the photographs and worked together with the most important European book publishers and art dealers. The photographer Alphonse Plumier kept a general supply of them in Brussels for the Belgian market, while the prints produced in Lille were distributed on the English market by M.P. Camus & Co and the Belgian art dealer Ernest Gambart. A little known fact to date is that in the 1850s Gambart was one of the big publishers of photograph albums, along with Goupil and Masson in Paris.[40] In 1857 Gambart published a *Jerusalem Album* of 32 photographs by James Robertson and Felice Beato who had travelled to Egypt and Palestine in 1856-57 [116]. The whole series was priced at approximately £ 10.10s or at 40 pence per individual motif.[41] Thus it is more than probable that Alma-Tadema acquired the photographs by Du Camp, Salzmann and Robertson & Beato via Gambart some time after 1864. This supposition is supported not only by the fact that Salzmann's photographs were available on the market for a long time due to poor sales, but also by the hand-written inscription 'specimen proof' on a number of the photographs by Robertson & Beato, which means that they must have been either sample items or remainders of a photographic archive.[42] Another folio of photographs of the Orient, several copies of which are present in Alma-Tadema's archive [115], is by the English photographer Francis Bedford and is regarded as one of the most outstanding series of travel photographs produced in the 19th century. Bedford had taken these 210 photographs of landscapes and monuments while accompanying Edward, Prince of Wales, on an educational trip to the East. Although Bedford and the English travel agent kept more or less to the main routes, the photographer had ample opportunity to seek out lesser known sites which were normally closed to tourists. A selection from Bedford's series was published in 1863 in a luxury edition of 172 motifs under the title

Photographic pictures of Egypt, the Holy Land and Syria, Constantinople, the Mediterranean, Athens, etc. The publisher was W. Day & Sons in London and the work was distributed by Marion & Co. in London either as a complete series costing 43 guineas, as a set on a specific country, costing between £ 12 and £ 19, as a selection of 20 photographs of 'particular Biblical or architectonic interest' costing £ 7.7s, or as individual motifs costing 7 shillings each.[43]

Alma-Tadema was particularly interested in the Acropolis in Athens. He owned photographs of it by William Stillman, Pascal Sébah and Félix Bonfils taken in the period between 1862 and 1882. It is quite probable that Alma-Tadema had social contact with Stillman (1828-1901), a rather colourful character who was a diplomat, artist, spy, journalist and photographer. Stillman had taken impressive photographs of modern and ancient Athens in 1868 which he was able to publish two years later with the support of the Hellenic Society of London under the title *The acropolis of Athens illustrated picturesquely and architecturally in photography*.[44] Some of the photographs were taken from the upper entablature of the Parthenon [121] and their unusual compositional perspective resembles that in Alma-Tadema's painting *Phidias showing the frieze of the Parthenon to his friends* [13]. However, given the later date of the photograph's publication, it cannot have acted as a model for the painting.[45]

Alma-Tadema's enthusiasm for collecting photographs of historically and culturally important buildings was not restricted to the Mediterranean region but also included the English cultural heritage. Numerous architectural studies of Norman churches and Gothic cathedrals, monasteries and cloisters in Wells, St. Alban's, Exeter, Durham, Winchester and Canterbury bear witness to this. Most of them were taken by Francis Frith, James Valentine, Francis Bedford and Frank Mason Good, and they inspired Alma-Tadema to drawings of wall elevations and architectural details such as consoles, wall buttresses, canopies and tracery.[46] The artist's interest in the historical and cultural roots of his chosen homeland is further illustrated by three portfolios containing 120 carbon prints of 'old' London. These photographs were taken between 1875 and 1886 by A. & J. Bool and Henry & Thomson J. Dixon under contract to the Society for photographing relics of Old London. The

117 Henry Stuart Wortley (attributed), *Study of clouds with city silhouette*, c. 1860, photograph from Alma-Tadema's collection, University of Birmingham (CXLVI, 11958)

118 Constant Famin, *Oak forest with woman*, c. 1870, photograph from Alma-Tadema's collection, University of Birmingham (CLVIII, 12406)

119 Frederick Hollyer, *Lily (Calla)*, c. 1880, photograph from Alma-Tadema's collection, University of Birmingham (LXI, 9283)

120 George Washington Wilson, *Kilt Rock – Loch Staffin*, *Skye*, c. 1870, photograph from Alma-Tadema's collection, University of Birmingham (XCVII, 10404)

motivation behind this commission was to document the 18th-century backyards, inns and public houses threatened by the process of urban development.[47]

A special case among the many travel views in Alma-Tadema's archive are the photographs of Indian temple architecture and landscapes by Jung & Fricke and from the India series by Bourne & Shepherd. These photographs were also published by Marion & Co in London and served the artist, who never travelled to India, as studies for watercolours of Indian costumes. An even more exotic flavour is provided by the photographs of South American and Oceanian cultures, plus an album of 45 outstanding photographs of the landscape, inhabitants and culture of Java which the photographer Isidore van Kinsbergen (1821-1905) donated to the artist in 1870 complete with a personal dedication. This would seem to indicate that Alma-Tadema's passion for collecting photographs was widely known.

A different nature

In view of the neo-classical emphasis in his paintings, at first glance it comes somewhat as a surprise that Alma-Tadema also owned an extensive collection of photographic studies of animals, flowers and plants. These included photographs of oxen and cows grazing or drawing carts, of goats, pigs, donkeys, horses, dogs and cats, some of which occasionally link up with studies of peasant scenes. He also possessed a wide selection of depictions of various birds, ranging from ducks, turkeys, chickens, geese, swans, peacocks, and cranes to parrots and falcons. This type of work, known as *études d'après nature* and pursued by photographers such as Constant Famin, Achille Quinet, Frederick Hollyer and Ottomar Anschütz, became very popular around 1860, especially among the French painters of the Barbizon School.[48] The same can be said of the numerous botanical studies and still lifes of plants and flowers such as tulips, primroses, lilies, irises, hyacinths, daisies, anemones, roses, foxgloves, crocuses, clematis, lilac and larkspur, mostly by Hollyer, James Valentine, S. Thompson, August Kotzsch, Tuminello, Quinet and Famin.[49] The archive also contains a range of photographs of trees in bloom, chestnut, apple, cherry, plum, pear and fig trees and individual studies of oak, cypress, olive, pine, cedar, beech or birch trees, most of which were taken in the forest of Fontainebleau.[50] The botanical studies, which were photographed both outdoors and in studios, possibly served as models for paintings. Beautiful flowers appear frequently as decorative components in Alma-Tadema's work, as in his *Confidences* [17], *The roses of Heliogabalus* [69] and *Spring* [6]. Furthermore, his own thriving flower garden provided him with actual examples which he copied with great application and care, often with the aid of a magnifying glass.

Among the nature photographs are sea, river and cliff views taken mostly in England by Francis Frith and George Washington Wilson. The dramatically heroic photographs of the Scottish highlands and the Shetland islands in particular – for example the steep angled views of Kilt Rock on the isle of Skye [120] – seem to have encouraged Alma-Tadema to opt for daring perspectives, as in his painting *Coign of vantage* [79].[51]

The archive also contains a portfolio of cloud studies, among which is a view by Robert Rive of the clouds of ash from the eruption of Vesuvius on 26 April 1872. Cloud photographs became part of the favoured repertoire of photographic studies for artists around 1851. Nevertheless, they represented a considerable technical challenge for the photographer given the fact that, due to the absence of colour sensitivity in the negative emulsions and the long exposure times, the sky in landscape photographs became a vacant area and could only be captured adequately by very short exposures. An unusual series of sea and cloud studies in Alma-Tadema's archive is presumably the work of Colonel Henry Stuart Wortley dating from around 1869 [117].

A dialogue between painting and photography

One question which naturally arises is the extent to which, and in what way, Alma-Tadema had recourse to these photographs as models for his paintings. There is no evidence that Alma-Tadema used the methods widespread in the 19th century of either drawing a transfer of a photographic model with the help of a grid, tracing it, or projecting it onto a light sensitive screen by means of slides. The photographic collection served the artist primarily as a source of inspiration for his paintings, as did his replicas of ancient sculptures, his extensive library of more than 4,000 mostly illustrated books on

121 William Stillman, *Interior view of the Parthenon from the entablature, Acropolis, Athens*, c. 1868, photograph from Alma-Tadema's collection, University of Birmingham (LXXVIII, 9890)

122 Guido Rey, *Pompeian scene*, 1895, photograph, private collection

123 Maxime Du Camp, *Médinet Habou. Peristyle of the Palace of Ramses Méiamoun*, c. 1852, photograph from Alma-Tadema's collection, University of Birmingham (XXXI, 8688)

124 Guglielmo Plüschow, *Three boys in a Pompeian house*, c. 1885, photograph from Alma-Tadema's collection, University of Birmingham (CXXIII, 11160)

archaeology and art history, his city guides and travel reports, and his wood engravings from illustrated newspapers such as *Le Monde Illustré* or the *London Illustrated News* which carried detailed reports on the latest excavations. His photographic collection of examples was often a substitute for close observation of the original, as in the case of the Egyptian monuments which Alma-Tadema only got to know directly during a trip to the Orient four decades after his Egyptian period. Furthermore, many of the ancient monuments had undergone serious alterations as a result of urban development and the damaging effects of tourism and were thus documented in a more original state in the photographs. For the artist in his studio, the photographs constituted a veritable garden of remembrance of past cultures, supporting him as he strove through his painting to translate the spirit of antiquity into a living present. In the course of that translation, the photographs functioned as a corrective, facilitating as they did the detailed reproduction of the exact proportions of ancient monuments and works of art.

'Alma-Tadema's compositions are the sums of their details'.[52] Taking the example of the painting *Spring* [6], Louise Lippincott has succeeded in presenting the artist's eclectic procedure convincingly as an imaginative interplay of various pictorial sources resulting in an 'ancient' composition. Yet in the case of Alma-Tadema, the 'reconstruction' of scenes from important cultural epochs could never be equated with an authentic depiction of a historical event. What he created in his art with the aid of photographs – deemed then to be objective – was a fiction of the ancient world which remains full of anachronisms.

Another interesting fact is that Alma-Tadema's neo-classicism exerted a profound influence on Art Photography at the turn of the century. In their attempts to imbue their ideas of an ancient Arcady with new life, not only the North American representatives of Pictorialism such as Fred Holland Day, Clarence H. White and Herbert Hess, but also and more especially those photographers living in Italy, namely Guglielmo Plüschow, Vicenzo Galdi, Wilhelm von Gloeden and Guido Rey, had recourse to the iconography of Alma-Tadema. For Art Photography this revitalization of antiquity, its everyday life and its myths, gained considerable importance against the backdrop of the omni-present urbanization, industrialization and destruction of the natural environment. In their desire for a life-style free of social and political contradictions, the art photographers often turned their eyes towards antiquity.[53] It was in this sense that between 1895 and 1898 the Turin art photographer Guido Rey produced a series of photographic re-enactments of life in Pompeii which were shown successfully at several exhibitions. The main actors in these meticulously staged compositions, such as *Pompeian scene* (1895) [122], *Conversation* (1898) and *Siesta on a Pompeian afternoon* (1898), were young women dressed in robes reminiscent of Roman antiquity and positioned among replicas of sculptures. According to a contemporary, they thus succeeded in allowing everyday life in ancient Rome to re-emerge, much in the style of the artist Alma-Tadema.[54] Rey understood his recourse to the iconography of antiquity as an attempt to raise his photographs to the noble status of art. In contrast to the physical immediacy of Plüschow's or Gloeden's 'ancient' models, whose subliminal homoeroticism appealed to a corresponding audience, Rey's re-enactments present an idealized and at the same time purified and ethereal vision of life in ancient times. Here white is the dominant tone, a symbol of innocence and a reference to a 'better' world irretrievably vanished in the past. This example of how the work of Alma-Tadema influenced Art Photography at the close of the last century clearly illustrates that painting and photography in the 19th century interacted, mutually inspiring and enriching one another.

SALVE

Catalogue

Alma-Tadema's opus numbers

Catalogue entries include two reference numbers for each picture: the opus number (in Roman numerals) assigned by Alma-Tadema himself, and the number (in Arabic numerals) assigned to the work in Vern G. Swanson, *The biography and catalogue raisonné of the paintings of Sir Lawrence Alma-Tadema*, London 1990.

The opus numbers had several functions; the numbering system allowed Alma-Tadema to keep track of each work, and also made forgery more difficult since each authentic Alma-Tadema had a unique number. The opus numbers obviated the need to inscribe a date on each picture; this permitted the exhibition of older works without making it obvious that they were not fresh from the easel.

By using the word 'opus' (Latin for 'work'), followed by a Roman numeral, Alma-Tadema was wittily relating the numbering system to the ancient Roman subject-matter typical of his work. However, the designation 'opus' also recalls the practice of composers. The musical reference may be deliberate, referring to the idea, current in Victorian aestheticism, that a painting should be considered a 'pure' work of art analogous to a piece of music.

Catalogue authors

Rosemary Barrow (RB), Teio Meedendorp (TM), Edward Morris (EM), Luuk Pijl (LP), Elizabeth Prettejohn (EP), Julian Treuherz (JT).

Alma-Tadema's photographic collection

Alma-Tadema amassed a vast collection of photographs, which he used as source material for his paintings. The photographs include thousands of artefacts, architecture, landscapes, plants, flowers, trees and animals; the scope is not limited to Greek and Roman material but also includes Byzantine and medieval, Near Eastern and Indian. Alma-Tadema had a scholarly urge for thoroughness, collecting and studying more material than he ever used.

The photographs, collected in 167 portfolios, are now held in the Heslop Room, Main Library, University of Birmingham. References to Alma-Tadema's photographs in the text are by Portfolio number, in Roman numbers, followed by the inventory number of the individual photograph in Arabic numerals; thus, a reference to 'LXXV, 9799' refers to Portfolio LXXV, photograph number 9799.

Notes to the reader

[00] refers to catalogue nos., [00] to illustrations, (S 00) refers to the catalogue nos. in Vern G. Swanson, *The biography and catalogue raisonné of the paintings of Sir Lawrence Alma-Tadema*, London 1990. Citations to exhibitions refer to the work's first public exhibition.

1

Portrait of Lourens Alma-Tadema

Opus II, S 7
15 March 1852
oil on canvas, 55.5 x 48.3 cm
Fries Museum, Leeuwarden

Exhibited Grosvenor Gallery, London, Winter 1882-83 (1)

Alma-Tadema painted this self portrait at the age of 16 as a birthday present for his mother. It displays a close affinity with the work of the Friesian portraitist and genre painter Willem Bartel van der Kooi (1768-1836), whose paintings the young Alma-Tadema had ample opportunity to study in Leeuwarden. Van der Kooi had a predilection for half-figures placed close to the surface of the picture and his paintings rarely lack columns partly hidden from sight by drapery. These elements are all to be found in Alma-Tadema's self portrait. In terms of painterly technique too, the young artist drew on the work of his late fellow townsman. The polished execution, particularly conspicuous in the face, and the subdued palette are obviously derived from Van der Kooi's work.

Although the portrait contains certain imperfections, for example in the perspective, it is admirably executed for a 16-year old. In particular, the head and chair are convincingly represented, revealing something of the great technical mastery which Alma-Tadema was to display in his later work.

The artist had pleasant recollections of this early picture. He told the following anecdote in 1901. He had completed the painting and was walking home with it when some boys called out: 'Look! He's carrying himself under his arm!' (Alma-Tadema 1901, p. 202). The prospective artist concluded from this that it was a good likeness and took this non-professional verdict as a compliment. TM/LP

2

Faust and Marguerite

Opus VII
1857
watercolour on paper, 45.2 x 50.1 cm
John Constable Esq., England

Exhibited Royal Academy, London, Winter 1913 (136)

This watercolour is one of the finest works from Alma-Tadema's Antwerp period. In particular. the Gothic architecture in the misty morning light is represented in

a highly successful fashion. The scene is taken from the 16th-century German Faust saga. which enjoyed great popularity thanks to Goethe. Alma-Tadema's interest in this subject is connected with his membership of the Antwerp 'Cercle Artistique'. Among the themes to which the members of this association devoted themselves were those of German history and myth such as the rediscovered Nibelungen legend.

Faust and Marguerite is the earliest watercolour that Alma-Tadema included in his list of works with an opus number. He had already acquired proficiency in this technique at a young age through copying water-

colours by the Friesian artist Eelke Jelles Eelkema. Throughout his life, Alma-Tadema continued to make works on paper in this delicate technique with a certain regularity. TM/LP

3

The education of the children of Clovis

Opus XIV, S 50
1861
oil on canvas, 127 x 176.8 cm
private collection

Exhibited Salon d'Exposition d'Anvers, Antwerp, 1861 (20)

The French Merovingian dynasty owed its name to Merovech, the grandfather of Clovis. At first they ruled the northern provinces of France and the Netherlands. Under Clovis (who reigned from 481 to 511) Gaul was overcome and the empire of the Franks expanded to more or less the size of present-day France.

This painting shows Clovis's wife, Queen Clotilde, watching her children being trained in the art of axe-throwing. The queen had a special intention in mind: she demanded that her children should campaign against Gondobald, the king of the Burgundians, who had murdered her parents. Revenge is thus the theme of what appears at first sight to be an innocent subject. As in other of his historical paintings, Alma-Tadema did not follow the textual source literally. In Book III, Chapter 6 of the *History of the Franks*, Gregory of Tours wrote that Clotilde summoned her three sons to do battle with the murderers of her parents. These sons, however, who bore the picturesque names Chlodomer, Childebert and Chlotarius, were already full-grown men. Chlodomer even had to pay for the act of vengeance with his life (524). *The education of the children of Clovis* refers to an earlier point in the story which must have seemed plausible to Alma-Tadema even though Gregory did not mention it: the children are trained for their subsequent mission. The artist had followed a similar procedure with his first Merovingian subject, *Clotilde at the tomb of her grandchildren* (1858, whereabouts unknown). In reply to the objection that Gregory did not describe such a scene, Alma-

125 *The education of the children of Clovis*, 1868,
      whereabouts unknown

Tadema observed that 'after the loyal Clotilde had lost all hope of influence through the death of her grandchildren, she is bound to have mourned at their grave, which is only natural and as such firmly historical' (Swanson 1977, p. 11).

The architectural decoration of the setting is particularly rich: the foreground and background are ingeniously linked by the diagonal pattern in the decorative tiled floor of the court. The columns support Corinthian capitals, relics of the Gallo-Roman period. In a smaller, later version of the work [125], the artist has replaced the capitals by others which bear a closer resemblance to the Ionic type. The figures are dressed more simply and the group on the left has been halved. The older warrior no longer leans on his shield, but on a well with early medieval decorations. The vista in the background and the view of the roof have been replaced by a sober, continuous white-grey wall and a gently arched piece of masonry above a marble architrave. The beautiful floor of the first version has become a dark brown floor of sand. Alma-Tadema probably intended the second version to be more in line with the widely accepted view that the early Middle Ages was a sober if not dark period. But there is another possibility. In the second version, the only fig-

ures depicted behind Clotilde are clerics. The large cross on the wall behind her, with the typical Merovingian stripes at the tips, has been replaced by three monograms of Christ. The space looks more like a simple cloister, while the first version portrayed the splendour of a royal palace. Alma-Tadema may have hit upon this discovery after re-reading Gregory. After the death of Clovis, Clotilde retired and exchanged the court in Paris for a life in the service of the church of Saint Martin in Tours. It is therefore not ruled out that she is having her children trained in the court of a monastery in the neighbourhood.

The education of the children of Clovis is one of Alma-Tadema's major Merovingian paintings and was of great importance for his early career. Highly praised at the 1861 exhibition, it was immediately acquired for King Leopold of Belgium, who hung it in a prominent position in his palace. This early success of Alma-Tadema did not prevent his tutor, Henri Leys, in whose studio the painting had been produced, from making the critical remark: 'Ah, it is better than I thought it would be, but the marble is cheese!' (Alma-Tadema 1901, p. 204). Alma-Tadema took this criticism to heart. Marble was later to become one of his specialities, earning him the nickname of 'marbellous' painter (see p. 106).

Alma-Tadema is one of the first 19th-century artists to have chosen the deeds of the ancient Franks as a theme for his paintings. In his biography of Alma-

Tadema. Georg Ebers calls the Merovingian period 'a period in European history which is monstrous and appalling as a whole, but whose details offer a wealth of material for a painter' (Ebers, p. 14). He also notes that, when Carel Vosmaer asked the artist why he had turned to the Merovingians, Alma-Tadema, who was 'a stranger to all gloom and monstrosity', replied: 'They are a "sorry lot", to be sure, still they are picturesque and interesting' (idem). TM/LP

4

The education of the children of Clovis

1861
black chalk on paper, 62.9 x 90.2 cm
private collection

This large-scale chalk drawing represents the same scene as the painting of 1861 [3], but the positions of the figures in relation to one another are somewhat different. Also, the vista and the door in the background have been reversed. In view of the changes that Alma-Tadema made, the drawing might be considered as a preliminary study for the work on canvas. However, the finished character of the drawing suggests that it was made after the painting, so perhaps the artist has elaborated his preliminary study.

A similar drawing for *The education of the children of Clovis* was given to his former tutor Louis de Taeye (Birmingham University Library, Heslop Room). Alma-Tadema gave preliminary studies to friends on more than one occasion. Another example of this practice are the drawings that he presented to Carel Vosmaer, who was also given a sketch in oil, *Exhausted maenides after the dance* [34]. TM/LP

5

Venantius Fortunatus reading his poems to Radegonda VI

Opus XV, S 51
1862
oil on canvas, 65 x 83.1 cm
Dordrechts Museum, Dordrecht

Exhibited Koninklijke Academie, Amsterdam, 1862 (5)

The adventurous Venantius Fortunatus, who was to become bishop of Poitiers at the end of the 6th century, is reciting his hymns to Radegonda. This German princess was forced to marry the youngest son of Clovis, Chlotarius I. Her sensitive religious character and erudition (she knew Latin and studied ancient texts and the writings of the church) formed a marked contrast with the barbaric behaviour of her husband, whose many murder victims included her own brother. After a while she left her spouse to found the convent of the

Holy Cross in Poitiers in 555 and to devote the rest of her life to God. This is when Chlotarius must have said: 'It is a nun that I have here, not a queen' (Thierry, p. 177).

Alma-Tadema took his information for this scene from Augustin Thierry's *Récits des temps mérovingiens*. Gregory of Tours does not mention the adventurer Venantius Fortunatus, who arrived in Poitiers in 565 and became a counsellor to Radegonda. This poet of Italian origin, who had travelled through France for years and frequented the local nobility and clergy, was known for his appetite for eating and drinking. The consumption of wine was particularly beneficial to the recital of his poems. Radegonda and her abbess Agnes gave him an abundant supply in return for his services. Alma-Tadema has expressed this by setting Venantius amid an exquisitely painted dinner-service and food. Thierry called Venantius a good Christian, but 'his way of life was indolent and sensual' (Thierry, p. 183).

The scene is set in an enclosed pergola into which some light falls from outside. As a result of the diffuse lighting, the whole is portrayed in subdued tones. Alma-Tadema seems to use this device to emphasize Radegonda's isolation. The Latin inscriptions on the edge of the partition indicate the setting of the convent in which the scene is situated. Alma-Tadema may here be deliberately contrasting the prevalent view of the 'barbaric' Middle Ages with a scene which explicitly illustrates a more refined intellectual and retiring life.

This picture won Alma-Tadema a gold medal in Amsterdam in 1862; he thus became a member of the academy in that city. The painting was acquired by the Amsterdam collector Jonkheer H.D. Hooft van Woudenberg in 1867. Thirteen years later it was purchased by the Dordrechts Museum for the considerable sum of 1400 guilders. There were few subsequent tokens of recognition in the artist's own country (see pp. 21-30). TM/LP

6

Interior of the church of San Clemente, Rome

Opus XIX, S 57
October 1863
oil on canvas, 63.5 x 51 cm
Fries Museum, Leeuwarden

Exhibited Grosvenor Gallery, London, Winter 1882–83 (9)

Alma-Tadema married Marie Pauline Gressin Dumoulin de Boisgirard in the autumn of 1863. The young couple honeymooned in Florence, Rome, Naples and Pompeii. During this trip Lawrence painted the interior of San Clemente in Rome. This early medieval church is situated behind the Coliseum and is famous for the mosaics inspired by Byzantine art. The choice of this subject reflects Alma-Tadema's fondness for early medieval art at the time.

At first sight there does not appear to be any human trace in this scene, but closer inspection reveals a woman in modern dress just disappearing between the columns in the background. Furthermore, the head of a bearded man is painted above the marble parapet. It is tempting to identify these figures with the young married couple. In this case Alma-Tadema painted a contemporary event instead of a historical situation. As far as we know, this is the only painting that he made on this trip. However, it is not completed; although some parts, such as the mosaic in the apse with the *Triumph of the Cross*, have been finished, a few of the columns are only roughly indicated.

The painting formed part of the Memorial Exhibition held in the Royal Academy shortly after Alma-Tadema's death. It was regarded by one critic as his best work (Clutton Brock, p. 285). The simplicity of the painting was praised in comparison with the extravagant compositions such as *The finding of Moses* [91] and *Caracalla and Geta* (S 415), which this critic did not rate very highly. According to Clutton Brock, the wealth of detail in the latter works detracted attention from the actual subject. Of course, Alma-Tadema would have been in complete disagreement. He must have regarded the paintings in question as the climax of his oeuvre, while he did not consider the *San Clemente* worth completing. TM/LP

7

Leaving church in the fifteenth century

Opus XXI, S 59
1864
oil on canvas, 57.1 x 39.4 cm
private collection

Exhibited French Gallery, London, April 1868

At the 1864 Paris Salon Alma-Tadema's debut, *Pastimes in ancient Egypt 3000 years ago* [13], had been awarded a gold medal. In the summer of the same year, an event of even greater importance occurred to him, in which his painting *Leaving church in the fifteenth century* played a crucial role. As story has it (see pp. 26-27), the influential art dealer Ernest Gambart acciden-

tally found himself in the painter's studio. Alma-Tadema described the encounter as follows:

'I remember him on that first visit to me, standing before my easel, on which I had posed my *Coming out of church* [sic], and instantly exclaiming; ... "Did you paint that church for the Vanderdoncks?" [Vanderdonck was an Antwerp art dealer] I assured him of the fact. He asked me if they had seen it and what was the price. I told him they had not seen it as yet. "Well then", said Gambart, "I'll take it; and let me have a couple of dozen of that kind at progressive prices each half dozen". It was really as if he was buying bales of cotton. Of course, I thought, and not without reason, that my fortune was as good as made' (Alma-Tadema 1909, p. 290).

The choice of theme is in line with the historicizing paintings which Alma-Tadema's tutor Henri Leys produced, often set in late medieval Antwerp, and which Gambart successfully exhibited in his French Gallery in England from the 1850s. However, Alma-Tadema had discovered ancient Rome on his journey to Italy in 1863 and preferred to choose his themes from that period. After a while Gambart agreed, and they eventually concluded a contract for 24 paintings (see p. 27).

The critic for the *Illustrated London News* dismissed the painting in 1868 as 'a rather heavy uninteresting thirteenth century church-porch scene' (Swanson, p. 133). The action in the painting certainly is rather sedate, though not lacking in charm. The two groups of richly dressed townspeople leaving the church are linked by the figure of the boy in the foreground. His short jacket, extremely pointed shoes and close-fitting tights are characteristic dress for the second half of the 15th century. The same is true of the striking tall headdresses of two women in the background: the one on the right is wearing a so-called 'butterfly head-dress', while the one on the left has a 'steeple head-dress'. The man walking out of the painting on the left can be identified by his clothing as a high-ranking cleric in his fur-lined mozzetta and high bonnet, the precursor of the dented cardinal's cap (Houston, pp. 173-78; Costume du moyen âge, pp. 78-79).

The church in question is that of Notre Dame de Paris; the setting is the north porch on the west side, 'le portail de la Vierge', completed between 1210 and 1220 and regarded as one of the most splendid examples of

126 *An Egyptian game*, 1865, private collection

Gothic sculpture in France. Alma-Tadema visited Paris for the first time in 1864 and had seen Notre Dame on that occasion. In *Leaving church in the fifteenth century*, Alma-Tadema seems to have deployed his well-known attention to detail to contrast the attractive colouring and folds of the costumes with the monochrome background of the 13th-century porch. TM/LP

8

An Egyptian game

1865
pencil on paper, 25 x 35 cm
Rijksprentenkabinet, Amsterdam

This is one of a group of drawings that Alma-Tadema gave to his friend Carel Vosmaer. It was published as *The Egyptian chess players* (*De verzameling van Mr. Carel Vosmaer*, pp. 128-30), but this title is incorrect as the game depicted here is clearly not chess. The drawing is a study for the painting with the same title [126].

Alma-Tadema's Egyptian works were his first attempt at representing genre figures from the remote past. Like all of his works with Egyptian themes, this pencil drawing betrays the influence of J.G. Wilkinson's *Manners and customs of the ancient Egyptians* (1837). The bald figures and their postures are taken from various reproductions from this publication (see Raven, p. 109, ill. 10). Characteristic of the technique of this sheet are the closed contours with which the figures are drawn. The artist has successfully managed to convey an Egyptian flavour to the drawing not only by the choice of theme but also by the technique. TM/LP

9

Entrance to a Roman theatre

Opus XXXV, S 74
April 1866
oil on canvas, 70.4 x 98.4 cm
Haussner Family Limited Partnership

Exhibited French Gallery, London, May 1866 (2)

This painting, still in its striking original frame with theatrical masks, depicts two patrician women of Pompeii at the entrance to a theatre. A woman in a red robe is standing on the pavement holding a child by the hand. A couple greet her, while an attendant helps another elegantly dressed woman to step out of her carriage. This picture is rich in minute social distinctions, the women descending from the carriage (in fact a *cisium*, or light bronze chariot) appear to be high-ranking patricians, while the couple greeting them are clearly rather vulgar (Pompeian *nouveaux riches?*) – the woman of the couple, in particular, is too gaudily dressed and has dyed hair. According to the inscription in the upper right, these well-to-do Romans are going to watch a performance of a comedy by Terence. A ticket seller can be seen behind a table in the semi-darkness of the entrance. Behind him are the stalls where members of the audience are trying to find a place.

Alma-Tadema based this section on a photograph of the Odeon in Pompeii which was already in his possession in 1863 (Cuypers 1991, pp. 41-42, fig. 31, Portfolio CXLIX, 12086). The artist has enriched the theatre with a few sculptures. For instance, he has reconstructed the marble figure of Atlas supporting the balustrade. Although he made use of a photograph,

Alma-Tadema later saw the Odeon at first hand. During a visit to Pompeii in the spring of 1883, he pointed this theatre out to Carel Vosmaer from the Via Stabiana and told his friend that this was the site he had used for his painting.

The composition consists of three zones: a frontal plane, a dark portico, and behind it a brightly illuminated area. Alma-Tadema often used this simple and effective device to suggest depth. A painting with a very similar construction is *Returning home from market* (s 70), painted a year earlier. In both paintings the figures are set on a pavement, and a dark passage connects the scene with a second one. The pavement forms a natural barrier between the world created by the artist and the surroundings of the spectator. This division confers on the painting the character of a scene from a play, reinforced by the shallow foreground.

Entrance to a Roman theatre was exhibited by Gambart in London immediately after it had been completed. It was thus one of the first paintings to be shown to the English public. The painting was acquired in 1877 by the millionaire William Vanderbilt and remained in the possession of his family until 1945 (see pp. 93-95).
TM/LP

10

My studio

Opus XLV, S 85
March – May 1867
oil on panel, 42.1 x 54 cm
Groninger Museum, Groningen

Exhibited Pictura, Groningen 1868 (160)

This painting from the spring of 1867 shows Alma-Tadema's wife Marie Pauline, with her mother and her daughter Laurense, in the Brussels studio. Marie Pauline, the only figure who is looking towards the spectator, accentuates her condition by placing both her hands on her pregnant belly: she was expecting Anna, who was born on 16 May 1867. Alma-Tadema created this picture at a time of growing prosperity, as can be seen from the luxurious furnishings and the heavy, mobile easel. The fashionable clothing of the figures in the portrait is also an indication that they are well-to-do.

The figures are sitting with their backs to a wall on which are four photographs of recent paintings by the artist. These works can easily be identified (s 60, 62, 81, 136), but it is less simple to identify the painting on the easel. The warrior in combat is closely related to the one in *A Pyrrhic dance* [16], which was completed in 1869, but it is not identical. Swanson (p. 142) takes it to be a painting by a colleague, but it is not impossible that it is a first version of *A Pyrrhic dance*.

My Studio was commissioned by Alma-Tadema's uncle, Klaas Mesdag. Klaas's son, Hendrik Willem Mesdag, studied in Brussels under Willem Roelofs and his cousin Alma-Tadema from the autumn of 1866. He painted a related work (Pennock, fig. 1) in the same year in which Alma-Tadema completed his studio scene. The influence of his cousin, however, was short-lived. Mesdag soon developed in a different direction as regards choice of theme and painterly technique: he became a master of the seascape. TM/LP

11

The siesta

Opus LV, S 99
February 1868
oil on panel, 13 x 34.2 cm
J. Nicholson, Beverly Hills, California

Exhibited Netherlands Benefit Exhibition, Brussels, 1868

Two men are reclining on cushions while a slave girl plays a double flute (*tibia*) for them. They have apparently drunk a large quantity of wine: one has fallen asleep, the other rests his head on his arm and drifts off. Because a table with food and drink is placed parallel to the surface of the picture and the figures hardly overlap,

127 *The siesta*, 1868, Museo Nacional del Prado, Madrid

the scene resembles a pictorial relief in a frieze. This similarity seems to be reinforced by the miniature replica of the famous Farnese Hercules which has been set on the table as a decoration.

The scene is a symposium, a Greek practice which was taken over by the Romans (*Empires restored*, p. 56). Plentiful eating and drinking were accompanied by musical and dance performances at these gatherings.

The small painting might have served as model for a very large-scale painting [127]. Alma-Tadema's art dealer, Ernest Gambart, wanted the large work to form part of a series of scenes of Roman eating and drinking customs, but the only painting in this series to be completed was *The siesta*. Gambart bequeathed this huge version to the Prado in Madrid in 1887. The composition is the reverse of its model, and the statue of Hercules has been replaced by a replica of the equally famous Medici Venus. TM/LP

12

Boating

Opus LVI, S 100
February 1868
oil on canvas, 82.5 x 56.3 cm
Museum Mesdag, The Hague

Exhibited Netherlands Benefit Exhibition, Brussels, 1868

This painting shows a young Roman hauling in a boat to the pier for his loved one. The light erotic tone of the scene is emphasized by the cupid on the boat. An older woman leans over a balustrade and witnesses the scene. The painting was exhibited in Brussels under the title *La promenade en barquette*. It is one of the earliest examples of a subject taken from the leisure and amorous activities of the more well-to-do Roman circles. The man in scenes of this kind is often a dark, Mediterranean type, while the woman has a Northern appearance [45].

A variant on *Boating* can be seen in a photograph of Alma-Tadema in his studio in Townshend House (repr. Swanson, p. 50). This painting (S 161), which was never completed, was not included by the artist in his list of works, so that we do not know from which year it dates. Since Alma-Tadema was apparently working on it

in Townshend House, it must have been started after 1871, and thus after *Boating* at any rate.

Soon after its completion the painting was acquired for less than Dfl. 1,000 by Hendrik Willem Mesdag. His father, Klaas, had commissioned *My Studio* [10], which Alma-Tadema had painted during the previous year: the Mesdag family can thus be regarded as early patrons of the painter. TM/LP

13

Phidias showing the frieze of the Parthenon to his friends

Opus LX, S 104
May 1868
oil on panel, 72 x 110.5 cm
Birmingham Museum & Art Gallery

Exhibited Grosvenor Gallery, London, 1877 (33)

Alma-Tadema's reconstruction of the Parthenon frieze, glowing with painted colours, makes a dramatic intervention into one of the most controversial debates of 19th-century classical studies. Archaeological evidence indicated that ancient marble sculpture had originally been adorned with painted decoration, or 'polychromy'. However, the notion of coloured sculpture was drastically at odds with the traditional reverence for Greek sculpture as an art of pure form: in particular, it seemed inconceivable to associate the 'primitive' practice of polychromy with the sculpture of Athens in the 5th-century B.C., regarded as the culmination of Greek civilization.

In 1816, the British Museum had acquired parts of the frieze and other sculptures from the Parthenon through the agency of Lord Elgin: the 'Elgin marbles' rose steadily in art-historical status until they were widely regarded as the finest extant examples of the greatest period in ancient art. A committee, appointed by the Trustees of the British Museum in 1836, had failed to find traces of colour on the Elgin marbles (Jenkins and Middleton, pp. 183-86). However, the issue refused to disappear, as evidence mounted that polychromy was a general practice in antiquity. On his visit to London in 1862, Alma-Tadema may have seen Owen Jones's coloured reconstruction of the Parthenon frieze

at the Crystal Palace in Sydenham, a major tourist attraction; Jones had found it necessary to justify his use of colour in a pamphlet of 1854, 'An apology for the colouring of the Greek Court in the Crystal Palace'. Alma-Tadema would certainly have seen the sculptor John Gibson's *Tinted Venus* (Walker Art Gallery, Liverpool) at the London International Exhibition of 1862; although Gibson used only the subtlest colours on his statue, the experiment proved controversial. Despite these precedents, then, it was still a daring project, in the late 1860s, to represent the most revered sculptures of Greek antiquity Athens completely covered with vivid polychromy.

Alma-Tadema's composition emphasizes the high status of the Parthenon frieze, glorifying its creator, Phidias, by placing him in the central position traditionally reserved for the hero of a history painting. Although the episode is invented, Alma-Tadema draws on Plutarch's account of Phidias's friendship with the most celebrated of Athenian statesmen, Pericles, who appears on the right with his mistress Aspasia (Plutarch, 'Pericles'). Georg Ebers speculated that the youthful figure at extreme left was Alcibiades, Pericles's political protegé, still in his teens when the sculptures were unveiled in the 430s B.C. (p. 47). Alma-Tadema thus shows two generations of Athenian statesmen, paying homage to the sculptor and his masterpiece.

The view of the northwest corner reunites sections of the frieze that had been sundered. Nearest the spectator are the British Museum's sections: slab XLII and part of slab XLI of the north side, parallel to the picture plane, with slabs I and II of the west side around the corner. The rest of the west side remained at Athens; probably working from photographs, Alma-Tadema reproduces the Athens section as meticulously as the British Museum slabs, despite extreme foreshortening. Moreover, he carefully repairs damaged areas, such as the horses' heads at top left, missing from the broken edges of the British Museum's slabs. Nonetheless, the composition alludes to the fragmentation of the surviving sculptures, with the Athens section receding rapidly, suggesting its physical distance from the picture's Western European audience, and the abrupt curtailment at the left edge, where only a sliver of slab XLI is visible.

Alma-Tadema's picture can be read as a demonstration of how polychromy might function to enhance

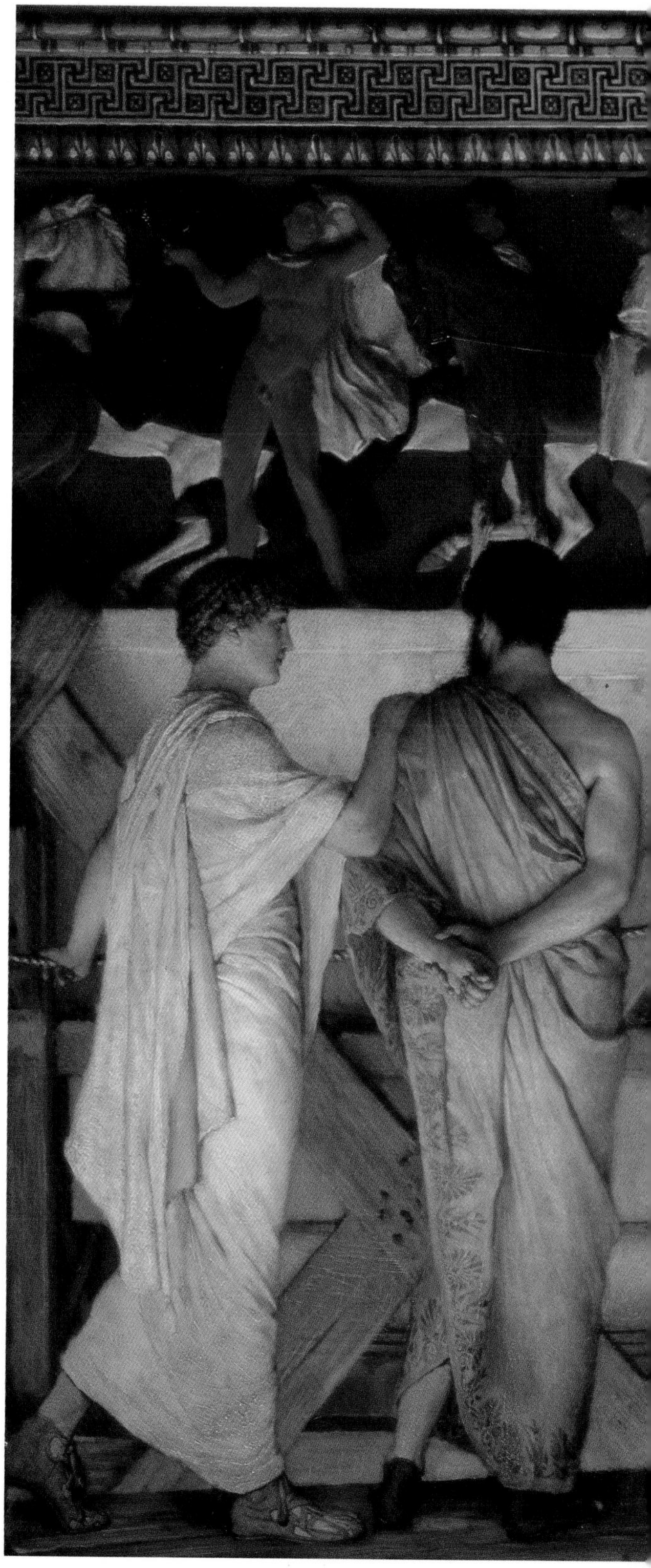

the legibility of the relief sculpture. The hues are limited to the four colours identified in classical texts as those
used by the great Greek painters: white, yellow, red, and
black (Pliny, XXXV.50). Moreover, they are organized to
define the successive planes of the relief. This is clearest
in the front section, where the nude figure on the top
plane is red, with his white cloak in the next plane
behind him, a black horse behind that, and a white
horse still farther back, against a darkish background.
The colour contrasts are abrupt, and startlingly conven-
tionalized in comparison with the more naturalistic
colouring of the human figures. However, they assist the
spectator to read the successive planes of the relief.

Legibility was a problem, as the picture indicates,
because the frieze was 40 feet from the ground and
underneath the ceiling of the colonnade, lit only from
below. The scaffolding on which the figures stand allows
them a privileged view; gaps between the planks admit

a moody light, leaving subordinate figures in shadow but
highlighting parts of the frieze. The illumination from
below is a tour de force of the painter's art, but it also
demonstrates how the polychromy could assist legibility
by catching reflected light.

Although the picture was finished and sold in
1868 to David Price, through the dealer Ernest Gambart,
Price was reluctant to lend it for exhibition. Accordingly,
it did not appear before the English public until the
inaugural exhibition of the Grosvenor Gallery, in 1877
[43]. Even at that late date, the polychromy proved a
major source of contention; despite the artist's reputation for archaeological accuracy, many critics found the
vividness and non-naturalism of the polychromy unpal-
atable. Subsequent scholarship has been more willing to
accept the notion of coloured sculpture, and Alma-
Tadema's picture is now often reproduced as an example
of how ancient polychromy might have looked (e.g.,

Jenkins 1994, colour plate II; for further discussion of the 19th-century debates on colouring sculpture, see *The colour of sculpture*). EP

14

The flower market

Opus LXII, S 106
September 1868
oil on panel, 42.1 x 58 cm
Manchester City Art Gallery

Exhibited Exposition de Gand, Ghent, 1868

In size and subject-matter *The flower market* is typical of the small works in the Dutch genre painting tradition that Alma-Tadema executed for the art dealer, Ernest Gambart; Gambart's first commission for 24 pictures, given in 1864, was soon followed by another for 52 more. Indeed, the dealer entirely financed the artist's early career, on a contractual basis that was a novel development in the mid-19th century art world. The prices were on an ascending scale starting from a modest level, appropriate for small-scale pictures by a young artist whose reputation was yet to be made (see Maas, pp. 172, 215-16). Since *The flower market* was one of the early pictures in the second commission, Gambart probably paid Alma-Tadema between £ 80 and £ 100 for it, on its completion in the autumn of 1868. It was not until about 1870 that prices for the artist's work suddenly began to soar, but when this picture was resold at auction in 1873 it fetched £ 640 10s – an increase of more than sixfold in only five years, and a high figure indeed for so small a picture.

Equally characteristic of the artist's early work is the Pompeian setting, elaborated by abundant accessories of Roman everyday life based on those unearthed in the Pompeian excavations (see pp. 35-39). The emphasis on commerce, including both a flower market and a wine-shop, reflects contemporary interest in ancient social and economic history, in antithesis to more traditional kinds of classical scholarship centred on ancient literary texts; Alma-Tadema explored themes of ancient commerce in several pictures of this period [25]; (S 70, 81, 116). The interaction between the young man and the flower girl may involve more than one kind of commer-

cial transaction: the patrician man buys flowers from the plebeian flower girl, but some contemporaries speculated that he may also be purchasing her sexual favours (see pp. 37-38). To associate the flower girl with prostitution may have seemed logical to 19th-century spectators, drawing on the widespread perception that flower girls in the modern city were often sexually available (Mayhew, vol. I, pp. 140-42).

The flower girl's wares pose problems, however. Alma-Tadema owned many photographs of actual flowers and plants (Portfolios LXI-LXIV), which he used to ensure botanical correctness; Sir W.C. Thiselton Dyer, of Kew Gardens, reported in 1906 that Alma-Tadema's drawing of plants was 'absolutely satisfying to the botanist' (Barrington, vol. I, p. 220). However, several of the species represented in *The flower market* are less satisfying to the classicist; although found in Italy by the 19th century, they were not native to Europe in the classical period (information from John Edmondson). It is unclear whether Alma-Tadema realized he was introducing anachronistic flora into this scene, otherwise scrupulously correct for its notional date in the 1st century A.D. EP

15

A birth chamber, seventeenth century

Opus LXVIII, S 110
1868
oil on panel, 49 x 64.8 cm
Board of Trustees of the Victoria & Albert Museum, London

Exhibited Arti et Amicitiae, Amsterdam, 1868 (6)

There are three versions of this subject, of which this one, from the Brussels period, is the earliest. In two other versions (S 139) and a watercolour (Walker Art Gallery, Liverpool), which were painted in London, the left-hand part with the bed is absent and Alma-Tadema confined himself to the midwife turned to face the window. The daylight entering the room falls on her in a very attractive way. In the watercolour the upright format is emphasized by representing the upper part of the stained glass as well.

128 Huib van Hove, *The listening servant*, c. 1853,
Victoria & Albert Museum, London

Both theme and execution are based to a large
extent on 17th-century Dutch models. In particular,
paintings by Pieter de Hooch must have served as a
source of inspiration. De Hooch painted this theme
many times, and motifs such as stained glass and a figure set against a bright light are common in his paintings too. It was probably its Dutch character which
earned the painting positive criticism during the exhibition of Living Masters in Amsterdam in 1868. The high
praise which Alma-Tadema received on this occasion
played a part in the conferral of a Knighthood in the
Order of the Dutch Lion.

Alma-Tadema's interest in 17th-century Dutch
painting was probably stimulated by Joseph Dyckmans,
who was teaching in the Antwerp Academy at the time
of Alma-Tadema's arrival. Dyckmans was known as the
'Dou of Belgium' for his meticulously rendered genre
paintings. At the time when Alma-Tadema was painting
the birth chamber, interest in genre scenes inspired by

the 17th century was on the wane in the Netherlands: the kinds of works most frequently displayed at the exhibitions of Living Masters were contemporary genre scenes and landscapes. Remarkably enough, two of the better-known Dutch practitioners of this genre, Petrus van Schendel and Huib van Hove [128], had moved to Belgium too, where figures like Pieter de Hooch, Gabriel Metsu, Nicolaas Maes and Gerard Dou continued to be revered as models. Henri Leys in particular, who sometimes worked with Van Hove, had initially drawn his inspiration from Rubens, but from 1839 on he concentrated more and more on Dutch *fine painting*. Dutch realism, however, was not a lasting influence on Alma-Tadema. From the mid-1860s, he was almost completely dominated by the idealized world of the Greeks and Romans. His second wife, Laura Epps, who also painted and received her first lessons from her husband, concentrated on 17th-century Dutch genre motifs.

A birth chamber, seventeenth century is dated to 1868, but it is listed under 1869 in the opus list. This minor discrepancy can be explained by the fact that Alma-Tadema did not start signing his works with an opus number until November 1872, when he also gave opus numbers to 105 works that he had already painted. It is thus understandable that he made some mistakes in the process. TM/LP

16

A Pyrrhic dance

Opus LXIX, S 111
April 1869
oil on panel, 40.6 x 81.3 cm
Guildhall Art Gallery, Corporation of London

Exhibited Royal Academy, London, 1869 (421)

A Pyrrhic dance, a striking evocation of the Hellenic world, was one of Alma-Tadema's first two works to be exhibited at the Royal Academy. Roman themes were to dominate the artist's work, but he continued to exhibit a small number of Greek subjects at significant points throughout his career [59 68]. This depiction of a ritualistic military dance may seem to involve a surprising choice of subject. It is, for instance, markedly different from the elegant mythological figures characteristic of Frederic Leighton's Greek subjects of a similar date.

The Pyrrhic dance was a stylized version of certain traditional battle moves, both attacking and defensive. The dance was of great antiquity and from an early period its origin was disputed: the list of its putative inventors included a Cretan soldier, Pyrrhicus, and Pyrrhus, the son of Achilles. In the Classical period the dance was performed annually at the public Attic festival, the *Panathenaea*.

In 1869 the painting received favourable reviews, but its exhibition at the Grosvenor Gallery in 1882-83 prompted Ruskin to offer a notorious criticism in which he compared it to 'a microscopic view of a small detachment of black-beetles, in search of a dead rat' (vol. 33, p. 321). For Ruskin Greek warfare was as the splendid heroism and individual quest for glory he found in Homer. In the same lecture he cites the passage from the *Iliad* (XVIII.203-09) where Achilles routs the enemy by showing himself in triumph on the Greek ramparts (p. 320). In effect Alma-Tadema challenges the Victorian equation of ancient warfare with a single named hero competing on the battlefield, and instead depicts a primitive theatrical display by anonymous performers.

129 *Figure in hoplite armour*, from a series of drawings after Greek vase paintings, late 1860s, University of Birmingham (LXXX, E.2141)

As the spectators watch from beneath a Doric portico, the formation enacts its dance, dramatically cut off at the left of the canvas. Behind the sturdy columns, we can see the facade of a Doric temple, with its outer frieze (*triglyphs* and *metopes*), painted in splendid polychromy [13]. Alma-Tadema is often criticized for the static nature of his figures, but in this early painting the exhilarating thrusts of the dance are powerfully conveyed through clouds of dust kicked up around the performer's feet. These dancers wear the armour of Classical Greek soldiers (*hoplites*): a large bronze shield (*hoplon*), helmet, corselet, leg greaves, and javelin. The undersides of the shields are meticulously rendered, down to the details of arm straps and stitching. Alma-Tadema's photographic collection includes numerous sheets of figure sketches in hoplite armour copied from

ancient vase paintings [129]. The sketches are undated but their French inscriptions suggest that they were executed in the 1860s (Alma-Tadema usually inscribed his drawings in French until his move to England in 1870) perhaps as preparatory studies for this very painting.

The audience is all male with high ranking figures seated in the front row while those of lower status stand behind. Mature bearded men and clean-shaven youths watch side by side. The two seated figures on the right of the canvas make a piquant comparison. The elder figure with his full beard and bare, slightly sagging chest resembles Greek sculptures of philosopher-types while his young companion's styled hair and pastel costume, with its floral border, more than hints at effeminacy. Greek social custom sanctioned relationships between an older man and a younger man or boy, the lover (*erastes*) and the beloved (*eromenos*). The *eromenos* would be chosen for his personal beauty and grace, as exemplified by this seated youth. The homosocial aspect of Greek life is also alluded to in *The dinner* [29]. In *A Pyrrhic dance* the theme is more pronounced, as if in acknowledgement of the well-attested models of homosexuality amongst Greek warriors, from the passionate relationship ascribed in later antiquity to Achilles and Patroclus in the *Iliad* to the 'Sacred Band of Thebes', an army of lovers living in the 4th century B.C. whose bravery and dedication to each other in battle were legendary. RB

17

Confidences

Opus LXXII, S 114
October 1869
oil on panel, 55.8 x 37.6 cm
Board of Trustees of the National Museums & Galleries on Merseyside
Walker Art Gallery, Liverpool

Exhibited Grosvenor Gallery, London, Winter 1882-83 (51)

This restful image of female Roman idleness is in marked contrast to the Greek manliness and athleticism evoked in *A Pyrrhic dance* [16], completed in the same year. The red painted walls and Roman artefacts place *Confidences* in a Pompeian setting typical of Alma-Tadema's early work. Until the 1870s brightly coloured

interiors and accessories of a broadly Pompeian cast remain characteristic of the artist's subjects. It is not until the 1880s that the artist uses outdoor settings whose distinctive bravura derives from Rome and the Bay of Naples [79]. This painting combines two of Alma-Tadema's favourite themes present in his early works: a pair of women smelling flowers and idly gossiping.

130 *Bronze head with corkscrew curls, from the Villa of the Papyri, Herculaneum, Museo Archeologico Nazionale, Naples*

Assorted artefacts are cluttered in a niche above the confidantes: a wool basket and spindle, perfume phial, bronze statuette, hair pins, gold mirror, bronze container, lamp and cosmetic jar and brush. These domestic objects not only place the women in their customary sphere but serve to remind the viewer of the Victorian conception of the irredeemable vanity of a rich woman in ancient Rome. 19th-century historical novels frequently represent such women at their elaborate toilet. These scenes are no doubt inspired by mocking depictions in Roman poets who point to expensive clothes and jewels, makeup and hair dye (Ovid, *The art of love* III; Juvenal, VI). The theme is taken up in Simeon Solomon's *The toilette of a Roman lady* [56], exhibited at the Royal Academy in the same year *Confidences* was completed.

The bronze statuette could be an image of the Egyptian goddess Isis (a similar statuette is also found in the Solomon painting). The cult of Isis was an important part of religious life at Pompeii as shown by the temple to the goddess in the forum and numerous cult objects excavated throughout the town. This mystery religion, like the cult of Bacchus [21 72], was especially popular amongst women. The worship of Isis was sometimes linked with the Roman Venus and hence eroticism. Isis herself was said to have been a prostitute for ten years at Tyre and her temples had a reputation for attracting prostitutes. The image of Isis lends an erotic undercurrent to the painting: perhaps the 'confidences' of the title concern some secret love tryst?

The lion-legged couch, footstool and elegant bronze table combine with the painted walls to create an accurate representation of a Pompeian dwelling. The artist does not, as has sometimes been claimed, merely place Victorian models in a precise archaeological framework: he uses appropriate classical prototypes for his figures. As in *The flower market* [14], the dark-haired woman resembles Pompeian painted portraits, while her companion's striking corkscrew curls (characteristic of representations of Isis), hair fillet and full face unmistakably imitate a bronze female bust from Herculaneum [130]. Other artists of the period are known to base their figure-types on well-known classical works, for instance, Frederic Leighton's *Daedalus and Icarus* of 1868 (The Faringdon collection, Buscot Park), inspired by celebrated sculptures of the ideal male nude and George Frederic Watts' *Ariadne on Naxos* of 1875 (Guildhall Art Gallery, Corporation of London), influenced by the 'Fates', figures K, L and M from the east pediment of the Parthenon. Alma-Tadema rarely does this. Instead he adopts lesser known or genre subjects which often exploit the latest archaeological discoveries [33]. RB

18

An exedra

Opus LXXV, S 117
December 1869
oil on panel, 38 x 59.8 cm
Frances Lehman Loeb Art Center, Vassar College, Poughkeepsie, New York (Gift of Mrs. Avery Coonley)

Exhibited Tekenacademie, The Hague, 1872

Just outside the city wall of Pompeii is the tomb of Mamia on the Via dei Sepulcri (Street of Tombs). The Mamia tomb has the form of an exedra, a semicircular marble

seat affording a wonderful panorama of the Bay of Naples. A photograph of this monument in the Alma-Tadema collection [131] probably served as a basis for the painting. Alma-Tadema had already begun collecting photographs of classical ruins during his first trip to Italy. The semicircular marble seat and the upright boundary marker in the foreground have been faithfully transferred to the painting. The naked youths in the photograph have been replaced by a company of distinguished Romans. In the foreground is a young slave with a parasol. His tunic bears the name of his master, Holconius.

Of course, the archaeologist Alma-Tadema has restored what had been ravaged by time. For instance, the stone which can be seen behind the seat in the photograph, a fragment of the tomb of the Istidacii, has been reconstructed as a simple temple. The corners of the seat have been decorated with palmettes; though they are to be found in Pompeii, they are not applied in this position. Alma-Tadema took this detail from F. Mazois, *Les ruines de Pompéi*, which was published between 1824 and 1838. He owned a copy of this expen-

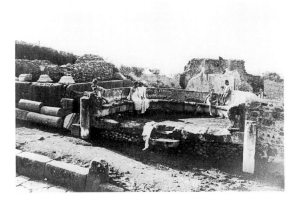

131 Guglielmo Plüschow, *The Mamia seat in Pompeii*, c. 1863, photograph from Alma-Tadema's collection, University of Birmingham (CLIX, 12477)

sive publication (Cuypers 1991, pp. 42-43). The low inscribed stele on the left is taken from the tomb of Porcius, which lies to the east of the Mamia tomb. The text refers to Porcius' right of ownership to the site of his tomb (Cuypers 1976, p. 86, note 15). The inscription on the seat is largely hidden from view, and is therefore difficult to interpret.

A watercolour painted in 1871 (Opus XCV; auctioned at Christie's, New York, 15 February 1985, lot 342) is a replica with the same dimensions as the Poughkeepsie painting. TM/LP

19

Sketches of coiffures from antique sculpture

Portfolio CXVII, no. E.2623
undated
pencil on paper, 22.6 x 31.8 cm
University of Birmingham

This delicate pencil drawing records a wide variety of Roman female portrait heads studied from the Uffizi collection, Florence; the artist's annotations identify some as members of the Imperial families of different dynasties. His principal interest is in the elaborate hairstyles of successive Imperial fashions, often attacked as

frivolous by Roman satirists such as Martial; the heads display unidealized facial features in the Roman tradition of 'realistic' portraiture. The drawing encapsulates Alma-Tadema's urge to collect information on classical antiquities, seen on a larger scale in his comprehensive collection of photographs. In photographs and drawings, Alma-Tadema collected much more data than he ever used; although he frequently depicted extravagant Imperial hairstyles (see p. 36) [14], he rarely used coiffures as detailed as the ones seen here.

The work is undated, but the drawing style suggests that it belongs to the late 1860s, also the period when Alma-Tadema was most interested in extravagant female hairstyles [17 20]. EP/RB

20

A juggler

Opus LXXVII, S 119
5 February 1870
oil on canvas, mounted on panel, 78.7 x 49.5 cm
Stanley J. Allen

Exhibited Royal Academy, London, 1870 (153)

Together with a few other works of around 1870 [21] (S 120), *A juggler* marks the culmination of Alma-Tadema's early fascination with the Pompeian-style

interior, the leading motive of the artist's Roman pictures for a decade after his first, revelatory visit to Pompeii in 1863. However, the preoccupation with Pompeii was no mere accident of the artist's biography. The 1860s were a particularly exciting period in the long history of the excavations at Pompeii, extending from the 1740s to the present. Under the superintendence, from 1860-75, of the Italian patriot and archaeologist, Giuseppe Fiorelli, excavation proceeded at a hectic pace, while new methods of display stressed restoration of the buildings, providing a more vivid experience of the Pompeian physical environment (see Layard, pp. 329-31). The most famous of Fiorelli's inventions was the technique of making plaster casts of the cavities, left in the volcanic debris by the decayed bodies of humans and animals; the casts still seem particularly compelling records of the 'real' victims of the eruption, but the casting technique was only one of a number of innovations aimed at enhancing the immediacy of the material remains of Pompeii. Alma-Tadema's emphasis on recreating the material specificity of the early Imperial domestic interior must owe much to the experiments of Fiorelli and his colleagues.

By 1870, though, Alma-Tadema was elaborating his painted recreations to a splendour exceeding that of the real buildings of Pompeii, a provincial town of modest dwellings: the interior of *A juggler* is more opulent than those found at Pompeii. Nonetheless, it is composed of Pompeian elements, many of which would have been recognizable to Victorian audiences, if not through first-hand experience of the site, then through the many books and articles of the 1860s on the Pompeian excavations, including Fiorelli's own scholarly publications. The present author's previous account of the picture misidentified the fresco on the rear wall as a Bacchanalian subject (*Imagining Rome*, no. 48); in fact, it is a close reproduction of the fresco of *Hercules and Omphale*, from the house of M. Lucretius in Pompeii (information from Eleanor Winsor Leach). Also instantly recognizable were the statue of a stag from Herculaneum, visible at the rear although its head is cut off by the colonnade, and the bronze group from the Naples Museum, of the infant Hercules strangling the serpents, on the left; the group reappears in *The sculpture gallery* (transformed into marble) [35]. Other accessory objects reproduce common types of artefact

from the Pompeian excavations: the wall and ceiling decorations; the bronze candelabrum; and the foreground bench, similar to the modern recreation of such a bench, used by Alma-Tadema as a studio prop [87]. Only one object is conspicuously non-Pompeian: the Egyptian *shabti* box, used in antiquity for storing funerary statuettes of the kind seen in *Prose* [53], but here wittily reinterpreted as a box for the juggler's equipment.

The intrusion of the Egyptian artefact is significant: it helps to identify the juggler, darker in complexion than his Roman audience, as a victim of Imperial oppression. At the rear is a household slave, identifiable by his closely cropped hair and short tunic, but fairer in complexion than the juggler and therefore perhaps European: his subordinate status is emphasized by the abrupt cropping of the figure, behind the colonnade. The references to Roman racial and social oppression appear almost incidental, but there is a sinister note to the depiction of slavery as routine in the Roman household, here and in other early works by the artist [29 35]: at this date the American Civil War and the attendant anti-slavery campaigns would have been fresh in the minds of the pictures' audiences. Moreover, the remaining figures do not form a nuclear family, as in many of the artist's later pictures [49]. Instead they illustrate the social patterns of the patrician class of the Roman Empire, as understood by Victorian social historians: a patrician family with an assortment of their clients, dependents, and parasites, crowded for instance into the left rear corner. At this early stage in his career, Alma-Tadema is interested in historically specific Roman social hierarchies [14], and not without a critical edge: the paterfamilias, surrounded by his dependents, appears complacent, with his flabby features and stolid pose, hands on knees, while the women in the background were interpreted by contemporary critics as frivolous, with their dyed red hair and elaborate coiffures [19]. Moreover, none of the figures has business more important than to watch a juggler's tricks, or to engage in desultory conversation. Although the artist's later pictures of Romans at leisure are not without their darker implications, the patrician figures can appear lovely in their idleness; here the unflattering characterizations give a sharper edge to the satire. As one critic put it, 'There is no idealization of the figures introduced, and no sacrifice to the attractive in the women' (*The Times*, 30 April 1870, p. 12).

To present the Romans as idle, overprivileged, and oppressive ran directly counter to the High Art tradition of painting the heroic actions of Roman antiquity [23]. Many of the art critics of 1870 accordingly found the subject-matter of *A juggler* distasteful, even when they praised its technical thoroughness. As one critic put it, 'sneer and irony discolour truth; moreover, this eccentric Dutchman dresses up history in so grotesque a garb that he casts ridicule on scenes which he might seem to honour' (*Saturday Review*, 18 June 1870, p. 801). EP

21

The vintage festival

Opus LXXXI, S 122
23 August 1870
oil on canvas, 77 x 177 cm
Hamburger Kunsthalle, Hamburg

Exhibited Ernest Gambart's gallery, London, spring 1871 (only picture in exhibition)

The vintage festival is Alma-Tadema's first exploration of the nature of Roman religious ritual, or Bacchanalia, dedicated to the Roman god Bacchus who was chiefly celebrated for his association with wine. Bacchanalia appropriated many elements of the Greek Dionysiac *orgia* such as the involvement of women devotees (maenads or bacchantes). Bacchanalian, and to a lesser extent Dionysiac subjects, are important themes throughout the artist's career [34 39 46 59 68 72] (S 132, 135, 194, 251, 265, 417, 432). The main classical source for the Roman worship of Bacchus is Livy's 'History of Rome' (XXXIX.8-18). Livy records that Bacchanalian rites were outlawed at Rome in 186 B.C. because of their connection with 'debauchery and murders'. Worshippers had to apply for a special permit and gatherings were limited to five people. However, inscriptions attest to the continuing existence of larger cult activities. Even though the foreground figures in this painting maintain a serene and ordered procession, the dancing throng in the background evokes the more riotous behaviour described by Livy.

This procession celebrating the year's vintage is headed by a priestess. Her hair is adorned with grapes and ivy leaves in a style attributable to Hellenistic and Roman statues of Dionysus or Bacchus. She is followed by a troupe of musicians playing double flutes (*tibiae*) tied around their heads by a leather band (*capistrum*) and dancing figures playing shallow drums similar to the modern tambourine (*tympana*). Two men carry the new wine in amphorae, followed by an attendant carrying a basket of vintage grapes. In the centre of the composition stands a huge terracotta pot, decorated with ivy, full of the new wine. A bronze tripod and silver *situla* of dedicatory wine stand on a marble altar. The altar is decorated with theatrical masks, appropriate to a Dionysiac context, and a relief of a maenad and satyr who were traditionally known as members of Dionysus' mythical entourage (*thiasus*). Dionysiac imagery is echoed in the huge ornamental *volute crater* on the far left, a vessel originally used for mixing wine. To the right of the painting stands a silver drinking cup (*rhyton*) and a jug (*askos*). On the marble step rests a staff topped with a pine cone (*thyrsus*) traditionally carried by a maenad.

The setting is the atrium of a Pompeian villa. An inscription on the marble floor at the left of the canvas relates to Marcus Holconius Rufus, a prominent Pompeian householder who is recorded as holding public office at the end of the 1st century B.C. A number of surviving inscriptions at Pompeii refer to the prestigious Holconii family. Alma-Tadema's allusion to Holconius Rufus, here and previously in *An exedra* [18], places these scenes in settings as precise and immediate as those involving well-known historical characters [13 23 40 64 69]. Although this grand processional scene would be more appropriate in a public setting, numerous portable household altars found at Pompeii and Herculaneum attest to the prevalence of private cults. Alma-Tadema seems to have been interested in the rituals of domestic religion as shown by numerous photographs of these altars in his collection (Portfolios I-II) [32 46 49 61]. The atrium is decorated in a highly extravagant manner with unfluted green Cipollino marble columns surmounted by ornate Corinthian capitals. For the dark red wall painting which characterizes his earlier Pompeian scenes [17], the artist has substituted a lighter decorative style and

greater use of marble. The delicate wall designs in the background and black and gold pilasters evoke third-style Pompeian wall painting dating roughly to the Augustan period. The statue in the background left is known as the *Prima Porta Augustus*. It is a statue of the Emperor Augustus in military uniform erected in 20 B.C. [40 51]. The setting and artefacts then are all exactly contemporaneous with the life of Holconius Rufus. The corresponding cuirassed statue on the right

may be that of Holconius Rufus himself, dressed in the uniform of a military tribune and found near the Stabian baths at Pompeii. As is characteristic of the artist's representations of ordinary individuals, the status of the Pompeian citizen in his own house is equal to that of the Emperor.

The painting hanging on the pilaster near the priestess copies a fresco fragment from Pompeii, depicting Hercules and Omphale [20]. Hercules was sold into

servitude to Omphale, Queen of Lydia, and while he stayed with her wore women's clothes and sat weaving amongst her maids. This effeminate portrayal of Hercules evokes long-haired and softly contoured Hellenistic sculptures of Dionysus and reminds us that Dionysus himself was raised in the all-female company of the nymphs of Mount Nysa. Lydia was also visited by Dionysus on his travels and consequently remained a centre of the cult.

The vintage festival was the first Alma-Tadema acquired by Heinrich Schröder, later Baron Sir Henry Schröder, the German proprietor of a London banking firm (now the international merchant bank, J. Henry Schroder & Co.). Schröder eventually owned ten Alma-Tademas, of which most had Bacchanalian or erotic subjects [33 43 46 72 78] (s 169); Schröder also owned one of the period's most notoriously salacious paintings in an antique setting, Jean-Léon Gérôme's *Phryné before the*

tribunal of 1861 (Hamburger Kunsthalle, Hamburg). He seems to have amassed his collection largely if not exclusively through Gambart and his successors, Pilgeram and Lefèvre [36]. The story has often been told of Gambart's generosity to Alma-Tadema; although *The vintage festival* was one of the early pictures in the second contract, Gambart was so pleased with it that he paid Alma-Tadema at the highest rate, at least £ 120, giving the artist an additional £ 100 as a present (Maas, pp. 215-16). However, Gambart's profits scarcely suffered, since Schröder gave £ 1,850 for *The vintage festival* in 1871: this was his first purchase of an Alma-Tadema, made at the moment when prices for the artist's work began to soar (see *Ein Hamburger sammelt in London*, pp. 16, 41). EP/RB

22

The Epps family screen

S 129

1870-71

oil on canvas, six hinged panels, each 182.9 x 78.7 cm

Board of Trustees of the Victoria & Albert Museum,
London

Exhibited The National Gallery of Art, Washington,
March – September 1984 (2)

This unfinished painted screen depicts the artist's in-
laws, the Epps family, in their London dining room, and
was painted jointly by Alma-Tadema and Laura Epps,
his future second wife. It includes her parents and her
five brothers and sisters, Hahnemann, Ellen, Amy,
Louisa and Washington. Her father, Dr. George
Napoleon Epps, was a noted homeopathic practitioner
and surgeon. He is seen seated at the head of the table
and the other figures are (left to right): his wife
Charlotte; Mary Epps, her husband Dr. Hahnemann

Epps (named after the founder of homeopathy) and their two children; Ellen Epps (later Mrs. Edmund Gosse); standing in front of the table in profile: Emily Epps; Charles Pratt and his wife Amy (née Epps); Louisa Hill (née Epps) with her baby Charlotte and her husband Rowland Hill (partially painted out, because of his subsequent involvement in a Stock Exchange scandal, though his figure is still visible); Frances Epps and her husband Dr. Washington Epps; Laura (in profile); Alma-Tadema; Mr. and Mrs. Franklin Epps. The unpainted section in the centre was intended for more of the grandchildren.

Alma-Tadema met Laura on Boxing Day 1869 at a dance held by Ford Madox Brown where according to Gambart, Alma-Tadema 'fell in love at first sight with Miss Epps' (letter to Holman Hunt; Swanson, p. 159). She received lessons from him and the screen seems to have been begun by Alma-Tadema as a way of teaching her to paint. According to Swanson, Alma-Tadema roughed out the figures for her to complete; however he points out that those of Emily, Amy, Louisa, baby Charlotte, Rowland Hill and the group on the extreme right seem to be in his hand. The screen was unfinished at the time of the couple's marriage in July 1871.

The scene is surrounded on two sides by a terracotta red border lettered with the names of some of the figures. Above runs an inscription on the theme of family unity: 'It was the hap of a very honest man to be the father of a brood of children. He call'd for a bundle of arrows and bad'em take it and try one after another with all their force, if they could break it. They try'd and could not. Well says he, unbind it now and take every arrow of it apart, and see what you can do that way. They did so, and with great ease, by one and one, they snap'd it all to pieces. This says he is the true emblem of your condition. Keep together and y'are safe'.

The screen is backed with Morris Pomegranate wallpaper. At least one pencil study is known, for the figure of Emily (repr. Swanson 1977, p. 13). JT

23

A Roman emperor, A.D. 41

Opus LXXXVIII, S 131
19 March 1871
oil on canvas, 83.8 x 174.2 cm
Walters Art Gallery, Baltimore

Exhibited Royal Academy, London, 1871 (210)

This was the first of Alma-Tadema's Royal Academy pictures to feature a significant event from Roman political history: the proclamation of Claudius as Emperor after the murder of his nephew, the corrupt Caligula. Subject-

matter from Roman history held the most exalted rank in the traditional hierarchy of pictorial categories, but Alma-Tadema reverses the orthodox emphasis on ancient Roman heroism to present a grotesque Claudius, cringing behind a curtain as the Praetorian guard approach. Claudius's red slippers make him ridiculous, elaborating a detail from the account of the Roman historian Suetonius, in which the Praetorian guard discover Claudius because his feet protrude beneath the curtain ('Claudius', v.x).

The composition also subverts the conventions of the history painting tradition. At centre stage, in the position traditionally reserved for the Roman hero,

appear the corpses of Caligula and his associates, ignominiously heaped on the ground while the action is displaced to the edges of the picture. On the left, an unruly crowd of armed guards and inquisitive women surge into the room; one figure clutches a bundle of precious objects, looted from the palace amidst the turmoil. The mock reverence of the Praetorian, saluting the cowardly Claudius on the right, parodies the hierarchical figural groupings of traditional history painting. In this corrupt Roman world, it is not the heroic individual, but the brutal Praetorian guard who wield the power of Empire.

Although subjects from Roman history remained rare in Alma-Tadema's oeuvre, this episode held special

fascination for the artist, who had first painted the subject in 1867 and would return to it in 1880 [15] (s 260); the present picture is much the largest of the three. One critic stressed that the subject epitomized ' "the beginning of the end" of the Roman Empire', the moment of transition from vitality to decadence (*The Times*, 5 December 1882, p. 8); this was the first occasion on which an Emperor had been chosen by the military rather than the Senate. The fresco of the Battle of Actium commemorates the valour of the Roman past; its abrupt cropping at the top edge suggests its irrelevance to the present scene of brute force. The terminal portrait of Augustus in the centre plays a similar role: its sculptured features are the only ones to display the dignity appropriate to a Roman hero, but the pedestal is bloodstained. Augustus's world of Roman heroism has been superseded by one of violence amidst excessive luxury, indicated by the opulent surroundings of the palace interior. The inscription on the floor, cut off by the bottom edge, reads '*genius huius loci*' ('the guardian spirit of this place'); this demarcates the Imperial

shrine on the right, with its lavish marble altar and mosaic floor decorations. The reference to traditional Roman piety again emphasizes the anarchy of the present scene by contrast.

Despite the sumptuous setting and vivid characterizations, the picture's interpretation of Roman history was perhaps too cynical to appeal to contemporary art collectors. It failed to find a purchaser until 1882, when it was sold to the American collector, William T. Walters. EP

24

Self portraits of Lawrence Alma-Tadema and Laura Theresa Epps

S 133
June - July 1871
oil on panel, 27.5 x 37.5 cm
Fries Museum, Leeuwarden

Exhibited Art Foundation, Rotterdam, May - June 1974

The two self portraits, by Alma-Tadema and Laura Epps, were painted at the time of their marriage in the summer of 1871: Laura, Alma-Tadema's pupil during their courtship, became a painter in her own right, exhibiting regularly at the Royal Academy between 1873 and her death in 1909. Each artist appears as an individual, but the design unites the two portraits, alluding not only to the couple's marriage but to their shared pursuit of painting: the two heads, facing each other, are executed with the same sketchy touch. Similarly, the inscriptions present information about each individual – name, current age, date and place of birth – but the lettering encircles both portraits.

The Latin lettering is in the elongated capitals typical of Pompeian inscriptions [14]; this places the couple's union in a classicizing context, although both wear contemporary dress. Moreover, the frame is of a common ancient type, with protruding cross-bars at the

132 *A family group*, 1896, Royal Academy of Arts, London

corners; Alma-Tadema's pictures often include representations of such frames [36]. The motif of combining two separate portraits in a single frame does not derive from classical precedent, but the two artists may have been alluding to the famous double portrait of a Pompeian man and wife, of which Alma-Tadema owned a photograph [20]; in the Pompeian portrait, the woman holds a stylus to her lips much as Laura holds her fan.

The reference was topical, since the Pompeian portrait was a recent discovery, unearthed in 1868 (see p. 36).

On the inside surfaces of the frame's doors, Alma-Tadema introduces more personal allusions, the Dutch tulip on his own side and the English rose on Laura's. The two flowers recur, no doubt as a deliberate echo, in the picture Alma-Tadema painted for Laura to commemorate their 25th wedding anniversary, *A family group* of 1896 [132]: in the later work, the tulip and rose appear on the reverse of the picture on the easel, contemplated by Laura and her siblings [35] while Alma-Tadema himself is glimpsed, at work, in the background mirror. EP

25

Pottery painting

Opus XCIV, S 138
23 September 1871
oil on panel, 39.2 x 27.3 cm
Manchester City Art Gallery

Exhibited French Gallery, London, 1871-72 (67)

Pottery painting evokes the busy activity of an ancient workshop. Alma-Tadema had already explored the theme of ancient commercial life a few years earlier in *The flower market* [14] and was to return to it again at the height of his career with *Hadrian in England* [63-65]. In *Pottery painting* the principal figure is a woman who leans back to admire the pot onto which she is copying a design from a tracing on parchment. This reminds us of the contemporary Victorian art world in which women were characteristically employed in the minor or decorative arts. Many women worked alongside men in the British pottery industry as semi-skilled and skilled workers (see Buckley).

The woman is working on an Apulian red-figure flask (*lekythos*), the seated man next to her on a wedding bowl (*lebes gamikos*). A red-figure drinking cup (*glaux*) and an oil-bottle (*aryballos*) rest on the window-ledge. The *lekythos* and the *glaux* have been identified as two pots now in the Louvre (Jenkins 1983, p. 602). The Alma-Tadema photograph collection includes a water-colour sketch of these vases (LXXXIV, 2325). Similar water-colours in the collection are signed

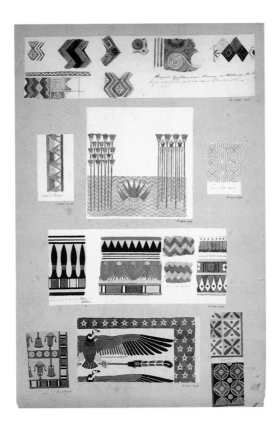

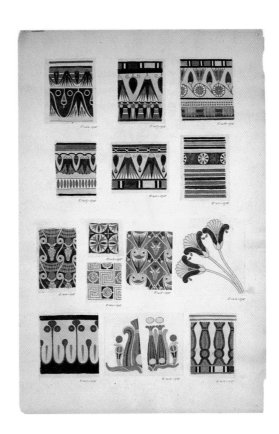

and dated 1886, which suggests that the sketches post-date the painting and neatly demonstrates that Alma-Tadema's interest in the classical world goes beyond the utilization of artefacts for his paintings.

The Apulian *lekythos* places the scene in southern Italy (Apulia was the centre of a school of vase painting from the late 5th century B.C.), and the Doric temple glimpsed through the window indicates that this setting is *Magna Graecia*, the area of southern Italy colonized by Greece from the 8th century B.C. and culturally part of the Hellenic world for hundreds of years. The woman wears Greek-style drapery with long vertical folds falling from a bunched overfold confirming a Greek setting. With his penchant for the unexpected the artist chooses to show the pottery industry of southern Italy rather than that of Athens, despite the much higher status accorded to Athenian pottery in the later 19th century. At all events, *Pottery painting* presents a creative and artistic culture, quite distinct from the rich and leisured world of Rome, but comparable to some of Alma-Tadema's few other representations of Greeks, such as *Phidias showing the frieze of the Parthenon to his friends* [13] and *Sappho* [98].

The painting was bought by the international financier José de Murrieta who acquired an impressive collection of modern British art including twenty paintings by Alma-Tadema (see pp. 92-95). RB

26

Sketches of Egyptian ornament

Portfolio XXXV
nos. E.1398 – 1405 (left)
nos. E.1406 – 1419 (right)
undated
mixed media on paper, various sizes
University of Birmingham

Both leaves display fragments of Egyptian wall and floor decorations, which Alma-Tadema partly copied from the three volumes of J.G. Wilkinson's richly illustrated *Manners and customs of the ancient Egyptians* (1837), 'the greatest review of ancient Egyptian civilization ever undertaken' (W.R. Dawson and E.P. Uphill, *Who was who in Egyptology*, London 1972, cited in Raven, p. 116, note 9). He used the studies for the details in his paintings, but the question remains why he copied them when he had the book itself in his possession.

The studies were probably executed before Alma-Tadema's move to London, as the texts on a number of the pages (nos. E.1398, E.1399, E.1401-E.1405) are in both Dutch and French (see p. 152). It is not certain when Alma-Tadema started compiling his portfolios, but his growing collection of individual studies probably more or less forced him to do so (see pp. 111-124). TM/LP

27

An Egyptian widow in the time of Diocletian

Opus XCIX, S 141

April 1872

oil on panel, 74.9 x 99.1 cm

Rijksmuseum, Amsterdam

Exhibited Royal Academy, London, 1872 (524)

This painting was still for sale in 1880. Alma-Tadema was keen for the Dutch government to purchase it, because he considered that his work was poorly represented in the Netherlands. He enlisted his friend Carel Vosmaer to his aid, but Vosmaer's efforts met with little response (*De verzameling van Mr. Carel Vosmaer*, p. 139). It was not until the beginning of the 20th century that the painting was donated to the Rijksmuseum by Mrs. J.C.J. Drucker-Fräser.

Despite the different composition, the painting is a repetition of opus XLII, *The mummy* (1867, whereabouts unknown, included as a wood engraving in Georg Ebers's *Aegypten in Bild und Wort*, 1880). Like *The death of the first-born* [28], this work combines a faithfulness to archaeological precision with a heightened sense of drama, although there is no direct literary source. Nevertheless, the theme is a familiar one in Egyptian funerary decoration, and appears in tomb paintings and in vignettes in the Book of the Dead. This is where Alma-Tadema must have found his source of inspiration (Raven, p. 107).

The Egyptian objects have been identified by Maarten Raven. They are almost all from the Egyptian collection in the British Museum. The large statue of Sachmet in the temple court is one of the museum's most priceless treasures. The coffin is based on one from the grave of the Theban archon Soter (BM 6712). The decoration on the low rear wall is inspired by the Djedhor Book of the Dead in London (BM 10017). Smaller objects, such as the canopic jars – used to hold the entrails of the deceased – in the lower right-hand corner of the painting, may also be based on artefacts in the British Museum (Raven, pp. 107-08). Almost all of the objects depicted date from the period of Greco-Roman rule. Alma-Tadema could also have found many of the British Museum objects, as well as other Egyptian artefacts in

27

J.G. Wilkinson's three-volume *Manners and customs of the ancient Egyptians* (1837). The numerous illustrations in this famous work were a rich source of inspiration, and were copied by Alma-Tadema on an incidental basis and kept with other studies in portfolios [26].

That borrowing motifs from a secondary source is not without its hazards can be seen from the following case. The large harp which the black slave is playing is

represented upside-down, just as in Gardner Wilkinson's book. Egyptian statues of the period indicate that this instrument was played with the shaft pointing downwards. Alma-Tadema's mistake is all the more surprising because he had represented this musical instrument correctly in one of his first Egyptian paintings [13]. Raven refers to other details which are incorrect in the light of our present-day knowledge of ancient Egypt. The floor,

for example, would appear to be a product of the artist's imagination, and the same is true of the door with a very anachronistic key-hole.

As is often the case in Alma-Tadema's paintings, the composition is very striking. His interiors almost always offer a glimpse, however infinitesimal, of the outdoor world. In this case a few square centimetres of blue sky prevent the upper part of the painting from forming a massive block. The lamenting singers and musicians are wedged between the mummy and coffin on a proportionately narrow base against the richly decorated rear wall, thereby leaving a free area for the widow, bent double in her grief. The foreground is largely vacant, but a wall on the left and a row of canopic jars on the right provide a precisely calculated balance. The extreme foreshortening of the canopic jars which lead the viewer into the 'more crowded' right-hand side of the painting is a particularly masterly touch.

Alma-Tadema visited Egypt for the first and last time in 1902-03. However, this did not lead to a deepening of his interest in ancient Egypt. He only painted one Egyptian scene afterwards [91], in which the Egyptian elements play a less prominent role. TM/LP

28

The death of the first-born

Opus CIII, S 145

July 1872

oil on canvas, 79.9 x 124.5 cm

Rijksmuseum, Amsterdam

Exhibited Salon des Beaux-Arts, Brussels, 1872

The death of the first-born is a *magnum opus* from Alma-Tadema's early period. It was hailed as the painting of the year by the *Pall Mall Magazine* in 1872. Six years later it was awarded a gold medal in Paris. The painter himself considered it to be one of his major works. It was commissioned by Ernest Gambart, but the artist bought it back for his own collection in 1879. Nevertheless, he tried to sell it to the museum in Dresden a few years later because he needed money for the renovation of his villa in Grove End Road. The price he asked – £ 2,000 – was too high. He was not prepared to offer it to another museum: 'but if not for so first rate a museum I won't part with it as we all love the picture and enjoy having it home' (letter to Ebers, 27 September 1884, cited in Swanson, p. 167).

He did not try to part with it again during his lifetime, and gave it a special place in his studio, where it was hidden from sight by a curtain. When visitors came to his richly furnished house, he could unveil his masterpiece with a dramatic gesture and receive their accolades. In 1911 this practice was described with due respect by Lita de Ranitz for the Dutch magazine *Het Huis: Oud en Nieuw*: 'Attached to a copper rod, a curtain of Italian embroidery, red and blue majolica colours on a ground of warm white tones, conceals a work of art. Suddenly Sir Lawrence has pulled the curtain aside! We stand before: "The Death of the Firstborn". [...] The value that Alma Tadema attaches to this painting borders on devotion. Seized with difficulty from the hands of an eager public, he has restored it to this shrine of his own studio' (De Ranitz, p. 29). After his death, it was bequeathed to the Rijksmuseum, Amsterdam.

The theme of the painting is the tenth plague of Egypt, the last which God visited upon the land of Egypt because he would not let the chosen children of Israel go (Exodus 12:29). Pharaoh and his wife are lamenting the death of their first-born son, whose lifeless body lies in Pharaoh's lap in the pose of a pietà. The skills of a physician, depicted to the left of Pharaoh with a basket of medicinal elixirs, are to no avail. In the background to the right we see Moses and Aaron entering the dark room from the moonlit courtyard. The heavy responsibility of leading their people in the Exodus awaits them. It has been suggested that the artist's fondness for this theme is connected with the death of his son in 1864, but Alma-Tadema had already completed a painting on the same theme in 1859, a fragment of which is now in the Johannesburg Art Gallery (S 40). In 1901 he repeated the central group of figures from the Amsterdam painting in a drawing (Opus CCCLXIV). This time, however, he set the figures out of doors, with the Nile Delta in the background.

Oriental themes, biblical and otherwise, were gaining in popularity in Europe from the beginning of the 19th century (see p. 65). Frederick Goodall, in whose house Alma-Tadema lived for six months when he arrived in England in 1870, was a specialist in Bedouins, and in 1867 Edward John Poynter, like Alma-Tadema, also chose a passage from the Book of Exodus for his *Israel in Egypt* (Guildhall Art Gallery, Corporation of London).

Raven identified the so-called ear stele to the left of the Pharaoh's head with an exemple in the British Museum (BM 25296). It is, however, certain that Alma-Tadema's model was not this particular stele itself, but

an illustration of it in J.G. Wilkinson's *Manners and customs of the ancient Egyptians* (Raven, pp. 111-12, figs. 13 and 14). Raven suggests that the representation of the stele is connected with the prayers that were uttered to save the young life. Alma-Tadema used to date his Egyptian works by including a cartouche in the painting referring to the period in which the scene is set, and by selecting objects as far as possible from a single stylistic period. To the left of the stele a cartouche from the reign of Ramses II can be seen. The reign of Ramses is dated to the 13th century B.C., the period in which Moses was placed by 19th-century scholars (Raven, p. 111). The gold chain with a green scarab worn by the dead youth can be found in Wilkinson, who used an exemple from the Rijksmuseum van Oudheden in Leiden as a model. Alma-Tadema also included this so-called deer scarab of Djehouty in Opus X (1859) and Opus XXVI (1865). It is therefore probable that he saw the object with his own eyes (Raven, p. 112).

Alma-Tadema's attachment to *The death of the first-born* is probably connected with its exceptional position within his oeuvre. He seldom painted themes with a deep emotional content – which was not always appreciated by the critics. Helen Zimmern, for example, whose admiration for Alma-Tadema did not cloud her critical judgement, wrote: '... here he has shown conclusively that he can paint pathos, and he is possessed of the deeper imagination which he puts forth so rarely' (Zimmern 1886, p. 16).

The Egyptologist Georg Ebers described the painting in glowing terms in 1885. He praised the archaeological accuracy and the lyricism of the work. He concluded his commentary with the words: 'If Tadema had only created this one work, this painting alone would have secured him a place as one of the greatest painters of our time' (Borger, p. 36). TM/LP

29

The dinner (Greek)

Opus CXI, S 153
31 March 1873
oil on panel, 16.5 x 58.5 cm
William Morris Gallery, Walthamstow

Exhibited Royal Academy, London, 1873 (577)

Between 1868 and 1880, Alma-Tadema painted a number of pictures with elongated horizontal formats, showing Greek figures reclining to enjoy the pleasures of the senses. These may have been intended to establish a practice in large-scale frieze decorations, particularly appropriate for dining rooms, but patronage was not forthcoming for large works of this type [11 41] [127] (S 196, 256). *The dinner* was one of a set of three small-scale versions of the theme, sold to the same patron, Frederick Thomas Turner, and exhibited together in 1873 (S 148, 154).

Unusually for Alma-Tadema, not only individual artefacts but the overall composition derives from a classical source, the 'symposium' scenes on Greek vases; the artist made many drawings of vase designs of this type (Portfolio LXXXI). *The dinner* is based on one such drawing [133], which is copied not once, but twice: the design is reproduced as a wall painting, but the 'real' figures also mimic the same composition. The picture therefore makes a double play on the notion of 'copying' from the ancient source [35 36].

Many critics objected to the hedonism of the subject: it may have seemed more objectionable to represent passive sensuous enjoyment in a context specifically identified as Greek, rather than the 'decadent' Roman period more usually associated with idle luxury. As one writer declared, 'The exhibition of post-prandial crapulosity is not rendered less repulsive by the very correct details' (Pollock, p. 79). Indeed, the 'correct' reproduction of the compositional formula of the Greek symposium scene may have been an underlying reason for critical objections. Although the subject can be read as an innocuous courtship scene of a kind common in Victorian genre painting, with the young pair about to ask the father's permission to marry, a different reading is available if the scene is interpreted as a Greek symposium, or drinking party for men. As classical texts indi-

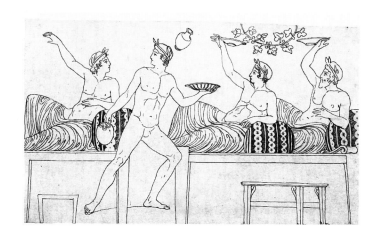

133 *Symposium scene*, from a series of drawings after Greek vase paintings, late 1860s, University of Birmingham (LXXXI, E.2172)

cated, the symposium was never attended by respectable women (e.g., Vitruvius, VI.vii.3-5); a classical scholar might accordingly identify the female figure as a courtesan or prostitute. There may be a hint of homoeroticism, also associated with the Greek symposium, in the depiction of young male slaves, carrying in the next course of the dinner at the extreme left; the juxtaposition of older with younger men carried similar connotations [16]. Victorian texts celebrating Greek political 'freedom' often glossed over the Greek practice of slavery, but

Alma-Tadema emphasizes the slaves' status, providing them with identity badges hanging around their necks; the badges were based on an artefact of which Alma-Tadema made a careful drawing (LXXXI, E.2215).

The possibility of a double reading is typical of Alma-Tadema's work (see pp. 37-38). In this case, the doubling of the 'real' figures with the vase scene, represented as a wall painting, parallels the possibility of double interpretation of the subject-matter. EP

30

Cherries

Opus CXIV, S 155
12 August 1873
oil on canvas, 79 x 129.1 cm
Koninklijk Museum voor Schone Kunsten, Antwerp

Exhibited Cercle Artistique, Antwerp, November 1873

Cherries was designed as Alma-Tadema's diploma picture for the Cercle Artistique in Antwerp, and first exhibited there in 1873. The picture's destination in the collection of an artists' society helps to account for the unusual boldness of its execution; bravura sketchiness was traditionally seen as appealing to artists and sophisticated amateurs. The unusually overt eroticism of the picture's subject-matter may also relate to its exhibition with the Cercle Artistique, rather than the larger public exhibitions in which Alma-Tadema's work ordinarily appeared. The woman's unabashed eye contact with the spectator and the gesture with which she offers the cherries unmistakably suggest a sexual invitation. The erotic symbolism of cherries, associated with women's lips and with the hymen, was well established in the later 19th century (see Reis, p. 203).

The composition, with a reclining figure behind a foreground table, is related to the 'symposium' type, perhaps drawing on the hedonistic and sensual connotations of such scenes [29]. However, the accessories are less archaeologically precise than usual in Alma-Tadema's work at this date. The fragment of a fluted pilaster, the clasping of the dress at the shoulder, and the woman's hairstyle are classical in an understated way, and the tiger skin was a common accessory in 19th-century scenes of ancient life, but the bold pattern of the woman's dress is not particularly classicizing. The picture is closer to 'aestheticizing' pictures, such as Frederic Leighton's *Mother and child* of 1865 (Blackburn Art Gallery) or Charles Edward Perugini's *Cherries* of 1869 (untraced), both of which used cherries in compositions combining female beauty with the gorgeous colours and

textures of accessory objects. However, Alma-Tadema's presentation of his female figure makes the erotic symbolism of the cherries more explicit than in the pictures by his English contemporaries. EP

31

This is our corner
(Portrait of Laurense and Anna
Alma-Tadema as children)

Opus CXVI, S 156
6 October 1873
oil on panel, 56.5 x 47 cm
Van Gogh Museum, Amsterdam

Exhibited Dudley Gallery, London, Winter 1873 (235)

At its first exhibition in 1873, the picture was titled *This is our corner*, indicating that it could function as a subject picture about childhood, as well as a double portrait of the artist's daughters, Laurense (born 1865, standing)

and Anna (born 1867, on the couch). This dual function was frequent in Victorian pictures of children [42]; a close parallel is John Everett Millais's *Leisure hours* of 1864, simultaneously a portrait of the two young daughters of Sir John Pender and a picture of well-to-do girls at play (Detroit Institute of Arts).

Although Laurense and Anna were the daughters of Alma-Tadema's first wife, they were integrated, apparently harmoniously, into the family circle of the artist's childless second marriage to Laura Theresa Epps, who had received this painting as a present [22 24]. The interior presumably represents a room in Townshend House, the family home from 1871 until 1885 (see pp. 46-49). The black-and-white striped rug recalls similar floor coverings in the pictures of James McNeill Whistler and Albert Moore, and the sketchy decorations on a cushion against the rear wall suggest Chinese or Japanese design; the Greek key border above the baseboard of the right wall introduces a classicizing note.

These eclectic elements characterize an 'aesthetic' interior belonging to a well-off middle-class family. The two figures are indeed enclosed in a 'corner', which the original title identifies as their own special enclave, suggesting the sheltered environment of Victorian middle-class girlhood. The wicker chair closes the space to the left; it is unoccupied, and may be Laurense's chair, or that of an unseen parent. Both girls are provided with books, appropriate accessories for their social class and sex [54]. They gaze with the wide eyes of childhood toward the spectator, implicitly placed in the role of the supervising parent. Anna buries her face in the cushion, suggesting shyness, but both expressions convey a childish artlessness, not without a hint of feminine charm. Recent scholarship has called attention to the subtle eroticism in Victorian pictures of young girls (see Reis); although it can scarcely have been Alma-Tadema's intention to present his daughters in eroticized terms, the soft textures of flesh and hair, together with the appealing vulnerability of the expressions, correspond to contemporary conventions for the representation of the fragile allure of pre-adolescent girls. EP

32

A votive offering (The last roses)

Opus CXVIII
1873
watercolour on paper, 47.3 x 39.4 cm
private collection

Like many of Alma-Tadema's watercolours, 51 of which he considered important enough to assign opus numbers, this is closely related to a previous oil, *The last roses* of 1872 [79]. Such watercolours presumably served as saleable repetitions, but invariably maintained the high technical standard of an artist as proficient in watercolour as in his more usual medium. This example combines the artist's interest in the quotidian religious rituals of antiquity with a mood of autumnal melancholy [37 46 61]: a woman is making a votive offering of 'last

roses', probably at a columnar tomb. The composition is similar to that of Frederic Leighton's *Electra at the tomb of Agamemnon* of 1869 (Ferens Art Gallery, Hull); but instead of invoking an elevated classical drama, Alma-Tadema uses the withered rosebush and autumnal setting to hint at themes of mortality and transience (see p. 84). EP

33

Fishing

Opus CXIX, S 158
4 November 1873
oil on panel, 19 x 40.6 cm
Hamburger Kunsthalle, Hamburg

Exhibited Amsterdam 1874 (8)

The title of the painting is ambiguous, as the woman is clearly not fishing but idly leaning against a pillar, fingering her necklace while the rod rests on a silk cushion. Dressed in her finery, is she hoping to attract lovers rather than fish?

The relief on her left shows a nude female figure fishing. It is copied from a Pompeian wall painting, 'Venus fishing', of which Alma-Tadema owned a photograph [134]. The other relief illustrates a cupid being drawn through the water by dolphins. Both reliefs confirm the fish theme and the picture's underlying erotic significance. Birds in flight, one with a wedding-ring, allude to an added symbolism of the transitory nature of love. The artist returned to the subject of fish-ponds in other paintings, all in opulent settings, with leisured women amusing themselves nearby [83] (S 150, 167, 171, 186, 396).

134 *Venus fishing*, mural decoration from Pompeii (Museo Archeologico Nazionale, Naples), photograph by Robert Rive from Alma-Tadema's collection, University of Birmingham (CXXXI, 11444)

135 *After the dance*, 1875, private collection

Alma-Tadema has utilized the latest archaeological discoveries rather than drawing on some well-known classical piece. Furthermore, he has modelled his figure on a mass-produced genre subject, not a work specially admired for its artistic merit [17].

Fishing was one of a number of the artist's works bought by Baron Schröder [21]. RB

34
Exhausted maenides after the dance

S 162
c. 1873-74
oil on canvas (unfinished), 59.1 x 132 cm
Van Gogh Museum, Amsterdam

Exhibited Art Foundation, Rotterdam, May - June 1974

Alma-Tadema's first essay in the painting of the nude was planned at a large scale appropriate for an exhibition picture, but abandoned before completion, presumably in favour of *After the dance*, shown at the Royal Academy in 1876 (untraced: [135]). *After the dance* was almost identical to *Exhausted maenides* in dimensions, but omitted the two rear figures to concentrate on the single nude, corresponding to the most finished figure in the abandoned work.

By the early 1870s, the female nude was an important category in the practice of English painters of classical antiquity, following the examples of Frederic Leighton and George Frederic Watts in the previous decade. However, Alma-Tadema joined the English revival of the nude with a subject representing the aftermath of a Bacchanalian revel [21], a scene of abandon far more likely to raise critical eyebrows than the chaste classical goddesses favoured by the English painters of the nude at this date. The representation of the sleeping maenad with one arm over her head was derived from ancient art (see Hedreen, pp. 82-83), but Alma-Tadema reinterprets the motif, using a modern technique that makes the figure vividly 'life-like'. Indeed, the treatment of the flesh in the unfinished picture suggests a warm colouring and pliancy of texture very different from the cool, polished surfaces characteristic of artists such as Leighton or Albert Moore (see pp. 59-66).

34

The figure's pose, drapery, jewellery and fan all conform to Tanagra figurine types[143]; Alma-Tadema may have been drawing on the very latest archaeological discoveries. From 1870 terracotta statuettes were excavated in huge quantities from graves in Tanagra, a city of ancient Boeotia in central Greece. By 1873 they were widely available on the Athenian antiquities market and were soon included in many private and public British collections (see Higgins, pp. 29-31, 163). The statuettes are mostly brightly-coloured figures of standing women adorned with jewels and sometimes wearing hats and holding fans. The small size of this canvas and playful nature of the subject reflect the light-hearted character of the Tanagra finds. Other artists, such as Jean-Léon Gérôme and James McNeill Whistler later developed an interest in Tanagra figurines.

The unfinished picture is particularly interesting for the evidence it affords about Alma-Tadema's working methods. Clearly visible are the dark outlines of the underdrawing, bold strokes that appear to have been swiftly applied, and in some cases corrected on the spot. Broad areas of pigment have been applied to establish the basic value relationships over the entire picture, with the flesh tones of the figures balancing a dark fur rug under the figures, bands of deep red, and a brilliant silver accent in the centre foreground. The artist has begun to model the figures in detail, leaving the finishing of the background and accessories for later.

Alma-Tadema gave *Exhausted maenides* to his Dutch friend, Carel Vosmaer, a lawyer and writer (see p. 29) [45] [16]. Vosmaer was the author of the first catalogue raisonné of the artist's works, in manuscript form (1885), as well as a novel whose principal character was based on Alma-Tadema (*The amazon*, 1880). A contemporary photograph of Vosmaer's house in The Hague shows *Exhausted maenides* hanging above his writing desk (see *De verzameling van Mr. Carel Vosmaer*, p. 7). EP

35

The sculpture gallery

Opus CXXV, S 164
20 March 1874
oil on canvas, 223.4 x 171.5 cm
Hood Museum of Art, Dartmouth College, Hanover, New Hampshire

Exhibited Salon, Paris, 1874 (19); Royal Academy, London, 1875 (26)

The sculpture gallery and its companion, *The picture gallery* [36], were Alma-Tadema's most important public exhibition pictures at the crucial moment in his career when success was beginning to seem a certainty. Much the largest of his pictures (along with a related work [63-65]), they were exhibited in alternation at the two major public forums for the artist, the Salon in Paris and the Royal Academy in London. Although the two pictures were exhibited together several times during Alma-Tadema's lifetime, they are here reunited for the first time since the artist's memorial exhibition in 1913.

The two paintings are also the largest versions of their compositional types, used in two other pairs (S 89-90, 157 and 193); Alma-Tadema transfers a traditional theme of genre painting, connoisseurs in an art gallery, to magnificent settings in ancient Rome. The complementary subjects may be read as the artist's twin homages to the great ancient arts of sculpture and painting, or as glorifications of the activity of art collecting with an implied compliment to the artist's Victorian patrons; connoisseurship was a frequent theme in Alma-Tadema's early work (S 102, 108, 120).

However, Ruskin noted another implication, asserting that in *The sculpture gallery* the artist 'sees in the Rome he studies so profoundly, only a central establishment for the manufacture and sale of imitation-Greek articles of virtu' (vol. 14, p. 272). The commercialism that Ruskin saw as degrading the grandeur of antique art is precisely Alma-Tadema's point: the two pictures present ancient Roman connoisseurship as a matter of buying and selling. This reflects stereotypes about the Romans as an acquisitive rather than a creative nation, drawing on a major theme in the Elder Pliny's history of ancient art: Pliny repeatedly complained that his Roman contemporaries valued works of art for their costliness rather than their artistic merit (e.g., XXXIV.5; XXXV.50).

Accordingly, expensive luxury objects are displayed for sale alongside celebrated sculptures. The critic J.B. Atkinson easily recognized the so-called Seated Agrippina on the far right; the infant Hercules strangling the serpents, on the left edge [20]; and the bust of Pericles, partly obscured behind the Hercules (p. 404). All of these were well-known sculptures of which Alma-Tadema owned photographs (CXXXV, 11557; LXIX, 9563-64; LXXXII, 10025-26). However, the Hercules is not quite the statue of the Naples Museum; it has been transformed from bronze to marble. The case of the Pericles is more complicated: extant versions of the bust, such as that in the British Museum, are indeed in marble, but contemporary scholars agreed that these were copies of a lost Greek original, usually identified with a bronze bust by Cresilas, praised by Pliny (XXIV.74). Thus, the depicted marble bust is indeed 'imitation-Greek', a Roman copy of an important Greek original. This suggests that the Hercules, too, should be read as a marble copy of the bronze original.

The depiction of marbles, rather than bronzes, permitted a bravura display of relieving white against white – a traditional tour de force of the painter's art, and one highly appropriate to the picture's role as a spectacular exhibition piece. However, the representation of marble copies also elaborates the commercial theme: as Ruskin noted, the objects appear to have been manufactured for sale in this ancient emporium. The Roman practice of making copies was a major issue in contemporary research on ancient sculpture, as 19th-century scholars increasingly acknowledged that the vast majority of extant ancient sculptures were Roman copies, rather than the unique Greek originals accorded high status in classical literary texts (Haskell and Penny, p. 122).

Alongside the important classical sculptures – or their copies – Alma-Tadema introduces a variety of humbler artefacts, some of which were equally recognizable to contemporaries interested in classical archaeology. The foreground table imitates a type most familiar in an example from the house of Cornelius Rufus at Pompeii, although it is not an exact copy, as has sometimes been claimed [136]: indeed, the fact that it does not quite correspond suggests that it is deliberately presented as a common type of merchandise, rather than a particular example. On the table is a large silver bowl; like the table, this is an example of applied rather than fine art, but one of exceptional luxury, as Pliny's comments on the value of silver vessels indicate (XXXIII.154-157). Around the doorway is a sculptured relief, reminiscent of the famous cryptoportico of Eumachia at Pompeii: the emporium evidently supplies everything from large-scale architectural sculpture to household objects. In the farther room is a variety of bronze statuettes, candelabra, and hanging lamps: these are luxury objects analogous to those found in many Pompeian houses, here apparently mass-produced for sale. The partially obscured figures in the background room represent customers examining the wares, with attendants waiting on them.

The foreground figures are more important customers, contemplating more important objects – or perhaps, following Pliny, more expensive ones, which might explain the prominence of the silver bowl. Indeed, the composition does not establish a hierarchy between elevated works of fine art and luxury objects for household

136 *Marble table from the House of Gaius Cornelius Rufus, Pompeii*, photograph from Alma-Tadema's collection, University of Birmingham (CXIX, 11080)

use: the unique statue of the Seated Agrippina is upstaged by the table that reproduces a common Pompeian type. Moreover, the principal focus of the figures' attention is a tazza with a carved figure of the mythological sea-creature, Scylla, on its base: although it is based on an identifiable artefact from the Naples Museum, of which Alma-Tadema made a careful drawing (CXIX, E.2672), the tazza was of far lower art-historical status than the works of figurative sculpture, displaced to the sides of the composition. It nonetheless occupies the central position traditionally accorded to the highest-ranking human figure in a Roman history painting, and it is huge in scale: the figures pay attention to it as the figures in a history painting might attend to a general or Emperor. Although this picture is one of very few by Alma-Tadema that approach the grand dimensions of traditional history painting, it mocks the conventions of that genre, placing the central focus on a material object.

The complex series of plays on the status of individual artefacts is further complicated by their assemblage, juxtaposing works of divergent dates and origins. One chronological inconsistency was probably unintentional: since Alma-Tadema's time, the so-called Seated Agrippina has been reassigned to the early 4th century A.D., much later than the other artefacts (Haskell and Penny, no. 1). However, Alma-Tadema may have known of doubts about the antiquity of the infant Hercules,

thought by some contemporary scholars to be a Renaissance imitation. This sculpture is fancifully placed on an artefact quite unrelated to it, even if Alma-Tadema believed it to be a Roman original: a Greek column drum from the 4th century B.C., an object of high status from the Temple of Artemis at Ephesus, unearthed as recently as 1869 (British Museum). The chronological diversity makes a special point; as Atkinson noted, Alma-Tadema 'avoids startling anachronisms, by choosing some late period when palaces and baths had received accumulated spoils from distant lands and ages' (p. 402). The assemblage characterizes the Romans as a conquering nation, plundering subject peoples for their works of art.

The most 'startling' anachronism, though, involves the figures. As contemporary critics reported, they are portraits – of Alma-Tadema himself, seated on the left and extending his arm protectively toward his two daughters and his wife, Laura, with Laura's sister, Ellen Gosse (wife of the author Edmund Gosse) seated at the left; her brother, Dr. Washington Epps, is glimpsed at extreme left. Only the slave seems not to be a portrait of a 19th-century individual; he is the only one to represent an ancient racial and social stereotype, with the close-cropped hair of the Roman slave and 'Mediterranean' colouring. The metal plate, hanging around his neck, is an identity badge similar in function to the smaller badges worn by the slaves in *The dinner* [29].

It might be called audacious to present oneself and one's family as the figures in the grandest of classicizing exhibition pictures; this demonstrates the confidence of an artist who now felt assured of fame. However, the systematic anachronism of incorporating contemporary portraits also calls attention to the composite nature of Alma-Tadema's 'reconstructions': the depicted artefacts may be authentically ancient, but their selection and juxtaposition is the result of modern archaeology and the choices of the modern artist. This implication is often hinted in Alma-Tadema's pictures, but in *The sculpture gallery* the presence of the modern artist and his family makes it unusually explicit. EP

36

The picture gallery

Opus CXXVI, S 165
30 March 1874
oil on canvas, 219.7 x 166 cm
Towneley Hall Art Gallery & Museums, Burnley
Borough Council

Exhibited Royal Academy, London, 1874 (157); Salon, Paris, 1875 (13)

The picture gallery complements *The sculpture gallery* in its large format and its role at public exhibition [35]. It too includes portraits, this time of the art dealers of contemporary London and Paris, reinforcing the commercial theme of both pictures. Contemporary critics informed their readers that the standing male figure in the centre was a portrait of Ernest Gambart, the dealer who had funded Alma-Tadema's early career and was now reaping his reward as prices for the artist's work soared: perhaps in celebration. Gambart had commissioned both this picture and *The sculpture gallery* for his private collection. The other male figures can tentatively be identified as portraits of Henry Wallis and Charles Deschamps at the easel; P.J. Pilgeram and Léon Lefèvre, the successors to Gambart's London business, standing at the rear; and perhaps Paul Durand-Ruel, now most famous as the important early dealer for the French Impressionists, seated and cut off by the right edge (Swanson, p. 175; Maas, p. 242). All were close business associates of Gambart's; their collective power in the international art world was formidable. In *The sculpture gallery*, the odd figure out is the slave; here it is the woman, not a dealer, but benefitting from the instruction of the figure representing Gambart. Maas argues persuasively that the figure is a portrait of Gambart's mistress, Mme Angelée.

Even for spectators ignorant of the dealers' identities, there are signs that this scene, like *The sculpture gallery*, represents a commercial emporium rather than a connoisseur's gallery. As the critic J.B. Atkinson noted, 'the walls are hung like a modern picture-gallery, from the ceiling downwards, as if, in ancient as in present days, artists painted pot-boilers for the dealers' (p. 404). The walls are indeed densely hung, with paintings as diverse in status as the sculptures in the companion picture. However, *The picture gallery* approaches the issue of copy *versus* original from the opposite direction: instead of copies, some of the works on the walls appear to be the lost originals of ancient paintings, known to the modern world only through verbal descriptions in classical literary texts, or through copies unearthed at Pompeii. Again, the clue is a change of medium: two of the depicted works reproduce the compositions of mosaics found at Pompeii, but they are paintings. Since both Pompeian works were thought to be mosaic copies of original Greek paintings, the paintings that Alma-Tadema depicts appear to represent the lost originals.

One of these transpositions is the scene of a theatrical rehearsal, on the upper tier at extreme right; Alma-Tadema owned a photograph of the Pompeian mosaic (CLI, 12121), but represented it here as a painting. More challenging to the spectator's erudition is the large work dramatically cut off by the left edge. Although only a few inches are visible, it is identifiable from one telling detail, the points of two spears meeting at an angle in the top corner. This derives from the famous Pompeian mosaic of the *Battle of Issus*, but again the work represented by Alma-Tadema is a painting. After the mosaic was unearthed in 1831, it was widely agreed that it was a copy of an original Greek battle painting of fine quality, although there was lively debate about exactly which of the battle paintings, mentioned in classical texts, it copied (Pliny, ed. Jex-Blake, footnote, p. 134).

Whichever one it was, the original painting had perished, leaving only fragmentary evidence in the form of verbal descriptions and the mosaic copy; the drastic cropping of the painting, in Alma-Tadema's picture, may be a visual metaphor for this. The problem of non-survival is also hinted in the presentation of the picture on the foreground easel, the principal object of attention for the figures within the picture, but unseen by the spectator since its back is turned. In the two previous versions of the picture gallery composition, the picture on the easel was identified by lettering, on the reverse, as a monochrome by Apelles (S 90, 157). Apelles was invariably described as the greatest painter in classical texts on art, but all of his works perished before the end of the classical era. The invisibility of Apelles's picture, in the earlier versions of *The picture gallery*, served as a reminder that a crucial part of the history of ancient art is forever unrecoverable; although the specific reference to Apelles is omitted from this final version, the reversed picture nonetheless alludes to the general issue of non-survival.

Indeed, not one of the paintings, identified as great works in classical texts, survived into the modern world. This created a powerful incentive for archaeologists to identify the much later paintings and mosaics, unearthed at Pompeii and similar sites, as copies of the lost works, as happened with the *Battle of Issus*. Similarly, the painting at the left of the rear wall in *The picture gallery* reproduces a painting from Herculaneum thought to copy the figure of Medea in a picture by the Greek painter Timomachos (Pliny XXXV.26, 136).

Next to the right, on the lower tier, is a reproduction of a Pompeian work associated with the most exalted of all ancient paintings, the *Sacrifice of Iphigenia* by Timanthes. According to classical texts, Timanthes had represented Agamemnon at the sacrifice of his daughter, Iphigenia, with his face veiled, because his extreme grief was inexpressible in painting (Pliny XXXV.73): art theorists from antiquity onwards had avidly debated the merits of this device. The Pompeian painting representing the sacrifice of a female figure, with a veiled male figure on the left, was logically identified as a later copy of Timanthes's composition, but there was one worrying discrepancy: Pliny states that the figure of Iphigenia was represented standing up, but in the Pompeian picture she is in a prone position. Alma-Tadema faithfully reproduces the composition of the Pompeian copy, but he conceals the discrepancy with the intervening head of a figure. Thus, the spectator cannot tell whether the painting corresponds to Pliny's description of the original, or to the Pompeian copy. Moreover, Alma-Tadema's device exactly parallels that of Timanthes: where Timanthes had concealed Agamemnon's problematic facial expression with a veil, Alma-Tadema conceals the problematic section of the Pompeian painting with an intervening head.

The *Battle of Issus* and Timanthes's *Sacrifice of Iphigenia* were the highest in status among the pictures Alma-Tadema represents, but none of the figures looks at either. Instead, the two figures at the rear are intent upon a picture in a much lower category in the traditional hierarchy of genres: an animal picture. This recalls a picture of an ox by Pausias, praised by Pliny for its expert foreshortening (XXXV.126; the last four letters of

Pausias's name are just visible on the frame). Alma-Tadema reproduces Pausias's perspectival tour de force, showing the animal in a head-on view; however, it is not an ox but a lion, prompting one critic to call it 'a wonderful beast by the Landseer of the day' (*Spectator*, 9 May 1874, p. 597). The comparison may be apposite, suggesting that the reason for the two male figures' interest in the picture is its saleability; Landseer was one of the most commercially successful artists of the Victorian period. Pliny and Victorian art critics alike complained that works in lower pictorial genres, such as animal painting, were more popular with art collectors than grand historical works, like the *Battle of Issus*, or elevated subjects from mythology, like the *Sacrifice of Iphigenia*.

The gallery includes two Roman works, both in genres particularly associated with Roman art: the portrait of Nerva above the doorway and the picture in the middle of the upper tier, identified by lettering on the frame as the work of Marcus Ludius, one of the few Roman painters given prominence in classical texts on art. Indeed, Ludius was credited with the invention of the genre of decorative landscape or seascape, the only pictorial category considered to have been originated by the Romans, categorically stigmatized as an uncreative nation in 19th-century histories of art. However, the decorative landscape was treated, in Pliny as in 19th-centu-ry texts, as a low category in comparison with the historical and mythological subjects of the Greek painters (Pliny, XXXV.116-18).

This commercial gallery therefore includes works in all genres, high and low, crowded together in a fashion analogous to the juxtapositions in *The sculpture gallery* between works of fine and decorative art. However, the predominance of original Greek paintings also alludes to the Roman practice of plundering Greek cities, documented in Pliny and other ancient sources (e.g., Pliny, XXXV.24-26; Cicero, 'Against Verres', II.v.48). The Roman despoliation of Greek cities was a frequent theme in 19th-century histories of art and historical novels; Tony Robert-Fleury's enormous painting of plundering Romans, *The last day of Corinth*, had been a dramatic success at the Salon in 1870 (Musée d'Orsay, Paris).

The picture gallery and *The sculpture gallery* display every possible variation on the theme of the original *versus* the copy, showing Greek originals, Roman copies of Greek originals, Roman originals, and Roman copies of Roman originals. Moreover, each of the works is 'copied' again by Alma-Tadema himself, so that in some cases the modern spectator is witnessing a modern copy of an ancient copy of a still more ancient original. This widens the ramifications to include the question of the originality of Alma-Tadema's own 'reconstructions',

37

Autumn

Opus CXXVIII

1874

watercolour on paper, 24.8 x 58.5 cm

Board of Trustees of the National Museums & Galleries
on Merseyside

Walker Art Gallery, Liverpool

Exhibited Royal Society of Painters in Water-Colours,
London, 1874 (249)

37

an issue widely debated in contemporary criticism of his work, and related to broader 19th-century debates about the nature of artistic originality. The inclusion of figures, openly acknowledged to be portraits of 19th-century individuals, makes the contemporary relevance of the theme overt.

Alma-Tadema 'copies' each of his artefacts precisely: the picture's 'originality' is a matter, instead, of compositional juxtapositions and 'modern' technical skill. Contemporary critics of *The picture gallery* particularly admired the light effects. Although the artist's extensive reworkings have caused cracking and darkening in some areas, it is still possible to observe the tour de force of the light from the high window, illuminating Gambart's bald head and his hand, outstretched in a foreshortened gesture worthy of Pausias himself: the light shines also on the head of the figure modelled on Wallis, on his clasped hands glimpsed below the easel, and, in a final bravura touch, on his toes in their classical sandals. This is a painter's virtuoso performance, appropriate for this large-scale public statement destined for Europe's major exhibitions. Even in this display of 'modern' technical brilliance, though, there may be a reference to an ancient source. Vitruvius's frequent comments on the importance of lighting in picture galleries (I.ii.7; VI.iv.2; VI.vii.3). At every level, from subject-matter to details of technique, Alma-Tadema

This ambitious watercolour was exhibited at the Royal Society of Painters in Water-Colours (the 'Old Water-Colour Society') in 1874, following Alma-Tadema's election to that prestigious institution the previous year. Like cat. 32, the work is closely related to an earlier oil, *A halt* of 1872 (destroyed; S 143). More broadly, the composition belongs to a common type in Alma-Tadema's work, organized around an outdoor marble bench or *exedra* (cf. S 117, 140, 142, 273, 280, 304, 367, 403, 425). The inscription of the marble seat refers to the Emperor Hadrian, adopted son of Parthicus (Emperor Trajan), adopted son of the Emperor Nerva.

In contrast to the suburban Pompeian setting of *An exedra* [18], the watercolour's exedra appears in a wooded, rural setting, reflecting Alma-Tadema's new interest in landscape in the 1870s [42 48]. The autumnal theme permits delicate colour harmonies among creamy marble, silvery bark, and russet leaves, as well as suggesting a melancholic mood for the figures, lost in reverie as they sit, resting from their travels. The male figures on the exedra, two youths and an isolated older man, are counterpointed against the pair of lovers, half concealed behind a tree on the right: however, the absence of legible narrative interactions leaves the scene enigmatic, evoking a mood rather than spelling out a story (see p. 85). EP/RB

38

Bacchus and Silenus

c. 1874

watercolour and white gouache on paper,
15.4 x 35.7 cm

Koninklijk Museum voor Schone Kunsten, Antwerp

Exhibited Musées royaux des Beaux-Arts de Belgique,
Brussels, 1995 (84)

This drawing is identical in composition to *Bacchus and Silenus* (s 210), one of the ceiling decorations executed between 1871 and 1877 for Alma-Tadema's studio at Townshend House (see p. 47). The ceiling, damaged after Alma-Tadema's departure from the house and finally destroyed during the Second World War, had a complex allegorical programme centring on the elevated subject of Apollo, the sun god: perhaps this was intended to suggest the theme, appropriate for an artist's studio, of the sun as the origin of light, and therefore of the art of painting. The surrounding decorations featured mythological or allegorical figures emblematic of eternal verities, such as Honour, Fame, Life, Death (for the artist's description of the programme, see Swanson, p. 192). It was characteristic of the artist's sense of humour, as well as the personal exuberance noted by friends, to include among these high-flown allegories the scene of drunken revelry represent-ed in the drawing: a youthful Bacchus, sprawled in startling foreshortening (a traditional tour de force for ceiling decorations) and clutching a wineskin, while a corpulent Silenus drinks from a wine-bowl, spilling most of the contents; the partly nude bodies of both figures are notably unidealized. The inscription on the chunky wine vat, behind the youthful figure's head, is enigmatic, but perhaps refers to Nehalennia, goddess of prosperity and fertility: many altars, dedicated to Nehalennia, were found in Zeeland, a province in Holland near the Belgian border.

This drawing may have been among those sent to Carel Vosmaer (see p. 29) late in 1874, when Alma-Tadema was working on a new phase of the ceiling decorations after an explosion had caused considerable damage to Townshend House (see p. 47). EP/TM

39

A bacchante ('There he is!')

Opus CLII, S 187
11 June 1875
oil on mahogany panel, 26.7 x 19.6 cm
Board of Trustees of the National Museums & Galleries
on Merseyside
Sudley House, Liverpool

Exhibited Grosvenor Gallery, London, 1878 (25)

39

137 *Scene of seduction*, also known as *Alcibiades among the courtesans*, or *Apollo and the Graces*, marble relief (Museo Archeologico Nazionale, Naples), photograph from Alma-Tadema's collection, University of Birmingham (LXVIII, 9529)

The figure is adorned with the attributes of the bacchante, derived from representations on ancient vases and bas-reliefs, and invariably reproduced in Alma-Tadema's Bacchanalian scenes: the ivy wreath, thyrsus, and leopard or panther skin [21 46 72]: the artist always referred to the animal skin as that of a panther, a traditional attribute of Bacchus, but as in many ancient representations he gave it the spots of the leopard). Despite the attributes, Alma-Tadema insisted that the figure 'is not a bacchante but a young Roman lady' (Swanson, p. 183). This transfers the scene from the realm of mythology to that of Roman social history: the young woman is acting the role of a bacchante in the rites that the Roman authorities tried ineffectually to control [21]. When first exhibited at the Grosvenor Gallery in 1878, the picture was accompanied by a fragment of poetry by the artist's brother-in-law, Edmund Gosse:

> She hears the marble floor repeat
> A measured sound of leopards' feet,
> Nor hardly dares for sweet desire
> To give her wild heart time to beat.

This suggests that the woman is about to abandon herself to the excitement of a large Bacchanalian festival. In his study of the artist, published in 1886, Georg Ebers described the figure as 'watching for her lover who will clasp her in his arms, and inspired by the god whirl along in the throng of frantic revellers' (p. 71): he interpreted the exhausted nude bacchante in *After the dance* (135) as the same figure, in the aftermath of the revel [34]. Perhaps, then, Alma-Tadema's picture was one inspiration for the similar scene in Ebers's own novel of 1881, *The emperor*, where two young lovers are caught up in a Bacchanalian procession. Although the present picture was first exhibited as *A bacchante*, on its reappearance at Alma-Tadema's Grosvenor retrospective of 1882-83 it was retitled '*There he is!*', making explicit the suggestion mooted by Ebers, that the woman has glimpsed the lover with whom she will join the festivities. The retitling also reflects Alma-Tadema's increasing tendency, after the mid-1870s, to use anecdotal titles, closer to English titling practices than the simple descriptive titles he had used earlier in his career [41 56].

The composition catches the figure unawares, in the corner of a splendid marble interior decorated with relief sculpture – a sign, perhaps, that she is the daughter of a wealthy patrician family. In the top left corner is part of a bas-relief from the Naples Museum, of which Alma-Tadema owned a photograph [137]. Alma-Tadema may have expected his more learned spectators to recognize the original relief, sometimes called 'Apollo and the

Graces', but more plausibly identified as a scene of seduction, appropriate to the theme of Alma-Tadema's painting, a woman about to engage in revelry with her lover. The relief is cut off by the picture's left edge, so that the spectator sees only two nude female figures and two lyres, in piquant juxtaposition with the clothed figure and her Bacchanalian accessories.

The view through the window shows a fragment of a grand Corinthian order, indicating that the scene is set on an upper floor, but the spectator is left to imagine the Bacchanalian festival forming in the street below. Most enigmatic of all is the minuscule figure, perched atop the exterior building and glimpsed in the triangle formed by the window shade and jamb; this appears to be a male figure, but it is impossible to tell whether he is observing the woman. Although this is one of the artist's smallest and least pretentious pictures, it epitomizes certain aspects of his approach, presenting a glimpse of ancient life that is archaeologically and socially specific, yet not completely revealed to the modern observer. Moreover, the less respectable implications of the subject would have been accessible only to spectators familiar with the connotations of Bacchanalian rites and of the Naples bas-relief. EP

40

An audience at Agrippa's

Opus CLXI, S 197
30 October 1875
oil on panel, 90.8 x 62.8 cm
Dick Institute, Kilmarnock, Scotland

Exhibited Cercle Artistique, Brussels, November 1875;
Royal Academy, London, 1876 (249)

An audience at Agrippa's helped to confirm Alma-Tadema's growing London reputation. It was rapturously received by the critics who particularly praised the exquisitely painted expanse of marble. It is one of the first paintings to demonstrate the artist's use of a stunning marble setting, which was to characterize many of his later works. It was commissioned in London and sold to the Murrieta family (see pp. 92-95). A sequel, *After the audience*, was completed in 1879 [51] (see *Imagining Rome*, no. 52).

Marcus Vipsanius Agrippa, the powerful political ally and son-in-law of the Emperor Augustus, leaves an impressive atrium followed by a retinue of clients. A small group of petitioners wait at the entrance with a tray of gold and silver plate. Tableware and ornaments wrought in precious metals were especially valued in Roman society (Pliny, XXXIII.141; Persius, II.52) [35]. Georg Ebers interprets the scene as follows: 'a noble-looking man in the costume of an Oriental prince, who with his wife or daughter has come to ask a boon of the citizen before whom kings bowed. The daughter holds in her hand a costly golden vessel, either to offer it as a gift to their exalted patron or to pour a libation before him as if he were a god (an inscription in Mytilene calls him "god and preserver"). Their young companion is calling to the prince, – who is pondering over the words with which he is to touch the heart of the omnipotent Roman, – that Agrippa is coming, and in fact he appears on the staircase' (p. 74).

The palatial grandeur of blue-veined Carrara and green Cipollino marble confirms Agrippa's high status. Vitruvius, writing in the late Republic, confirms the necessity of a show of luxury in private dwellings belonging to men of rank and official importance (VI.V.1-2). In an article entitled 'Marbles: their ancient and modern application' Alma-Tadema discusses the extravagant marble buildings of Rome in the late Republic. He cites the example of Scarus, whose ostentatious atrium, according to Pliny, was supported by 38 ft high columns of black Lucullian marble (p. 174). In a reaction against such displays of wealth Augustus attempted to curb the lavish use of marble in domestic architecture and instead encouraged a public building programme. The scheme was so successful that the Roman historian, Suetonius, writes that Augustus 'could justly boast that he found [Rome] built of brick and left it in marble' ('Augustus' XXVIII). Agrippa was the most conspicuous financier of Augustus' rebuilding programme; his projects included a Pantheon, the Basilica of Neptune, the baths of Agrippa, and a host of aqueducts and sewers. Here the dome of the surviving Pantheon, at the time of the painting credited as Agrippa's building but later found to be Hadrianic, is glimpsed in the distance. Alma-Tadema perhaps hints at political hypocrisy as, despite Augustus' clear views on extravagant private dwellings, Agrippa's house (even

allowing for a reasonable show of wealth) is quite as spectacular as his public buildings.

Agrippa's costume and pose are reminiscent of standard Roman togatus statues while his distinctive features are modelled on surviving portraits. A marble bust is included amongst Alma-Tadema's photographs (CXXXIV, 11505). The figure of Agrippa appears diminutive compared with the huge statue of Augustus in the foreground. This statue, known as the *Prima Porta Augustus*, now in the Vatican, was discovered intact in 1863 at the villa of Livia, in Prima Porta outside Rome (the same statue appears in cat. 21). It is a copy of an original statue erected to celebrate Augustus' military victory over the Parthians in 20 B.C. Augustus is presented as a youthful military hero in contrast to the much older Agrippa who is preoccupied with civil matters. Despite Agrippa's lavish private setting and the allusion to his grand public buildings he is completely overshadowed by the statue of Augustus, reminding us that the real power in Rome is held only by the Emperor himself. RB

41

Between hope and fear

Opus CLXIII, S 204
6 September 1876
oil on canvas, 78.1 x 128.2 cm
An anonymous lady, Texas

Exhibited Royal Academy, London, 1877 (597)

The composition repeats elements of *The dinner* [29], but concentrates on the two figures of young woman and gray-bearded man. When the picture was first exhibited, at the Royal Academy in 1877, art critics readily interpreted the subject as a daughter asking her father's permission to marry. They were prompted by the title, among the first in Alma-Tadema's work to adopt the English practice of hinting at anecdotal content [39]; a comparable example is John Everett Millais's *Yes or No?* of 1871, showing a young woman deliberating over a proposal (Yale University Art Gallery, New Haven). The title's narrative hint helped

Between hope and fear to escape the accusations of hedonism levelled at *The dinner* and similar compositions of figures reclining to indulge in the pleasures of food and drink [11 29]. Indeed, critics moralized the Greek armour, seen in the left rear corner, as indicating the man's right to a life of ease and enjoyment in old age, after a career of military service (e.g., *Academy*, 2 June 1877, p. 495).

Critics paid less attention to the mural painting, on the rear wall where a mural had also appeared in *The dinner*. The mural in *Between hope and fear* also derives from a vase painting (drawing in Portfolio LXXXI, E.2231), but in this case it represents an ecstatic Dionysiac procession with dancing and music-making figures: a group of nude youths carry a large ritual phallus, traditionally associated with Dionysiac worship, on a litter. The motif is perfectly appropriate to the subject of a young woman who wishes to marry, and the practice of bearing the ritual phallus was acknowledged in standard Victorian sources on Dionysiac imagery, such as William Smith's *Dictionary of antiquities* (entry on 'Dionysia'): nonetheless, its introduction was daring for a Royal Academy picture, and it is scarcely surprising that art critics chose to ignore it. Moreover, the entire picture might be given a different reading by spectators conversant with the connotations of the Greek symposium, to which the composition unmistakably alludes: in the context of a symposium, the woman would be a courtesan, invited to offer her favours to the older man [11].

It is not impossible that the more risqué connotations of the picture contributed to its rejection by the patron to whom it was first offered, the Newcastle armaments manufacturer and art collector Sir William Armstrong. However, the stated reason was Armstrong's disappointment that the picture omitted the expanse of white marble characteristic of the artist's most recent works, such as the much admired *An audience at Agrippa's* [40] (see Swanson, p. 50). *Between hope and fear* is a late example of the sombre colouring and dim interior lighting typical of Alma-Tadema's 'Pompeian' phase, although the symposium composition, the wall painting, and other accessories clearly identify the setting as Greek. EP

42

94° in the shade

Opus CLXIV, S 205
7 September 1876
oil on canvas, mounted on mahogany panel,
35.5 x 21.6 cm
Lent by the Syndics of the Fitzwilliam Museum,
Cambridge

Exhibited Grosvenor Gallery, London, Winter 1882-83 (64)

The boy in the foreground is strongly characterized even though his face is not visible: his white clothes, catching the sunlight in a bravura demonstration of the painter's skill, indicate his gentle birth. His casual and abruptly foreshortened pose captures his absorption in a boyhood enthusiasm, as he reads a book on butterflies with his net before him. The butterfly theme hints at the transience of youth as well as the 19th-century fascination with natural science.

The golds and ochres of the colour scheme evoke the extreme heat of a summer day, while the perspective recession of the landscape conveys a sense of extensive space despite the picture's small dimensions. The agricultural landscape relates to studies of English hayfields made in 1875 (S 188, 192), at the beginning of a new interest in landscape [37]. The delicate handling of the foreground foliage and the hay in the background, with carefully judged tonal gradations to suggest atmosphere and space, indicates that the artist might have become a successful landscapist. Nonetheless, the scene is dominated by the figure, seen at large scale against the rapid perspective diminution, although he occupies barely the bottom quarter of the composition.

The picture can easily be read as a subject-picture about contemporary upper-middle-class boyhood, as well as a landscape, but it is also a portrait of the son of Alma-Tadema's friend and doctor, Sir Henry Thompson. Although there is no hint in the picture of the artist's usual preoccupation with the ancient world, there is a fortuitous *a posteriori* connection: the depicted boy, Herbert Thompson, grew up to become a distinguished Egyptologist. EP

43

A bath (An antique custom)

Opus CLXV, S 206

29 September 1876

oil on panel, 28 x 8 cm

Hamburger Kunsthalle, Hamburg

Exhibited Grosvenor Gallery, London, 1877 (32)

A bath was among the earliest of Alma-Tadema's Roman bath scenes to appear at public exhibition (cf. S 191, 214). It was shown in 1877 at the first exhibition of the Grosvenor Gallery, a new London exhibiting institution that quickly became associated with 'aestheticism' (see Newall). Artists participated in the Grosvenor exhibitions only by invitation of the proprietor, Sir Coutts Lindsay; the invitation indicates Alma-Tadema's reputation in the later 1870s as an artist of exceptional sophistication and indeed of progressive aims.

Although the nude was no longer a rarity in Victorian painting, since its revival from the late 1860s in the circle associated with Leighton, most exhibition nudes were presented in 'ideal' mythological contexts [34]. Alma-Tadema's socially specific representation of nudes in Roman baths may therefore have been daring: it was perhaps partly to offset this that his first bath scenes were tiny in scale. Alma-Tadema shows a fully-clothed balneatrix, one of the female slaves in attendance at the baths, carrying a tray laden with towels, and introduces archaeologically specific accessories such as the *strigil*, or scraping implement, held by the figure in the right foreground [140]. The phallic connotations of the strigil may also be implied: the artist's Bacchanalian pictures demonstrate his alertness to the sexual symbolism of ancient accessories. The fountain in the shape of a sphinx is probably imitated from a decorative detail on a piece of Roman furniture [21]. Alma-Tadema introduces a characteristic play on scale by blowing up the motif to the huge dimensions of the fountain. However, the sphinx had more complicated resonances; combining the forms of woman and beast, and associated with the story of Oedipus, its connotations of threatening female irrationality were explored by many artists of the later 19th century (see p. 87; Dijkstra, pp. 325-35). The prominence of the oversize sphinx in the all-female environment of the bath, with its middle-

ground group of gossiping figures, introduces a note that is at least bizarre, perhaps disturbing.

The composition as a whole, with its unexpected cut-offs and extreme vertical elongation, produces the sense of an illicit glimpse through a keyhole: the statue of a male figure clad in armour, high in the background, seems to be observing the scene from the rear, through a narrow vertical space between two columns. It was perhaps this picture in particular that prompted the critic Sidney Colvin, in his review of the Grosvenor exhibition, to object to the artist's 'trick of ... looking at nature ... as it were through some queer slit or out of some queer corner' (p. 825). EP

44

Portrait of Aimé-Jules Dalou with his wife and daughter

Opus CLXVI, S 207

4 November 1876

oil on canvas, 61 x 30 cm

Musée d'Orsay, Paris

Exhibited Grosvenor Gallery, London, Winter 1882-83 (113)

The portrait of the French sculptor Aimé-Jules Dalou (1838-1902) with his family was painted in gratitude for Dalou's terracotta portrait busts of Alma-Tadema (1873; accidentally destroyed in Alma-Tadema's house, c. 1905) and Laura Alma-Tadema (1874; Musée d'Orsay, Paris). Dalou lived in exile in England after his involvement in the events of the Commune in 1870-71, returning to France after the amnesty of 1879; although he practised monumental public sculpture later in his career, he was most famous for naturalistic genre subjects, often featuring mothers and children. Alma-Tadema's portrayal of Dalou in the context of a closely-knit nuclear family is therefore appropriate to the sculptor's professional reputation.

The portrait was purchased for the French national collection at the sale of the contents of Dalou's studio, after his death, as a 'precious document by a celebrated foreign painter on a great sculptor of France' (Bénédite, p. 131). The portrait's status, then, was seen to rest on the two male artists; nonetheless, it is Madame Dalou, née Irma Vuillier, who dominates the

painting in her role as the central figure of the bourgeois family. Both she and her daughter Georgette, aged nine at the time of the portrait, epitomize middle-class respectability, with sober clothes buttoned to the neck. The sculptor presides over his family by virtue of his compositional position, but his body is hidden behind the more substantial figure of his wife; his smoking cigarette, in the hand resting on his wife's shoulder, is the only hint of artistic 'bohemianism'. The compact composition, placing each figure behind the next, emphasizes family unity, while its simplicity marks the picture as a document to friendship, in contrast to contemporary conventions for society portraiture [66]. The absence of an elegant surrounding environment may also refer to Dalou's own unostentatious lifestyle, notable in an age of opulent studio houses such as Alma-Tadema's own (for the austerity of Dalou's house and studio, see Bénédite, p. 129). EP

45

Pleading

Opus CLXVII, S 208
November 1876
oil on canvas, mounted on mahogany panel,
21.5 x 35.5 cm
Guildhall Art Gallery, Corporation of London

Exhibited Grosvenor Gallery, London, Winter 1882-83 (125)

This picture is one of about two dozen scenes of courtship, executed in a steady stream throughout Alma-Tadema's career [12 73]. Generally unpretentious in scale, these works must have been a consistently saleable product for the artist; *Pleading* was purchased by Charles Gassiot, owner of a large collection of Victorian genre pictures and landscapes (Gassiot also owned cat. 16).

Courtship was a frequent theme in Victorian novels and genre paintings (see Casteras, Kern). The hopeful deference of the 'pleading' man, and the woman's apparent, or feigned, indecision, correspond rather to the rituals of Victorian middle-class life than to the mores of Roman patricians, whose marriages would ordinarily have been arranged. Indeed, Georg Ebers found it necessary to justify his depiction of ancient romantic love, attacked by critics of his first historical novel, *An Egyptian princess* of 1864. In the preface to the novel's second edition of 1868, Ebers argued that classical texts, such as Apuleius's story of Cupid and Psyche, Sappho's love poems, and Theocritus's *Idylls*, proved that the ancients did possess an ideal of romantic love.

Alma-Tadema and Ebers subsequently exchanged ideas for scenes of ancient courtship. An engraving of *Pleading* appeared as the frontispiece to a tale of courtship by Ebers, published in 1880 as *Eine Frage* ('A question'). In the final chapter, where the two young lovers are reunited, they assume the positions of the figures in Alma-Tadema's picture. There has been considerable debate about the relationship between novella and picture: Ebers's original inspiration, as he stated himself in his later study of Alma-Tadema's work (p. 86), was another picture with a similar composition (s 226). However, Ebers must have been looking closely at the engraving of *Pleading* when he wrote the last chapter of the novella: the male character is described as wearing sandals and covering his head with a cloak, details that match *Pleading* but not the other picture. In 1883, Alma-Tadema returned the compliment in a watercolour that illustrated the characters of Ebers's novella, *Xanthe and Phaon* (Walters Art Gallery, Baltimore).

The composition of *Pleading* features in yet another novel, *The amazon* by Alma-Tadema's Dutch friend, Carel Vosmaer (see p. 29) [34]. Here the hero, an artist based on Alma-Tadema himself, paints the woman he loves seated in the position of the female figure, with himself in the 'pleading' role of the man. These fictional repetitions indicate that contemporaries found the composition a particularly compelling evocation of romantic love [48 62]. The subservience of the man's pose presented courtship as reversing the usual power relations between the sexes; this added a poignancy that appealed strongly to 19th-century spectators. In pictures of this type, the male figure is ordinarily more 'Mediterranean' in colouring, while the female figure is an 'English rose', introducing a hint of racial difference that may also have intrigued contemporaries; Ebers's novella stresses Xanthe's golden hair, *versus* Phaon's dark colouring. EP

46

Autumn

Opus CLXXIII, S 213
3 April 1877
oil on canvas, 74.9 x 38 cm
Birmingham Museum & Art Gallery

Exhibited Royal Academy, London, 1877 (119)

A single bacchante dances in celebration of the year's vintage. She wears a leopard-skin and ivy wreath, traditional symbols of the cult of Bacchus, and included by Alma-Tadema in many of his Bacchanalian scenes [21 39]. Unlike the artist's other bacchantes, this figure imitates a particular classical prototype; her Greek-style drapery, falling in vertical sculpture-like ripples and grooves, and her leaping pose are based on dancing maenad relief figures. Dancing maenads are known from numerous Roman copies of a Greek original dating to the 5th century B.C. Alma-Tadema possessed a photograph of such a relief which decorates a Roman marble drinking cup (rhyton) from the Conservatori Museum, Rome [138]. In the late 19th century nine maenad types were identified as relating to the Greek original (see Touchette, p. 5). Alma-Tadema does not imitate an identified type but uses a general pose, drapery and figure-style, based on all the dancing maenads.

Set in a Roman wine cellar, this scene, like *The vintage festival* [21] is one of domestic ritual. Perhaps the viewer is allowed an intimate glimpse of a larger Bacchanalia being celebrated outside the boundaries of the canvas. The bacchante offers a libation of wine from a ram's head rhyton over a flaming brazier. A burnished bronze term of Bacchus oversees the proceedings. The amphora labelled 'Herculaneum' could relate to Pliny's identification of intoxicating wine from the region of Vesuvius while the lids of storage jars protruding from the sandy cellar floor conform to his description of wine being traditionally stored in the ground (*N.H.* XIV.22, XIV.133).

Autumn is one of a series of four paintings exhibited under the titles of the seasons. *Winter* (S 212) shows a poor family huddling round a brazier, *Summer* (S 214) a bath scene, and *Spring* (S 215) [82] young girls gathering flowers. All four paintings demonstrate appropriate colour harmonies; the red and gold hues in this painting are chosen to suit to the autumnal theme. The whole series was bought for the Murrieta collection (see pp. 92-95). *Winter* and *Summer* are now severely damaged and *Spring* was destroyed during Word War II making *Autumn* the only painting of the series to be preserved in its original condition. RB

138 *Marble rhyton, decorated with relief figures of maenads (detail)*, Roman (Museo dei Conservatori, Rome), photograph from Alma-Tadema's collection, University of Birmingham (XII, 8006)

47

A sculptor's model (Venus Esquilina)

Opus CLXXIX, S 219
2 August 1877
oil on canvas, 195.5 x 86 cm
private collection

Exhibited Königliche Kunstakademie, Berlin, June 1877;
Royal Academy, London, 1878 (255)

The second and larger of Alma-Tadema's two large-scale exhibition nudes [34], *A sculptor's model* draws on the archetypal theme of male artist and female model. Alma-Tadema's contemporaries often explored that theme through the myth of Pygmalion, as in the two versions of Edward Burne-Jones's *Pygmalion and the Image* (1868-70, private collection; 1878, Birmingham Museum & Art Gallery), and Jean-Léon Gérôme's *Pygmalion and Galatea* (c. 1890, The Metropolitan Museum of Art, New York). By contrast, Alma-Tadema abandons the mythological context to present a scene ostensibly from 'real' life. Although the sculptor's costume clearly indicated a classical setting, the *Athenaeum* critic saw the scene as 'a masterly life-size study of a nude female figure in a modern Roman studio' (4 May 1878, p. 577). The mistake is telling: the critic missed the distancing effect of a mythological pretext and could see only a 'life-like' nude.

This helps to explain why *A sculptor's model* proved more controversial than other classicizing English nudes of the period: the representation did not appear distanced enough to preempt debates about the status of the nude model in contemporary society. Moreover, some elements in the picture would have reminded 19th-century spectators of the contemporary life-drawing class: the wooden platform on which the model stands resembles those in contemporary use, and the palm branch on which she leans recalls the poles used in life-drawing classes, to help the model sustain the pose.

The debate over *A sculptor's model* was widely reported in the contemporary press (e.g., *Magazine of Art* (January 1879), p. xxxiii). In a private letter, the Bishop of Carlisle voiced one contemporary attitude: 'for a living artist to exhibit a life-size, life-like, almost photographic representation of a beautiful naked woman strikes my inartistic mind as somewhat, if not very, mischievous' (Stirling, p. 63) The Bishop's self-charac-

terization as 'inartistic' indicates the issues involved: this was one of a series of Victorian debates on the nude, polarized between those who advocated the representation of the nude as the epitome of 'High Art' and those who opposed it as a threat to public morality (see A. Smith). It was not only in Victorian England that the picture proved controversial: in Holland, Lodewijk van Deyssel took issue with Alma-Tadema's friend, Carel Vosmaer, for his praise of the work (Swanson, p. 196).

Alma-Tadema's composition does nothing to neutralize the implications of the subject-matter. Indeed, it develops the theme of male voyeurism: the spectator sees the nude from the front, while the sculptor sees her from the back, so that her body is available to the gaze from both sides. This may allude to ancient descriptions of the celebrated nude statue by Praxiteles, the Aphrodite of Cnidus, placed in an open shrine so that it could be seen from all directions (Pliny XXXVI.21). Moreover, the nude figure appears twice, once as a 'real' woman in the foreground, and again as the sculptor's marble creation, glimpsed behind the palm branch on which the 'real' model leans.

The repetition of the figure, in flesh and marble, also introduces another of Alma-Tadema's characteristic themes, twice 'copying' a particular ancient statue, unearthed on the Esquiline hill as recently as 1874 and accordingly dubbed the 'Venus Esquilina' (Capitoline Museum). Alma-Tadema had seen the work on his visit to Rome in 1875-76, and owned photographs of both front and back views (LXVII, 9499-9500). Although some hailed the Venus Esquilina as a fine Greek original, others claimed that it was an inferior Roman copy; as in *The sculpture gallery* and *The picture gallery* [35 36], Alma-Tadema introduces a play on 'copying' what may already be a copy. Moreover, the controversy over the Venus Esquilina may have influenced the reception of Alma-Tadema's modern repetition. In 1884 and 1885, Edward John Poynter exhibited two pictures of the female nude, both titled *Diadumenè* and based on the Venus Esquilina (Royal Albert Memorial Museum, Exeter; private collection); these nudes also proved controversial (see *Imagining Rome*, no. 56). EP

48

Roman gardens

Opus CLXXXIV, S 225
22 October 1877
oil on canvas, mounted on mahogany panel,
20.2 x 53.5 cm
Museum Mesdag, The Hague

Exhibited Levende Meesters, Groningen, 1880 (2)

In his opus list, Alma-Tadema describes this work as 'A Pannel [sic] for Mr. H.W. Mesdag's Studio door', but the painting was never used in this way (Pennock, p. 17). For unknown reasons Mesdag had it framed and send it to the exhibition in Groningen in 1880, where it received the title *Garden in a Florentine palace*. This title is also found in Vosmaer's manuscript (Rijksprentenkabinet, Amsterdam). The prominent fountain, however, is the Fontana dei Cavalli Marini, designed by Christofor Unterberger around 1790, and which is still in the park of the Villa Borghese in Rome (see *Empires restored*, p. 71). The same is true of the statue of Hercules in the background of the painting. The statue of Hermes with the young Dionysus is in the Vatican Museum.

Hendrik Willem Mesdag (1831-1915), was Alma-Tadema's cousin and a painter of the Hague School, well known for his seascapes and beach scenes. Like their mutual friend Carel Vosmaer, Mesdag was one of the circle of Dutch artists and connoisseurs who remained close friends of Alma-Tadema's throughout his life [34] (p. 29). The tiny figures on the background bench repeat in reverse the composition of *Pleading* [45] that was such a favourite among the artist's friends. Evidently, the composition came to serve almost as a badge of the friendships in the circle: Vosmaer, too, would refer to it in his novel, *The amazon*.

In Vosmaer's novel, the relevant scene takes place in the Borghese Gardens, where Alma-Tadema had sketched during his visit to Rome in the winter of 1875-76 (S 202). Although the location of the present scene has been queried (see Swanson, p. 199), the general aspect of the outdoor setting, with its classical statuary and seahorse fountain, clearly alludes to the Borghese Gardens. This setting, like the *Pleading* composition, appears to have had romantic or evocative associations for Alma-Tadema and his circle. The same setting appears as the background in two works of 1877, identified with the Borghese Gardens and featuring fore-

ground female figures plucking flowers (s 224 and the watercolour, *Flora*. Opus CLXXXVII, private collection).

However, in the present picture the figures take a subordinate role in what is essentially a landscape, a new interest of Alma-Tadema's in the later 1870s [42]. EP/LP

49

A hearty welcome

Opus CXC, S 236
15 February 1878
oil on canvas, 30.5 x 92.7 cm
Ashmolean Museum, Oxford

Exhibited Exposition Universelle, Paris, 1878 (8)

This domestic scene, set in the garden (*peristyle*) of a Roman villa, is one of the artist's last paintings which uses a Pompeian setting. The mother or eldest daughter, still in her travelling cloak, has just returned home. The whole family of two young girls, nurse and baby, paterfamilias descending from the house and even the family pet, are present to greet her. In *An audience at Agrippa's* [40] Alma-Tadema painted the atrium, the portion of the Roman house designed as a public showcase while here

he gives us a glimpse of the inner sanctum of a Roman dwelling. The warm colouring of the flowers and painted decoration in the enclosed garden are set against an imposing white marble structure of a public building outside the walls. A candle burns in the shrine to the household gods (*lararium*), the focal point of Roman family life. The hearth and home are common themes in paintings of Victorian domesticity.

The covered arbour is reminiscent of a similar structure in the garden of the villa of Diomedes at Pompeii. Painted walls and pillars evoke Pompeian-style wall decoration while the painted garland hanging between pillars imitates a painting from the House of Livia on the Palatine, Rome, which although not Pompeian is of a similar date (CXXIX, 11358). The fountain, decorated with a statuette of a cupid, tiled *lararium* and sundial on the garden wall are all similar to ancient artefacts included in Alma-Tadema's photographic collection.

Shafts of sunlight fall onto sunflowers growing against the garden wall, across the pillars, to a brilliant array of poppies. The spectacular colour of the flowers complements the brightly painted walls but some are anachronistic in this otherwise precise Pompeian setting [14]. The painting was commissioned by a friend of the artist's family, Sir Henry Thompson [85] [42]. RB

50

In the time of Constantine

Opus CXCII, S 238
6 March 1878
oil on mahogany panel, 32.2 x 16 cm
William Morris Gallery, Walthamstow

Exhibited Royal Academy, London, 1879 (627)

Unusual care is taken to indicate a precise historical context for the scene, not only in the title, but in visual allusions to the 4th-century Emperor: the inscription of his name, cut off on the right, and the fragmentary view of the Arch of Constantine, of which the distinctive sculptured roundels can just be glimpsed through the foliage. This establishes a contrast between the significant historical figure of the Emperor, celebrated equally for his military heroism and for proclaiming Christianity as Rome's official religion, and the utterly trivial incident represented in the picture, two male figures teaching a dog to 'sit up and beg'. The critic for the *Athenaeum* described the figures as 'senators' (17 May 1879, p. 637); although there is no overt indication of the figures' senatorial status, the critic evidently read the picture as involving a theme of political duty *versus* private leisure.

The setting makes nonsense of the map of ancient Rome, and seems designed instead to introduce as many recognizable monuments as possible, in a compact composition. A fragment of the Colosseum is sliced off at the right edge, while the dome of the Pantheon is glimpsed through the Arch of Constantine, beyond a view of what appears to be part of the Roman Forum, with the interpolation of a grandiose fountain that resembles those in Alma-Tadema's pictures of the Borghese Gardens [48]. The architecture therefore repeats the basic theme of the picture: the important public monuments are relegated to the background or cut off, to be upstaged by a marble bench of a common Roman type in the foreground.

Above the figures, and presiding over the scene, is a Roman marble copy of a famous statue, the *Spinario*, best known in a bronze version in the Capitoline Museum. This, too, elaborates the picture's theme about the contrast between public duty and private interests: in the 19th century, the statue was popularly believed to represent a boy who had carried an important message

to the Senate, without stopping to remove the thorn from his foot until he had fulfilled his duty (Haskell and Penny no. 78). In the middle ages the *Spinario* had been displayed on top of a column, so that its genitals could be seen from below, and were remarked upon by a 13th-century writer (ibid.): the elevated position of the statue suggests that Alma-Tadema was making a covert reference to this engaging anecdote, comprehensible only to his most erudite spectators. EP

51

After the audience

Opus CXCVI, S 244
2 January 1879
oil on panel, 91.4 x 66 cm
private collection (courtesy of Christie's, London)

Exhibited Royal Scottish Academy, Edinburgh, 1879 (332)

The sole example in Alma-Tadema's work of a picture expressly designed as a sequel to a previous work. *After the audience* is testimony to the growing fame, in the 1870s, of the artist's work in general, and of his rendering of marble in particular. The success of *An audience at Agrippa's* [40] at the Royal Academy in 1876 inspired Sir William Armstrong, the Newcastle armaments manufacturer, with an urgent desire to possess a similar work for his own art collection. Under pressure from the patron, the artist offered *Between hope and fear* [41], but the 'Pompeian' manner of that picture, typical of Alma-Tadema's work up to the early 1870s, failed to please in the autumn of 1876: Armstrong summarily rejected the picture. *After the audience* was the artist's witty retort, repeating the sumptuous marble setting of *An audience at Agrippa's* but reversing the figures of Agrippa and his attendants so that they are seen from the back. Armstrong did not appreciate the joke: *After the audience* was also rejected, and the Newcastle patron never acquired a work by Alma-Tadema (see Swanson, p. 50).

The anecdote provides an intriguing insight into the workings of the contemporary art market: Armstrong was evidently unwilling to accept a work in a manner he regarded as even slightly outdated, but insisted on possessing a picture in the artist's most recent style. Alma-Tadema was scarcely reluctant to satisfy the market with

variations on a popular compositional formula, as the numerous repetitions of the *Pleading* composition indicate [45 48 62]. Nonetheless, he chafed at the commercial pressures that encouraged commodification of his most recognizable motifs: 'I paint a bit of marble, and they always want marble; a blue sky, and they always want blue skies; Agrippa, and they always want Agrippas; an Oleander, and they want nothing but Oleanders. Bah! A man isn't a machine!' (Hind, p. 136). The wording suggests that the incident involving *After the audience* particularly rankled with the artist.

The picture itself registers a protest against such commercial constraints on the artist's freedom, not only through the impudent device of confronting the spectator with the figures' backs, but in more subtle ways as well. It was a well-established practice, in Victorian painting, to provide a sequel for a successful picture, as Abraham Solomon had done when he followed *Waiting for the verdict*, of 1857, with '*Not guilty*' two years later (Tate Gallery, London). However, Alma-Tadema's sequel breaks the unwritten rules observed in the Solomon pair and similar examples. *After the audience* refuses to resolve the narrative established in the earlier picture: the foreground group of petitioners has disappeared without trace, along with their costly gift, conspicuous by its absence from the expensive bribes strewn on the tiger rug in the sequel picture. The spectator is thus left in ignorance of the fate of the group: this was in abrupt contrast to the procedure of a Solomon, whose sequel unambiguously announced the resolution of the narrative with the title, '*Not guilty*'. Indeed, *After the audience* offers no definite evidence that the petitioners' gifts will lead to any tangible benefit for their causes, suggesting the arbitrary character of Roman Imperial power as well as disrupting the standard conventions of Victorian narrative painting.

Furthermore, the later picture teases the spectator's memory of its predecessor by altering numerous details. Although the setting is instantly recognizable as the same marble interior as that of *An audience at Agrippa's*, no part is identical with the previous picture: the undecorated roundel at top right has metamorphosed into an oblong bas-relief, the pilaster has acquired fluting, the upholstery on the bench, just behind the statue of Augustus, has changed colour, and there are similar alterations throughout the composition.

The *Prima Porta Augustus* might be expected to be exempt from this process of metamorphosis, since it is closely based on an extant Roman statue, but even here there are minute changes, notably the addition of a putto astride the dolphin that supports one leg. The putto is a feature of the Roman statue found at Prima Porta, so the second rendition is in fact more accurate than the first. However, the *Prima Porta Augustus* was itself understood to be a copy of an absent original [40]; once again, Alma-Tadema appears to be introducing a play on his favourite theme of original *versus* copy [35 36]. If the second version is closer to the extant statue, that merely means it is more like the copy: the absent original remains forever elusive, dispite the virtuoso realism of its painted reproduction, twice in succession. EP

52

Strigils and sponges

Opus CXCVII
1879
watercolour on paper (A), mounted with etching of same (B), 31.8 x 14 cm
The British Museum, London

Exhibited Society of Painters in Water-Colours, London, 1879 (241)

The frolicsome poses of the three female nudes create circling rhythms around the fantastic fountain, with its winged amorino tumbling upside-down in the coils of a dolphin's tail. The composition is the most playful variant of a favourite type of Alma-Tadema's at this period, presenting nude bathing figures in an elongated vertical format, as in *A bath* of 1876 [43]. The watercolour is still closer to an oil of 1878, *A safe confidant* (untraced; S 241), following the artist's standard procedure of repeating compositions in watercolour. Although the watercolour is slightly smaller, the variations to the earlier oil in fact expand the subject: the artist adds two figures to the oil's single female nude (corresponding to the figure on the left), and presents the entire fountain, cropped at the top in the earlier oil. The latter alteration makes the source for the fountain more recognizable; it is based on a marble group in the Naples Museum, transformed into bronze for the watercolour [35 72]. Alma-

Tadema makes the group more playful still: the amorino appears to be scrutinizing the gesture of the right figure, scraping her arm with a strigil, as the dolphin spurts water onto the back of the central nude. With characteristic attention to detail, Alma-Tadema paints minute bubbles where the jets of water splash into the pool; the nude legs and feet of the women are visible through the ripples. As in the artist's other scenes of Roman bathing [43 84], the baths appear a place more for luxury and revelry than utilitarian purposes of hygiene.

On the same mount is a trial proof for an etching of the watercolour, by the French engraver Paul Adolphe Rajon, a reminder that Alma-Tadema's pictures, like those of many 19th-century artists, were widely circulated as prints, accessible to many who could not afford the soaring prices of the original works. The marginal notes, in French, from Alma-Tadema to Rajon show how closely the artist supervised the preparation of prints after his works; he makes many minute suggestions for improvements, including delicate pencil sketches to illustrate his points [1]. Most of the suggestions relate to the difficulty of achieving clear relief for forms in the monochromatic linear medium of the etching (see p. 12); however, in his general comment at the bottom, Alma-Tadema declares himself pleased with Rajon's work. EP/RB

53

Prose

Opus CXCIX, S 246
11 March 1879
oil on panel, 35.5 x 24.2 cm
National Museum of Wales, Cardiff

Exhibited Royal Glasgow Institute, 1880 (516)

Prose and its companion *Poetry* [54] draw on one of Alma-Tadema's favourite themes: reading. In early pictures, the artist had presented the great writers of antiquity reading from their own works [5] (S 121): later works often featured figures with books or papyrus rolls [67 71] (S 286, 354, 421). The pictures play on the traditional authority of written classical texts, the classicism of 'words', *versus* Alma-Tadema's archaeologically based classicism of 'things' (see Sandys, p. 89). In the later pictures, anonymous figures read equally anonymous texts, which appear as archaeologically specific 'things' rather than the authoritative 'words' of authors celebrated in the classical literary tradition.

The two small pictures of 1879 contrast masculine and feminine kinds of reading. The male figure in *Prose* intently studies a papyrus roll, neatly wound on its wooden roller. Indeed, he has been industrious, having read and rewound most of the roll; the light shines through the final section, from a sunshiny exterior world to which the hooded figure is oblivious, absorbed as he

is in his task. The masculine sphere is further dramatized by the inclusion of the famous sculpture of *The wrestlers* (Haskell and Penny, no. 94), abruptly cut off at top left so that only the learned can recognize its disconnected limbs. More enigmatic is the Egyptian shabti figure, or funerary statuette in the shape of a mummy, on the ledge; perhaps this is intended as a *memento mori*, or perhaps it is simply meant to appear an appropriately masculine accessory, along with the chunky pot on the right, and in contrast to the more delicate accessories of *Poetry*. EP

54

Poetry

Opus CCIII, S 249
28 May 1879
oil on panel, 34.8 x 24.2 cm
National Museum of Wales, Cardiff

Exhibited Royal Glasgow Institute, 1880 (44)

Poetry is the dreamy province of the female figure; although she sits next to a box of papyrus rolls of a common ancient type, she ignores them to gaze through the window, in abrupt contrast to the concentration of the male figure in the companion picture, *Prose* [53]. The untidy folds of papyrus next to her make a similar antithesis to the male figure's carefully wound roll. Holding a plectrum in her right hand, she idly plucks the strings of a square-based cithara, an instrument of the lyre family, associated with the recitation of poetry (hence 'lyric poetry').

The theme of women reading was much more common in 19th-century painting than that of men reading: reading was a quiet pursuit associated with the domestic sphere rather than the man's sphere of action, and many unpretentious Victorian genre pictures presented single female figures reading, in a wide variety of historical and modern-life contexts (Flint). In a classicizing context, Albert Moore frequently painted pictures of Grecian maidens reading, such as *A reader* of 1877 (Manchester City Art Gallery). EP

55

Portrait of the singer George Henschel

Opus CCII, S 248
1879
oil on canvas, 48 x 34.2 cm
Van Gogh Museum, Amsterdam

Exhibited Grosvenor Gallery, London, 1879 (2)

In January 1877 Alma-Tadema went to The Hague for the wedding of the daughter of Hendrik Willem Mesdag. He met the talented Silesian baritone and conductor George Henschel there, and a lifelong friendship was born. The Tademas regularly visited Henschel's home in Scotland during brief holidays, while the singer often added lustre to the well-attended soirées in St. John's Wood with his music. He describes these evenings in his memoirs: '... in that uniquely beautiful studio, the most celebrated musicians of the day, players and singers, happening to be in town, could be heard giving of their best to a rare assembly of men and women prominent in all branches of science, literature, and the arts' (Henschel, p. 148).

In this portrait, Henschel is seated at the grand piano which Alma-Tadema had specially designed for himself by George Fox in 1878 (see pp. 48-49). The backrest of the piano-stool is decorated with the painter's monogram. The singer is portrayed from the side, with his head facing the audience. Since Henschel is depicted in the act of accompanying himself as he sings, it is not a formal portrait at all. Most attention is lavished on the head and the very carefully modelled hands, the parts of the body which produce the music, while the background is left somewhat undefined.

Alma-Tadema gave the painting to the singer in 1879. Ten years later Tadema coyly pointed out in a letter to Henschel that 'The price of a portrait like yours is £ 600, full length £ 800' (Swanson, p. 207). A comment of this kind is completely in harmony with his direct approach, as many of his contemporaries remarked.
TM/LP

56

'Not at home'

Opus CCX, S 255
28 September 1879
oil on panel, 40.5 x 31.2 cm
Walters Art Gallery, Baltimore

Exhibited Royal Academy, London, 1880 (195)

The subject parallels that of *Idyll: my sister is not there* by the French 'néo-Grec' painter, Jean-Louis Hamon, exhibited at the Salon in 1853 and subsequently famous through reproduction as an engraving [139] (see pp. 73-75). In Hamon's picture, as in Alma-Tadema's, the title indicates that the male suitor is being told that the object of his attentions is 'not there', but the spectator can see that the female figure is in fact present. The narrative twist is more specific than usual for Alma-Tadema, who ordinarily preferred to suggest rather than spelling out an anecdote [37 78]. The anecdotal specificity, in this case, suggests a deliberate reference to the famous picture by Hamon.

However, Hamon had represented a group of children, in a playful composition typical of 'néo-Grec' practice. Alma-Tadema changes the episode into one of courtship among young adults of marriageable age, comparable to his many other scenes of courtship. Alma-Tadema's scene is therefore less fanciful than Hamon's, although the courtship ritual it represents corresponds more closely to Victorian than to ancient customs, as in his other courtship pictures [45]. Hamon includes some archaeologically specific accessories, but his 'idyllic' Italianate setting is more generalized than Alma-

139 Jean-Louis Hamon, *Idyll; my sister is not there*, 1853, engraving

Tadema's interior scene of 26 years later. reflecting a general trend toward more minute specificity in archaeological detail. in the third quarter of the 19th century. as well as Alma-Tadema's personal enthusiasm for archaeological precision. The couch is reminiscent of a common ancient type. on which Alma-Tadema based the reproduction he later had made for his own studio [87]. but it is a particularly elaborate example. incorporating a sculptured figure of the infant Hercules strangling the serpents. EP

57

Pandora

Opus CCXXVIII
1881
watercolour on paper, 26 x 24.3 cm
(originally enclosed in an oval mount)
Royal Watercolour Society, London

Exhibited Royal Society of Painters in Water-Colours,
London, Winter 1881-82 (334)

Alma-Tadema's diploma work for the Old Water-Colour Society is unusual for the artist. in both its oval format and its mythological subject. The beautiful Pandora. who disobeyed a divine command by opening her box to release all evils into the world. became an archetypal *femme fatale* in the later 19th century (see Dijkstra. pp. 364. 366); the subject was frequently painted. including versions by Dante Gabriel Rossetti (1871. private collection) and John William Waterhouse (1896. private collection). Alma-Tadema's Pandora exchanges an intense stare with the sculptured sphinx on the box. The sphinx is a fanciful invention. but appropriate to contemporary interpretations of the Pandora myth. stressing dangerous female irrationality (see p. 87) [43]. The corners of the square sheet of paper were intended to be concealed by the oval mount: Alma-Tadema used the space to experiment with the colours as he worked on the picture. EP/RB

58

Tepidarium

Opus CCXXIX, S 269
2 August 1881
oil on panel, 24.2 x 33 cm
Board of Trustees of the National Museums & Galleries
on Merseyside
Lady Lever Art Gallery, Port Sunlight

Exhibited Galerie Georges Petit, Paris, 1882 (82)

58

The few nudes painted by Alma-Tadema were not large mythological scenes, of the sort usually exhibited on the Academy walls, but studies of 'real' Roman women. Archaeological reconstructions of actual baths sanctioned nudity and informed the viewer of the environment and social customs of the ancient Romans. Even though no elaborate reconstruction distracts the viewer's gaze from this nude the small dimensions of the canvas diminish what would be an overwhelming eroticism if she were a life-size figure.

Bathing was considered one of the great pleasures of Roman life. The line 'baths, wine and women' (*balnea, vina, Venus*) is a set phrase used in numerous Roman verse inscriptions (Griffin, p. 88). The Roman attitude to bathing conveyed through this sentiment as one of enjoyment and eroticism is nowhere more vividly revealed by Alma-Tadema than in this painting. A woman reclines beside the luke-warm bath (*tepidarium*). Her flushed face and exhausted attitude would be more suited to the hot bath (*caldarium*). So great is her lassitude that the ostrich feather fan almost slips from her hand. She holds a bronze scraping instrument (*strigil*) in the other hand. Strigils, found in large numbers at the baths of Pompeii [140], were applied by slaves to scrape oil off the body and were used mainly by men after exercise. Here it is the one archaeological artefact which confirms an ancient setting as well as being an explicitly phallic image.

Each detail of this tiny picture is exquisitely painted. The ruffled hair of the animal skin contrasts with the smooth marble, soft flesh, and silk pillow. The pale tones of both skin and marble are relieved by the bright azalea and rosy flush of the woman's face. Although *Tepidarium* is not reminiscent of any surviving piece of ancient art its small size and erotic nature

140 *Bronze decorated strigil*, photograph from Alma-Tadema's collection, University of Birmingham (XII, 8037)

recalls Pliny's reference to the acclaimed Greek painter Parrhasius who, as well as large ambitious pictures, 'also painted small pictures of licentious subjects, seeking relaxation in this wanton humour' (XXXV.72: trans. Jex-Blake). RB

59

The way to the temple

Opus CCXXXIX, S 277
19 April 1882
oil on canvas, 101.5 x 53.5 cm
Royal Academy of Arts, London

Exhibited Royal Academy, London, 1883 (296)

For his 'diploma picture', submitted to the Royal Academy following his election as a full Royal Academician, Alma-Tadema chose a setting in ancient Greece, higher in status, according to contemporary notions, than his more familiar settings in the Roman 'decadence'. However, the picture does not idealize ancient Greek art or religion: the foreground figure is selling mass-produced votive images, one of which she displays in the palm of her hand, with other accessories of pagan worship beside her. As usual, Alma-Tadema's use of archaeological evidence is scrupulous: vast numbers of votive statuettes were being unearthed in excavations of Greek temples (Murray, p. 6). The manufacture

and sale of votive images in antiquity was a theme explored in other paintings, such as Edwin Long's *The gods and their makers*, in an Egyptian setting, of 1878 (Towneley Hall Art Gallery & Museums, Burnley Borough Council), and historical novels such as John Henry Newman's *Callista* of 1856. The trade in votive images was presented as an activity for women in these works as in Alma-Tadema's painting, recalling Alma-Tadema's depiction of a woman employed in another of the applied arts, *Pottery painting* [25].

The theme of the image-seller combines religious idolatry with commercialism, drawing on archaeological evidence in antithesis to traditional conceptions of ancient Greek culture as rational and idealistic. As in *Phidias showing the frieze of the Parthenon to his friends* [13], the vivid polychromy transforms the traditional notion of Doric gravity into exotic colour, while the complicated spatial organization rejects the simplicity usually attributed to Greek architecture: the architectural fragments hint at a vast temple complex lying beyond the borders of the scene. The angle of view makes the massive polychromed entablature jut dramatically into nothingness: through the open doorway a fragment of an ecstatic Dionysiac procession is glimpsed. Although Alma-Tadema had often represented Roman Bacchanalia [21 46], this was his first excursion into the older Greek rituals associated with Dionysus [68]. The red-figure vase implies a date no earlier than about 530 B.C.: nonetheless, there are hints in the architecture, as well as the religious ritual, of the survival of more primitive religious forms. Dimly visible behind the figure is a metalwork relief representing a winged Artemis with lions, similar to small decorative plaques, such as an example in the British Museum from c. 625 B.C. However, the motif is drastically enlarged in scale to become an architectural relief.

For his diploma work, Alma-Tadema had at first planned a larger picture, nearly two metres wide, representing the male priests of Apollo on the Acropolis (Swanson, p. 55). Abandoning this ambitious scheme, the artist nonetheless retained the general theme of Greek religion. It would be fascinating to know whether Alma-Tadema planned to present the male priests engaging in a more rational or 'civilized' form of religious ritual than this scene of feminine idolatry and Dionysiac ecstasy. EP

60

Portrait of Anna Alma-Tadema

Opus CCXLVIII, S 285
8 February 1883
oil on canvas, 112 x 76.2 cm
Royal Academy of Arts, London

Exhibited Royal Scottish Academy, Edinburgh, 1883 (401)

This portrait of Alma-Tadema's younger daughter at the age of 15 was one of many portraits of members of the artist's family [31]; in this case, though, the picture may not have been merely a private document. Exhibited repeatedly between 1883 and the artist's death, it served as a demonstration of the artist's skill as a portraitist, an increasingly important category in English painting in the later 19th century. The subtle colours are in the silvery and grayish greens that were particularly fashionable among patrons with 'aesthetic' tastes in this period; the unpretentious necklace of gleaming seashells, more appropriate than expensive jewellery for a portrait of a teenaged girl, adds a delicate coppery hue to the colour harmony. Anna's unstructured dress, with its sash, rippling folds, and soft ruffles at neck and sleeves, also reflects 'aestheticizing' fashions, and is particularly reminiscent of the contemporary book illustrations of Walter Crane (information from Charlotte Gere). The setting is Townshend House, where the Alma-Tadema family lived until 1885; the green wooden door, with ebonized decorations and oval painted panels representing the artist and his wife, was in the entrance passage (see p. 49). EP

61

A street altar

Opus CCLVI

1883

watercolour on paper, 34.7 x 17.3 cm

Trustees of the Cecil Higgins Art Gallery, Bedford

Exhibited Royal Society of Painters in Water-Colours, London, 1884 (247)

Domestic or popular religious customs appear frequently in Alma-Tadema's watercolours, in contrast to the large-scale religious festivals in a number of his important oil paintings [21 59 72]. Although a few oils presented quotidian religious rites [46], the theme was particularly suitable for the small scale and spontaneity associated with the watercolour medium. In this example, a female figure fixes a garland of roses on a humble street-corner shrine, decorated with rustic painting, while a male flute-player is glimpsed around the corner. The offering of roses recalls the earlier watercolour, *A votive offering* [32], but in contrast to the sombre mood and autumnal setting of the earlier picture, ancient popular religion here appears joyful and carefree. The narrow glimpse of the sunny street on the left, with its brightly polychromed buildings, produces the sense of encountering the scene by chance; the female figure looks around as if she has just been interrupted in her task, again emphasizing the informality of the scene. EP

62

A declaration

Opus CCLVIII
1883
watercolour on paper, 21.5 x 46.1 cm
The British Museum, London

Exhibited Royal Society of Painters in Water-Colours,
London, Winter 1883-84 (349)

A declaration is one of a number of variations on the courtship composition established in the oil. *Pleading* of 1876 [45]. The compositional type was a favourite among the artist's friends [48]. but the repetitions indicate that it also appealed to art collectors (cf. S 413): indeed. courtship compositions with a male figure gazing at a female who averts her glance were highly popular in 19th-century painting (see Kern).

Whether in oil or watercolour. Alma-Tadema's variants preserve the basic characteristics of the saleable type: the chivalrous deference of the male figure counterpointed with the female figure's shy submissiveness. and the setting on a marble bench or exedra with a glimpse of the sea behind. Predictability was important to the category's saleability. but each picture also has unique features. *A declaration* might be considered a watercolour repetition of the oil of 1881. *Amo te ama me* (S 273: the title derives from Vosmaer's novel. *The amazon* [45]). Nonetheless. there are subtle changes: the

claw-footed armrest is more extravagant in the watercolour. and the man's glance has been altered to suggest that he is looking beseechingly at the woman. The hooded traveller's cloak and heavy sandals. in both works. suggest that the man has come some distance to make his 'declaration'. but otherwise the narrative remains vague: as in other compositions of this type. the romantic mood is enhanced by the viewer's uncertainty about what the woman's response will be. The watercolour also uses the characteristic distinction between fair woman and darker man [12]: indeed. the woman's brilliant red hair introduces a startling accent into a colour scheme based on delicate shades of white. blue. and lilac. EP/RB

63-65

Hadrian in England: visiting a Romano-British pottery

Opus CCLXI, S 295
April 1884
oil on canvas, original dimensions approx. 220 x 167 cm

Exhibited Royal Academy, London, 1884 (245)

Cats. 63-65 are parts of what was originally one large picture. exhibited at the Royal Academy in 1884 as *Hadrian in England: visiting a Romano-British pottery* [141]: the artist subsequently cut the picture into three

141   *Hadrian in England: visiting a Romano-British pottery,*
       1884, engraving

pieces. Swanson states that the picture was cut apart after August 1886 (p. 223). However, the picture must have been intact at the time of its exhibition at the Glasgow Institute of the Fine Arts in the winter of 1890-91, and it may also have been the whole picture that was exhibited at the New Gallery's autumn exhibition in 1892. The precise date of the dismemberment is therefore uncertain, but the present exhibition is probably the first occasion on which the three pieces have been reunited.

The dimensions of the original picture, about 220 by 167 cm, matched those of *The sculpture gallery* and *The picture gallery* [35 36]. Moreover, the subject is complementary, adding a third ancient art form, pottery, to the previous two. The later picture continues the commercial theme, showing a factory for the production of pottery, with the wares displayed for sale on the upper level. In this case there is a particularly overt clue to the message; the inscription on the wall, just to the left of the staircase, reads *'Salve Lucri'* ('Hail to Gain').

As early as 1871, Alma-Tadema had painted a small picture of the commercial production of vases, set in the Greek colonies of Southern Italy [25]. However,

142 Joe Parkin Mayall, *Alma-Tadema in his studio at Townshend House*, c. 1883, photograph, private collection (courtesy Bob Haboldt, Paris)

pottery was not a luxury product in the Rome of the Empire, nor did the Romans covet Greek pottery as they did Greek paintings and sculpture. It was not, then, until the early 1880s that Alma-Tadema conceived the idea of using a provincial setting to expand the picture and sculpture gallery pair into a trilogy; he would no doubt have noticed examples of Romano-British pottery on his visits to English museums.

The immediate cue for *Hadrian in England*, though, seems to have been Georg Ebers's novel of 1881, *The emperor*, which stresses Hadrian's support for the local industries of the provinces. Ebers had described Hadrian's visit to a papyrus factory in Alexandria; shortly afterwards, Alma-Tadema devised the parallel scene of Hadrian visiting a pottery factory, presumably on his documented trip to Britain in about 121 A.D. The result was Alma-Tadema's only picture set in Roman Britain, a setting used occasionally by English painters (see Smiles).

The composition of the original picture was one of the artist's most audacious. A contemporary photograph of the artist in his studio shows the painting in progress, with elaborate chalk markings indicating Alma-Tadema's care in planning the organization (Blotkamp, p. 51) [142]. As exhibited in 1884 [141], the composition juxtaposes a view up to the Emperor's party with one down into the lower room where workmen ply their wheels. The disjuncture between the spaces establishes a social hierarchy with the higher-ranking figures at the top and the working men below. However, this orderly hierarchy is disrupted by the two foreground working men: although their presence on the staircase is explained by their action, carrying trays of pottery, their placement gives them a compositional prominence that is quite inappropriate to their low rank, according to the conventions of traditional art theory. Indeed, the half-nude figure on the right, seen from the back, dramatically upstages the Emperor himself. The anecdote that the Queen of Holland objected to this figure may be apocryphal (Swanson, p. 224), but the fact that it has gained wide currency is telling: there is a certain logic to the notion of a Queen objecting to a figure of a working man who upstages an Emperor. Indeed, the reversal of the hierarchy between Emperor and working man is perhaps the clearest example in Alma-Tadema's work of a compositional device that can be given a political reading. Contemporary critics did not raise this issue explicitly, but the many complaints about the incoherence of the composition suggest some underlying unease with the political or social implications of the compositional juxtapositions. EP

63

The Roman potters in Britain

section A of Opus CCLXI, S 296
April 1884, cut and repainted, probably after 1890
oil on canvas, 76.2 x 119.4 cm
Royal Collections, The Hague
By gracious permission of H.R.H. Princess Juliana of the Netherlands

This section isolates the pottery workers, stripped to the waist to work at the wheels. Despite the ancient setting, the row of potters at work makes a compelling image of industrial labour. The spectator looks down at the workers, made minuscule by the perspective recession: the hanging lamp on the arch appears as large as the heads of the workers. The plays on scale and the unconventional angle of vision are compositional tricks typical of Alma-Tadema's work, but they also emphasize the low social status of these anonymous working men.

In the foreground is a drastically cropped figure carrying a tray of pottery on his head. In preparation for *Hadrian in England*, Alma-Tadema made a systematic

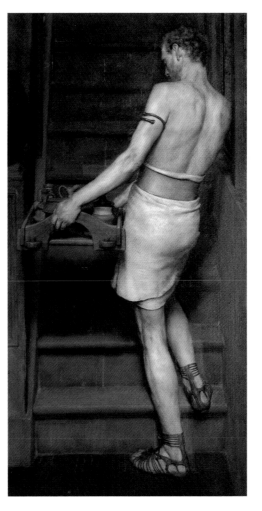

study of Romano-British pottery; as usual, he collected photographs, also employing a draughtsman, J.J. Gaul, to make drawings of Romano-British pots in English collections (Portfolio CXXXVIII). The photographs and drawings include a wide range of types, but the artist selected a much narrower group for inclusion in the picture, omitting the many pots with representations of armed men and violent hunting scenes, and instead favouring more elegant depictions of animals and spiralling decorations. This is typical of the artist's use of his photograph collection: although he amassed photographs of every kind of artefact he could find, he included only a small proportion in his pictures. In this case the result is to present Romano-British pottery as more elegant and refined, according to 19th-century tastes, than it might otherwise have appeared. The juxtaposition of the working men with their products indicates that they are highly skilled labourers. EP

64

Hadrian visiting a Romano-British pottery

section B of Opus CCLXI, S 297
April 1884, cut and repainted, probably after 1890
oil on canvas, 159 x 171 cm
Van Gogh Museum, Amsterdam (on loan from the Stedelijk Museum, Amsterdam)

This section isolates the highest-ranking figures, drawn from the cast of characters of Ebers's novel, with the addition of the proprietor of the pottery on the right and his wife in the group of women on the left. Although the world of labour in cat. 63 is exclusively masculine, the patrician group includes separate spheres for men and women. Conversing with the proprietor of the pottery, the emperor wears his famous beard, a Hellenic fashion introduced by Hadrian in contrast to the clean-shaven faces of previous Roman Emperors; brandishing a papyrus roll, he appears in the character of a Greek philosopher or orator. The Empress Sabina and her companion, the patrician female poet Balbilla, also sport the latest fashion, the elaborate construction of curls at the front of the head [19]. Alma-Tadema's characterization of the Imperial party is not unsympathetic, presenting them as

genuinely interested in the local industry they are inspecting. This corresponds to Ebers's characterization of Hadrian, drawing on evidence in classical sources, of Hadrian's interest in the local communities and activities of the Roman provinces. 19th-century writers also celebrated Hadrian's activities as a patron of the fine arts (e.g., Robinson). EP

65

A Romano-British potter

section C of Opus CCLXI, S 298
April 1884, cut and repainted, probably after 1890
oil on canvas, 152.5 x 80 cm
Musée d'Orsay, Paris

The final section isolates the single figure of the working man ascending the stairs. If this figure had seemed to usurp the attention due to higher-ranking figures, in the original composition, it was not only because of his prominent placement, but also because of the virtuoso painting of the figure, whose action appears strikingly 'life-like' in comparison with the rather stiff gesture of Hadrian. Although the figure's back is turned, he is strongly characterized, his averted head indicating absorption in his task, his body suggesting a man who is tall and fit. The figure has ordinarily been identified as a slave, and it is possible that the bracelet on his upper arm is intended as an identity badge analogous to the badges worn by slaves in other pictures [29 35]. However, his hair is not closely cropped in the manner characteristic of a Roman slave, and the bracelet resembles many articles of Celtic jewellery found in excavations in Britain; he may therefore be intended to represent a freeborn Briton. Some critics of the original picture, in 1884, described the figure as a slave; others identified him simply as a working man.

Alma-Tadema never sold this section of *Hadrian in England*. Perhaps he was reluctant to place it on the market, since it had been the most controversial section; alternatively, he may have wished to keep it for himself, since it is one of his most successful paintings of the human figure. He apparently thought highly of the painting, eventually donating it to the Musée du Luxembourg to represent his work in the French national collection. EP

66

Portrait of Alice Lewis

Opus CCLXII, S 299

May 1884

oil on canvas, 83.7 x 56 cm

Zanesville Art Center, Zanesville, Ohio

Exhibited Grosvenor Gallery, London, 1884 (15)

Portraiture was an increasingly important category in English painting from the 1870s onward, as the art market shifted away from the earlier Victorian fascination for the subject picture: like most of his English contemporaries, Alma-Tadema painted more portraits after about 1880. The elegance of his characterization of Alice Lewis suggests that he could have built a career as a society portraitist, as successful as contemporaries such

as John Everett Millais and John Singer Sargent. The pose flatters the sitter's slenderness, and the background drapery, as well as her dress, introduce opulent textures worthy of Sargent himself, just beginning his English exhibiting career at this date. The sitter is seen, not in her own everyday environment, but in a sumptuous fantasy world created for the portrait. The background drapery, described by one contemporary as 'a gorgeous Chinese silk curtain' (Meynell, p. 187), hung in the Gold Room at Townshend House, where there were also chairs similar to the one depicted here (ibid., p. 188) [31]. Alma-Tadema formed a large collection of antique textiles, some of which were used to furnish the interiors of his houses (see pp. 45-56); they were also available as exotic accessories for pictures, particularly suitable for creating the opulent environment appropriate for society portraiture.

However, the continuing saleability of Alma-Tadema's scenes of classical antiquity made a large portrait practice unnecessary; most of his portraits continued to be of friends and associates. Alice Lewis was the daughter of Sir George Lewis, the solicitor who acted for many artists, including Alma-Tadema as well as a far more litigious client, James McNeill Whistler. EP

67

A reading from Homer

Opus CCLXVII, S 305
April 1885
oil on canvas, 91.4 x 183.8 cm
Philadelphia Museum of Art
(The George W. Elkins Collection)

Exhibited Royal Academy, London, 1885 (276)

The composition recalls *Sappho* of 1881 [98], but here the poet is not present. Although Homer's name appears in a cropped inscription in the top right corner, his poet-

ry is read aloud by an anonymous male figure, seated on the right where the poet Alcaeus had appeared in *Sappho*; the reader's chair derives from the same source as in the previous picture, the Theatre of Dionysus in Athens (for Alma-Tadema's photographs of the Theatre (Portfolio LXXV), see Tomlinson, nos. 51-60).

Since the *Prolegomena ad Homerum* of 1795, by the German classicist F.A. Wolf, the question of Homer's historical existence had been one of the most contentious issues in classical scholarship, analogous to the debate about polychromy in sculpture [13]. On one side was philological and historical evidence that the Homeric epics were too diverse to have been composed by a single individual, on the other was the authoritative tradition of Homer's authorship of the *Iliad* and *Odyssey*. The debate was by no means exhausted in Alma-Tadema's period, when writers in favour of Homer's individual authorship included the statesman, William Ewart Gladstone (see Turner, Chapter 4). The non-appearance of Homer in Alma-Tadema's picture may be a witty contribution to this debate; Alma-Tadema's stance on other issues in classical scholarship suggests that he was likely to favour the anti-traditional notion of collective authorship.

Alma-Tadema was fond of subjects involving reading [5 53 54 71], but the theme has special resonances in the context of the Homeric controversy, in which one focus was the question of when the epics had been recorded in written form. Here the reader dramatically unfurls a papyrus roll, while the cithara that might have accompanied an oral recitation lies silent on the ground; the implication would seem to be that the scene occurs at a late period, after the epics had been committed to writing. The variety of costumes and poses among the listening figures suggests the universal appeal of Homer's poetry; the elegantly dressed figure, half cut off at the left edge, contrasts sharply with the figure in rustic goat skins. The critic Claude Phillips complained that the facial types were 'of a low order', inappropriate to the dignity of the subject (*Academy*, 9 May 1885, p. 336). However, this suggests Alma-Tadema's sympathy with one 19th-century view of Homer, as a popular rather than an elitist poet; as one writer put it, Homer was a 'minstrel, who addressed his narrative songs to the ear of the masses for their amusement – not a ... modern poetic man of genius, who addresses his epos to the cultivated understanding and the polished taste of the reading public, or, it may be, only a small fraction of that public' (Blackie, p. 272).

Alma-Tadema may have wished his own 'epics' to reach a broad public, and indeed *A reading from Homer* was widely disseminated in the form of independent engravings as well as reproductions in school texts and other books. However, the prices the artist could command meant that his original paintings were available only to the wealthy few. Beginning in the early 1880s, many of Alma-Tadema's important pictures went to American collectors, reflecting the increasing importance of American money on the international art market, as well as the popularity of Alma-Tadema's works in America [79]. The purchaser of *A reading from Homer* was the New York banker Henry G. Marquand, as usual through a dealer, Gambart's nephew Charles Deschamps. Marquand also employed Alma-Tadema, along with Frederic Leighton, in the design of the music room in his New York mansion, where *A reading from Homer* hung (see pp. 49-51) [33]. EP

68

The women of Amphissa

Opus CCLXXVIII, S 317
April 1887
oil on canvas, 121.8 x 182.8 cm
Sterling and Francine Clark Art Institute, Williamstown

Exhibited Royal Academy, London, 1887 (305)

For this large and impressive painting, Alma-Tadema was awarded the gold medal at the Paris Exposition Universelle in 1889. The scene depicted purports to be set in northern Greece during the 4th century B.C. It is the artist's only major exploration of a Greek Dionysiac, as opposed to a Roman Bacchanalian, subject [59]. The source is Plutarch's *Moralia* (249-50) which was quoted without ascription in the Royal Academy exhibition catalogue: 'During the holy war that followed the taking of Delphi by the Phocians, it chanced that the Thyades, women sacred to Dionysos, were seized with religious frenzy, and, wandering aimlessly, came at night to the city of Amphissa, which was in league with Phocis, and their enemy. But, being weary, and unconscious of danger, they lay down in the market-place and slept. When

the wives of Amphissa heard this, they hastened to the spot, fearing lest the Thyades should suffer insult or injury; and standing round the sleepers, waited till they had awakened, then tended them and gave them food. After which, having asked leave of their husbands, they led the wanderers from the city, safe unto the boundaries of their own land'.

Plutarch's story is part of a series primarily concerned to demonstrate the bravery of women. George Eliot, in *Daniel Deronda* (1876: bk.II, ch.xvii), alludes to this story to highlight the moral of like-minded female charity in the face of adversity. The painting's title suggests that Alma-Tadema follows both Plutarch and George Eliot with a study of female compassion and courage. However, it is not the women of Amphissa but the more striking thyades or maenads who engage the viewer's attention. Unlike the heavily draped townswomen on the periphery, the maenads slowly awakening after the night's revel lie centre stage, in abandoned positions, their hair loose, their clothing in disarray.

Stalls laden with refreshments – eggs, poultry, wine, honeycomb and cucumbers – stand in the corner of the market place. The market place itself is equipped with an array of classical accessories (see *Empires restored*, no. 37). Archaeological details are drawn from a variety of sources including, appropriately, the 4th-century Greek world. Artefacts are combined ingeniously to produce novel, even whimsical, effects, albeit in pursuance of the theme of the painting. A 4th-century funeral stele is used as a column capital. Below the capital hangs a 4th-century Sicilian fish plate, outdoors and near a string of real fish. The maenads sport their usual ivy wreaths, animal skins and *tympana* [21]. *Thyrsoi* in maenadic scenes are usually carried by the women themselves; here they support an awning covering the food. Architectural detail includes metopes copied from the temple of Hera at Selinus in Sicily, discovered in 1877. They depict Heracles fighting the Amazons, and Actaeon attacked by his own hounds for spying on Artemis bathing. The metopes not only illustrate the artist's knowledge of recent archaeological discoveries but are especially significant in this setting as both myths portray female subjects who, like the maenads, are outside the traditional perimeters of society.

The pale tones of marble, skin and drapery are chosen to complement a clear and cool early morning light. Both the townswomen and maenads are either of a distinctly dark or fair skin and hair type favoured by the artist [86]. The sleeping maenads evoke earlier paintings, *Exhausted maenides after the dance* [34] and *After the dance* [135]. These sleeping nudes confirm that for Alma-Tadema, as for most Victorian painters, eroticism is a connotation of the maenadic nature. In *The women of Amphissa* the pose of the reclining foreground figure resembles that of the artist's nude maenads but her clothing and less languorous attitude dilute a powerful eroticism found in the earlier paintings (see Hedreen, pp. 86-87).

If there are no overt indications of eroticism in *The women of Amphissa* the shape and configuration of the painting, nevertheless, suggests a comparison with an aspect of Victorian sexuality which the antique subject does not ostensibly allow. The line of serious townswomen queuing to offer food to the waking maenads is quaintly reminiscent of a group of Victorian matrons dispensing charity to their fallen sisters. RB

69

The roses of Heliogabalus

Opus CCLXXXIII, S 321
1888
oil on canvas, 132.1 x 213.9 cm
private collection

Exhibited Royal Academy, London, 1888 (298)

Alma-Tadema's most extravagant vision of a supremely decadent Rome is inspired by an episode from the colourful life of Heliogabalus recorded in the *Scriptores Historiae Augustae* as follows:

In a banqueting-room with a reversible ceiling he once overwhelmed his parasites with violets and other flowers, so that some of them were actually smothered to death being unable to crawl out to the top.
('Antoninus Elagabalus', XXI.5)

Like the much earlier painting, *A Roman emperor, A.D. 41* [23] (also a Roman history subject based on ancient texts) this picture displays a moment of inglorious corruption. *A Roman emperor, A.D. 41* hailed the beginning of the decline of the Roman Empire while *The roses of Heliogabalus*, a scene of almost two hundred years later, shows the Empire in the throes of dissipation and fast approaching its end.

Marcus Aurelius Antoninus became Emperor of Rome at the age of fourteen: his more familiar name, Heliogabalus or Elagabalus, was derived from the Syrian sun god whose worship, along with Eastern court practices, he attempted to introduce to Rome. He was a voluptuary in the style of Nero and ruled Rome amidst venality and debauchery until he was murdered by the Praetorian guard after a reign of only four years (218-222 A.D.).

19th-century scholarly and literary texts tend to judge Heliogabalus severely following Edward Gibbon's scathing account of his reign and character in *The history of the decline and fall of the Roman Empire* (1776-88). William Smith writes that during his short reign Heliogabalus rendered himself 'alike odious and contemptible by all manner of follies and abominations', (Biography, vol. II, p.7), while Walter Pater declares him 'an embodiment of pure and unmodified evil' (p. 120). An alternative notion of Heliogabalus as a sensualist who revelled in the greatest extravagances of Eastern luxury is evinced by J.K. Huysmans who describes him 'treading in silver dust and sand of gold, his head crowned with a tiara and his clothes studded with jewels' (p. 45). Simeon Solomon's water-colour, *Heliogabalus, high priest of the sun* of 1866 (Forbes Magazine Collection, New York), evokes a similarly luxuriant and sensuous image of the Emperor, in which he is portrayed as an effete and languorous young man set in a highly decorated and rich interior. On the other hand, the Dutch writer Louis Couperus was not so much fascinated by the superficial and opulent decadence, but more by the tormented soul of the androgynous sun-priest (*De berg van licht*, The mountain of light, 1905).

Alma-Tadema's young Emperor, dressed in saffron silk, reclines on a couch placed on a raised platform and gazes impassively at the scene below. Beside him sits his mother, Julia Soaemias Bassiana, 'a most depraved woman and one worthy of such a son' (*SHA.*, XVIII.3). The other court favourites at the Emperor's table include an old roué ('at his banquets he preferred to have perverts placed next to him', *SHA.*, XII.4) and a bevy of young beauties. The guests, lazily reclining on silk cushions, in an arena of pain and pleasure calmly succumb to a sea of petals and their exquisitely decadent deaths.

The artist's choice of episode allows both a cruel and a voluptuous reading of Heliogabalus' character: he is murdering his guests but they suffer the sweetest of deaths. The painting itself implies no moral stance as the spectator is utterly intoxicated by the richness of detail. Fabulous marbles, silks, jewels, fruits and flowers assuage us and distance the potentially horrifying subject. An outdoor setting of rolling hills and a soft twilight complement the seemingly serene mood. Significantly, only rose petals fall from a silken canopy, rather than the 'violets and other flowers' mentioned in the classical source. To a Victorian audience roses had Swinburnean associations of sensual beauty, corruption and death. In the well known lines from Swinburne's *Dolores* the poet speaks of the 'sweet lips' of his cruel mistress which:

> change in a trice
> The lilies and languors of virtue
> For the raptures and roses of vice

Alma-Tadema reproduces the sumptuous display of Roman wealth detailed in the *Scriptores Historiae Augustae*: Heliogabalus wore a tunic of silk and gold thread and adorned himself with jewels and a diadem (XXIII.3-5, XXVI.1), he had couches made of solid silver (XX.4) and coverlets of gold (XVIX.1), and embellished his palace with expensive variegated marble such as red porphyry and green Laconian marble (XXIV.6).

The Emperor's reputation for depravity was matched by that for his beauty. In this painting his handsome face, with Eastern features and a wispy moustache and beard, must have been copied from his only securely identified portrait in the Capitoline Museum, Rome. Ancient sculptural portraits were also closely studied for the artist's other depictions of historical characters including Agrippa [40] and Hadrian [64].

A bacchante plays the double flute or *tibia* in the background and in the distance stands a sculptural group of Dionysus, faun and panther. As elsewhere the artist has modified his source [52] and in effect has improved it. The original marble statue (Vatican Museum, Rome) is transformed into bronze allowing the exclusion of a clumsy tree trunk and struts needed to support marble but unnecessary in bronze. Dionysiac-Bacchic motifs enliven many of Alma-Tadema's paintings and are fully appropriate to the scene of revelry here.

Alma-Tadema obviously valued *The roses of Heliogabalus* as an important picture. A study for the painting [70] was shown at the New Gallery in the same year it was exhibited at the Royal Academy. The comparatively huge scale of the painting places it amongst the largest of the artist's canvases. As in the smaller paintings details are meticulously rendered including each delicate rose petal. Roses were even shipped over from the French Riviera during the winter providing a continual fresh supply for the artist to work from (Swanson, p. 70).

Following its exhibition the majority of critics admired the technical proficiency of detail demonstrated in the painting. The more progressive critics discussed execution and technique rather than subject, while for others a moral discrepancy seemed to arise between subject and mood. Aware of Heliogabalus' infamous reputation, critics were unable to reconcile this cruel incident in the life of a seemingly insane despot with such a sumptuous and entrancing treatment. Many seemed to avoid the moral issue by following F.G. Stephens's interpretation of the subject, in a preview article, as merely 'one of those practical jokes in which the emperor delighted' (*Athenaeum*, 14 January 1888, p. 58).

Of the original critics only M.H. Spielmann of the *Magazine of Art* saw *The roses of Heliogabalus* as the artist's *chef d'oeuvre* while today it is judged as one of

Alma-Tadema's most important works. The painting was commissioned by the wealthy engineer, Mr (later Sir) John Aird, for the large sum of £ 4,000. J.F. Boyes, in an article on Aird's collection for the *Art Journal* of 1891, writes that it was considered the collection's prize painting (p. 138). An illustration in the same article shows it hanging in the back drawing room, a private room of the Airds' London house [90]. Perhaps the subject was considered too risqué to be displayed in full public view. However, as the illustration includes Mrs Aird and two of her daughters the more likely supposition is that the Airds, like many of the critics, preferred to appreciate the painting as an accomplished representation of a fantastic prank rather than as a glorious revel in the ultimate realization of Roman decadence: Heliogabalus' beautiful banquet of death. RB

70

Study for The roses of Heliogabalus

S 320
c. 1888
oil on panel, 23.5 x 38.2 cm
private collection

Exhibited New Gallery, London, 1888 (132)

Alma-Tadema considered this study important enough to exhibit in its own right at the New Gallery, simultaneously with the exhibition of the finished painting of the same subject at the Royal Academy [69]: the exhibition of the study also enhanced the status of the painting, marking it as a major work that had required extensive preparation. By showing the two works simultaneously, Alma-Tadema was capitalizing on growing contemporary interest in artists' working procedures. In a general sense, this reflects the celebrity status accorded to major late Victorian artists, evident in extensive press coverage of artists' lives and careers; more particularly, it demonstrates the glamorization of the process of artistic creation, as periodicals such as the *Magazine of Art* published detailed accounts of the working procedures of artists such as Frederic Leighton (see Prettejohn).

However, comparison of the study with the finished picture indicates that Alma-Tadema used a much more informal working procedure than the traditional academic method of a Leighton (see ibid.): Alma-Tadema freely alters not only details, but larger compositional elements from study to finished work. The finished picture substitutes an airy landscape background for the tentlike closed background of the study; the dais is no longer distanced by a flight of steps; the silver vessels, prominent in the study (on the table, and centrally among the rose petals), are absent from the finished work; and there are numerous changes to the disposition of the foreground figures. Cumulatively, the changes bring greater unity to the composition: they relate the foreground and background groups more tightly, eliminate the potentially distracting accents of the silver vessels, and create a more unified rhythm among the abandoned limbs in the foreground. The airborne rose petals, scattered rather at random in the sketch, are organized into an elegant curving pattern in the final painting. Alma-Tadema would seem to have used the study merely as a preliminary step, from which he refined and reworked the composition as he transferred it to the larger canvas of the finished picture. However, as the critic F.G. Stephens stressed, the more varied composition works well at the smaller scale of the study (*Athenaeum*, 19 May 1888, p. 636): it was perhaps in recognition of the independent merit of the study that the artist chose to exhibit it separately. EP

71

A favourite poet

Opus CCXC, S 327
October 1888
oil on panel, 36.9 x 49.6 cm
Board of Trustees of the National Museums & Galleries on Merseyside
Lady Lever Art Gallery, Port Sunlight

Exhibited New Gallery, London, 1889 (8)

A woman stretches languorously on a cushioned marble bench listening to her seated companion reading from a papyrus roll. Ancient papyri were unrolled with the right hand and rolled up with the left but here the roll falls in an untidy heap beside the reader as if she has hastily opened it to find some special poem. The papyrus provides no clue to the identity of the 'favourite poet' as the writing is indistinct. However, even though the bronze wall inscription is mischievously obscured by the reclining figure it can be identified as a fragment of lines 18-19 from Horace's *Ode*, I, XXXI:

dones ac, precor, integra cum mente

Lines 18-20 translate as follows: Grant, son of Latona, that I may enjoy what I have with good health and, I pray, with sound mind, and that my old age may not be squalid and not without the lyre (trans. West).

The subject matter of the ode is the poet's prayer to Apollo ('son of Latona') on the occasion of Augustus's dedication of a new temple to the god on the Palatine, Rome. The listener's flushed cheeks and dreamy gaze suggest that she is thinking of a Roman love elegy rather than the earnest message from Horace. Perhaps the verse is more appropriate for the now firmly established and ageing artist.

The rear wall is decorated with bronze panels, carved in relief, which pivot to act as open windows. Three of the nine muses are depicted on medallions: Thalia, the muse of comedy [82], Urania, muse of astronomy and Polyhymnia, muse of the sacred song and inventor of the lyre. Only the lower crossed legs of a standing figure are visible on the first panel. They could belong to Apollo, who is often represented in company with the muses, but the exact position of the legs next to a goose imitates a free-standing figure of *Pothos* (Desire)

143 *Tanagra terracotta group of two seated women from Asia Minor, c. 100 B.C., The British Museum, London*

known from numerous marble Roman copies of a 4th-century B.C. Greek original [144]. The presence of this half-hidden figure surely evokes the erotic reverie in which the listener is utterly lost despite Horace's sobering entreaty.

An elaborate Corinthian capital and familiar Mediterranean seascape can be seen through the open window. As often, Alma-Tadema gives a glimpse of an exterior through an open space [39 78]. Sunlight streams into the room illuminating the marble and highlighting the body of the seated figure outlined through her dress. The figures both wear Greek-style drapery of transparent Coan material (a kind of silk made on the island of Cos) falling in beautiful sculpture-like ripples. The listless atmosphere, pastel colour

144 *Pothos (Desire)*, Roman marble copy of an original by Scopas, c. 330 B.C., Musei Capitolini, Rome

harmonies and reading theme echo the aesthetic paintings of Albert Moore.

Many of Alma-Tadema's later works depict two women talking or merely resting. It is probable that these works are influenced by Tanagra statuettes, small genre subjects often of two women exchanging gossip [143]. The artist had earlier made use of these figurines in *Fishing* [33]. His renewed interest may be connected with an exhibition of Tanagra statuettes at the Burlington Fine Arts Club from June 1888. RB

72

A dedication to Bacchus

Opus CCXCIII, S 330
2 May 1889
oil on canvas, 77.5 x 177.5 cm
Hamburger Kunsthalle, Hamburg

Exhibited L.H. Lefèvre Gallery, London, Spring 1889
(only picture in exhibition)

An exhibition at the Lefèvre Gallery was dedicated solely to this large picture which was commissioned for the collection of Baron Schröder as a companion piece to *The vintage festival* [21]. The occasion is the initiation of a child into the cult of Bacchus. Sunlight shines through a canopy casting a violet shadow on the solemn figures of a veiled priest and priestess who await the child in front of a marble altar. Beside them a group of musicians play the cymbals, *tibiae* and *tympana*. To the left of the altar the child waits with a crowd of worshippers including four men carrying a huge wineskin to be offered as a libation to the god. F.G. Stephens, in a pamphlet accompanying the painting's exhibition, stresses that *A dedication to Bacchus* has no connection with what he calls 'the beastly orgies' described in Livy's account of the Bacchanalian scandal in 186 B.C. [21]. In the initiation scene religiosity is certainly more apparent than Bacchanalian fervour. However, in an attempt to sanitize the subject Stephens has chosen to ignore the crowd of ivy-wreathed celebrants waving *tympana* cut off at the edge of the canvas. As in *The vintage festival* the behaviour of these background figures indicates the wild revelry described by Livy and suggests that beyond the immediate scene a more riotous Bacchanalia is being enjoyed.

A bacchante dressed in a leopard skin stands by a silver *crater* used for mixing the dedicatory wine with water. This imitates a famous piece from the Hildesheim treasure, discovered in 1868, of which Alma-Tadema was known to have owned a copy (Meynell, p. 187) and which is reproduced in many of his paintings [84]. Another bacchante in a tiger skin waves a branch decorated with silver flowers, a bell and ribbon. Stephens suggests that it is a more elaborate version of the traditional *thyrsus*. He also informs us that the two dancing bacchantes are approaching the altar on which they will ritually hang the garland. Dancing was an important part of Bacchanalian ritual, already explored by the artist in *Autumn* [46].

The setting is the precinct of an altar overlooking the sea, perhaps with a temple on the right. A frieze in the upper right corner, depicting the battle between Lapiths and centaurs, is copied from the 5th-century B.C. Temple of Apollo at Bassae (acquired by the British Museum in 1818). Below the frieze stands another centaur, known through a number of Roman marble copies

of a pair of Hellenistic bronze originals. As in *The sculpture gallery* [35] the artist plays with the notion of copies and represents either the Hellenistic original or an imagined bronze Roman copy. Either way, he has managed to eliminate an ugly support at the statue's stomach, an integral part of the marble copies, by obscuring this part of the figure behind the priest's head. In ancient art, centaurs were traditionally depicted in mythological representations as members of Bacchus-Dionysus' band of followers (*thiasus*). Such a *thiasus*, of satyrs (known for their excessive sexual appetites) and bacchantes, can be glimpsed on the balustrade's frieze.

The porphyry statue on the left of the canvas is of a kneeling man lighting a fire beneath a brazier. Similar ancient sculptural groups exist of fire-lighters preparing a brazier while the sacrificial animal is slaughtered. Along with the battle frieze this image reminds us of the violent nature of certain aspects of the ancient world. On an initial reading *A dedication to Bacchus* appears as a respectable and ordered representation of ancient religious ritual but with a closer inspection imagery of sexuality, Bacchanalian revelry and cruelty reveal a more violent and irrational vision of Roman life. RB

73

A silent greeting

Opus CCXCIX, S 336
November 1889
oil on panel, 30.5 x 23 cm
Tate Gallery, London

Exhibited New Gallery, London, 1892 (15)

A silent greeting was commissioned by Sir Henry Tate as a companion picture to another courtship scene, *A foregone conclusion* of 1885 [145], which Tate had given to his wife as a wedding present. According to Alma-Tadema the title is a line from a poem by Goethe suggested to him by a friend (Swanson, p. 240). From the mid-1880s the artist chooses titles of an increasingly anecdotal or literary cast [74 83].

A Roman soldier leaves a bunch of roses in the lap of his sleeping sweetheart. Even in his cumbersome metal armour he leaves quietly, careful not to wake her.

The male figure from the world of heroic action enters the domestic sphere in which the woman has been occupied with the traditional female activity of sewing.

Alma-Tadema secured a lucrative market with a number of scenes of what seem to be Victorian courtship rituals in ancient settings [45 62]. There was no corresponding convention of courtship as a prelude to marriage in ancient Rome. Freeborn girls of the higher classes would have had little contact with men who were not relatives and marriages were usually arranged while girls were still young. It was only after marriage that a woman gained power and status as mistress of the house. The household slaves were often complicit in their mistresses' affairs. Roman love poets describe their relationships with women who are married or of dubious reputation. In his earlier career Alma-Tadema painted scenes of lovers and mistresses based on the lives of love poets. Catullus and Tibullus (S 66, 77, 80, 121).

To the viewer with a knowledge of ancient social customs *A silent greeting* is open to two different readings. If we interpret the scene in a Roman rather than Victorian context it is not as innocent as it first appears. The soldier, on leave, paying a visit to his betrothed becomes a lover hastily bringing a gift to his mistress while the slave, waiting at the curtain, acts as a lookout for the husband. RB

145 *A foregone conclusion*, 1885, Tate Gallery, London

74

An earthly paradise

Opus CCCVII, S 345
April 1891
oil on canvas, 86.5 x 165 cm
private collection

Exhibited Royal Academy, London, 1891 (298)

The subject is one of the most familiar in Victorian genre painting; a close comparison is William Quiller Orchardson's *Master baby* of 1886 (National Gallery of Scotland, Edinburgh). Indeed, the more progressive art critics of the later Victorian period complained bitterly about the prevalence of pictures of mothers with babies at the public exhibitions. The theme, at first associated with the painting of contemporary life, had become rou-

poem 'Olive', published in 1889 in the third series of A.C. Swinburne's *Poems and Ballads*: 'All the heaven of heavens in one / Little child'. As in other late Victorian pictures, by Alma-Tadema and other artists, the fragment of poetry serves to create a general mood rather than marking a specific relation to the quoted source [73 83]: the picture is quite independent of Swinburne's poem, about a nine-year-old girl.

Nonetheless, the hint of religious fervour, in the line from Swinburne, is appropriate to Alma-Tadema's version of the Victorian ideal of the sanctity of motherhood, with the mother kneeling reverentially to kiss the baby's hand; the glowing colour harmonies create an aura around the figures, most brilliant in the crucial central area where the flesh-tones of mother and baby meet. Alma-Tadema had frequently represented ancient Roman families [20], or members of his own family in Roman guise [35], but *An earthly paradise* is almost unique in his oeuvre for its concentration on the relationship between mother and baby, without additional figures (although cf. s 127, 274). The picture weaves together archaeologically specific elements from Alma-Tadema's Roman repertoire with the iconography of Victorian babyhood. The baby's cushion rests on a Roman bench of a type familiar in Alma-Tadema's pictures [87]; the baby's bath, glimpsed through the curtains on the right, is a Roman marble basin set into the floor. Most piquant of all is the tiny Roman sandal, prominent in the foreground to the left of centre. The motif of an adorably small child's shoe was a frequent adjunct to Victorian pictures of childhood, as, for example, the little black slippers in virtually the same foreground position in Frederic Leighton's *Mother and child* of 1865 (Blackburn Museum and Art Gallery). With characteristic inventiveness, Alma-Tadema reinterprets the conventional motif in terms of Roman archaeological accuracy. The same might be said for the picture as a whole: the humble Victorian subject type of mother and baby is transformed into a scene of Roman magnificence. At over a metre and a half in width, the picture is not only unusually large for Alma-Tadema's work, but one of the grandest Victorian pictures of the mother-and-child theme. EP

tine even in pictures with Roman settings, such as Edward John Poynter's *A corner of the marketplace* of 1887 (private collection): in Alfred Elmore's *Pompeii anno Domini 79*, a mother plays with an older child before an ominously smoking Vesuvius (1878; Yale Center for British Art, New Haven). The theme was equally familiar in literature: indeed, Alma-Tadema appended to the picture's title a quotation from the

75

Portrait of Ignacy Jan Paderewski

Opus CCCXI, S 350
August 1891
oil on canvas, 45.7 x 58.4 cm
Muzeum Narodowe w Warszawie, Warsaw

Exhibited Royal Birmingham Society of Artists,
Autumn 1891 (503)

Although this small portrait appears to be a vivid private glimpse of the sitter, it also captures the crucial aspects of Ignacy Jan Paderewski's public persona: his famous shock of hair and his intense gaze, seen also in contemporary photographs of the Polish pianist. Portraits of musicians were a noticeable subcategory in Victorian and Edwardian portraiture; Alma-Tadema, a lover of music, painted a number of such portraits [55] (s 259, 268, 325, 355, 378, 424). The genre reflects the increasingly high status of musical celebrities, encouraged by the dramatic growth in the international market for musical performances, parallel to the internationalization of the art market at the same period and mediated by impresarios who played a role similar to that of international art dealers. Paderewski's brilliant piano technique and flamboyant persona were in the tradition of Liszt, one of the first international celebrities of the piano; his romantic public image was enhanced by his well-known activities as a Polish patriot.

Alma-Tadema's characterization suggests sympathy with both sides of Paderewski's career. Paderewski performed at musical evenings at Alma-Tadema's house, and the artist's older daughter, Laurense, became a supporter of the Polish cause. Laurense had been present at the sittings for the portrait, vividly described by Paderewski in his memoirs (pp. 188-89). Not only Alma-Tadema, but his wife Laura and the Princess Louise painted portraits of Paderewski on the same occasion: 'Each one was constantly begging me to turn *his* way!' However, the point of view in the present portrait suggests that Alma-Tadema was directly facing the pianist; as the most famous of the three artists and the only man, he was perhaps permitted the privileged central position. In the same summer of 1891, the sculptor Alfred Gilbert made a portrait bust of Paderewski (plaster, Manchester City Art Gallery; bronze cast, Tate Gallery, London). EP

76

A kiss

Opus CCCXII, S 351
18 December 1891
oil on panel, 45.7 x 62.7 cm
private collection (courtesy of Christie's, London)

Exhibited Royal Academy, London, 1892 (258)

A kiss presents a familiar scene of Roman women bathing. but by comparison with the artist's usual scenes of bathing customs set in accurate ancient buildings [84][26]. the women here are swimming for pleasure in the sea.

The artist asserted that the background was painted from a oil sketch. *A lake in Bavaria* (untraced: s 340). made at the villa of Georg Ebers at Tutzing the previous summer (Swanson. p. 246). Nevertheless.

despite a hint of northern pallor. the clear sea and sparkling marble evoke the balmy Mediterranean world of a series of paintings which represent the Roman aristocracy taking its leisure along the Bay of Naples [79 83]. The fine garments and conspicuous gold and silver bracelets worn by these women suggest that they share the same wealth and status.

In *A kiss*. Alma-Tadema has ingeniously combined the sentimental with the risqué. The central group. from which the title derives. shows a young woman kissing a golden-haired child goodbye before joining the swimmers. Her identity. like that of the older woman standing behind. is unclear. but the configuration is reminiscent of Victorian genre scenes involving children with their mothers and governesses. In piquant contrast to this group. at the far left of the canvas. a nude bather gazes directly at the viewer. As elsewhere. the artist allows the spectator a forbidden glimpse of this nude as if through a keyhole [43].

As with many of the later paintings, few artefacts clutter the composition: only a familiar bronze tripod, a skilfully foreshortened inscription on the left wall, and a marble relief of a satyr playing pan pipes beneath a tree alongside what seems to be a term of Dionysus. The nude satyr is a surprising, if discreet, intruder into an otherwise all-female sphere. Through the inclusion of Dionysiac accessories, the artist often adds erotic connotations to seemingly innocent scenes [39 41 59].

The painting was commissioned by Sir Max Waechter. His collection included two other paintings by Alma-Tadema: *An apodyterium* of 1886 (S 312) and *The frigidarium* of 1890 (S 339). Both are bathing scenes and, like *A kiss*, afford a glimpse of the nude in a private, female world. RB

77

In my studio

Opus CCCXIX, S 356
April 1893
oil on canvas, 61.6 x 47 cm
private collection

Exhibited Royal Academy, London, 1893 (113)

In my studio depicts a model in classical costume amidst the splendours of Alma-Tadema's studio in his Grove End Road house (see pp. 51-56). The painting is unusual in his oeuvre in that it is neither a classical scene nor a portrait in modern dress (like [66], also seen in the studio). Though on one level it shows a specific moment in time, the mixture of ancient and modern, the eclectic surroundings and the 'exquisite half-light' (*Magazine of Art*, 1893, p. 258) from the onyx windows combine to create a self-contained world removed from everyday life. *In my studio* embodies the artist's aestheticism. It evokes the aesthete's pleasures of the senses: sight is expressed in the visual richness, touch in the model's hand resting on the textured cloth and smell in her attitude, taking a deep draught of perfume from the roses. However the picture is probably not intended as a representation of the Five Senses, as taste is absent, and hearing is only indirectly (and probably unintentionally) referred to by the piano hidden under the embroidered cloth.

The model depicted is Blanche Tueski (Swanson, p. 247). She stands in front of the studio alcove lit by the Mexican onyx window panes, the design of which includes the artist's name spelt out in Greek characters. The alcove contains a raised platform for Alma-Tadema's grand piano (see pp. 54-55) reached by a step covered in gleaming brass. The objects in the painting include some that can be identified from the catalogue of the studio sale of 1913. The piano (lot 17) is draped with an Indian tablecloth of rose-coloured silk velvet, its borders encrusted with gold and silver embroidery (lot 1238). On the inlaid capital (top right) is a copy of a blue-rimmed Byzantine glass vase with a gold centre medallion (lot 178), and at the back of the alcove below the window is a 14th-century Chinese temple screen 'finely painted to represent Buddha and the 27 Singers and Dancers of Heaven' (lot 1440). This screen also appears in several of the artists's portraits [75 80].

Alma-Tadema gave this picture to Frederic Lord Leighton in return for the latter's gift of his small *Bath of Psyche* [52], one of the collection of paintings presented to Alma-Tadema by his artist friends to hang in the hall of his house (see pp. 53-54). Of the many studio-houses in London, those of Leighton and Alma-Tadema were the most remarkable and this painting thus has special significance as a tribute from the creator of one to the creator of the other. JT

78

Unconscious rivals

Opus CCCXXI, S 358
June 1893
oil on panel, 45.1 x 62.8 cm
Bristol City Museum & Art Gallery

Exhibited New Gallery, London, 1893 (12)

A spectacular barrel vault, an azalea and dazzling white marble encompass two women. Their relationship and the whole subject of the picture can only be inferred from the title and hints in the imagery. While the decorative nature of the painting is pronounced the enigmatic narrative is merely suggested.

The gorgeous painted ceiling can have no ancient prototype as no decorated ceiling on such a scale

remains intact. The closest equivalents are the vaulted ceilings from Nero's Golden House in Rome which was discovered in the 16th century. By the late Victorian age much of the paint had deteriorated but a general idea of the design could be grasped from Raphael's paintings (in the loggia of the Vatican and the Villa Madama) inspired by the Golden House.

A Bacchic relief of swags and masks supported by cupids embellishes the balcony wall. Alma-Tadema owned a photograph of a section of the original relief [24]. The artist has here supplied additional portions and made the masks more prominent. The Bacchic imagery is echoed and a theme of disguise is suggested by the statue of a Cupid trying on a mask of Silenus from the Capitoline Museum, Rome (LXVI, 9418).

The statue cut off at the right of the picture is known as a seated gladiator (LXX, 9618)[25]. The artist has restored the figure to pristine condition and supplied a missing left hand. The same sculpture is depicted in full in *The voice of spring* of 1910 (S 425). Although Alma-Tadema's paintings often include easily recognizable statues familiar to an educated audience, the seated gladiator was not a well-known work, but perhaps a favourite of the artist. Furthermore, in this flirtatious Roman setting the image of a gladiator has a special significance. Respectable imperial women were notorious

for their passionate support of favourite combatants and for affairs with gladiators outside the ring (Juvenal, *Satires* VI.110ff.). The wife of Marcus Aurelius, Faustina, was even said to have conceived the future Emperor Commodus with a gladiator (*Scriptores historiae Augustae*, 'Marcus Aurelius Antoninus', XIX). *Unconscious rivals* was one of the paintings bought for the Schröder collection [21]. RB

79

Coign of vantage

Opus CCCXXXIII, S 371
1895
oil on panel, 64 x 44.5 cm
private collection

Exhibited The Metropolitan Museum of Art, New York, March 1973 (27)

From the 1880s Alma-Tadema began a series of paintings which depict women high up on lofty marble terraces overlooking a brilliant Mediterranean sea [76 83] (S 359, 361, 367, 409, 420, 423). Even though there are few archaeological artefacts in these paintings they appear to be set in a definite time and place: the Roman

146 *Villa San Michele (Axel Munthe)*, Capri, photograph, private collection

254

Bay of Naples. Ancient sources describe this coastline as a popular resort dating from the early Empire. The wealthy built luxury villas (*villae maritimae*) along the Bay, many of which came to be spectacularly placed on the edges of cliffs (see D'Arms, ch. 5). *Coign of vantage* is one of the most striking paintings in this series. The artist exploits a bravura display of spectacular perspective with a remarkable view of the dizzying drop from terrace to sea far below.

Frédéric Bastet has identified the bronze animal as a free copy of an Egyptian sphinx from the Villa San Michele at Capri (the home of Swedish writer and physician, Axel Munthe, built in 1890 on the site of an ancient Roman house). Furthermore, Bastet places this scene at the precise location of Munthe's villa overlooking the sea in the direction of Sorrento (p. 82): a view which was also popular with 19th-century tourists in Italy. Alma-Tadema's choice of Capri, the site of the most ostentatious *villa maritima*, that of the Emperor Tiberius, clearly indicates that his intention is to evoke the luxurious and leisured world of the imperial Bay of Naples.

The three women are represented as fashionable and rich aristocrats taking a holiday. Their silken garments and gold jewellery confirm their high status. From their elevated position the women watch the ships sailing into the Bay. These are often described as the Roman fleet returning home (e.g., Swanson, p. 253). The women could be awaiting a visit from their lovers who are home on leave, a scene depicted in *A silent greeting* [73], or alternatively, the ships may merely be pleasure boats. The latter reading is strengthened by the location, known for leisure and amusement rather than military exercises. Seneca mentions exuberant sailing parties in his disapproving description of riotous living that he encountered on a visit to Baiae along the Bay (*Epistles*, LI.12). Similarly, in Cicero's vivid account of the scandalous life of the aristocratic Clodia Metelli (the real woman identified as Catullus's Lesbia), he lists amongst her indulgences trips to Baiae, beach-parties and boating picnics (*Pro Caelio*, XV.35).

This painting, like many of Alma-Tadema's later works, was bought by a wealthy American patron [67]. As a consequence it was little known in Europe until the 1970s but has since become one of Alma-Tadema's best known works. Proliferated through countless reproductions *Coign of vantage* is today for many people the quintessential Alma-Tadema. RB

80

Self portrait

Opus CCCXLI, S 379
12 November 1896
oil on canvas, 65.7 x 52.8 cm
Galleria degli Uffizi, Collezione degli Autoritratti, Florence

Exhibited Royal Academy, London, Winter 1913 (212)

Alma-Tadema executed self portraits throughout his career, from the youthful example of 1852 [1] through one finished in the year of his death (S 431; S 229, 293, 315, 418) [24]. However, the present picture was of unusual public importance: its commission for the celebrated gallery of painters' self portraits at the Uffizi in Florence reflected the artist's growing international reputation. Few contemporary English painters were represented in the Uffizi collection, although commissions for John Everett Millais and George Frederic Watts had followed the honour first accorded to Frederic Leighton in 1880, two years after his election to the Presidency of the Royal Academy (*Frederic Leighton*, no. 84).

147 Frederic Lord Leighton, *Self portrait*, 1880, Galleria degli Uffizi, Collezione degli Autoritratti, Florence

For his Uffizi portrait [147], Leighton had represented himself in the robes of his honorary doctorate from Oxford University, with the gold medal of his Presidency; his pose before a section of the Parthenon frieze referred to his status as England's most eminent painter in the classical tradition. Alma-Tadema, however, characterizes himself not as a magisterial elder statesman, but an energetic working artist, mahlstick and paintbrush in hand; at sixty, he appears still youthful, the blonds of his hair and beard picking up the gold accents of the overall colour scheme. Although his clothing shows no sign of 'bohemian' disorder, the suit is simple and unpretentious. In place of Leighton's representation of the most elevated work of ancient fine art, the Parthenon frieze, Alma-Tadema relieves his head against a work of decorative art, an Oriental antiquity of the kind he collected for his house (see pp. 45-56). Alma-Tadema would certainly have seen Leighton's self portrait at the Royal Academy in 1881, when his own *Sappho* was on view [98]; his own less portentous self-characterization may have been in deference to the eminence of his friend, Leighton (Alma-Tadema also chooses a somewhat smaller format than Leighton's, which measures 76.5 x 64 cm). Even if it was not Alma-Tadema's specific intention to distinguish his self portrait from Leighton's, the differences

between the two works aptly express the contrasting reputations of the artists: Leighton, the painter of the Greek ideal, and Alma-Tadema, the painter of ancient everyday life. EP

81

Interior of Caius Martius's house

1901
watercolour, with pencil and bodycolour,
on paper, 36.3 x 50.7 cm
Manchester City Art Gallery

Exhibited Royal Society of Painters in Water-Colours,
London, Spring 1901 (113)

In 1879 the actor Henry Irving asked Alma-Tadema to provide stage designs for Shakespeare's *Coriolanus*, and the artist was working on drawings for it with the help of an architectural assistant in 1880. The production did not finally reach the stage of the Lyceum Theatre, London until 1901, when it was much praised for its spectacle and its authentic appearance. Irving himself and Ellen Terry took the leading roles. Alma-Tadema set the play in the Etruscan period, rather than in the more usual but less correct classical Rome.

This is a finished exhibition watercolour, rather than a set design, and shows the appearance of the stage for act I scene ii. The interior of the house, with an open courtyard, is based on Vitruvius's description of a Greek house, and not on Roman models from Pompeii. The painted sundial on the back wall, similar to one in the British Museum, is also as described by Vitruvius, and many of the details are taken from Etruscan tombs (Spiers, pp. 17-18). Alma-Tadema worked out his designs with the help of a small model of the Lyceum stage, making cardboard cut-outs of his sets; a design for the Capitol (Victoria & Albert Museum, London) has cut out columns over a blue sky backdrop. Rosenfeld (pp. 87-89) conjectures that on the stage the illusion of solidity, noted by contempories, was achieved not by a three-dimensional built up set but by a flat backcloth for the courtyard, with lateral flats and ceiling borders. The set was painted by Joseph Harker, a professional scene-painter, and was lit by electric light, not the usual gas. The watercolour was owned by Irving (sold Christie's, London, 16 December 1905, lot 24). JT

82

The crowning of Aesculapius

c. 1903
pencil on beige paper, 24.2 x 33.7 cm
Musée d'Orsay, Paris

Exhibited Musée du Louvre, Paris, March – May 1977 (1)

There is no specific mythological tale to connect Thalia, Muse of comic and pastoral poetry (identifiable by the theatrical mask she carries) to Aesculapius, god of medicine (identifiable by his luxuriant beard as well as the inscription), but the fanciful juxtaposition allows Alma-Tadema to use one of his favourite devices in his later years, the contrast between a male marble statue and a living female figure [78]. The sightless stare of the bust is in playful counterpoint with both Thalia's attentiveness and the grotesque features of the mask. The valetudinarian aspects of the Roman cult of Aesculapius attracted some attention in the Victorian period, as in John William Waterhouse's painting of *A sick child brought into the Temple of Aesculapius* (1877, private collection) and the similar scene in Walter Pater's Roman historical novel of 1885, *Marius the Epicurean*. Alma-Tadema, at other times interested in such religious practices [32 72], here abandons social history; the approach is closer in spirit to that of Edward John Poynter's famous picture of 1880, *A visit to Aesculapius* (Tate Gallery, London), where Venus displays a thorn in her foot to Aesculapius, bearded and draped as a figure of masculine medical authority in piquant juxtaposition with the nude figures of Venus and her attendants. The drawing is either closely related or identical to a pencil drawing entitled *Thalia's homage to Aesculapius* in Rudolf Dircks's catalogue of the artist's works (Opus CCCLXXVI; see Dircks, p. 32). It was given by the artist to the Musée du Luxembourg in 1903, his first gift to the French national collection (see Bénédite, p. 131); later he would also give the section of *Hadrian in England* featuring the single male figure [65]. EP

83

Silver favourites

Opus CCCLXXIII, S 407
11 February 1903
oil on panel, 69.1 x 42.2 cm
Manchester City Art Gallery

Exhibited Royal Academy, London, 1903 (203)

Silver favourites is a notable example of a series of paintings which depict women set against glistening marble and the clear Mediterranean sea and sky. Like the fig-

ures in *Coign of vantage* [79] these are wealthy Roman women idly amusing themselves whilst enjoying the luxurious setting and splendid view afforded by a *villa maritima*. The standing figure crumbles bread for fish in a sparkling marble pond while another watches and the third lolls on the marble *exedra*. The bread is carried in a *tympanum*, an often used artefact from Alma-Tadema's Bacchanalian paintings [21 68 72].

Fish ponds were fashionable extravagances built by the rich in their *villae maritimae*. Such ponds were often executed on a grand scale as an ostentatious display of wealth as well as for their decorative and amusement function [33]. The keeping of fish as pets in such a grand manner is mentioned contemptuously by such Roman writers as Cicero and Pliny. Cicero bemoans the sorry state of political affairs when 'the Senate has been deserted by the knights ... Our leading men think they have transcended the summit of human ambition if the bearded mullet in their fish-ponds feed out of their hands, and let all else go hang' (*Letters to Atticus*, II.1.7). Pliny writes of yet worse excesses: fish were named, decorated with jewels and tears were shed at their deaths (IX.172).

The fish theme is emphasized by the four lines of verse, attached to the frame, from William Wordsworth's *Gold and silver fishes in a vase*:

> When, sensitive of every ray
> That smites this tiny sea,
> Your scaly panoplies repay
> The loan with usury.

19th-century British picture-titles were often gleaned from texts by English poets. Lines of verse were also attached to picture frames or quoted in exhibition catalogues. Alma-Tadema began to use literary titles in the mid-1880s [73] (S 310, 382, 400) and first attached lines of verse to a frame with *Spring* of 1894 [6].

The women wear shades of blue, mauve and purple, harmonizing with the clear sea and sky and also confirming their high status: only the wealthy could afford expensive purple dye. Their garments are distinctive and are used by Alma-Tadema in other paintings [33 76]. The shawl pulled tightly across the tunic at cross axis is characteristic of 4th-century B.C. Greek sculpture and Hellenistic Tanagra statuettes [143]. RB

84

A favourite custom

Opus CCCXCI, S 422
April 1909
oil on panel, 66.1 x 45 cm
Tate Gallery, London

Exhibited Royal Academy, London, 1909 (181)

A favourite custom is the last of Alma-Tadema's paintings of Roman baths. It was bought for the nation by the Chantrey Bequest and represents one of the artist's most successful subjects. In the foreground is a cold bath (*frigidarium*), in which one woman playfully splashes another; the eye is drawn through the undressing room (*apodyterium*), to a glimpse of a sunlit peristyle beyond the open door.

Like the *Thermae Antoninianae* [26] this is largely a reconstruction of an actual building, the 1st-century A.D. Stabian baths at Pompeii, excavated in 1824. Alma-Tadema has combined elements of different rooms in the baths, which were divided into men's and women's sections. As depicted here the women's *apodyterium* led straight into the *frigidarium*. The exact stucco work above the door, shape of the room and niches around the walls (fancifully supplied with numbered cupboards by the artist) are based on the well preserved men's *apodyterium*, while the fluted ceiling is copied from the men's hot bath (*caldarium*). Alma-Tadema owned photographs of the men's *apodyterium* and other exterior and interior sections of the bath (Portfolio X). The artist has made the setting more luxurious than the Stabian baths through the use of marble walls and flooring associated with the larger imperial *thermae* such as the Baths of Caracalla.

A few favourite ancient objects found in other paintings, the Hildesheim crater [72] and a lion-legged table [35], are both appropriately placed in their early imperial setting. The small dimensions, also employed in *Tepidarium* [58], minimize the potential impact of the graceful nudes. Their slender, girlish body-types are similar to other Edwardian representations of the nude as seen in works by Edward John Poynter, John William Waterhouse and Herbert Draper. By the turn of the century Royal Academy exhibitions usually included large canvases of classicizing, mainly mythological nudes.

Poynter, like Alma-Tadema, also painted more 'realistic' nudes in accurate ancient settings. For example *Water babies* of 1900 depicts two adolescent nudes splashing each other in a Roman fountain (*Imagining Rome*, no. 62). Alma-Tadema only painted a small number of nudes, and here they appear almost as accessories to his archaeological reconstruction. RB

85

A summer offering

Opus CCCCIII, S 428
March 1911
oil on panel, 35.5 x 52.1 cm
Museum of Art, Brigham Young University, Provo, Utah

Exhibited Royal Academy, London, 1911 (208)

The title suggests a seasonal ritual, but one unlike the archaeologically specific religious festivals of Alma-Tadema's earlier works [21 72]. The roses are not offered at an altar or shrine, as in earlier depictions of Roman popular religion [32 61], but thrust forward, as if to the spectator. Each of the three intense tints of the flowers – golden yellow, pink, and white – is linked to one of the women; this promises some kind of symbolism but there is no definite clue to what is being symbolized. The roses might be interpreted as emblems of summer, as visual equivalents for the beauty of women [86], or as elements in a religious ritual whose purpose remains enigmatic. Their associations finally resist specific definition, in a fashion that has affinities with continental Symbolism (see pp. 84-87). The vagueness, or perhaps universality, of the rose symbolism parallels the elusive drama of the subject as a whole: the rapt expressions, the sense of forward processional movement, and the gestures of offering or smelling the roses hint at some nature ritual, enacted in the glowing atmosphere of midsummer, in the midst of a vast landscape dominated by an expanse of sky.

Further ambiguities surround the characterizations of the figures; there is no obvious explanation for the flagrant asymmetry of the grouping, with one figure almost hidden at lower left, while the other two appear at startlingly close range, as if they are about to burst forth from the picture space. The faces appear to be

portraits, and there has been some debate about whether the three women should be identified as Alma-Tadema's wife, Laura, and his two daughters (see Swanson, p. 274). To identify the left figure as Laura, who had died in 1909, might account for its strange curtailment, behind the central figure and drastically cropped by the lower left corner; the golden roses have been interpreted as wilted (e.g., *Empires restored*, no. 49). However, this figure's facial features are largely obscured, and the other two faces do not closely resemble the Alma-Tadema daughters, much older than the figures by the time the picture was painted; the artist might, of course, have used young professional models as proxies, to evoke his memories of his daughters at a younger age. The difficulty of verifying the identifications is perhaps its own answer. Any composition of three women, by an artist whose close-knit family consisted precisely of three women, inevitably has personal resonances at some level. However, it is left to the spectator's imagination whether to read the figures as the 'real' Alma-Tadema women, as dream figures in the artist's memory of some lost summertime, or as altogether fictive evocations of female beauty.

Alma-Tadema's late works include a number of meditations on the seasons, a theme explored earlier in the series of 1877 [46] as well as a number of watercolours [32 37]. Most of the late examples focus on spring, with its suggestion of renewal or rebirth [6] (s 425-26). Indeed, *A summer offering* was paired with a companion picture on a springtime theme, *When flowers return* (s 427). Both were commissioned by the artist's faithful patron and friend, Sir John Aird, the owner of *The roses of Heliogabalus* [69]. They appeared together at the Royal Academy exhibition of 1911, the last but one of Alma-Tadema's lifetime. EP

86

In beauty's bloom

Opus CCCCIX
1911 (unfinished)
watercolour on card, 16.5 x 23 cm
Board of Trustees of the National Museums & Galleries
on Merseyside
Lady Lever Art Gallery, Port Sunlight

Exhibited Royal Academy, London, Winter 1913 (98)

The composition compares women and flowers [85]: the faces overlap as do the stalks and leaves of the arum lilies. The exaggerated scale of the lilies, as well as emphasizing the comparison, indicates cultivation in a greenhouse (information from John Edmondson). This suggests the artificial and exotic environment of the hothouse, a frequent theme in European Symbolist literature. The pairing of fair and dark figures is a characteristic motif for the artist [68 71], also frequent in other 19th-century pictures: here the contrasting hair colours have no evident narrative or symbolic meaning, but seem instead to suggest varieties of beauty. This late work, unfinished at the time of the artist's death, demonstrates his continuing interest in the watercolour medium. EP/RB

87

Studio seat

c. 1890
cedar, sycamore and ebony, with mother of pearl inlay
and brass mounts
the cushion, held in by the original leather straps,
is upholstered in modern silk
height 35.5, length 162.5, depth 76.2 cm
Board of Trustees of the Victoria & Albert Museum,
London

Exhibited Arts and Crafts Exhibition Society, London,
1893 (84)

One of a pair of seats made for the artist's studio, and sold in the studio sale of 1913 (lots 10 and 11). The seat appears in several paintings [74] [26]. It is unusual in that one side is in the Egyptian style and the other Pompeian. The design of the Pompeian side is inspired by a bronze bedstead in the Naples Archeological Museum discovered at Pompeii in 1868. A photograph of the bedstead is in the artist's collection [148]. The seat was probably made to Alma-Tadema's design by Johnstone, Norman & Co., the London firm previously employed by the artist to make the suite of furniture for Henry Marquand (see pp. 49-51).

Alma-Tadema showed the seat at the 4th Exhibition of the Arts and Crafts Exhibition Society in 1893, thus demonstrating his affinity with the Arts and Crafts Movement and its belief in breaking down the artificial distinction between artists and designers. Nevertheless, a critic of *The Studio* disapproved of the seat's artifice while admiring its craftsmanship (1893, II, p. 17): 'even this, perfect as are its proportions, and cunning as is its fashioning, affects one with a subtle sense of unreality, almost of theatricalism'. JT

88

Edward Onslow Ford (1852-1901)
Bust of Lawrence Alma-Tadema

1895
bronze
height 52.1, width 63.5 cm
(height including marble base 73.7 cm)
Royal Academy of Arts, London

Exhibited Royal Academy, London, 1896 (1880)

148 *Bronze bed*, discovered at Pompeii in 1868, photograph from Alma-Tadema's collection, University of Birmingham (XLIV, 9066)

M.H. Spielmann (1901, p. 63) thought that Ford was at his best in his busts which do indeed well demonstrate how the vivid surface detail and realistic spontaneous characterization of the 'New Sculpture' were able to transform and re-vivify the English portrait bust of the 1880s. This new informality was particularly appropriate for busts of fellow artists and these were a speciality

of the sculptor (Dixon, p. 296) – he also provided the busts of great watercolour painters of the past for the façade of the Royal Society of Painters in Water-Colours in Piccadilly. This bust was given by the sculptor to the Royal Academy as his 'diploma' work – again reflecting the high status he accorded to the portrait bust.

Although bronze was the favoured material of the 'New Sculpture' for its surface detail and versatility of form, there was also a marble version of this bust (Ford, n.p.) which was acquired by Alma-Tadema for his famous house (Swanson, p. 93) and was apparently given to Birmingham University in 1947 by the Victoria & Albert Museum. It must also date from 1895-96 as it, and not the bronze bust, was wrongly reproduced in *Royal Academy Pictures* (1896, p. 44) and in the *Art Journal* (1896, p. 168) as the bust exhibited at the 1896 Royal Academy. Another bronze version was presented to the Antwerp Academy by Alma-Tadema in 1900; the Academy lent it to the Koninklijk Museum voor Schone Kunsten, but it was destroyed during the Second World

War. Yet another version was in the sculptor's studio at his death (Rinder, p. 61).

Onslow Ford and Alma-Tadema both lived and worked in St. John's Wood and the sculptor presided over the great banquet of 1899 in which the most celebrated men of arts, letters and music celebrated the painter's knighthood.

For this bust, Alma-Tadema wears academic dress, presumably reflecting his honorary doctorate of letters awarded by Dublin University in 1892 or his honorary doctorate of civil law from Durham University of 1893. He was notoriously proud of his many awards, medals and honours, but academic dress also permitted artists to claim intellectual as well as merely practical distinction – a tradition going back at least to Reynolds's famous self-portrait also in the Royal Academy, showing the artist as an Oxford University doctor of civil law. Academic dress also reflected a traditional compromise between obtrusively modern and anachronistically classical dress. EM

Notes

Introduction to Alma-Tadema

Julian Treuherz

1 *Dictionary of National Biography 1912-1921*, London 1927, p. 5.

2 Sir Lawrence Alma-Tadema, 'My reminiscences', *Strand Magazine* 27 (1909), p. 295.

3 Frederick Dolman, 'Illustrated interviews, LXVIII: Sir Lawrence Alma-Tadema', *Strand Magazine* 18 (December 1899), p. 607.

4 Cosmo Monkhouse, 'Some English artists and their studios', *Century Magazine* 24 (August 1882), p. 568.

5 Theodore Reff, 'Some unpublished letters of Degas', *Art Bulletin* 50 (1968), p. 89; letter of 22 August 1875. For Deschamps see below note 14.

6 Ellen Gosse, 'Laurens Alma-Tadema', *Century Magazine* 47 (February 1894), pp. 491, 496.

7 'Mr. Alma-Tadema RA on art training', *Journal of the Royal Institute of British Architects* 2, 3rd s. (August 1895), no. 18, pp. 623-24.

8 R. Phené Spiers, 'The architecture of "Coriolanus" at the Lyceum Theatre', *Architectural Review* 10 (July 1901), pp. 2-21.

9 Vern G. Swanson, *The biography and catalogue raisonné of the paintings of Sir Lawrence Alma-Tadema*, London 1990, p. 99.

10 'trop de lumière sur le jet d'eau ... la strigyle dans l'ombre plus foncée ... un peu plus de dessin dans les cheveux sur le bronze ... l'éponge pourrait avoir des trous plus variées et plus profondes' (inscribed on impression in the British Museum).

11 Alma-Tadema, op. cit. (note 2); see also Georg Ebers, *Lorenz Alma Tadema: his life and works*, trans. Mary J. Safford, New York 1886, pp. 1-23; Percy Cross Standing, *Sir Lawrence Alma-Tadema O.M., R.A.*, London 1905, pp. 9-29; Swanson, op. cit. (note 9), pp. 19-22.

12 Alma-Tadema, op. cit. (note 2), p. 289.

13 Ibid., p. 290.

14 Jeremy Maas, *Gambart, prince of the Victorian art world*, London 1975, pp. 171-72, 215-16. Gambart was succeeded by the firm of Pilgeram and Lefèvre on 25 March 1871. Léon Lefèvre was Gambart's nephew; his other nephew Charles Deschamps managed Durand-Ruel's London gallery but continued to act for Alma-Tadema occasionally. For portraits of Deschamps and Gambart see cat. 36.

15 R. Phené Spiers, 'Archaeological research in the paintings of Sir Lawrence Alma-Tadema', *Architectural Review* 33 (March 1913), pp. 45-48.

16 Dolman, op. cit. (note 3), p. 612.

17 Sibyl Rosenfeld, 'Alma-Tadema's designs for Henry Irving's "Coriolanus"', *Deutsche Shakespeare-Gesellschaft West Jahrbuch* (1974), pp. 84-95; see also Phené Spiers, op. cit. (note 8).

18 Bram Stoker, *Personal reminiscences of Henry Irving*, 2 vols., London 1906, vol. 2, p. 66.

19 'A chat with Miss Julia Neilsen', *The Sketch* (1 March 1893), p. 301. See also Robyn Asleson, *Classic into modern: the inspiration of antiquity in English painting, 1864-1918*, diss. Yale University (1993), pp. 266-78.

20 *Daily Telegraph* (24 January 1898).

21 Monkhouse, op. cit. (note 4), p. 566.

22 John H.G. Archer, 'A classic of its age', in: John H.G. Archer (ed.), *Art and architecture in Victorian Manchester*, Manchester 1985, p. 147.

23 W.R. Dawson and E.P. Uphill, *Who was who in Egyptology*, 2nd ed., Egypt Exploration Society, London 1972, p. 94. I owe this reference to Piotr Bienkowski.

24 Andrew Graham-Dixon, 'Victorian vices' (review of the Lord Leighton exhibition at the Royal Academy), *The Independent* (20 February 1996), section 2, p. 8.

25 Louise Lippincott, *Lawrence Alma Tadema: Spring*, Malibu (California) 1990, pp. 59-71.

26 Gosse, op. cit. (note 6), p. 490.

27 Ibid., pp. 492-93.

28 Several drawings of this type were exhibited by the London dealer Peter Nahum 1995.

29 Examples are reproduced by Swanson, op. cit. (note 9), pp. 37 and 64; and in exhib. cat. *De verzameling van Mr. Carel Vosmaer (1826-1888)*, Amsterdam (Rijksmuseum) 1989, pp. 128 and 129 (see cat. 8).

30 Letter to Ebers, 27 December 1883, quoted by Swanson, op. cit. (note 9), p. 62.

31 Philip Carr, 'Alma-Tadema and his friends', *The Listener* (9 December 1954), pp. 1013-14.

32 Gosse, op. cit. (note 6), p. 494.

33 C. Lewis Hind, *Naphtali*, London 1926, p. 136, quoted by Swanson, op. cit. (note 9), p. 99.

34 Gosse, op. cit. (note 6), p. 495.

35 Philip Burne-Jones to the editor, *The Times* (7 January 1913), p. 9, quoted by Jennifer Gordon Lovett in exhib. cat. *Empires restored, Elysium revisited: the art of Sir Lawrence Alma-Tadema*, Williamstown (Sterling and Francine Clark Art Institute), Baltimore (Walters Art Gallery), Cincinnati (Taft Museum) & Memphis (Dixon Gallery and Gardens) 1991-92, p. 27.

36 Vern G. Swanson, *Alma-Tadema: the painter of the Victorian vision of the ancient world*, London 1977, p. 43; Lippincott, op. cit. (note 25), p. 89.

Alma-Tadema's artistic training

Teio Meedendorp and Luuk Pijl

Translated from the Dutch by Peter Mason

1 Johan Braakensiek, Het Engelsche lokaas, reproduced in: *De Amsterdammer* (10 February 1895), no. 920, p. 11.

2 Information from Pieter A. Scheen, *Lexicon Nederlandse beeldende kunstenaars, 1750-1880*, The Hague 1981, pp. 14, 515; Eduard Reeser, *Een eeuw Nederlandse muziek*, Amsterdam 1950, pp. 191-92.

3 It is not clear why Alma-Tadema did not gain admission to the academies. Frederick George Stephens, *Artists at home*, London 1884, p. 29, suggests that he was turned down because he came from 'provincial' Friesland, but this seems implausible. Alma-Tadema's fellow townsman and later friend Christoffel Bisschop, for example, was admitted to the Academy in The Hague in the same period. It is quite possible that his godparents, who were responsible for his social welfare after the death of Alma-Tadema's father in 1840, wanted nothing but the best – that is, the most prestigious – for their protégé (he was the son of a solicitor, after all), and that this was the reason why their choice fell on Antwerp.

4 Letter to an anonymous woman, 12 October 1885, Royal Library, The Hague, manuscript collection, P. Hofstede de Groot collection.

5 On the situation in Belgium see: Saskia de Bodt, *Halverwege Parijs: Willem Roelofs en de Nederlandse schilderskolonie in Brussel 1840-1890*, Ghent 1995.

6 Ibid., pp. 49-52.

7 Ibid., p. 18.

8 Lawrence Alma-Tadema, 'Laurens Alma Tadema, R.A.' in: *In the days of my youth...*, containing autobiographies of thirty-four well known men and women of today, Thomas Power O'Conner (ed.), London 1901, p. 203. On Leys and his contemporaries see Henri Hymans, *Près de 700 biographies d'artistes belges*, Brussels 1920, vol. 2, pp. 602-13; exhib. cat. *Schilderkunst in België ten tijde van Henri Leys (1815-1869)*, Antwerp (Koninklijk Museum voor Schone Kunsten) 1969; exhib. cat. *Van Gustaaf Wappers tot Henri Leys*, Brussels (Koninklijk Museum voor Schone Kunsten van België) 1973.

9 Louis Pfau, cited by Huysmans, op. cit. (note 8), p. 603.

10 See, e.g., J. Knoef, *Van Romantiek tot Realisme*, The Hague 1947, pp. 239-42.

11 Huysmans, op. cit. (note 8), p. 609.

12 In a letter to his Dutch friend A.J. Kruseman dated 11 April 1862 (now in The Netherlands Institute for Art History in The Hague), Alma-Tadema expressed his admiration for Henri Leys in connection with the painting *Announcement of the Edict of Charles V*, which was a great success at the International Exhibition in London in that year. And when Alma-Tadema first exhibited a work in the Salon in Paris in 1864, he had the following recommendation included in the catalogue: 'Laurens Alma Tadema (élève de M. Leys)'; Catalogue of the Salon des Beaux-Arts, 1864, p. 6.

13 It was only in the 1870s that a number of artists in France associated with Jean-Paul Laurens (1838-1923) tackled Merovingian themes on a large scale; see: exhib. cat. *Le moyen-âge et les peintres français de la fin du XIX siècle: Jean-Paul Laurens et ses contemporains*, Cagnes-sur-Mer (Château-Musée du Haut de Cagnes) 1989 (does not mention Alma-Tadema). Ary Scheffer and Octave Tassaert painted Merovingian subjects for the halls in Versailles in the 1830s; see Leo Ewals, *Ary Scheffer: sa vie et son oeuvre*, Nijmegen 1987, p. 280 and Clare Constanse and Jean-Pierre Babelon, *Musée national du château de Versailles: la peinture*, Paris 1995, vol. 2, pp. 817, 847.

14 Respectively opus numbers: IX (watercolour, whereabouts unknown), XIII (watercolour, private collection, USA), XI (watercolour, whereabouts unknown), and X (oil on canvas, Johannesburg Art Gallery, South Africa).

15 Constant Cuypers, 'Alma Tadema's "Fredegonde en Praetextatus" (1871)', in: *Bouwkunst: studies in vriendschap voor Kees Peters*, Amsterdam 1993, pp. 145, 153. Presumably Alma-Tadema drew more on Thierry than on Gregory for his information about the Merovingians. Thierry only covered the period from 561 to c. 590: Alma-Tadema took his themes from this period except for two cases (the first Merovingian paintings with Queen Clotilde).

16 Cited by Georg Ebers, 'Lorenz Alma Tadema', *Westermanns Deutsche Illustrierte Monatshefte* 30 (October 1885), no. 349, p. 5.

17 Cited by Rulon Neph Smitson, *Augustin Thierry: social and political consciousness in the evolution of a historical method*, Geneva 1972, p. 223.

18 Augustin Thierry, *Récits des temps mérovingiens précédés de considérations sur l'histoire de France*, 2 vols., Brussels 1840, vol. 1, p. 5.

19 Cited by Jo Tollebeek, 'Horror vacui: Barante, Stendhal en de romantische geschiedschrijving', *Feit en fictie* 2 (1995), no. 2, p. 27.

20 Thierry, op. cit. (note 18), vol. 2, p. 124. Specifically on this painting see Cuypers, op. cit. (note 15).

21 Gregory of Tours, *Historia francorum* (VIII.31).

22 Paul Mantz, 'Salon de 1865', *Gazette des Beaux-Arts* 7 (1865), vol. 18, pp. 508, 510.

23 Ibid.

24 J.J. Guiffrey, 'Exposition à Anvers', *Gazette des Beaux-Arts* 6 (1864), vol. 17, pp. 370-71.

25 Helen Zimmern, 'Laurence Alma-Tadema R.A.: his life and work', *Art Journal*, Special Number (1886), p. 28.

26 Georg Ebers, *Aegypten in Bild und Wort: dargestellt von unseren besten Künstlern*, 2 vols., Leipzig 1879-80, vol. 1, p. 277; vol. 2, pp. 113, 139, 165, 309, e.g., cats. 27, 28. On Ebers himself see: Rykle Borger, *Drei Klassizisten: Alma Tadema, Ebers, Vosmaer*, Leiden 1978, pp. 30-36. The Dutch writer Conrad Busken Huet recognized the conception of history shared by Thierry and Ebers in Alma-Tadema's work: 'As Augustin Thierry wrote, as Mommsen and Ebers write, so does Alma Tadema paint', from: *Parijs en omstreken*, Amsterdam 1878, p. 258.

27 Constant Cuypers, 'Twee testamenten van Lourens Alma Tadema', in: *Nader beschouwd: een serie kunsthistorische opstellen aangeboden aan Pieter Singelenberg*, Nijmegen 1986, pp. 107-28.

28 Constant Cuypers, 'De droom van Alma Tadema', *Kunstschrift* 35 (July-August 1991), no. 4, pp. 38-47.

29 Percy Cross Standing, *Sir Lawrence Alma-Tadema, O.M., R.A.*, London 1905, p. 24.

30 Jeremy Maas, *Gambart, prince of the Victorian art world*, London 1975.

31 Standing, op. cit. (note 29), pp. 25-26; Helen Zimmern, *Sir Lawrence Alma Tadema*,

R.A., London 1902, p. 11; Edmund W. Gosse, 'Alma-Tadema', in: F.G. Dumas, *Modern artists*, London 1882-83, p. 80.

32 Gosse, ibid.

33 An extremely useful source for exchange rates in the 19th century is: N.V. Posthumus, *Nederlandsche prijsgeschiedenis*, 2 vols., Leiden 1943, vol. 1: Wisselkoersen te Amsterdam 1609-1914, pp. 579-638 (with thanks to Chris Stolwijk).

34 Chris Stolwijk, ' "Benden van rampzaligen?": de economische positie van de Haagse kunstschilders in de tweede helft van de negentiende eeuw', *Kunstlicht* 15 (1994), no. 3/4, p. 19. The income is estimated on the basis of the income tax due. The wage of an educated worker at this time was around 400 guilders a year.

35 On Leighton and the Classicists see the essay of Edward Morris in this catalogue; Christopher Wood, *Olympian dreamers: Victorian classical painters 1860-1914*, London 1983 and exhib. cat. *Frederic Leighton 1830-1896*, London (Royal Academy of Arts) 1996.

36 Information on Brussels from De Bodt, op. cit. (note 5), pp. 35-70.

37 Teio Meedendorp,' "Ik ben toch eigenlijk een lompert...": Zeven brieven van Lourens Alma Tadema aan Christoffel Bisschop', *Jong Holland* 9 (1993), no. 1, pp. 20-27.

38 Hanna Pennock, 'De levens van twee neven, Hendrik Willem Mesdag en Lourens Alma Tadema', *Jong Holland* 9 (1993), no. 1, pp. 8-19.

39 De Bodt, op. cit. (note 5), p. 155.

40 H. van Wickevoort Crommelin, *Dutch painters of the nineteenth century*, London 1898, vol. 1, p. 158.

41 Although Maas, op. cit. (note 30), p. 215, states, that the second commission consisted of forty-eight pictures, Alma-Tadema himself, op. cit. (note 8), p. 205, mentions the number of fifty-two.

42 Letter to H.W. Mesdag, 8 June 1868, Rijksarchief at The Hague, S. van Houten archive.

43 1864 Salon, gold medal for *Pastimes in ancient Egypt 3000 years ago* (fig. 13); second-class medal for the same work at the 1867 Exposition Universelle; 1868 Salon, third-class medal for *The siesta* (fig. 127), opus LVII, large version (130 x 360 cm) of cat. 11.

44 See exhib. cat. *De Haagse School: Hollandse meesters van de 19de eeuw*, Paris (Galeries nationales du Grand Palais), London (Royal Academy of Arts) & The Hague (Haags Gemeentemuseum) 1983.

45 Chris Stolwijk, 'De tentoonstellingen van Levende Meesters in Amsterdam en Den Haag 1858-1896', *De Negentiende Eeuw* 19 (December 1995), no. 4, p. 210.

46 'De tentoonstelling te 's Gravenhage 1866', *Kunstkronijk* 8 (1867), p. 58.

47 'A propos van de tentoonstelling van schilderijen van levende meesters in Arti et Amicitiae', *Kunstkronijk* 10 (1868), p. 4.

48 Unpublished, continued by his son in close collaboration with the artist and kept in the archive of the Rijksprentenkabinet in the Rijksmuseum Amsterdam, Vosmaer archive. This archive also contains the correspondence and a few drawings. The relation between Vosmaer and Alma-Tadema is extensively described in Frédéric Bastet, *Met Carel Vosmaer op reis*, Amsterdam 1989 and idem, 'Carel Vosmaer en Lourens Alma Tadema', in: exhib. cat. *De verzameling van Mr. Carel Vosmaer (1826-1888)*, Amsterdam (Rijksmuseum) 1989, pp. 130-47.

49 Carel Vosmaer, 'Eene schilderij van Alma Tadema: Bezoek van Hadrianus aan een Romeinsch-Britse pottenbakkerij', *De Nederlandsche Spectator* (1886), p. 294.

50 Bastet, *Met Carel Vosmaer op reis*, cit. (note 48), pp. 117-43.

51 B.D.H. Tellegen, 'Mr. J.R. Thorbecke, Parlementaire redevoeringen, 1862-1863, Deventer 1867', *De Nederlandsche Spectator* (9 November 1867), no. 45, p. 356.

52 *De Nederlandsche Spectator* (5 October 1867), no. 40, pp. 314-15.

53 J. Maalman in: *De Nederlandsche Spectator* (2 January 1869), no. 1, p. 6.

54 Jenny Reynaerts, 'Van atelier naar Academie: schilders in opleiding 1850-1900', exhib. cat. *De schilders van tachtig*, Amsterdam (Van Gogh Museum) 1991, p. 95; exhib. cat. *'Waarde heer Allebé': leven en werk van August Allebé (1838-1927)*, Haarlem (Frans Hals Museum), Dordrecht (Dordrechts Museum) & Assen (Drents Museum) 1988, pp. 31, 49; Pennock, op. cit. (note 38) 1993, p. 13.

55 He sent a copy of the letter to H.W. Mesdag, now in the Rijksarchief in The Hague, S. van Houten archive; see also Pennock, op. cit. (note 38), p. 13.

56 Letter to Verwee, from London, 26 January 1870, in The Netherlands Institute for Art History, The Hague, artists documentation.

57 Gambart in a letter to William Holman Hunt, 6 December 1871: 'Tadema went last Boxing day to a Danse at Maddox Brown's, fell in love at first sight with Miss Epps, the Surgeon's daughter, & is going to marry her as soon as she names the day', cited by Maas, op. cit. (note 30), p. 226.

58 J. Staphorst (pseud. Jan Veth), 'Iets over Alma Tadema', *De Nieuwe Gids* 1 (1887), vol. 2, pp. 94-96.

59 Ibid.

Antiquity fragmented and reconstructed

Elizabeth Prettejohn

I am grateful to Rosemary Barrow for many excellent suggestions.

1 'The Royal Academy Exhibition', *The Times* (30 April 1870), p. 12.

2 Sidney Colvin, 'The Grosvenor Gallery', *Fortnightly Review* n.s. 21 (1 June 1877), p. 825.

3 Editor [Marion Henry Spielmann], 'Current art', *Magazine of Art* 23 (1899), p. 388.

4 Cosmo Monkhouse, 'The Grosvenor Gallery. III', *Academy* (23 December 1882), p. 457.

5 See, e.g., Linda Nochlin, 'Manet's *Masked ball at the Opera*', in: *The politics of vision: essays on nineteenth-century art and society*, London 1991, p. 81. Nochlin and others relate the new compositional techniques to the inspiration of Japanese art. This may also be relevant to Alma-Tadema, an enthusiastic admirer and collector of Japanese prints and decorative objects from an early date; see William Michael Rossetti's diary entry for 20 February 1871, in Odette Bornand (ed.), *The diary of W.M. Rossetti: 1870-1873*, Oxford 1977, pp. 45-46.

6 Stephen Bann, *The clothing of Clio: a study of the representation of history in nineteenth-century Britain and France*, Cambridge 1984, p. 74. For another discussion of the sources for *The flower market*, see Constant Cuypers, 'De droom van Alma Tadema', *Kunstschrift* 35 (July – August 1991), no. 4, pp. 44-47.

7 For the inscription, see Cuypers, op. cit. (note 6), p. 46.

8 For the notice-board, see ibid., pp. 44-46.

9 Arthur Clutton Brock, 'Alma Tadema', *Burlington Magazine* 22 (February 1913), p. 286.

10 See Euphrosyne Doxiadis, *The mysterious Fayum portraits: faces from ancient Egypt*, London 1995.

11 For Alma-Tadema's visit to Pompeii before June 1868, see Vern G. Swanson, *The biogra-*

phy and catalogue raisonné of the paintings of *Sir Lawrence Alma-Tadema*, London 1990, pp. 34-35. It is uncertain when Alma-Tadema acquired the photograph. An account of the portrait, with an engraving, was published the month after Alma-Tadema finished *The flower market*; see G. de Petra, 'Domus et pistrinum P. Paqui Proculi (*Regio* VII. *Insula* II. n. 3. 6)', *Giornale degli Scavi di Pompei* n.s. 1 (October 1868), p. 63 and plate II. For the history of the portrait, see M. della Corte, 'Publius Paquius Proculus', *Journal of Roman Studies* 16 (1926), pp. 145-54.

12   Alma-Tadema's collection of more than 4000 books, now at the University of Birmingham, must have been one of the period's most extensive libraries on classical archaeology; a complete list is held in the Heslop Room, Main Library, University of Birmingham.

13   I am grateful to Dr. Catharine Edwards of the University of Bristol for deciphering the inscription and identifying the historical figures it mentions: Marcus Epidius Sabinus stood for local elections in 74 and 77 AD; Titus Suedius Clemens was a tribune sent by the Emperor Vespasian to undertake land clearance around Pompeii. For information on elections posters, see James L. Franklin Jr., *Pompeii: the electoral programmata, campaigns and politics, AD 71-79*, Rome 1980.

14   Swanson, op. cit. (note 11), p. 150.

15   Georg Ebers, *Lorenz Alma Tadema: his life and works*, trans. Mary J. Safford, New York 1886, pp. 47-48.

16   For the plants, see cat. 14.

17   See, e.g., the unsigned article by the archaeologist A.H. Layard, 'Pompeii', *Quarterly Review* 115 (April 1864), p. 319.

18   See, e.g., Alfred Woltmann and Karl Woermann, *History of painting*, ed. Sidney Colvin, London 1880, vol. 1, pp. 35-36.

Alma-Tadema, aesthete, architect and interior designer

Julian Treuherz

1   Frederick Dolman, 'Illustrated interviews, LXVIII, Sir Lawrence Alma-Tadema', *Strand Magazine* 18 (December 1899), p. 612.

2   Georg Ebers, *Lorenz Alma-Tadema: his life and work*, trans. Mary J. Safford, New York 1886, p. 42.

3   O. Roelandts, *Les peintres décorateurs belges décédés depuis 1830*, Académie Royale de Belgique, Classe des Beaux-Arts, Mémoires, 2nd s. 4 (1937), p. 45. Alma-Tadema's painting *The siesta* (S 101, see fig. 127, cat. 11) is an echo of the Leys murals; it was intended as the first of a series of scenes depicting a feast, intended to decorate a dining room.

4   Louise Campbell, 'The design of Leighton House: the artist's "Palace of Art"', *Apollo* 143 n.s. (February 1996) no. 408, pp. 10-16.

5   Andrew Saint, *Richard Norman Shaw*, London 1976, pp. 153-62; Mark Girouard, *Sweetness and light*, London 1977, pp. 90-119; Giles Walkley, *Artists' houses in London 1764-1914*, Aldershot 1994.

6   Vern G. Swanson, *The biography and catalogue raisonné of the paintings of Sir Lawrence Alma-Tadema*, London 1990, pp. 41, 47 states that Burges, Aitchison and Godwin assisted Alma-Tadema, but gives no source.

7   Joseph Hatton, 'Some glimpses of artistic London', *Harper's New Monthly Magazine* 47 (November 1883), no. 32, p. 844.

8   I am grateful to Charlotte Gere, who identified the interior shown in Verhas's painting on the basis of a comparison with the illustration in Moncure Daniel Conway, *Travels in South Kensington*, London 1882, p. 194. Charlotte Gere, 'Alma-Tadema in St. John's Wood', paper presented at Leighton House, 1992. The date of 1870 on the painting is puzzling for the artist is thought to have moved in only shortly before his marriage in July 1871.

9   Odette Bornand (ed.), *The diary of W.M. Rossetti: 1870-1873*, Oxford 1977, p. 46. See also the large group of oriental works of art included in the sale catalogue of the artist's collection auctioned after his death: London (Hampton & Sons), *Catalogue of ... antique furniture and objets d'art*, 9-16 June 1913.

10   Conway, op. cit. (note 8), pp. 193-94.

11   Cosmo Monkhouse, 'Some English artists and their studios', *Century Magazine* 24 (August 1882), pp. 567-68.

12   *Illustrated London News* (10 October 1874), pp. 349-50; Percy Cross Standing, *Sir Lawrence Alma-Tadema O.M., R.A.*, London 1905, p. 39.

13   W. Minto (ed.), *Autobiographical notes of the life of William Bell Scott*, 2 vols., London 1892, vol. 2, pp. 207-08.

14   The chief sources of my description are: Mary Eliza Haweis, *Beautiful homes*, London 1882, pp. 23-33; Wilfrid Meynell, 'Artists' homes: Mr. Alma-Tadema's at North Gate, Regent's Park', *Magazine of Art* 5 (1882), pp. 184-88; Monkhouse, op. cit. (note 11); Ebers, op. cit. (note 2), pp. 52-60.

15   Meynell, op. cit. (note 14), p. 186; Ebers, op. cit. (note 2), p. 55.

16   Charlotte Gere, *Nineteenth century decoration*, London 1989, pp. 256-57; see also exhib. cat. *The Second Empire 1852-1870: art in France under Napoleon III*, Philadelphia (Museum of Art) 1978, nos. I.22 (Drawing by Alfred Normand) and VI.12 (Painting by Gustave Boulanger).

17   Conway, op. cit. (note 8), pp. 206-10.

18   The columns are clearly visible in the engraved view in Meynell, op. cit. (note 14), p. 184.

19   The artist formed a large collection of antique textiles. See the sale of the artists' collection, op. cit. (note 9). The birdcage was lot 803 in the sale.

20   *Athenaeum* (22 June 1878), p. 806; ibid. (29 June 1878), p. 835; *Graphic* (16 August 1879), p. 147.

21   Adam Zamoyski, *Paderewski*, London 1982, p. 56.

22   Michael Wilson, 'The case of the Victorian piano', *Victoria & Albert Museum Yearbook*, London 1962, pp. 137, 151, note 13.

23   Haweis, op. cit. (note 14), p. 25. The painted screen by Alma-Tadema in the Victoria & Albert Museum (cat. 22) uses this paper as a backing.

24   Sold London (Christie's), 4 November 1994, lot 69.

25   Described as 'batiste' by Haweis, op. cit. (note 14), p. 25, but Charlotte Gere ingeniously suggests this was a mishearing for 'batik'. Charlotte Gere, *Nineteenth century interiors: an album of watercolours*, London 1992, p. 96, no. 34.

26   Daniëlle O. Kisluk-Grosheide, 'The Marquand Mansion', *Metropolitan Museum Journal* 29 (1994), pp. 151-81.

27   Four settees, two armchairs, four side chairs, two stools, two tables, two corner cabinets, one music cabinet and the piano; made of ebony, boxwood, sandalwood, cedarwood, ivory, mother of pearl and brass, see Kisluk-Grosheide, op. cit. (note 26). For Johnstone, Normand and Co. see Elizabeth Aslin, *Nineteenth century English furniture*, London 1962, p. 86.

28   The piano is on loan to the Boston Museum of Fine Arts, but the locations of the works by Onslow Ford and Lord Leighton are unknown.

29 *Building News* (24 July 1885), p. 122.

30 Ellen Gosse, 'Laurens Alma-Tadema', *Century Magazine* 47 (February 1894), pp. 494-95.

31 The studio-seat was shown at the 4th exhibition of the Arts & Crafts Exhibition Society, London 1893, cat. 84.

32 RIBA Drawings Collection, *Catalogue*, 1968, vol. 20, pp. 21-22.

33 Helen Zimmern, 'Laurence Alma-Tadema R.A.: his life and work', *Art Journal*, Special Number (1886), p. 30.

34 E.g. measured drawing inscr. 'Seat with cupboard over Cornice & c in Bath Pompeii 23/5/83 JJG' (X, 1006); drawing of brick column inscr. 'Pompeii May 1883 JJG' (XIV, 1027); sketch inscr. 'Section of Pilaster Base & Step Pompeii 5/83 JJG' (XVI, 1045); sketches of windows with dimensions inscr. 'sizes of Window Glass found in Pompeii 5/83 JJG' (XVII, 1060); all at the University of Birmingham.

35 Zimmern, op. cit. (note 33). Inglis also drew Alma-Tadema's theatre designs for Julius Caesar, 1898, for a programme booklet (Theatre Museum, London).

36 Ebers, op. cit. (note 2), p. 55.

37 Walkley, op. cit. (note 5), p. 126-27; James Laver, *Vulgar society: the romantic career of James Tissot*, London 1936, pp. 60-61.

38 The chief sources of my description are: Zimmern, op. cit. (note 33); illustrations in *The Architect* 41 (31 May 1889), pp. 104-08; Marion Henry Spielmann, 'Laurence Alma-Tadema R.A.: a sketch', *Magazine of Art* (1896-97), pp. 42-50; Dolman, op. cit. (note 1), pp. 603-14; Standing, op. cit. (note 12), pp. 42-44.

39 *Builder* (18 September 1886), p. 412.

40 Rudolph de Cordova, 'The Panels in Sir Laurence Alma-Tadema's Hall', *Strand Magazine* 24 (1902), pp. 615-30.

41 Variously described as silver and platinum, but likely to have been aluminium, which is documented as having been used by the artist for his decoration of the Athenaeum Club (Tender from Hindley, 19 June 1893, no. 176 in 'Buildings, furniture and decoration books', mss., vol. 2, Athenaeum Club, London).

42 Reproduced by Kisluk-Grosheide, op. cit. (note 26), p. 167. See also lot 418 in the sale catalogue of the artist's collection, op. cit. (note 9).

43 Now in the Liverpool Museum: Pauline Rushton (ed.), *European musical instruments in Liverpool Museum*, Liverpool 1994, pp. 2-6.

44 Alfred Lys Baldry, 'The decorations of London Clubs: the Athenaeum', *Art Journal* (1898), pp. 21-25.

45 Athenaeum internal decorations album', bound volume of drawings, drawings 5-9, 22-23, Athenaeum Club, London.

46 5 and 23 April 1893, nos. 151 and 155 in 'Buildings, furniture and decoration books', mss., vol. 2, Athenaeum Club, London.

47 John Belcher, 'The Royal Gold Medal 1906: presentation to Sir Lawrence Alma-Tadema', *RIBA Journal*, 3rd s. 16 (30 June 1906), no. 13, pp. 437-45.

Alma-Tadema and the English Classical Revival

Edward Morris

1 Edward Armitage, *Lectures on painting*, London 1883, p. 216.

2 Edward John Poynter, *Ten lectures on art*, London 1879, p. 196.

3 Joseph William Comyns Carr, *Some eminent Victorians*, London 1908, p. 98.

4 Frederic Leighton, *Addresses*, London 1896, p. 56.

5 E.V. Lucas, *The Colvins and their friends*, London 1928, p. 8.

6 Sidney Colvin, 'Ford Madox Brown', *The Portfolio* (1870), vol. 1, p. 84.

7 Poynter, op. cit. (note 2), pp. 3-25; 252-72; Frederic Leighton, 'Presidential address', *Transactions of the National Association for the Advancement of Art and its Application to Industry*, Liverpool Meeting, London 1888, pp. 18-33; M.S. Watts, *George Frederic Watts*, 3 vols., London 1912, vol. 3, pp. 258-71.

8 Edmund W. Gosse, 'Alma-Tadema', in: F.G. Dumas, *Modern artists*, London 1882-83, vol. 2, pp. 73-96.

9 William Bell Scott, *Autobiographical notes*, London 1892, pp. 202-09.

10 Leighton, op. cit. (note 4), p. 124.

11 John Ruskin, *The art of England*, London 1887, p. 103.

12 Lawrence Alma-Tadema, 'Presidential address', *Transactions of the National Association for the Advancement of Art and its Application to Industry*, Liverpool Meeting, London 1888, pp. 37-40.

13 Poynter, op. cit. (note 2), p. 91.

14 Joseph A. Kestner, 'Correspondence: Edward J. Poynter, Lord Wharncliffe and others on the Wharncliffe murals', *Victorians Institute Journal* (1994), vol. 22, p. 211.

15 Cosmo Monkhouse, 'Sir Edward J.Poynter, P.R.A.: his life and work', *Easter Art Annual* (1897), p. 22.

16 Mrs. Russell Barrington, *The life, letters and work of Frederic Leighton*, 2 vols., London 1906, vol. 2, p. 208.

17 Alfred Lys Baldry, *Albert Moore: his life and works*, London 1894, p. 37.

18 J.B. Atkinson, 'The London art season', *Blackwood's Edinburgh Magazine* 106 (August 1869), p. 224.

19 Watts, op. cit. (note 7), vol. 2, p. 82.

20 Patricia Mainardi, *Art and politics of the Second Empire*, New Haven 1987, pp. 154-74.

21 Pierre Vaisse, *La Troisième République et les peintres*, Paris 1995, pp. 175-322.

22 Edward Morris, *Victorian and Edwardian paintings in the Walker Art Gallery and at Sudley House*, London 1996, p. 267.

23 Atkinson, op. cit. (note 18), p. 223.

24 *Athenaeum* (12 May 1866), pp. 640-41.

25 William Bell Scott, *Gems of modern Belgian art*, London 1872, pp. 90-91.

Alma-Tadema and the néo-Grecs

Jon Whiteley

1 'Painters in their studios, III: Lawrence Alma-Tadema', *The Graphic* (26 January 1895).

2 Louise Lippincott, *Lawrence Alma-Tadema: Spring*, Malibu (California) 1990, pp. 51-53.

3 Théophile Gautier, *Tableaux à la plume*, Paris 1880, pp. 35-36.

4 Georges Vignes, *Ingres*, Paris 1995, pp. 225-28.

5 Exhib. cat. *Hippolyte, Auguste et Paul Flandrin: une fraternité picturale au XIXe siècle*, Paris (Musée du Luxembourg) & Lyon (Musée des Beaux-Arts) 1984-85, no. 3; Philippe Grunchec, exhib. cat. *Les concours des Prix de Rome 1797-1863*, 2 vols., Paris (Ecole nationale supérieure des Beaux-Arts) 1986, vol. 1, pp. 139-41, vol. 2, pp. 114-17.

6 Exhib. cat. *Charles-François Jalabert 1819-1901*, Nîmes (Musée des Beaux-Arts) 1981, no. 33.

7 Gerald M. Ackermann, *The life and work of*

Jean-Léon Gérôme with a catalogue raisonné, Paris 1986, pp. 186-87, no. 14.

8 Claude Vignon, *Salon de 1852*, Paris 1852, ch. IV: L'école néo-Grecque, pp. 109-26.

9 Ackermann, op. cit. (note 7), pp. 54-55, no. 11.

10 Ibid., no. 109.

11 Edmund W. Gosse, 'Alma-Tadema', in: F.G. Dumas, *Modern artists*, London 1882-83, p. 82.

12 Ackermann, op. cit. (note 7), no. 168.

13 Ibid., no. S 21.

14 Vern G. Swanson, *The biography and catalogue raisonné of the paintings of Sir Lawrence Alma-Tadema*, London 1990, p. 209.

15 François Pupil, *Le style troubadour ou la nostalgie du bon vieux temps*, Nancy 1985.

The soul of things

Edwin Becker

Translated from the Dutch by Peter Mason

1 Helen Zimmern, *Sir Lawrence Alma-Tadema, R.A.*, London 1902, p. 42.

2 Roger Fry, 'The case of the late Sir Lawrence Alma-Tadema', *Nation* (18.1.1913), pp. 666-67.

3 'The works of Laurence Alma-Tadema, R.A.', *Art Journal* n.s. (February 1883), p. 36.

4 J. Winkler Prins, 'Tadema's denkbeelden over kunst', *De Leeswijzer* 4 (1887), no. 6, p. 81.

5 *Vor dem Theater von Taormina auf Sizilien*, oil on canvas, 240 x 400 cm, central ceiling painting in the left staircase, *Der Altar des Dionysos*, oil on canvas, 160 x 1200 cm, ceiling lunette in the right staircase, *Der Thespiskarren*, ceiling painting in the right staircase, and *Das Globetheater in London während einer Aufführung von William Shakespeares 'Romeo und Julia'*, ceiling painting in the right staircase. Fritz Novotny and Johannes Dobai, *Gustav Klimt: Oeuvrekatalog der Gemälde*, Salzburg 1967, cat. nos. 38-41.

6 Werner Kitlitschka, *Die Malerei der Wiener Ringstraße*, Wiesbaden 1981, p. 208.

7 Werner Hofmann, *Gustav Klimt*, Boston 1977, p. 20. Lisa Florman, 'Gustav Klimt and the precedent of ancient Greece', *Art Bulletin* 72 (June 1990), no. 2, pp. 315-16.

8 Zimmern, op. cit. (note 1), p. 50.

9 Richard Muther, *La peinture belge au XIXe siècle*, Brussels 1904, p. 134: '... the aesthete, the blue-blooded scion of ancient Belgian civilization, who derives the morbid and decaying scent of his works not from life, but from the art

of the ancients'.

10 *A travers les âges*, illustrated in: *The Studio* 4 (1894), no. 20.

11 Ludwig Hevesi, *Acht Jahre Secession*, Vienna 1900, p. 33.

12 Hugo von Hofmannsthal, *Sämtliche Werke III: Dramen 1*, Frankfurt am Main 1982, pp. 47-48.

13 Carl E. Schorske, *Fin-de-Siècle Vienna: politics and culture*, New York 1981, pp. 16-19.

14 Hofmann, op. cit. (note 7).

15 Monika Wagner, 'Gustav Klimts "verruchtes Ornament"', in: Susanne Deicher (ed.), *Die weibliche und die männliche Linie: das imaginäre Geschlecht der modernen Kunst von Klimt bis Mondrian*, Berlin 1993, p. 28.

16 Susan M. Canning, 'Fernand Khnopff and the iconography of silence', *Arts Magazine* 54 (December 1979), no. 4, p. 173.

17 Werner Fenz, *Kolo Moser*, Salzburg 1976, p. 176.

18 Michael Pabst, *Wiener Graphik um 1900*, Munich 1982, p. 50.

19 See Klimt's *Nuda Veritas*, 1899, oil on canvas, 252 x 56 cm, Österreichisches Theatermuseum, Vienna.

20 Zimmern, op. cit. (note 1), p. 51.

21 Michel Draguet, *Khnopff ou l'ambigu poétique*, Brussels 1995, p. 65-68. See also Jean-David Jumeau-Lafond, 'Le langage des fleurs, une contribution à l 'Art Nouveau', in: idem, *Carlos Schwabe: symboliste et visionnaire*, Paris 1994, pp. 158-73.

22 Georg Ebers, 'Lorenz Alma Tadema', *Westermanns Deutsche Illustrierte Monatshefte* 30 (October 1885), vol. 349, p. 12.

23 Carel Vosmaer, *Onze hedendaagsche schilders*, The Hague 1881, vol. 1, no. 4, p. 5.

24 Vern G. Swanson, *The biography and catalogue raisonné of the paintings of Sir Lawrence Alma-Tadema*, London 1990, p. 150.

25 Compare Alma-Tadema's detail with the tangle of threads at the foot of the adulterous woman in William Holman Hunt's famous *The awakening conscience*, 1853-54, Tate Gallery, London; exhib. cat. *The Pre-Raphaelites*, London (Tate Gallery) 1984, pp. 120-21.

26 Ebers, op. cit. (note 22), p. 183.

27 Ludwig Hevesi, *Acht Jahre Secession*, Vienna 1906 (reprint Klagenfurt 1984), p. 33.

28 Louise Lippincott, *Lawrence Alma Tadema: Spring*, Malibu (California) 1990, p. 13.

29 Ibid., p. 60.

30 See Edwin Becker, exhib. cat. *Franz von Stuck (1863-1928): Eros & Pathos*, Amsterdam (Van Gogh Museum) 1995-96.

31 Georg Habich, 'Villa Stuck', *Kunst und Handwerk*, 49 (1899), no. 7, pp. 185-207.

32 Rops and Alma-Tadema met during a soirée at Alma-Tadema's: Saskia de Bodt, *Halverwege Parijs: Willem Roelofs en de Nederlandse schilderskolonie in Brussel 1840-1890*, Ghent 1995, p. 155.

33 Fernand Khnopff, 'Des souvenirs à propos de Sir Lawrence Alma Tadema', *Annexe aux Bulletins de la Classe des Beaux-Arts (1915-1918)*, Brussels, Académie Royale de Belgique, 1919, pp. 9-16.

34 Paul Errera, 'En souvenir de Fernand Khnopff', *Revue de l 'Université Libre de Bruxelles* (1921/22), no. 3-4, p. 4. Richard Muther, *Geschichte der englischen Malerei*, Berlin 1903, p. 208.

35 Albert Mockel, *Propos de littérature*, Paris 1894, in: idem, *Esthétique du Symbolisme*, with an introduction by Michel Otten, Brussels 1962, pp. 89-91.

36 Fernand Khnopff, op. cit. (note 33), pp. 10-11.

37 Charles de Maeyer, 'Fernand Khnopff et ses modèles', *Bulletin des Musées Royaux des Beaux-Arts de Belgique* 13 (1964), no. 1-2, p. 46.

38 Wolfram Waldschmidt, 'Das Heim eines Symbolisten', *Die Kunst* 14 (1906), p. 164.

39 Khnopff, op. cit. (note 33), pp. 13-14.

40 Joseph A. Kestner, *Mythology and misogyny: the social discourse of nineteenth-century British classical-subject painting*, Madison 1989, p. 281.

The new centurions

Dianne Sachko Macleod

1 Full biographical references for these collectors can be found in the appendix of my *Art and the Victorian middle class: money and the making of cultural identity*, Cambridge 1996, pp. 382-489.

2 Lawrence Alma-Tadema, 'Laurens Alma Tadema, R.A.' in: *In the days of my youth..., containing autobiographies of thirty-four well known men and women of today*, Thomas Power O'Connor (ed.), London 1901, p. 205; Jeremy Maas, *Gambart, prince of the Victorian art world*, London 1975, pp. 172-73, 216.

3 Zachary Cope, *The versatile Victorian: being the life of Sir Henry Thompson, bt. 1820-1904*, London 1951, p. 51. For the Alma-Tademas owned by Thompson, see Vern G. Swanson, *The* biography and catalogue raisonné of the paintings of Sir Lawrence Alma-Tadema, London 1990, nos. 65, 91, 184, 192, 205, 228, 234, and 236.

4   A catalogue of blue and white Nankin porcelain forming the collection of Sir Henry Thompson, drawings by James Whistler, Esq. and Sir Henry Thompson, London 1878. For Whistler's role in this project, see Richard Dorment and Margaret F. Macdonald, James McNeill Whistler, London (Tate Gallery) 1994, nos. 83-89. Thompson also took lessons from artists George Bernard O'Neill and Alfred Elmore.

5   Cope, op. cit. (note 3), p. 103.

6   Ibid, p. 93.

7   On the attitudes of Aesthetic patrons, see my 'Art collecting and Victorian middle-class taste', Art History, vol. 10 (September 1987), pp. 338-43.

8   H. Osborne O 'Hagan, Leaves from my life, 2 vols., London 1929, vol. 1, p. 262.

9   Frederic Boase, Modern English biography, 6 vols., Truro 1892-1921, vol. 3, p. 1058.

10   Marquis de Ruvigny, Titled nobility of Europe, London 1914, p. 1304; Enciclopedia universal ilustrada, 70 vols., Madrid 1908-30, vol. 54, pp. 434-35 and Julio de Atienza, Nobiliario español, Madrid 1959, p. 971.

11   The Metropolitan (22 November 1890), in: F.H.W. Sheppard (ed.), Survey of London, 42 vols., London 1900 – , vol. 37, p. 161. See also Mark Girouard, 'Town houses for the wealthy: Kensington Palace Gardens. I', Country Life (11 November 1971), vol. 150, no. 5, pp. 1268-71 and 'Gilded preserves for the rich: Kensington Palace Gardens. II', ibid. (18 November 1971), vol. 150, no. 5, pp. 1360-63. Girouard states that the Murrietas decamped in the late 1880s and bought two houses on Carlton House Terrace (p. 1363).

12   Survey of London, cit. (note 11), vol. 37, p. 165. Although none survives, studies for the drawing room figures are preserved in the Victoria & Albert Museum, London and the Royal Institute of British Architects, London. See Helen Smith, Decorative painting in the domestic interior in England and Wales c. 1850-1890, London 1984, no. 76. See also Hugh Stannus, Alfred Stevens and his work, London 1891, pp. 13-15 and plates 28-30.

13   Walter Crane, An artist's reminiscences, London 1907, p. 156. A watercolour and pencil study for the design is in the collection of the Royal Borough of Kensington and Chelsea Library and Arts Service.

14   The Builder 35 (19 May 1877), no. 2, p. 502. José's and Mariano's two younger bachelor brothers, Adriano and Cristobel (junior) made the house their primary residence. Their names appear in electoral registers and local directories in the parish of Wadhurst between the years 1871-99. My thanks to Roger Davey, County Archivist, East Sussex Record Office for providing this information. The house was demolished in 1952. The present owners of Wadhurst Park purchased the property in 1975 and have restored the gardens. See Anthony du Gard Pasley, 'From ruins to romance', Country Life (18 July 1991), vol. 35, no. 2, pp. 60-63.

15   Thomas Hay Sweet Escott, Society in the country house, London 1907, pp. 95-96.

16   Märit Rausing, Some notes about the history of Wadhurst Park, Wadhurst, Sussex n.d. The author notes that the Murrietas owned two other houses nearby, Southover at Burwash Common and what is now Wadhurst College for Girls in Mayfield Lane. I am grateful to Mrs. Rausing for sharing her knowledge of the Murrieta family with me and for putting me in touch with their descendants.

17   For Murrieta's Alma-Tademas, see S 73, 80, 86, 88, 102, 107, 108, 117, 119, 120, 127, 135, 138, 174, 197, 212, 213, 214, 215, and 441. One wonders if Murrieta used his influence to win Gambart's appointment as Spanish consul in Nice in 1878, only one year after Murrieta was made a marqués by the king. Murrieta's name, however, does not appear in Jeremy Maas's study of Gambart, op. cit. (note 2).

18   A third version of the erstwhile art amateur, Un amateur romain (A lover of art), Glasgow Art Gallery and Museum, was one of the three Alma-Tademas owned by José's brother Mariano. The connoisseur, in this picture, according to Helen Zimmern, is attempting to pass off a fake silver statue as genuine to two young guests, while his dealer looks on impassively. See Helen Zimmern, 'Laurence Alma Tadema R.A.: 'his life and work', Art Journal, Special Number (1886), p. 13. That art was a family matter to the Murrietas is evident in the separate sales of the collections belonging to Mariano and Adriano at Christie's. See note 27 below.

19   Madeleine Fidell Beaufort, Herbert L. Kleinfield, and Jeanne K. Welcher (eds.), The diaries 1871-1882 of Samuel P. Avery, art dealer, New York 1979, pp. lii-liii. See also Edward Strahan, Mr. Vanderbilt's house and collection, 3 vols., New York 1883-84.

20   For Vanderbilt's Alma-Tademas, see S 74,

157, 163, 193, and 247.

21   S.G.W. Benjamin, 'An American palace', Magazine of Art 6 (1883), p. 141. For Vanderbilt's background and life, see Louis Auchincloss, The Vanderbilt era: profiles of a gilded age, New York 1989.

22   For Vanderbilt's reliance on Samuel Avery, see The diaries 1871-1882 of Samuel P. Avery, art dealer, cit. (note 19), pp. lviii-xl.

23   Ibid., pp. xlvii-xlviii.

24   Henry James, 'The American purchase of Meissonier's "Friedland" 1876', in: John L. Sweeney (ed.), The painter's eye: notes and essays on the pictorial arts, Madison 1989, p. 109. Vanderbilt's version is now in the Metropolitan Museum of Art, while Murrieta's large watercolour is untraced. See Gerald Reitlinger, The economics of taste, New York 1961, p. 162 and note 27 below.

25   Stanley Chapman, The rise of merchant banking, London 1984, p. 171. On the bankruptcy proceedings, see The Times, 3 December 1892, 15 December 1892, and 9 July 1896.

26   Chapman, op. cit. (note 25), p. 80. See also The Statist 29 (1892), pp. 207 and 321. Boase, op. cit. (note 9) registers the fact that the Murrietas claimed limited liability.

27   It is difficult to arrive at the precise number of paintings in José de Murrieta's collection, because the brothers held several joint sales at Christie's. Of the twelve Murrieta sales staged between 1873-94, Lugt identifies six as the property of 'Messrs. Murrieta'. He lists a further two each for José and Mariano, and an additional two as the property of the 'Marques de Santurce (Adrien de)'; however, none of the directories of Spanish nobility, op. cit. (note 10), records Adriano as the possessor of a title. See Frits Lugt, Répertoire des catalogues de ventes, 4 vols., The Hague 1938-87. To complicate matters further, Roberts notes that a number of items in the two picture sales of 1892 were bought in. See William Roberts, Memorials of Christie's: a record of art sales from 1766 to 1896, 2 vols., London 1897, vol. 2, pp. 181-84. Moreover, the Art Journal noted that José did not sell the majority of his French paintings at auction, stating that they were 'purchased en bloc and privately by one of the largest Art dealing firms in the world'. Art Journal (September 1893), p. 270. The dealer may have been Georges Petit who exhibited the large watercolour version of Meissonier's Friedland in Paris in 1893 that had formerly been in the collection of José de Murrieta. See Charles Sterling and Margaretta M. Salinger, French paintings: a catalogue of the collection of the Metropolitan Museum of Art: XIX century, Greenwich 1966, p. 153. I wish to thank Melissa De Maderios, the librarian at Knoedler's in New York, for verifying that Knoedler's was not involved in the Murrieta transaction.

28   See the entry for Baron Rudolph Bruno Schröder in David J. Jeremy (ed.), Dictionary of business biography, 5 vols., London 1984-86, vol. 5, p. 71.

29   For Schröder's collection, see exhib. cat. Ein Hamburger sammelt in London: die Freiherr J. H. von Schröder Stiftung 1910, Hamburg (Hamburger Kunsthalle) 1984.

30   For Schröder's Alma-Tademas, see S 122, 158, 169, 206, 212, 213, 214, 215, 330, and 358.

31   Schröder's bequest did not include Alma-Tadema's four-part The seasons which the collector sold in 1894. See S 212-15.

32   For Cassel see Dictionary of business biography, cit. (note 28), vol. 1, pp. 604-14 and Kurt Grunwald,'"Windsor-Cassel" – the last Court Jew, prolegomena to a biography of Sir Ernest Cassel', Year Book of the Leo Baeck Institute 14 (1969), pp. 119-61. Cassel's granddaughter Edwina Ashley married Lord Louis Mountbatten.

33   Survey of London, cit. (note 11), vol. 40, p. 281 and Grunwald, op. cit. (note 32), p. 155.

34   Grunwald, op. cit. (note 32), p. 155.

35   Dictionary of business biography, cit. (note 28), vol. 1, pp. 607-08.

36   Ibid., vol. 1, pp. 17-20.

37   For the placement of art in the Aird residence, see George Potter, The monthly record of eminent men, 4 vols., London 1890-91, vol. 1, p. 18.

38   See, for instance, Anne Higonnet, 'Secluded vision: images of feminine experience in nineteenth-century Europe', Radical History Review 38 (1987), p. 17 and passim.

39   The Married Woman's Property Act was finally passed in 1882. See L. Crispin Warmington (ed.), Stephens commentaries on the laws of England, 4 vols., London 1950, vol. 2, pp. 495 ff.

40   Leonore Davidoff and Catherine Hall, Family fortunes: men and women of the English middle class 1780-1850, Chicago 1987.

41   See my 'Pre-Raphaelite women collectors and the female gaze', Journal of Pre-Raphaelite Studies n.s. 5 (Spring 1996), pp. 43-52.

42   Art and the Victorian middle class, cit. (note 1), pp. 289-90.

43   Potter, op. cit. (note 37), p. 18.

44   J.F. Boyes, 'The private art collections of London: Mr. John Aird's, in Hyde Park Terrace',

Art Journal (May 1891), p. 140.

45   Art Journal (May 1907), p. 136 and Bruce Arnold, Orpen: mirror to an age, London 1981, pp. 216-20.

46   S 148, 153, and 154.

47   See Ann Douglas, The feminization of American culture, New York 1977 and Albert Boime, 'Sargent in Paris and London: a portrait of the artist as Dorian Gray', in: Patricia Hills (ed.), exhib. cat. John Singer Sargent, New York (Whitney Museum of American Art) 1986, pp. 75-109.

48   Harriet Foote of Chicago married George Allison Armour c. 1894 and they moved to Princeton in 1895. See S 397 and Harper Leech and John Charles Carroll, Armour and his times, Freeport (New York) 1938; rpt. 1971.

49   Robert Isaacson, exhib. cat. William-Adolphe Bouguereau, New York (New York Cultural Center) 1975, p. 26. For the Morgan family, see Dictionary of American biography, 22 vols., New York 1928-58, vol. 7, pp. 164-65.

50   See William Bradford Browne, The Babbitt family history, 1643-1900, New York 1912; John William Leonard, History of the city of New York, New York 1901, p. 872, and National cyclopaedia of American biography, 63 vols., New York 1893, vol. 26, pp. 194-96.

51   Dictionary of business biography, cit. (note 28), vol. 3, p. 746.

52   For the influence of American collectors on Lever, see Edward Morris, 'Paintings and sculpture', in: exhib. cat. Lord Leverhulme: a great Edwardian collector and builder, London (Royal Academy of Arts) 1980, pp. 31-32. For Walters, see exhib. cat. The taste of Maryland: art collecting in Maryland 1800-1934, Baltimore (Walters Art Gallery) 1984, p. 50. Walters owned seven Alma-Tademas (S 66, 131, 140, 255, 266, 307, and 384).

53   Allen Funt, 'Foreword', in: exhib. cat. Victorians in togas: paintings by Sir Lawrence Alma-Tadema from the collection of Allen Funt, New York (Metropolitan Museum of Art) 1973, n. p.

Art and 'materialism'

Elizabeth Prettejohn

1   Edmund W. Gosse, 'The Royal Academy in 1881', Fortnightly Review n.s. 29 (June 1881), p. 692. Gosse proves his own point by misspelling the word 'cithara' (presumably unintentionally).

2   The attack on Alma-Tadema's archaeological accuracy in the New York Nation has often been cited, but the article was exceptional. The overtly anglophobic critic's quibbles were trivial in any case; his statement that the togas in The picture gallery are reversed is not correct, and his observations on orthography are debatable. See 'The archaeologist of artists', Nation (16 September 1886), pp. 237-38.

3   See exhib. cat. Imagining Rome: British artists and Rome in the nineteenth century, Bristol (City Museum & Art Gallery) 1996, pp. 64-68 and nos. 43-45.

4   See, e.g., 'French Exhibition', Athenaeum (15 April 1865), p. 527; J. Beavington Atkinson, 'Art in the Paris Exhibition', Contemporary Review 6 (October 1867), pp. 161-62.

5   'Exhibition of the Royal Academy', The Times (21 May 1872), p. 7.

6   'The Royal Academy', Art-Journal n.s. 8 (1 June 1869), p. 168.

7   William Bell Scott, 'Alma Tadema's Vintage: ancient Rome', Academy 2 (1 May 1871), p. 237.

8   'Exhibition of the Royal Academy', Illustrated London News (6 May 1871), p. 447.

9   Reynolds's Discourses, delivered to the Royal Academy from 1769-90, remained one of the most widely read works on art theory in 19th-century England. See Sir Joshua Reynolds, Discourses on art, ed. Robert R. Wark, New Haven & London 1959.

10   'The Royal Academy', Art Journal n.s. 10 (1 July 1871), p. 175.

11   John Ruskin, 'Notes on some of the principal pictures exhibited in the rooms of the Royal Academy: 1875', reprinted in E.T. Cook and Alexander Wedderburn (eds.), The works of John Ruskin (library edition), London 1903-12, vol. 14, pp. 271-72.

12   John Ruskin, 'Classic schools of painting: Sir F. Leighton and Alma Tadema', lecture delivered May 1883, in: idem, op. cit. (note 11), vol. 33, p. 321.

13   Ibid., p. 322.

14   'The Royal Academy', Athenaeum (1 May 1875), p. 592.

15   Wilfrid Meynell, 'Our living artists: Laurens Alma-Tadema, R.A.', Magazine of Art 2 (1879), p. 193.

16   Sidney Colvin, 'The Grosvenor Gallery', Fortnightly Review n.s. 21 (1 June 1877), p. 825.

17   See Christopher Newall, The Grosvenor Gallery exhibitions: change and continuity in the Victorian art world, Cambridge 1995.

18   'The works of Laurence Alma-Tadema, R.A.', Art Journal n.s. (February 1883), p. 36.

19 'The Grosvenor Gallery – (Alma Tadema)',
Spectator (23 December 1882), p. 1651.

20 'The Grosvenor Gallery', *The Times*
(5 December 1882), p. 8.

21 Op. cit. (note 18), p. 36.

22 'The Grosvenor Gallery', *Spectator* (16
December 1882), p. 1615.

23 Ibid., p. 1614.

24 'Contemporary art – poetic and positive:
Rossetti and Tadema – Linnell and Lawson',
Blackwood's 133 (March 1883), p. 403.

25 Cosmo Monkhouse, 'The Grosvenor
Gallery. III', *Academy* (23 December 1882), p.
457.

26 'Exhibitions of the month', *Magazine of Art*
12 (June 1889), p. xxxiv.

27 Op. cit. (note 11), vol. 33, p. 319.

28 'Our guide to the Academy',
Punch (14 May 1881), p. 217.

29 'At the New Gallery', *Punch* (27 May 1893),
p. 244.

30 Editor [Marion Henry Spielmann], 'Current
art', *Magazine of Art* 12 (1889), p. 271.

31 'The Royal Academy',
The Times (5 May 1894), p. 16.

32 D.S.M., 'The New Gallery',
Spectator (6 May 1893), p. 607.

33 R. Phené Spiers, 'Archaeological research
in the paintings of Sir Lawrence Alma-Tadema',
Architectural Review 33 (March 1913), pp. 45-48.

34 Arthur Clutton Brock, 'Alma Tadema',
Burlington Magazine 22 (February 1913), p. 286.

35 Ibid.; 'The Royal Academy', *Athenaeum*
(11 January 1913), p. 50; 'Royal Academy',
Globe (6 January 1913), p. 10.

36 'Alma-Tadema', *Connoisseur* 35
(February 1913), p. 114.

37 Ibid., p. 113.

38 'The Royal Academy', *Athenaeum*
(11 January 1913), p. 49; 'Studio-Talk', *Studio* 58
(February 1913), p. 56.

39 Roger Fry, 'The case of the late Sir
Lawrence Alma Tadema, O.M.',
Nation (18 January 1913), pp. 666-67.

40 Op. cit. (note 11), vol. 33, p. 321.

41 'The Royal Academy',
Athenaeum (15 May 1909), p. 592.

42 Exhibitions have included *Victorians in
togas: paintings by Sir Lawrence Alma-Tadema
from the collection of Allen Funt*, New York
(The Metropolitan Museum of Art) 1973; *Sir
Lawrence Alma-Tadema O.M., R.A. 1836-1912*,
Sheffield (Mappin Art Gallery) & Newcastle-
upon-Tyne (Laing Art Gallery) 1976; *Empires
restored, Elysium revisited: the art of Sir
Lawrence Alma-Tadema*, Williamstown (Sterling
and Francine Clark Art Institute), Baltimore
(Walters Art Gallery), Cincinnati (Taft Museum)
& Memphis (Dixon Gallery and Gardens)
1991-92.

Alma-Tadema and photography

Ulrich Pohlmann

Translated from the German by Pauline Cumbers

1 Cf. Aaron Scharf, *Art and photography*,
London 1968; Van Deren Coke, *The painter and
the photograph: from Delacroix to Warhol*,
Albuquerque 1973; Josef A. Schmoll gen.
Eisenwerth (ed.), exhib. cat. *Malerei nach
Fotografie: von der Camera obscura bis zur Pop
Art*, Munich (Stadtmuseum) 1970; Erika Billeter
(ed.), *Photographie und Malerei im Dialog, von
1840 bis heute*, with texts by Josef A. Schmoll
gen. Eisenwerth, Zürich & Bern 1977.

2 Richard Tomlinson, *The Athens of Alma-
Tadema*, Stroud (Gloucestershire) 1991; Ken and
Jenny Jacobson, *Études d'après nature: 19th
century photographs in relation to art*, Petches
Bridge 1996, p. 13.

3 Prince Albert and Queen Victoria began collecting photographs (architecture, landscapes,
portraits, genre scenes, the Crimean War, art
reproductions) around 1840, among them works
by Roger Fenton, William Bambridge, Oscar
Gustave Rejlander, Fox Talbot, Francis Bedford,
Lake Price, Charles Clifford, Gustave Le Gray,
Eugène Disdéri, Caldesi, William E. Kilburn,
Cundall & Howlett. Cf. Francis Dimond and
Roger Taylor, *Crown and camera: the royal family
and photography 1842-1910*, London 1987.

4 *Reports* by the juries on the subjects in the
thirty classes into which the exhibition was divided, London 1852, p. 243.

5 Cf. *Official descriptive and illustrated catalogue of the Great Exhibition of the works of
industry of all nations*, London 1851, vol. 2,
p. 429.

6 *Reports*, op. cit. (note 4), p. 244.

7 Cf. Michael Bartram, *The Pre-Raphaelite
camera*, Boston 1985, and the literature mentioned under note 1.

8 Quoted in Jeremy Maas, *Victorian painters*,
London 1969, p. 195.

9 Cf. detailed commentary by Karl Raupp in
1889 on the occasion of the international art
exhibition in the Munich Crystal Palace and the
articles by Julius Raphaels published in the periodical *Die Kunst für Alle*. Cf. Ulrich Pohlmann
(ed.), *Frank Eugene: the dream of beauty*,
Munich 1995, p. 36.

10 Quoted in Wolfgang Kemp (ed.), *Theorie
der Fotografie I, 1839-1912*, Munich 1980,
p. 194. Frederic Leighton, W.P. Frith, John
Gilbert, George Reid, W.D. Richmond, Wyke
Bayliss, Walter Crane, Joseph Pennell and Walter
Sickert also took part in that survey.

11 Cf. Josef A. Schmoll gen. Eisenwerth,
'Lenbach und die Photographie', in: Rosel
Gollek and Winfried Ranke (eds.), *Franz von
Lenbach 1836-1904*, Munich 1987, pp. 63-97;
Jo-Anne Birnie-Danzker, Ulrich Pohlmann and
Josef A. Schmoll gen. Eisenwerth (eds.), *Franz
von Stuck und die Photographie: Inszenierung
und Dokumentation*, Munich 1996.

12 Cf. for example Maas, op. cit. (note 8),
p. 208; Christopher Wood, *Olympian dreamers:
Victorian classical painters 1860-1914*, London
1983, p. 109.

13 Cf. exhib. cat. *Empires restored, Elysium
revisited: the art of Sir Lawrence Alma-Tadema*,
Williamstown (Sterling and Francine Clark Art
Institute), Baltimore (Walters Art Gallery),
Cincinnati (Taft Museum) & Memphis
(Dixon Gallery and Gardens) 1991-92, p. 25.

14 The collection of photographs, drawings
and prints is numbered 7637 to 12899. Cf. *Alma-
Tadema library: list of photographs, drawings,
prints, bust by E. Onslow Ford, R.A.*, 1915.

15 Alma-Tadema's library and photograph col-
lection contained several folders documenting
ancient sculptures such as those in the
Königliche Glyptothek in Munich
(A. Furtwaengler, *Ein hundert Tafeln nach den
Bildwerken der Kgl. Glyptothek zu München*,
Munich 1903), the Gizeh Museum, the British
Museum, the Museum Plantin-Moretus in
Antwerp, and the Pergamon Museum in Berlin.

16 Cf. Wilfrid Meynell, 'Artists' homes: Mr.
Alma-Tadema's at North Gate, Regent's Park',
Magazine of Art 5 (1882), p. 188.

17 Cf. Vern G. Swanson, *The biography and
catalogue raisonné of the paintings of Sir
Lawrence Alma-Tadema*, London 1990, p. 33.

18 Lovett's claim that Alma-Tadema only
began collecting photographs of architectural
monuments in 1875 during a trip to Italy seems
too late to me. Cf. exhib. cat. *Empires restored,
Elysium revisited*, cit. (note 13), p. 19.

19 Tomlinson, op. cit. (note 2), p. 4.

20 Cf. CXXIII, 11161 and 11162. Another photograph shows Alma-Tadema on the Strada
delle Tombe, sitting inside the Tomba delle
Ghirlande.

21 The archive contains photographs by J. Laurent of the excavation of the Roman altars in Murcia in Spain and of the Roman thermae in Bath, discovered and excavated between 1879 and 1882 by C.E. Davis.

22 Cf. Robert E. Lassam and Michael Gray, *The Romantic era: la calotipia in Italia 1845-1860*, Florence 1988.

23 Cf. Marina Miraglia, Pino Piantanida, Ulrich Pohlmann and Dietmar Siegert (eds.), *Giorgio Sommer in Italien: Photographien 1858-1887*, Heidelberg 1992.

24 Cf. Hans Christian Adam, 'Heinrich Schliemann und die Photographie', in: Bodo von Dewitz (ed.), *Das Land der Griechen mit der Seele suchen*, Cologne 1990, pp. 38-41.

25 Parker was director of the Ashmolean Museum of History and Archaeology in Oxford from 1870. Cf. *Un inglese a Roma: la raccolta Parker nell' Archivio Fotografico Comunale*, Rome 1989.

26 *Historical photographs: a systematic catalogue of Mr. Parker's collection of photographs illustrative of the history of Rome, etc.*, Part I, London 1873. Cf. *Alma-Tadema library: shelf list of books*, 1915, p. 215. Parker's bibliography makes no reference to such a catalogue.

27 Cf. Simelli's photographs *Gates of Rome. Details of the North Gate of the Praetorian Camp, with windows of terracotta* (12434), and by Colamedici (XIV, 8089).

28 Cf. Giuseppe Pisani Sartorio, 'La documentazione fotografica negli studi di archeologia', in: *La fotografia a Roma nel secolo XIX: la veduta, il ritratto, l'archeologia*, Rome 1990, pp. 87-89.

29 Alma-Tadema's collection contains the following photographs by Plüschow: I, 7638 / 7645 / 7646 / 7648; XI, 7987 / 7988 / 7990 / 7991 / 7992 / 7993 / 8001; LXXIV, 9767 / 9768 / 9770; 10295; 10444; CXVIII, 11053 / 11058; CXXII, 11131 / 11132/ 11141; CXXIII, 11160; 11997 / 11998 / 12279 / 12287; 12420; 12477 / 12478 / 12479 / 12480. Cf. Swanson, op. cit. (note 17), p. 98.

30 In the Hauser estate in the Munich Archaeological Institute there are numerous photographs by Plüschow. On Gloeden and Plüschow see Ulrich Pohlmann, *Wilhelm von Gloeden: Sehnsucht nach Arkadien*, Berlin 1987; Ulrich Pohlmann, *Guglielmo Plüschow (1852-1930): ein Photograph aus Mecklenburg in Italien*, Schloß Plüschow 1995.

31 Cf. Piero Becchetti, *Giacomo Caneva e la scuola fotografica romana*, Rome & Florence 1989; Bodo von Dewitz, Dietmar Siegert and Karin Schuller-Procopovici (eds.), *Italien sehen und sterben: Photographien der Zeit des Risorgimento (1845-1870)*, Heidelberg 1994, pp. 182-87. Presumably Alma-Tadema purchased the calotypes by Caneva via the Roman photographer Ludovico Tuminello who had taken over Caneva's archive in 1870.

32 Rykle Borger, *Drei Klassizisten: Alma-Tadema, Ebers, Vosmaer*, Leiden 1978, p. 24.

33 Exhib. cat. *Empires restored, Elysium revisited*, cit. (note 13), p. 20.

34 Cf. Wood, op. cit. (note 12), p. 121. A similar opinion is expressed in exhib. cat. *Empires restored, Elysium revisited*, cit. (note 13), p. 25. According to the library inventory Alma-Tadema owned not Muybridge's *The human figure in motion* (London 1901) but his *Animals in motion* (London 1899).

35 H. Baden Pritchard, 'Instantaneous photography', *Magazine of Art* 5 (1882), pp. 70-73. Meynell's article on Alma-Tadema's home appeared in the same volume of that magazine, cf. note 16.

36 On the theme of archaeology and photography see Michel Frizot (ed.), *Nouvelle histoire de la photographie*, Paris 1995; Hertha Wolf, 'Das Denkmälerarchiv Fotografie', *Camera Austria* (1995), no. 51/52, pp. 133-45. The following photographs by Maxime Du Camp contained in Alma-Tadema's archive are clearly identifiable: *Palais de Karnak. Promenoir de Tothmès III*, pl. 45 (XXXI, 8656), *Médinet Habou. Vue générale des ruines*, pl. 46 (XXXI, 8682), *Médinet Habou. Péristyle du Palais de Ramses Méiamoun*, pl. 5 (XXXI, 8688), *Médinet Habou. Partie orientale du peristyle du Palais de Ramses Méiamoun*, pl. 51 (XXXI, 8689), *Gournah. Statue de Memnon*, pl. 55 (XXXII, 8712), *Rive septentrionale du Nile*, pl. 84 (XXXI, 8667) and *Jérusalem Porte Dorée* (CI, 10520).

37 Quoted in Isabelle Jammes, *Blanquart-Evrard et les origines de l'édition photographique française: catalogue raisonné des albums photographiques édités 1851-1855*, Geneva & Paris 1981, p. 95.

38 Ibid., p. 97-99.

39 The following works by Auguste Salzmann could be identified beyond a doubt: *Jérusalem Saint Sépulcre. Colonne du parvis* (XXIV, 8477), *Jérusalem. Tombeau de la Vierge* (XXXVIII, 8880).

40 Together with French colleagues, Gambart published, among other things: *Photographie zoologique ou représentation des animaux rares des collections du Musée d'Histoire Naturelle*, publiée par L. Rousseau et A. Devéria. Procédés des plus habiles photographes: imprimerie photographique de Lemercier, *Oeuvre d'Albert Dürer* (photographs by Bisson Frères, 1854), *Egypte et Nubie, sites et monuments les plus intéressants pour l'étude de l'art et de l'histoire. Atlas photographié accompagné de plans et d'une table explicative servant de complément à la grande description de l'Egypte* (photographs by Félix Teynard, 1858).

41 Cf. Colin Osman, 'Felice Beato: Dichtung und Wahrheit über sein Leben', in: Claudia Gabriele Philipp, Dietmar Siegert and Rainer Wick (eds.), *Felice Beato in Japan: Photographien zum Ende der Feudalzeit 1863-1873*, Heidelberg 1991, p. 21. Cf. also Bahattin Öztuncay, *James Robertson: pioneer of photography in the Ottoman Empire*, Istanbul 1992, p. 26.

42 Alma-Tadema's archive contains the following photographs by Robertson and Beato: *Jerusalem* (10433), *Jews at the Wailing Wall* (CI, 10518), *Wall of the Castle of A. ...* (name indecipherable) (CI, 10519), *Tombs of St. James and St. Zachariah* (CI, 10521), *St. Stephen's Gate* (CI, 10524), *Porch of the Church of the Holy Sepulchre* (CI, 10525).

43 A complete list of Bedford's photographs is contained in: Cuthbert Bede, *Photographic pleasures*, London n.d. (around 1863), no page reference. The following photographs from the cycle are in Alma-Tadema's archive: *Philae. The lily of Pharaoh and small temple* (XXXI, 8671), *Philae. Temple of Isis* (XXXI, 8673), *Thebes. Médinet Habou* (XXXI, 8681), *Denderak Temple. Great Gateway* (8699), *Edfu. Temple of Horns* (XXXII, 8706), *Esnah Temple* (XXXII, 8708), *Olive trees in the Garden of Gethsemane near Jerusalem* (LXIII, 9350 and 9351), *Athens Propyleon* (LXXV, 9792), *The ancient Capernaum* (10423), *Damascus. The Street called 'Straight', Christian quarter* (CI, 10515), *Tower of Galata with Turkish cemetery*, Constantinople (12338), *The El Aksa mosque, Jerusalem* (CLVII, 12339). Alma-Tadema also owned numerous photographs taken in the Orient by Francis Frith, James Mason Good, Pascal Sébah, Félix Bonfils, Antonio Beato and G. Saboungi. These were available in the 1860s and 1870s in large numbers and in varying formats.

44 For more details cf. Tomlinson, op. cit. (note 2). On the photographic presentation of Athens and the Acropolis in the 19th century see exhib. cat. *Athens 1893-1900: a photographic record*, Athens (Benaki Museum) 1985.

45 Cf. Stillman's photographs 9890 and 9891

in the Alma-Tadema archive.

46 Cf. Portfolios XXXIX, CIII, CIV and CV in the Alma-Tadema archive.

47 Cf. Portfolios CLXV-CLXVII in the Alma-Tadema archive.

48 Cf. Ulrich Pohlmann, 'Études d'après nature. Barbizon und die französische Landschaftsphotographie 1849-1875', in: Christoph Heilmann, Michael Clarke and John Sillevis (eds.), *Corot, Courbet und die Maler von Barbizon*, Munich 1996, pp. 403-16, plate section pp. 417-67. Alma-Tadema's collection contains numerous animal photographs taken by Famin, Quinet, Hollyer, Sommer, Rive, Beato, Anschütz and the Société Royale de Photographie de Bruxelles. Cf. for example IV, 7704 / 7706; VII, 7855 / 7856 / 7857; 8397 and 8398.

49 The most famous flower still lifes taken before 1860 were by Charles Aubry, Eugène Chauvigné, Eugène Colliau, Adolphe Braun, Francis Bedford and Roger Fenton. Cf. William A. Ewing, *Flora photographica 1835-1990*, London & Paris 1991. The flower photographs are in portfolios nos. LXI, LXII and LXIII.

50 Cf. the photographs by Quinet (CVII, 10712 / 10723 and CLV, 12376) and by Famin (CLVIII, 12378 / 12382 / 12385 / 12394 / 12398 / 12400 / 12403 / 12404 / 12405 and 12406).

51 The view from the writer Axel Munthe's villa San Michele on the isle of Capri is strikingly similar to the landscape in the painting *Coign of vantage*. Cf. Frédéric Bastet, 'Een gunstig uitkijkpunt op Capri', *Origine* 6 (December – January 1995), pp. 81-82.

52 Louise Lippincott, *Lawrence Alma-Tadema: Spring*, Malibu (California) 1990, p. 40.

53 Cf. for more details Ulrich Pohlmann, 'The dream of beauty, or Truth is beauty, beauty truth: Photography and Symbolism, 1890-1914', in: Jean Clair (ed.), *Lost Paradise: Symbolist Europe*, Montreal 1995, pp. 428-47.

54 E. Thovez: 'L'ispiratore ideale di queste scene romane è visibilmente il flemmatico fiammingo britannizzato che mai non vide la Grecia, Alma-Tadema', quoted by Marina Miraglia, *Culture fotografiche e società a Torino 1839-1911*, Turin 1990, p. 413. On Rey see also Sadakichi Hartmann, 'Guido Rey: a master of detail composition, 1907', reprinted in: Harry W. Lawton and George Knox (eds.), *The valiant knights of Daguerre*, Berkeley & Los Angeles 1978, pp. 250-55. Hartmann compares the aesthetics of the photograph *Feeding the pigeons* with that of the artist Alma-Tadema.

Bibliography

Alma-Tadema 1901
Lawrence Alma-Tadema, 'Laurens Alma-Tadema, R.A.', in: *In the days of my youth...*, containing biographies of thirty well-known men and women of today, Thomas Power O'Connor (ed.), London 1901.

Alma-Tadema 1907
Lawrence Alma-Tadema, 'Marbles: their ancient and modern application', *RIBA Journal* 3rd s (January 1907), vol. 14, pp. 169-80.

Alma-Tadema 1909
Sir Lawrence Alma-Tadema, 'My reminiscences', *Strand Magazine* 27 (1909), pp. 286-295.

Mario Amaya, 'The Roman world of Alma-Tadema', *Apollo* 76 (December 1962), pp. 771-78.

Russell Ash, *Sir Lawrence Alma-Tadema*, London 1989.

Atkinson
J.B. Atkinson, 'Contemporary art – poetic and positive: Rossetti and Tadema – Linnell and Lawson', *Blackwood's Edinburgh Magazine* 133 (March 1883), pp. 392-411.

Alfred Lys Baldry, *Albert Moore: his life and works*, London 1894.

Barrington
Mrs. Russell Barrington, *The life, letters and work of Frederic Leighton*, 2 vols., London 1906.

Bastet
Frédéric Bastet, 'Een gunstig uitkijkpunt op Capri', *Origine* 6 (December-January 1995), pp. 81-82.

Bénédite
Léonce Bénédite, 'Un portrait de Dalou et sa famille par Sir Lawrence Alma Tadema (Musée du Luxembourg)', *Musées et Monuments de France* 2 (1907), no. 9, pp. 129-31.

Blackie
John Stuart Blackie, 'Homer and his translators', *Macmillan's Magazine* 4 (August 1861), pp. 268-80.

Blotkamp
Carel Blotkamp, 'De Werkplaats: Joe Parkin Mayall fotografeert Alma Tadema', *Kunstschrift* 38 (March-April 1994), no. 2, pp. 50-51.

Borger
Rykle Borger, *Drei Klassizisten: Alma Tadema, Ebers, Vosmaer*, Leiden 1978.

Boyes
J.F. Boyes, 'The private art collections of London: Mr John Aird's, in Hyde Park Terrace', *Art Journal* (May 1891), pp. 135-40.

Clutton Brock
Arthur Clutton Brock, 'Alma Tadema', *Burlington Magazine* 22 (February 1913), pp. 285-87.

Buckley
Cheryl Buckley, *Potters and paintresses: women designers in the pottery industry 1870-1955*, London 1990.

Carter
A.C.R. Carter, 'The Royal Academy of 1899', *Art Journal* (June 1899), pp. 161-84.

Casteras
Susan P. Casteras, 'John Everett Millais'"Secret-Looking Garden Wall" and the courtship barrier in Victorian art', *Browning Institute Studies* 13 (1985), pp. 71-98.

John Collier, 'The art of Alma-Tadema', *Nineteenth Century and After* 73 (March 1913), pp. 597-607.

Colvin
Sidney Colvin, 'The Grosvenor Gallery', *Fortnightly Review* n.s. 21 (1 June 1877), pp. 820-33.

Costume du moyen âge
Costume du moyen âge d'après les manuscripts, Brussels 1847.

H. van Wickevoort Crommelin, *Het Schildersboek I*, Amsterdam 1898, pp. 138-64, reprinted *Dutch painters of the nineteenth century I*, London 1898, pp. 139-64.

Cuypers 1976
Constant Cuypers, 'The Question by Lourens Alma Tadema', *Nederlands Kunsthistorisch Jaarboek* 27 (1976), pp. 73-90.

Cuypers 1991
Constant Cuypers, 'De droom van Alma-Tadema', *Kunstschrift* 35 (July-August 1991), no. 4, pp. 38-49.

D'Arms
John D'Arms, *Romans on the Bay of Naples*, Cambridge (Massachusetts) 1970.

Lodewijk van Deyssel, *Verbeeldingen*, Amsterdam 1908.

Frederick Dolman, 'Illustrated interviews, LXVIII: Sir Lawrence Alma-Tadema', *Strand Magazine* 18 (December 1899), pp. 602-14.

Dijkstra
Bram Dijkstra, *Idols of perversity: fantasies of feminine evil in fin-de-siècle culture*, New York & Oxford 1986.

Dircks
Rudolf Dircks, 'Sir Lawrence Alma-Tadema, O.M., R.A.', *The Art Journal Christmas Number*, London 1910.

Dixon
M.H. Dixon, 'Onslow Ford R.A.', *Art Journal* (1898), pp. 294-96.

Ebers
Georg Ebers, *Lorenz Alma Tadema: his life and works*, trans. Mary J. Safford, New York 1886.

Ellen Epps Gosse, 'Laurens Alma-Tadema', *Century Magazine* 47 (February 1894), pp. 482-97.

Flint
Kate Flint, *The woman reader 1837-1914*, Oxford 1993.

Ford
Works by E. Onslow Ford R.A. from 1875 to 1901, MSS Courtauld Institute of Art, London.

Roger Fry, 'The case of the late Sir Lawrence Alma Tadema, O.M.', *Nation* (18 January 1913), pp. 666-67.

William Gaunt, *Victorian Olympus*, London 1952.

Edmund William Gosse, 'Alma-Tadema', in: F.G. Dumas, *Modern artists*, London 1882-83, vol. 2, pp. 73-96.

Griffin
Jasper Griffin, *Latin poets and Roman life*, London 1985.

Haskell and Penny
Francis Haskell and Nicholas Penny, *Taste and the antique: the lure of classical sculpture 1500-1900*, 2nd printing, New Haven & London 1982.

Hedreen
Guy Hedreen, 'Sir Lawrence Alma-Tadema's *Women of Amphissa*', *Journal of the Walters Art Gallery* 52/53 (1994), pp. 79-92.

Henschel
George Henschel, *Musings & memories of a musician*, London 1918.

Higgins
Reynold Higgins, *Tanagra and the figurines*, London 1986.

Hind
Charles Lewis Hind, *Naphtali: being influences and adventures while earning a living by writing*, London 1926.

Anthony Hobson, *The art and life of J. W. Waterhouse, R.A., 1849-1917*, London 1980.

Houston
Mary G. Houston, *Medieval costumes in England and France*, London 1939.

Huysmans
Joris-Karl Huysmans, *Against nature*, trans. R. Baldick, London 1966 (first published 1884).

Jenkins 1983
Ian Jenkins, 'Frederic Lord Leighton and Greek vases', *Burlington Magazine* 125 (October 1983), pp. 597-605.

Jenkins 1994
Ian Jenkins, *The Parthenon frieze*, London 1994.

Jenkins and Middleton
Ian Jenkins and A.P. Middleton, 'Paint on the Parthenon sculptures', *Annual of the British School at Athens* 83 (1988), pp. 183-207.

Ian Jenkins, *Archaeologists and aesthetes in the sculpture galleries of the British Museum 1800-1939*, London 1992.

Richard Jenkyns, *The Victorians and ancient Greece*, Oxford 1980.

Richard Jenkyns, *Dignity and decadence: Victorian art and the classical inheritance*, London 1991.

Kern
Stephen Kern, *Eyes of love: the gaze in English and French paintings and novels 1840-1900*, London 1996.

Joseph A. Kestner, *Mythology and misogyny: the social discourse of nineteenth-century British classical-subject painting*, Madison 1989.

Fernand Khnopff, 'Des souvenirs à propos de Sir Lawrence Alma Tadema', *Annexe aux Bulletins de la Classe des Beaux-Arts (1915-1918)*, Brussels, Académie Royale de Belgique, 1919, pp. 9-16.

Lanciani
Rodolfo Lanciani, *The ruins and excavations of ancient Rome*, Boston & New York 1897.

Layard
A.H. Layard, 'Pompeii', *Quarterly Review* 115 (April 1864), pp. 312-48.

Louise Lippincott, *Lawrence Alma-Tadema: Spring*, Malibu (California) 1990.

Maas
Jeremy Maas, *Gambart, prince of the Victorian art world*, London 1975.

Mayhew
Henry Mayhew, *London labour and the London poor*, 4 vols., London 1865.

Meynell
Wilfrid Meynell, 'Artists' homes: Mr. Alma-Tadema's at North Gate, Regent's Park', *Magazine of Art* 5 (1882), pp. 184-88.

Cosmo Monkhouse, 'Laurens Alma Tadema, R.A.', *Scribner's Magazine* 18 (December 1895), pp. 663-81.

Cosmo Monkhouse, 'Sir Edward J. Poynter, P.R.A.: his life and work', *Easter Art Annual* 1897.

Murray
A.S. Murray, 'Greek bronzes', *Portfolio Monograph*, no. 36, London 1898.

Newall
Christopher Newall, *The Grosvenor Gallery exhibitions: change and continuity in the Victorian art world*, Cambridge 1995.

Paderewski
Ignace Jan Paderewski and Mary Lawton, *The Paderewski memoirs*, London 1939.

Pater
Walter Pater, 'A fragment on *Measure for Measure*' (1874), repr. in *Essays on literature and art*, ed. Jennifer Uglow, London 1973, pp. 117-24.

Pennock
Hanna Pennock, 'De levens van twee neven, Hendrik Willem Mesdag en Lourens Alma Tadema', *Jong Holland* 9 (1993), no. 1, pp. 8-19.

Pollock
W.F. Pollock, 'Royal Academy exhibition', *Fraser's Magazine* n.s. 8 (July 1873), pp. 74-85.

Prettejohn
Elizabeth Prettejohn,'Painting indoors: Leighton and his studio', *Apollo* 143 (February 1996), pp. 17-21.

Richard Quick, *The life and works of Edwin Long, R.A.*, County Borough of Bournemouth Art Gallery and Museums 1970 (first published 1931).

De Ranitz
Lita de Ranitz, 'Het Huis van Alma Tadema', *Het Huis: Oud en Nieuw* 9 (1911), pp. 20-30.

Raven
Maarten Raven, 'Alma Tadema als amateur-egyptoloog', *Bulletin van het Rijksmuseum* 28 (1980), no. 3, pp. 101-17.

Reis
Pamela Tamarkin Reis, 'Victorian centerfold: another look at Millais's *Cherry Ripe*', *Victorian Studies* 35 (winter 1992), pp. 201-05.

Rinder
Frank Rinder, 'Edward Onslow Ford, R.A.', *Art Journal* (1902), pp. 59-62.

Robinson
F. Mabel Robinson, 'Art patrons: Hadrian', *Magazine of Art* 2 (1888), pp. 329-32.

Rosenfeld
Sibyl Rosenfeld, 'Alma-Tadema's designs for Henry Irving's "Coriolanus"', *Deutsche Shakespeare-Gesellschaft West Jahrbuch* (1974), pp. 84-95.

Ruskin
John Ruskin, *The works of John Ruskin (library edition)*, ed. E.T. Cook and Alexander Wedderburn, 39 vols., London 1903-12.

Sandys
John Edwin Sandys, *A history of classical scholarship*, 3 vols., Cambridge 1908, vol. 3 ('The eighteenth century in Germany, and the nineteenth century in Europe and the United States of America').

Smiles
Sam Smiles, *The image of antiquity: ancient Britain and the Romantic imagination*, New Haven & London 1994.

A. Smith
Alison Smith, *The Victorian nude: sexuality, morality, and art*, Manchester 1996.

Smith Antiquities
William Smith, *A dictionary of Greek and Roman antiquities*, London 1842.

Smith Biography
William Smith, *Dictionary of Greek and Roman biography and mythology*, 3 vols., London 1854-59.

Spielmann
Marion Henry Spielmann, 'Laurence Alma-Tadema, R.A.: a sketch', *Magazine of Art* 20 (1896-97), pp. 42-50.

Spielmann 1901
Marion Henry Spielmann, *British sculpture and sculptors of today*, London 1901.

Spiers
Richard Phené Spiers, 'The architecture of "Coriolanus" at the Lyceum Theatre', *Architectural Review* 10 (July 1901), pp. 2-21.

Richard Phené Spiers, 'Archaeological research in the paintings of Sir Lawrence Alma-Tadema', *Architectural Review* 33 (March 1913), pp. 45-48.

Standing
Percy Cross Standing, *Sir Lawrence Alma-Tadema O.M., R.A.*, London 1905.

Frederick George Stephens, *Laurence Alma-Tadema, R.A.: a sketch of his life and work*, London 1895.

Frederick George Stephens, *Selected works of Sir Laurence Alma-Tadema, O.M., R.A.*, London 1901.

Stirling
A.M.W. Stirling, *The Richmond papers*, London 1926.

Swanson
Vern G. Swanson, *The biography and catalogue raisonné of the paintings of Sir Lawrence Alma-Tadema*, London 1990.

Swanson 1977
Vern G. Swanson, *Sir Lawrence Alma-Tadema: the painter of the Victorian vision of the ancient world*, London 1977.

Thierry
Augustin Thierry, *Récits des temps mérovingiens précédés de considerations sur l'histoire de France*, 2 vols., Brussels 1840.

Tomlinson
Richard Tomlinson, *The Athens of Alma Tadema*, Stroud (Gloucestershire) 1991.

Touchette
Lori-Ann Touchette, *The dancing maenad reliefs*, London 1995.

Turner
Frank M. Turner, *The Greek heritage in Victorian Britain*, New Haven & London 1981.

Carel Vosmaer, *Amazone*, The Hague 1880, trans. E.J. Irving, *The amazon*, London 1884.

Wilkinson
J. Gardner Wilkinson, *Manners and customs of the ancient Egyptians*, 3 vols., London 1837.

Christopher Wood, *Olympian dreamers: Victorian classical painters 1860-1914*, London 1983.

Yegül
Fikret Yegül, *Baths and bathing in classical antiquity*, Cambridge (Massachusetts) & London 1992.

Baroness von Zedlitz, 'An interview with Mr. Laurence Alma-Tadema, R.A.', *The Woman at Home* (1895), pp. 491-500.

Zimmern 1886
Helen Zimmern, 'L. Alma-Tadema R.A.: his life and work', *The Art Annual (Art Journal)*, Special Number (1886).

Helen Zimmern, *Sir Lawrence Alma-Tadema, R.A.*, London 1902.

Exhibition catalogues

Sir Lawrence Alma-Tadema, O.M., R.A., 1836-1912, Sheffield (Mappin Art Gallery) & Newcastle-upon-Tyne (Laing Art Gallery) 1976.

The colour of sculpture 1840-1910, Amsterdam (Van Gogh Museum) & Leeds (The Henry Moore Institute) 1996-97.

Empires restored, Elysium revisited: the art of Sir Lawrence Alma-Tadema, Williamstown (Sterling and Francine Clark Art Institute), Baltimore (Walters Art Gallery), Cincinnati (Taft Museum) & Memphis (Dixon Gallery and Gardens) 1991-92.

Ein Hamburger sammelt in London: die Freiherr J.H. von Schröder-Stiftung 1910, Hamburg (Hamburger Kunsthalle) 1984.

Imagining Rome: British artists and Rome in the nineteenth century, Bristol (City Museum & Art Gallery) 1996.

Frederic Leighton, London (Royal Academy of Arts) 1996.

Albert Moore and his contemporaries, Newcastle-upon-Tyne (Laing Art Gallery) 1972.

Ary Scheffer, Sir Lawrence Alma-Tadema, Charles Rochussen of de vergankelijkheid van de roem, Rotterdam (De Rotterdamsche Kunststichting) 1974.

De verzameling van Mr. Carel Vosmaer (1826-1888), Amsterdam (Rijksmuseum) 1989.

Victorian High Renaissance, Manchester (City Art Gallery) & Minneapolis (Institute of Arts) 1978.

Victorians in togas: paintings by Sir Lawrence Alma-Tadema from the collection of Allen Funt, New York (The Metropolitan Museum of Art) 1973.

De wereld van Alma Tadema, Leeuwarden (Gemeentelijk Museum Het Princessehof) 1974.

Classical Texts

Catullus, text ed. R.A.B. Mynors, Oxford 1958.

The poems of Catullus, trans. Guy Lee, Oxford 1990.

Cicero, *Letters to Atticus*, text and trans. D.R. Shackleton Bailey, 5 vols., Cambridge 1965-66.

Cicero, *Pro Caelio*, text and trans. R. Gardner, Loeb Classical Library, Cambridge (Massachusetts) & London 1987.

Cicero, *The Verrine orations*, text and trans. L.H. Greenwood, Loeb Classical Library, 2 vols., Cambridge (Massachusetts) & London 1988.

Homer, *Iliad*, text ed. David B. Monro and Thomas W. Allen, Oxford 1976.

Homer, trans. Martin Hammond, Harmondsworth 1987.

Horace Odes I, text and trans. David West, Oxford 1995.

Juvenal, text and trans. G.G. Ramsay, Loeb Classical Library, Cambridge (Massachusetts) & London 1979.

Livy, text and trans. E.T. Sage, B.O. Foster, F.G. Moore, A.C. Schlesinger, Loeb Classical Library, 13 vols., Cambridge (Massachusetts) & London 1982-88.

Ovid, *The art of love*, text ed. E.J. Kenney, Oxford 1994.

Ovid, *The love poems*, trans. A.D. Meriville, Oxford 1990.

Persius, *Satires*, trans. Niall Rudd, Harmondsworth 1979.

Pliny, *The Elder Pliny's chapters on the history of art*, trans. K. Jex-Blake, with commentary and historical introduction by E. Sellers, London 1896.

Pliny, *Natural history*, text and trans. H. Rackham, D.E. Eichholz, W.H.S. Jones, Loeb Classical Library, 10 vols., Cambridge (Massachusetts) & London 1989-91.

Plutarch, *Lives*, text and trans. B. Perrin, Loeb Classical Library, 11 vols., Cambridge (Massachusetts) & London 1984-89.

Plutarch, *Moralia*, text and trans. F.C. Babbitt, W.C. Helmbold *et al.*, Loeb Classical Library, 15 vols., Cambridge (Massachusetts) & London 1989-95.

Scriptores Historiae Augustae, text and trans. D. Magie, Loeb Classical Library, 3 vols., Cambridge (Massachusetts) & London 1982.

Seneca, *Epistles*, text and trans. Richard M. Gummere, Loeb Classical Library, 2 vols., Cambridge (Massachusetts) & London 1991.

Suetonius, text and trans. J.C. Rolfe, Loeb Classical Library, Cambridge (Massachusetts) & London 1989.

Tibullus, *Elegies*, text and trans. Guy Lee, Leeds 1990.

Vitruvius, *On architecture*, text and trans. F. Granger, Loeb Classical Library, 2 vols., Cambridge (Massachusetts) & London 1995.

Index

Colophon

First published in the United States
of America in 1997 by Rizzoli
International Publications, Inc.
300 Park Avenue South, New York,
NY 10010

First published in the Netherlands
in 1996 by Van Gogh Museum,
Amsterdam / Walker Art Gallery,
Liverpool / Waanders Publishers,
Zwolle

Library of Congress
Cataloging-in-Publication Data
Sir Lawrence Alma-Tadema (edited by) Edwin
Becker, Edward Morris, Elizabeth Prettejohn,
Julian Treuherz
Includes bibliographical references and index
ISBN 0-8478-2001-7
1. Alma-Tadema, Lawrence, Sir, 1836-1912 –
Criticism and interpretation. I. Becker, Edwin.
II. Morris, Edward. III. Prettejohn, Elizabeth.
IV. Treuherz, Julian.
ND497.A4S55 1997
759.2–dc20   96-30853
                                          CIP

Translators
Pauline Cumbers
Peter Mason

Design
Studio Pieter Roozen, Amsterdam
(Nicola Lengsfeld)

Printing
Waanders Printers, Zwolle

Printed in the Netherlands

Photographs
All photographs have been generally provided
by the museums or owners of the works. With
special thanks to Agnew's, London [135],
Archivo Fotografico dei Musei Capitolini [144],
Bridgeman Art Library, London [**16 20 36 45**],
Trustees of the British Library [100], Christie's
Images, London [91], Courtauld Institute,
London [3], Haboldt & Co. [142], Manchester
Public Libraries [39-41, 43-46], Mr. Arturo Piera
[**7 74**], Simon Reynolds [57 58], Royal Institute
of British Architects Library [86], Sotheby's,
London [4 42 50 51 52 56], Sotheby's Inc., New
York [**47 77**], Spink & Son [32], Verlag Galerie
Welz, Salzburg [71 72], Elke Walford, Hamburg
[88] [**21 33 43 72**],.Christopher Wood [27]

Cover pages
p. 6 *Sir Lawrence Alma-Tadema*, photograph,
National Portrait Gallery, London
p. 9 *Self portrait*, 1896, Galleria degli Uffizi,
Collezione degli Autoritratti, Florence
p. 19 *The education of the children of Clovis*
(detail), 1861, private collection
p. 31 *Unconscious rivals* (detail), 1893, Bristol
City Museum & Art Gallery
p. 43 *The Epps family screen* (detail), 1870-71,
Board of Trustees of the Victoria & Albert
Museum, London
p. 57 *A sculptor's model (Venus Esquilina)*,
detail, 1877, private collection
p. 67 *A reading from Homer* (detail), 1885,
Philadelphia Museum of Art
p. 77 *A votive offering (The last roses)*, detail,
1873, private collection
p. 89 *The sculpture gallery* (detail), 1874, Hood
Museum of Art, Dartmouth College, Hanover,
New Hampshire
p. 99 *A Roman emperor, A.D. 41* (detail), 1871,
Walters Art Gallery, Baltimore
p. 109 Giorgio Sommer, *Advertising photograph*,
c. 1875, Dietmar Siegert collection, Munich
p. 125-27 *Alma-Tadema's House, 17 Grove End
Road*, from *The Art Journal*, 1910
p. 129 *Exhausted maenides after the dance*,
c. 1873-74, Van Gogh Museum, Amsterdam